Secession

by Western Australia

Second edition, revised and expanded

SECESSION BY WESTERN AUSTRALIA

By

Julian Gillespie

LLB, BJuris

Professor Gigi Foster

BA Ethics, Politics and Economics, PhD Economics

Michael Baker

BA (Econ)

Professor Ian Brighthope

Dip Ag Sci, MBBS, FACNEM

Editors

Julian Gillespie, Gigi Foster & Michael Baker

Hardcover ISBN 978-1-7644851-4-2

Paperback ISBN: 978-1-7644851-5-9

eBook ISBN: 978-1-7644851-6-6

Printed on demand by IngramSpark.

First published March 2026

Second edition, revised and expanded, published July 2026

This revised edition contains an expanded and clarified Chapter 2 addressing the legal processes by which Western Australia may pursue independence.

Copy Editing: Gigi Foster & Julian Gillespie

Text design: Julian Gillespie

Cover design: Julian Gillespie

Visuals: Julian Gillespie

To the People of Western Australia,

whose untapped potential inspires this vision of sovereignty.

There has been no *common* wealth delivered
to the People of Western Australia
under the Commonwealth.

ACKNOWLEDGEMENTS

This manuscript, *Secession by Western Australia*, has been shaped by the generosity, rigour, and courage of many, transforming a bold vision into a once-in-a-generation call to revitalise the West, empower ordinary Western Australians, and confront fractures in our nation's halls of power. We are profoundly grateful for the scholarly and professional input of colleagues whose rigour sharpened our arguments, and for the clinical insight and decades of medical experience that helped ground our reflections in enduring principles of health and resilience.

We are indebted to Professor Paul Frijters for his patient review of early drafts, invaluable feedback, and guiding insights on pivotal proposals, which fortified the manuscript's intellectual foundation. We likewise extend sincere thanks to Dr Ciara O'Sullivan, Adrian McRae, Jillian Fisher, Camilo Blanco, and Simon Barnett for generously providing workspaces, accommodations, and frank input as the manuscript progressed through countless iterations, and to Pip Clayden and Andrew Hughes for their practical support in Perth and for helping ensure the final steps of this long process were completed.

Finally, we acknowledge all those who pushed back during the covid years and insisted on accountability and open debate; your resolve helped clarify the underlying questions this work seeks to confront, inspiring us to advocate boldly for a sovereign, self-determined future. We also thank Andrew (Gigi's husband) for his patience through the many hours devoted to this manuscript, and for his reflections on the heart of Western Australians, of whom he is one. This work is for you all, and for the West we cherish.

PREQUEL

Each author who has contributed to this book has been deeply concerned at the deterioration in the quality of governance, including reckless economic management, in Canberra, which is to the detriment of the people of Australia. Each of us believes a better future is possible, and that the time is upon us to design that future. We see Western Australia as the most viable territory within Australia's national borders in which to develop and implement that design.

What you are about to read should be viewed as a conversation starter: a collection of initial ideas about how an independent Western Australia might be constituted and might operate, drawing on the authorship team's collective expertise about human nature and human societies in the domains of law, economics, politics, health, sociology, psychology, human development, and democracy. Having studied history and humans for decades, we lay down this book as a gauntlet to spur Western Australians to envision what an existence independent from Canberra and the eastern states could look like. We want those who read this book to take away the belief that secession can be done, and the desire and courage to be part of doing it. Ultimately, we also want Australia's eastern populations to be inspired by this book to build a better future for all Australians.

Within these 400 pages you will find placeholders for new systems of education, health, democracy, defence, finances, and energy; proposals for new institutional structures designed to minimise corruption; a new vision for community responsibility and rights guided by the principle of subsidiarity; and a draft new Constitution. None of these elements should be considered final. One of the great opportunities presented in establishing a new country is the chance to craft that country's institutions so that they reflect what its people want and need, tempered by wisdom and experience about what design elements are effective, feasible, and sustainable. Unlike many new nation-builders of past eras, we have the great fortune to be operating in a time of peace, giving us the time and space to survey and select the best ideas the West has delivered while accommodating modern technology into our designs.

We look forward to the next few years of refining and piloting the ideas presented herein collaboratively with the people of Western Australia. We envision establishing a new research institute whose sole job will be to further develop plans for the new country, drawing on the ideas of the best scholars and designers in the Western world, in consultation with the Western Australian community. We see this nation-designing-and-building process as the most exciting opportunity for Western Australia, and the one most likely to lead to a better life for its people, since the discovery in the middle of the last century of its vast deposits of natural resources.

The idea of secession has been lurking in the back of Western Australians' minds for generations. The assertion that the federal structure is inviolable is not supported by constitutional law, which leaves room for states like Western Australia to reassess their position within the Commonwealth. The High Court has yet to definitively rule on the issue of secession. The absence of explicit prohibition within the Constitution itself opens the way for Western Australia to pursue secession in a legally grounded and orderly manner, particularly if it reflects the democratic will of the state's population. Having borne witness to the betrayals of the covid era and seeing the decay and corruption of our once-great institutions and culture, we believe that now is the moment to turn our minds to making secession a reality, guiding WA to become reborn institutionally and culturally. Let us not pass this opportunity by abrogating our responsibility to craft a stronger, happier, more sustainable future for our children.

We ask all WA residents who wish to contribute their ideas and efforts towards the new country to send a message to SecessionWA@proton.me . We will add you to our secession mailing list, using which a detailed plan for community consultations and institutional piloting will be built. We need and welcome all those who are committed to establishing a free, joyful, healthy, tolerant, strong and confident Western Australia.

We love this state and we love its people, and this great love is what motivates us in this project. Please join us.

The Authorship Team

CONTENTS

Professor Paul Frijters

The authors in this book have guts, you have to give them that.

These four horsemen—ok, three men and a woman actually—not only seek to separate the richest state in Australia from the hangers-on profiting, but also present extensive designs to prevent her bounties falling to anyone else but the people of Western Australia. The authors present timelines and blueprints for introducing anti-corruption authorities with teeth, official-appointments-by-citizen-juries systems to shut out the lobbyists, and community-based health and education systems displacing the bloated bureaucracies. The authors present no less than a revolution in who governs Western Australia and how, neither shy to offer a draft constitution or a government budget. Their 400-page plans are more detailed than most actual budgets and draft legislative proposals, telling you they are serious and mean for you to take it seriously also.

They think secession can be achieved. Their opinion is backed up by constitutional experts and the legacy of a 1933 referendum in which WA already once before expressed a determination to be free, later thwarted in the distant halls of Westminster. This time they mean to push through.

Do the economic proposals in this document make sense, to the degree an outside economist like me can actually check their books? Yes, of course they make sense. It is not that hard to work out how the richest state could run its affairs once independent. Other places with smaller populations than WA have broken from larger countries and thrived, so why not WA? The authors essentially urge Western Australians to adopt an economic model similar to that of Norway, Dubai, and Singapore, three well-run rich places. Roughly put, Western Australia can impose a basic royalty revenue tax of 20% (like Norway), thereby avoid income tax (like Dubai), and trim the government of bloat (like Singapore). The authors throw into the bargain a sensible transition plan for how Western Australia could exchange the Australian Dollar as its current currency for a Western Australian Talent as a new currency. Both the transition paths and the particular economic policies proposed are based on successful examples from other countries, giving confidence in the feasibility of the plans laid out. The authors have simply paid attention to what economic ideas have worked elsewhere. They want Western Australia to have the best that others already have.

So, take it in: four good people—two economists, a lawyer, and a health expert—have put a huge effort into revolutionary proposals to make Western Australia a great independent nation. Backed by many others, they mean for you to join them: to help them work out even more detailed plans and to organise the road to independence. That is history in the making. As such the book is a call to action, a call for Western Australians to believe they can live freer and better than today.

What drove these eminent authors to do such a thing, one may wonder? Why were they not happy with their steady careers?

At a deeper level, this book is driven by rage and disappointment. Rage at the mismanagement and arrogance of Canberra over the last few decades, and in the covid period in particular. Disappointment at how the only policy Canberra can come up with invariably consists of lots more bureaucracy and worse health, education, housing, and other benefits to ordinary citizens. Rage at being belittled by far-away bureaucrats. Disappointment that decades of loyal compliance have merely worsened the exploitation of Western Australia, robbing its youth.

Yet, the authors chose not to dwell on their rage and disappointment but to instead channel their rage into hope. They want Western Australia to become a proud independent nation of its own, with citizens who step up and take matters into their own hands. They took their own hope seriously and worked out how independence might be achieved and what its benefits could be.

What they call for and what they propose then includes a call to Western Australians to take themselves seriously, to adopt a democracy that is about much more than ticking a box every few years in some election. They want a whole new separate institution to guard independent media, and to have oversight of the bureaucracy, run by people not put in place by (dubious) politicians but put in place by citizen juries. Read carefully what they propose, for they mean to set you free by putting actual power into your hands regularly as members of powerful oversight committees.

That is no small proposal, but a sea change in how democracy works. It ensures government of the people, for the people and by the people, promising blessings through imposing an obligation on the citizens to do their duty on these citizen bodies.

So grasp your chance to be more than a follower of regulations who once every few years votes for parties that one needs a microscope to tell apart. Read, reflect, and add your own energy and talents to this cause.

PROFESSOR WILLIAM COLEMAN

Tainted, illegitimate, harmful (and soon regretted): The accession of Western Australia to the 1901 federation

By William Coleman

Origins matter, and this volume finds one easy rationale in the fact that Western Australia's accession to the Federation of 1901 was tainted in provenance, illegitimate in process, harmful in consequence, and soon regretted by even its partisans.[1]

Tainted in Provenance

The impulse to WA's accession lay not in dreams of nationhood, but in the status-striving of a tiny elite, led by the premier John Forrest, and filled out by the youngish, ambitious, well-educated lawyers of genial aspect and easy circumstances, epitomised by two premiers-to-come, George Leake and Walter James. These found in Federation the promise of a grander stage, and brighter honours.[2] To these banal motivations was added a second vital spur, also quite remote from dreams of national unity: the glaring resentment of Perth by the goldfields' population, who saw in Federation a gratifying humiliation of the WA government.

Illegitimate in Process

The Australasian Federation Convention of 1897-8, which formulated the federal Constitution, gave no voice to the people of Western Australia. No delegates were chosen by WA voters; all 14 were WA parliamentarians, chosen, in effect, by the Premier, John Forrest. So Forrest chose himself. Neither did many of these delegates take trouble to make their voice heard at the Convention: Forrest missed 24 percent of the Convention's divisions, Leake 38 percent and James, incredibly, 75 percent.

The constitution Bill which the Convention ultimately drafted was opposed by a majority of WA's delegates. A majority of Forrest's ministry was also emphatically and publicly opposed. Since, according to Forrest, only two of his 30 followers in the Assembly supported it, he wanted it reworked. But 'Federal leaders in other colonies were bombarded with telegrams and letters from Leake and James imploring them not to make any concessions to Forrest or even enter into discussion with them on the subject'. Alfred Deakin gladly acquiesced. 'Forrest has appealed again to the eastern colonies',

---

[1] Unless otherwise provided, the sources for all quotations and quantitative statements may be found in the author's 2021 work *Their Fiery Cross of Union: A Retelling of the Creation of the Australian Federation, 1889-1914*, Brisbane, Connor Court, pp. 160, 218, 256-262, 271, 306-307, and 423.

[2] Made a Privy Councillor in 1897, and elevated from K.C.M.G. to G.C.M.G. in January 1901, Forrest in 1917 was created Baron Forrest of Bunbury.

Deakin told James, 'and has received an absolute refusal to treat with him'. Evidently, this 'federation', devoid of any spirit of compromise, would be an annexation.

At the same time James and Leake, in egregious bad faith, were successfully steering the goldfields' grievances into a demand for a new colony, 'Auralia', which would supposedly join the Commonwealth. In truth, Federationists were hostile to any 'Auralia': for, if it became a reality, the rest of WA, being anti-Federation, would be lost to the Commonwealth. But they seemed confident that separation would not come to pass, and yet WA's Federation sceptics would worry that it might. So Auralia was a useful, if bogus, threat to sponsor. Thus James told Barton that Auralia was a legal impossibility, but 'because our object would be obtained' if Federationists 'declared themselves' for it, Edmund Barton should 'beat up the separation movement'. Similarly, Leake told Barton separation was a 'bogey', but one worth ventilating, and pressed Barton to do so.

In the face of Forrest's aspiration to modify the Bill, Leake even took the extraordinary step of proposing that the Governor of Victoria persuade the Governor of WA—the dubious Sir Gerard Smith, whom the Colonial Office would soon force to resign—to dismiss Forrest, the premier of an elected government, with a majority in both the Assembly and the Council.

Browbeaten, Forrest retreated: the Bill was to be accepted *in toto,* save for four modest concessions. But WA's federationists found any concessions abhorrent. So Forrest sought to have the concessions implemented at the behest of the Colonial Secretary, Joseph Chamberlain, since 'Forrest ... knew from his private correspondence with them that several of the premiers would agree to the WA amendment if Chamberlain asked them to do so ...'. But Deakin, en route to London, had conferred with federationists in Albany—Leake's constituency—had absorbed there their resolutions, and advised Chamberlain to tell WA there would be no revision. Thus Chamberlain, by a telegram to Forrest of 27 April 1900, pointedly raised the costs to WA of only joining the Federation at a later date. So at Chamberlain's 'instigation', Forrest summoned parliament to enact a referendum on 30 July 1900. 'Many things in the scheme', declared Forrest publicly of the Constitution, 'had been carried out, as it were, at the point of the bayonet'.

In the subsequent referendum, Victorian federationists funded the Yes campaign. Deakin plainly entreated his comrades in the west, 'Tell us what sum you would require from us to enable you to carry out the campaign efficiently but of course as economically as possible'. But regardless of such tonics, the goldfields' dizzying 95 percent Yes vote would have carried the day for federationists. A haze of dubiety does enfold the precise dimensions of the Yes vote, since expedients intended to enlarge voter participation occasioned multiple voting and roll-packing. The fact that the electoral roll actually contracted by 20 percent in the nine months between the referendum of 1900 and the first federal election suggests a good deal of fraudulent enrolments. But ballot fraud could hardly have altered the Yes result. The lack of legitimation of the Yes majority of July 1900 lies not in any supposed numerical inauthenticity of it, but in the fact that the majority obscures how badly split was WA. In 18 of her 44 Assembly seats, 66.5 percent of votes were cast for No. So the great question is whether the goldfields had any right to a say in WA's fate as a whole? The right to vote on constitutional issues, surely, has a price greater than mere residence. Constitution-making is so deep a transaction, allegiance must be the price of participating in constitutional change. Palpably, no gold miners felt anything approaching 'allegiance' to WA. The only constitutional referendum which the goldfields would have a good claim to be part of would have been one regarding their own secession.

Harmful Consequences

Federation injured WA as soon as the new Commonwealth passed the *Customs Tariff Act 1902*. By this Act Victoria made captive markets of Australia's unindustrialised states, including WA, to its own benefit and their cost. Even Leake, by then WA Premier, protested, 'the tariff that had been placed before them by the Federal Ministry was neither a free trade nor a revenue tariff, but was an all round protectionist tariff. ... Victoria under the circumstances of the Federal tariff would be able to trade where she liked in Australia, while all the other states would only be able to trade with Victoria'.

Further crude and brutal exploitations of WA followed, climaxing perhaps in the High Court's extraordinary judgement of 1920 (*W & A McArthur Ltd v Queensland* HCA 77), that Section 92 did not apply to Commonwealth legislation, 'leaving the Commonwealth free to impose any embargo it desired on interstate transport', thereby causing 'untold losses' to WA, by permitting the Commonwealth to forbid 'either goods or passengers to travel by ocean-going steamers' to WA.

The sad truth is that Federation had left WA the ill-cast, minor character of a drama written by others, for their own profit.

Soon Regretted

Second thoughts on the wisdom of Yes seem to have been felt almost immediately. The turnout in WA in the inaugural Federal election of 1901 was spectacularly low: only a bit more than one in three voters saw any benefit in voting for their new Commonwealth representatives. Only one Convention delegate from WA entered the 1901 parliament (Forrest), reflecting the Constitution's near complete repudiation by members of WA's parliament. By contrast, six of the NSW delegates would become members of the new federal parliament, seven of the SA delegates and eight of the Victorian delegates.

Disillusion is best exemplified by Walter James, once an irrepressible partisan of Federation. As Premier from 1902, "he was soon embroiled with the Commonwealth in disputes: occupancy of transferred buildings; channels of communication; disentanglement of governmental functions; State debts; refunds of customs revenue to the State...leading to clashes between James and Federal ministers Deakin and C. C. Kingston."[3]

30 years later, on the eve of the Secession referendum, James was to recall how in the controversies over Federation in the 1890s,

> *There was much expressed anxiety by the smaller States at the grant of these powers [to the Commonwealth], but time after time we were urged to trust the honour of the Federal Parliament and its sense of moral responsibility to all the States, large or small, rich or poor. In that trust we entered the Commonwealth. For years past we have seen how vain that trust has been:*

[3] Lyall Hunt, 1983. 'James, Sir Walter Hartwell (1863–1943)', *Australian Dictionary of Biography*, 9, Melbourne, Melbourne University Press.

> *how the honour to which we looked has lost itself in the quicksand of power-loving parties and office-loving Ministries who know not the West.*

He then asked,

> *what are we to do in this State? If we are content to see the spirit of our Constitution outraged and our interests and feelings ignored then we should vote against Secession—content to be men and women without self-respect. If we are not content then we should let that fact be known in no indecisive manner.*[4]

James' sentiment would well serve Western Australians today.

[4] *West Australian* 6.4.1933.

Professor Augusto Zimmermann

Secession by Western Australia: Is it Constitutionally Possible?

By Augusto Zimmermann*

It is a pleasure to write this Foreword for 'Secession by Western Australia'. The arguments set out in this Foreword relate specifically to the legal possibility of secession by the people of this State from the Commonwealth of Australia.

Western Australians have long contemplated the possibility of seceding from the Australian federation. Secession can be defined as follows: 'The action of one of the component regions of the Federation concerned in withdrawing from that Federation, thereby asserting independence of the Federal Government and law'. [1]

Although the secessionist movement of the 1930s was ultimately unsuccessful, secessionist feelings continue down to this day. State grievances over ever increasing centralisation of power in Canberra are long-standing and, if anything, have intensified in recent times.[2]

The origins of the secession debate in Western Australia can be traced to the era leading up to Federation and its initial reluctance to become a member State.[3] In the 1890s, the colony was invited to attend constitutional conventions for the purpose of joining the other colonies of Australia to make up a Federation. Throughout those years Western Australian political leaders, such as the redoubtable Premier John Forrest, often expressed serious reservations about joining the new Commonwealth.

There were several reasons for such hesitancy. For example, Western Australians were extremely concerned that their economy would be crippled for the benefit of continental neighbours with whom they had little affinity.[4] The colony of Western Australia generated almost half of its revenue from inter-colonial tariffs,[5] and there was widespread concern that this income would be lost, since one of the main driving forces behind federation in the eastern colonies was the creation of a Australian 'free

---

* Dean and Professor of Law, Alphacrucis University College. This article includes material previously published in A. Zimmermann, 'The Still Reluctant State: Western Australia and the Conceptual Foundations of Australian Federalism', in: G. Appleby, N. Aroney and T. John, *The Future of Australian Federalism: Comparative Interdisciplinary Perspectives* (Cambridge University Press, 2012), p. 75-95.

[1] G. Craven, *Secession: The Ultimate States Right* (Melbourne, Vic: Melbourne University Press, 1986), p.4.

[2] See L. Curtis, 'Tax Review Stokes WA Secession Whispers', *ABC News*, Friday, 30 April, http://www.abc.net.au/news/stories/2010/04/30/2887478.htm. See also A. O'Brien, 'Tempers Flare but no Tanks Across the Nullabor Yet', *The Australian*, 8 May 2010, 2010, http://www.theaustralian.com.au/news/nation/tempers-flare-but-no-tanks-across-the-nullarbor-yet/story-e6frg6nf-1225863645688

[3] T. Musgrave, 'The Western Australian Secessionist Movement', *Macquarie Law Journal*, 3 (2003), 95.

[4] Musgrave, above n.3, p. 96.

[5] A. Shaw, *The Story of Australia* (New York, NY: Faber and Faber, 1961), p. 195.

trade' zone, something which in fact eventuated when the Commonwealth Constitution's requirement that trade, commerce and intercourse among the States be 'absolutely free' came into force.[6]

Mainly due to these concerns, Western Australia did not participate in the referendums of 1898 and 1899 for the approval of the proposed Federal Constitution. Despite its initial unwillingness, however, Western Australia did join the Commonwealth as an original member State—but only just. It was only in 1900, at the last gasp as it were, that the colony reluctantly agreed, in the face of threats by the people of Kalgoorlie and surrounding areas—most of whom had recently moved over from the eastern colonies in search for gold—to secede from Western Australia and join the new federation if the colony did not do so.[7]

With the promise of a train line to the east, and a specially negotiated five-year transitional decrease in inter-colonial tariffs, Western Australia held a referendum on 31 July 1900, and decided by a majority of 44,800 to 19,691 to join the Commonwealth. As the referendum did not take place until after the Commonwealth Constitution had been finally enacted, however, the agreement of Western Australia to federate *was not mentioned in the preamble.*

This omission of Western Australian in the preamble to the Commonwealth Constitution continues to undermine the unity expressed in those words.[8] Arguably, if the presence of Western Australia 'had not been necessary in the creation of the Federation, neither would its withdrawal affect its ongoing existence'.[9]

The Dominion League and the 1933 Secession Referendum

The call for Western Australia to secede has been a recurring theme throughout federation. As early as 1906 the Legislative Assembly passed by 19 votes to 8 a resolution which declared that the Commonwealth had 'proved detrimental to the best interest' of Western Australia, and called for a referendum to canvass public support for secession.[10] However, the resolution was not greeted with sufficient enthusiasm by the youthful Premier, Newton James Moore, and no further action was taken at that stage.

---

[6] Commonwealth Constitution, s.92.

[7] C. Besant, 'Two Nations, Two Destinies: A Reflection on the Significance of the Western Australian Secessionist Movement to Australia, Canada, and the British Empire' (1990) 20 *University of Western Australian Law Review* 209, p. 226.

[8] G. Williams, 'Too Rich, Too Weak to Succeed Seceding', *The Sydney Morning Herald*, Sydney, 31 September 2010, http://www.smh.com.au/opinion/politics/too-rich-too-weak-to-succeed-seceding-20100510-uoma.html

[9] Musgrave, above n.3, p.119.

[10] Legislative Assembly Debates, vol.29, 1906, p.1871. See also 'Secession', *The Sydney Morning Herald*, Sydney, 19 July 1906, p.6; 'Western Australia and the Commonwealth: Is Federation Detrimental? Discussion in the Legislative Assembly', *The West Australian*, Perth, 2 August 1906, p.4; 'Western Australia and Secession, Interview with Walter James', *The West Australian*, Perth, 29 September 1906, p.11.

After the special fiscal benefits of section 95 came to an end in 1905,[11] the Western Australian budget faced several fundamental problems.[12] In 1921, a local committee was appointed by the government of Western Australia to inquire into the effects of federation on the State's economy. The committee found that the economic difficulties of the State stemmed largely from the policies being pursued by the federal government.[13] The findings made by this committee were effectively confirmed by a federal agency, the Commonwealth Tariff Board, which even went on to describe Western Australia as being 'on the road of serfdom' under the tariff policy.[14]

To add to Western Australia's woes, the trend in High Court constitutional cases effectively expanded the Commonwealth's power at the expense of the States, particularly following the landmark decision in *Engineers* (1920).[15] This no doubt served to aggravate the State's dissatisfaction. To make matters worse, as a result of the decision in *Victoria v Commonwealth* (1926)[16] the Commonwealth was able to make section 96 grants—upon which Western Australia was heavily dependent—conditional upon virtually any terms and conditions that it saw fit.

Between 1900 and the early 1930s Western Australian confidence in the benefits of being part of the Commonwealth diminished dramatically. The Secession League, established in 1926 by James MacCullum Smith, editor of the local newspaper *The Sunday Times*, was the first organisation to advocate that Western Australia secede from the Australian Federation. However, the Secession League had a rather short life and soon was succeeded by a far more successful organisation, the Dominion League. Inaugurated at His Majesty's Theatre on 30th July 1930, the Dominion League's aim was simple: to have Western Australia secede from the Commonwealth of Australia and become an independent Dominion within the British Empire.[17]

In December 1932, the Western Australian Parliament enacted the *Secession Referendum Act 1932* (WA), a statute declaring that a referendum on secession was to be held in conjunction with the next State general election. On 8 April 1933, the referendum was held, and no less than 68 per cent of Western Australian electors (138,654 to 70,706) voted in favour of seceding from the Commonwealth. The goldfields were the only major region in the State to reject the call to secede, voting instead for an alternative proposition which called for a national convention to alter the Constitution 'as may appear to such convention to be necessary'. This second question was added to satisfy the Labor Opposition which was opposed to secession.

---

[11] Section 95 enabled Western Australia, on condition that it entered the federation as 'an original State', to continue to impose customs duties, on a diminishing scale and only over a period of five years. It also permitted Western Australia to maintain its inter-colonial tariff within the federation for a period of five years, in a formula which decreased the tariff by twenty percent each successive year.

[12] J. Robertson, '1930-39', in F.K. Crowley (ed.), *A New History of Australia* (Melbourne, Vic: Heinemann, 1974), p.432.

[13] Besant, above n.7, p.234.

[14] Id.

[15] (1920) 28 CLR 129

[16] (1926) 38 CLR 399

[17] C. Court, *Charles Court, The Early Years – An Autobiography* (Fremantle, WA: Fremantle Arts Centre Press, 1995), p. 169.

Paradoxically, on the very day that Western Australians decided to secede they also voted to replace the government that had openly supported secession.[18] The newly elected Labor government of Premier Collier did not support secession but recognised that it was politically impossible to go against the will of a very substantial majority of voters. The Premier was therefore quick to promise that his government would take 'all necessary steps to give effect to the majority decision of the people'.[19]

As Western Australians did not wish to sever ties with the United Kingdom, and as the amendment process required a dual majority of voters across the entire country and was therefore unlikely to be successful, the government chose to proceed by way of petition to the Imperial Parliament (UK), requesting that Western Australia be re-established as an independent self-governing colony.[20]

The delegation sent to London to petition the House of Lords and House of Commons for secession was led by the Agent General for the State, Sir Hal Colebatch, with Matthew Lewis Moss as legal advisor. The delegation presented *The Case for Secession* to the British Parliament in November 1934.[21] The petition was presented in the House of Lords by the Marquis of Aberdeen and in the House of Commons by Captain Adrian Mooring, MP, on 17 December 1934. The Parliament announced, however, that it was unable to consider the petition until it had determined whether it was properly receivable under the constitutional law and conventions of the time, and appointed a Joint Select Committee in early 1935 to consider the issue.[22] The Joint Select Committee received submissions on behalf of both Western Australia and the Commonwealth.[23]

After eighteen months of negotiations and lobbying, the petition from Western Australia was formally rejected, in November 1935. The Joint Select Committee affirmed that the doctrine of parliamentary sovereignty enabled the Parliament to legislate for the 'whole Empire' and receive any petition it saw fit. Yet, a practice had been developed whereby the Parliament would not legislate on matters relating to the affairs of Dominions unless specifically requested to do so by the Dominion in question,[24] a practice that was summarised in the 1926 *Balfour Declaration* and later enacted into law in the *Statute of Westminster 1931* (Imp).

Based on this line of reasoning, the committee concluded that to pass the Act desired by Western Australia would be incompatible with the 'Constitutional conventions of the Empire unless the demand for such legislation came as the clearly expressed wish of the Australian people as a whole'.[25] Although the former Australian colonies retained the right to petition the Parliament directly on matters that fell solely within their powers and responsibilities, the committee considered that the

---

[18] H.G.P. Colebatch, *Steadfast Knight: A Life of Sir Hal Colebatch* (Fremantle, WA: Fremantle Arts Centre Press, 2004), p. 170.
[19] E. Watt, 'Secession in Western Australia', *University Studies in Western Australian History*, 3 (1958), 64.
[20] K. Booker, A. Glass and R. Watt, *Federal Constitutional Law: An Introduction* (Sydney, NSW: Butterworths, 1998), p. 14.
[21] Musgrave, above n.3, p. 109.
[22] Id.
[23] Id., pp. 31-37, 40-41, 52-57.
[24] Musgrave, above n.3, p.109.
[25] Colebatch, above n.18, p.174.

question of secession was relevant to the whole of the Australian Commonwealth and its people, and as such the Imperial Parliament was prevented from receiving the petition without a direct request to do so from the federal government.[26] And it went without saying that there was no intention on the part of the federal government to request this.

Following the failure of the petition and negotiations surrounding it, secessionists were initially disheartened but soon started lobbying the Western Australian government, calling for unilateral secession. The request, however, was ignored by a Labor government that was never very enthusiastic about secession, and the Dominion League gradually lost support in the community. By 1938 the League had virtually ceased to exist. [27]

The Secession of Western Australia: Is it legally possible? How is it legally possible?

Although the British Parliament rejected the attempt to secede made by Western Australia in 1935 on the ground that it would not interfere with internal matters of a Dominion without the request of the Dominion government itself, an amendment to the Constitution by an Act of Parliament in the United Kingdom was still conceptually possible, though highly unlikely, until 1986.[28]

In that year, with the simultaneous enactment of the *Australia Act 1986* by the British and Australian Parliaments, the remaining, though remote, possibility that Western Australia might secede through parliamentary enactment came to a decisive end. Section 1 of the Act states that 'no Act of Parliament of the United Kingdom passed after the commencement of this Act shall extend, or be deemed to extend, to the Commonwealth, to a State or to a Territory as part of the law of the Commonwealth, of the State or of the Territory'.

This effectively puts an end to any further request for British intervention, such as occurred in 1934.[29] It basically means that Western Australia can now secede from the Australian Federation without the approval of the British Parliament.

The Legal Status of the Preamble

Held between 1891 and 1899, constitutional conventions that agreed on the elaboration of a federal Constitution were attended by representatives of every colony. Upon the request of these colonies *except for Western Australia, which only accepted to join Federation afterwards*, the *Commonwealth of Australia Constitution Act (Imp)* was first drafted by representatives of the citizens of the colonies in Australia, and then passed by the British Parliament on 5 July 1900, with Queen Victoria assenting to

---

[26] Musgrave, above n. 3, p. 120-22.
[27] Besant, above n.4, p. 229.
[28] For a discussion of the point at which the UK Parliament finally lost or abdicated the capacity to legislate for Australia, see R.D. Lumb, 'The Bicentenary of Australian Constitutionalism: The Evolution of Rules of Constitutional Change' (1988) 15 *University of Queensland Law Journal* 1.
[29] On the *Australia Act 1986*, see *Sue v Hill* (1999) 199 CLR 462 and *Attorney-General (W.A.) v. Marquet* (2003) 217 CLR 545.

the Bill four days later. In September 1900, the Queen proclaimed that the Commonwealth of Australia would come into existence on 1 January 1901.

The preamble to the Commonwealth Constitution is the only place in the entire document where there is any reference to the idea of secession.[30] The preamble recites the agreement of the people of the Australian colonies 'to unite in one *indissoluble* Federal Commonwealth'.[31]

In accordance with the traditional principles of legal interpretation, the preamble typically occupies a position of secondary importance, being only of relevance in the interpretation of an ambiguous provision within the main body of legislation statute.[32] In *Bowtell*, Griffith CJ stated that the plain words of an enactment could 'never be affected' by the preamble.[33] Only where the words were uncertain, and then only 'in a proper case', should the preamble be consulted to resolve the ambiguity. This was confirmed by the High Court in *Wacando.*[34]

As a result, the preamble could never operate as a direct prohibition of the unilateral secession of an Australian State. What is more, The Preamble only says that 'the people of New South Wales, Victoria, South Australia, Queensland and Tasmania.. agreed to unite in one indissoluble Federal Commonwealth'.

As can be seen, the people of Western Australia are not even mentioned in the Preamble to the Constitution. Now, if the presence of Western Australia was unnecessary for the formation of the Australian Federation, it can be easily said, for the same reason, that the permanence of the State in the Federation is legally non-obligatory. Above all, the statement in the Preamble regarding "indissolubility" certainly does not apply to the State of Western Australia.

It is also often said that the vast majority of the constitutional drafters intended the Australian federation to be 'permanent and indestructible'.[35] This may well be so but the fact is that they also neglected to include an explicit bar to secession in the substantive provisions of the Constitution. While the preamble may arguably act as a guide to the intention of the drafters, it cannot act alone to bar a State such as Western Australia from seceding, provided some independent legal basis for secession can be established. Indeed, the Joint Select Committee that scrutinised the matter in the 1930s agreed that secession was constitutionally possible in some circumstances, despite the existence of the preamble.[36]

---

30 G. Craven, "The Constitutionality of the Unilateral Secession of an Australian State', *Federal Law Review* 15 (1985), 124.

31 Emphasis added.

32 *Stowel v Lord Zouch* (1562) 75 ER 536; *Overseers v West Ham Iles* (1883) 8 App Cas 386, 388; *Sussex Peerage Claim* (1884) 11 CL & Fin 85, 143.

33 *Bowtell v Goldsborough, Mort & Co Ltd* (1906) 3 CLR 444, 451.

34 *Wacando v Commonwealth of Australia* (1981) 148 CLR 1, 15-6.

35 Eg, *Convention Debates*, Adelaide, 1897, p.128. (J. Symon)

36 Musgrave, above n.2, p. 126.

The Legality of Unilateral Secession

The possibility that a State might unilaterally secede has 'always held an ambiguous position in the political and constitutional folklore of Australia'.[37] Since nothing is said explicitly in the Constitution about the matter, much is left to speculation about how the Constitution is best interpreted. At stake is the possibility that a State might seek to leave the federal union lawfully and peacefully, just as it entered the union in the first place. In other words, unilateral secession can be regarded as the means by which a State regains its former independence. Secession, as such, is the counterpart of accession, the manner in which a State joined the federation in the first place.

Prior to the American Civil War (1861-1865), a great number of American jurists believed that since the individual States had created the federal Union, each State retained the right to secede. They also relied on the absence of any specific declaration of indissolubility in the U.S. Constitution.[38] This was particularly the approach taken by the secessionists in the American South, who invoked State sovereignty as the basis of a claim to an implied right to secede unilaterally, coupled with an extra-constitutional, non-justiciable right to secede said to be enshrined in the American Declaration of Independence, particularly in the following terms:

> Governments are instituted among Men, deriving their just Powers from the Consent of the Governed, that whenever any Form of Government becomes destructive of these Ends, it is the Right of the People to alter or to abolish it, and to institute new Government, laying its Foundation on such Principles, and organizing its Powers in such Form, as to them shall seem most likely to effect their Safety and Happiness.

The proposition aimed at here was that the American States individually enjoyed a right to unilateral secession as an implication of the right of all free people to self-government. The argument was developed by Thomas Jefferson, author of the Declaration, who wrote in 1816: 'If any State in the Union will declare that it prefers separation ... to a continuance in union ... I have no hesitation in saying, 'let us separate''.[39]

In the United States, the doctrine of the indestructibility of the Union is an idea that was imposed upon the States ultimately not by means of legal argumentation but by 'blood and iron', so to speak. It is a doctrine that was imposed during the Civil War at the cost of the lives of a million people. Professor Laurence Tribe has observed that it is 'a ban etched in the blood of civil war rather than in ink on parchment'.[40] Tribe also explains that Article V of the American Constitution, 'by allowing measures

---

[37] Craven, above n.62, p. 123.

[38] This was the argument presented by John Calhoun and Robert Hayne of South Carolina in their debates with Daniel Webster of Massachusetts, and in a series of congressional addresses formulating their view of the relations which the states and the federal government bore to each other. To Webster, the Union was an indivisible expression of the will of one nation of people. To Hayne and Calhoun, the Union was a voluntary compact among sovereign States. See H. Belz (ed.), *The Webster-Hayne Debate on the Nature of the Union.* (Indianapolis/IN: Liberty Fund, 2000).

[39] T. Jefferson, 'Letter to W. Crawford' (20 June 1816), quoted from C.R. Sunstein, 'Constitutionalism and Secession', *University of Chicago Law Review*, 58 (1991), 657.

[40] L.H. Tribe, 'American Constitutional Law, Vol.1', (3rd ed., New York, NY: Foundation Press, 2000), p. 1246.

to strip a state of its equal franchise in the Senate so long as the state consents, might be thought to imply that Congress may permit or ratify a state's secession from the Union'.[41]

The perpetuity of the federal Union received judicial sanction only after the Civil War. In the landmark case of *Texas v White* (1869) the Supreme Court held that the attempt of Texas to secede was unconstitutional on the ground that the States' agreement to join the federation amounted to a waiver of the right to withdraw.[42] Once the States decided to join the federation, the Court said there was 'no place for reconsideration or revocation, except through revolution, or through the consent of the States', meaning the consent of the *other* States.[43] Marchildon and Maxwell comment:

> Although the southern states were defeated militarily, the legal validity of their compact argument was never successfully challenged until *Texas v. White*. The compact argument was denied in that particular case, but Chief Justice Chase's tortuous reasoning can hardly be employed as a general legal argument against the operation of the compact theory and the implicit right of secession in other circumstances.[44]

Thomas Cooley, a distinguished nineteenth-century American constitutionalist, once stated that the theoretical postulate of indissolubility 'by no means implies the loss of distinct and individual existence, or of the right of self-government by the States'.[45] As Cooley pointed out, it is equally important to recognise that there must be 'no loss of separate and independent autonomy to the States through their union under the Constitution... [because] the preservation of the States and the maintenance of their governments are as much within the design and care of the Constitution as the preservation of the Union and the maintenance of the national government'.[46]

From what has been said it might be argued that secession could be justified if it is possible for a State to demonstrate that its legal capacity to exist as an autonomous entity has been violated. As far as federalism is concerned, when a State is unfairly treated and gravely prejudiced, and its financial independence grossly attacked, all contrary to the letter and spirit of the original compact, such a State could possibly claim an implied right to secede on the ground that that the central government has radically undermined the integrity of the federal system.

This is what Western Australia argued in the 1930s to support the cause of secession. Since the federal division of powers in the Constitution had been violated by the central government (with the connivance of the High Court), the Australian Commonwealth was no longer the same kind of federation that Western Australia had agreed to enter into. Hence, the State claimed that it was entitled to

---

[41] Id. Tribe however recognises that today few American lawyers 'would deny that the Constitution forbids secession from the Union by any state – the axiom over which the Civil War was fought – even though that principle of national indissolubility is nowhere written into [this] fundamental charter'. Id., p. 32.
[42] *Texas v White* (1869) 74 US 700, p. 724-26
[43] Id, p.726. Of course, the High Court is not bound to *Texas*. In fact, no Australian court has ever considered the issue of whether a right of secession exists, although it is likely that the High Court would follow the American Supreme Court's decision.
[44] G. Marchildon and E. Maxwell, 'Quebec's Right of Secession Under Canadian and International Law', *Virginia Journal of International Law*, 32 (1992), 594.
[45] T.M. Cooley, *Principles of Constitutional Law* (3rd ed., Boston, MA: Little, Brown & Co., 1898), p. 29.
[46] Id. Cooley's statement is taken from *Texas v White* (1869) 74 US 700, 725.

be relieved from its constitutional obligation to remain within the federation. However, the possibility of unilateral secession was not pursued mainly because on the same day the secessionists had won the secession referendum, an anti-secessionist Labor Government was returned to power.[47]

The Principle of Self-Determination

Finally, the right of secession might also be said to derive from self-determination as a principle of international law. Many international instruments proclaim the principle of self-determination. For instance, the United Nations' International Covenant on Civil and Political Rights (1966), which has been signed and ratified by Australia, declares: 'All peoples have the right of self-determination. By virtue of that right they freely determine their political status and freely pursue their economic, social and cultural development'.[48]

The principle of self-determination appears to be founded upon essentially democratic premises. The principle bestows a right upon a local community to 'determine itself', meaning to determine for itself that it has the capacity and status of a self-governing community. Similarly, secession has been said to represent 'the ultimate sovereignty of a national group or groups over the territory which they inhabit'.[49] It has even been suggested that self-determination can encourage the development of human rights, including those of voting, assembly, speaking out and holding office.[50]

In this sense, depending on the emphasis to be attached to the competing legal considerations, a case could be made that Western Australia has a fundamental right to secede *if* the people of that State were to indicate democratically and clearly an unmistakable desire to govern themselves independently. It is barely possible that in such a case the rest of the Commonwealth might even acquiesce with the State's decision to secede. If that were to happen Australia would make a very substantial contribution to the development of a 'new customary international law respecting secession'.[51]

What about a Confederal Model?

A possible secession of Western Australia would not necessarily have to break all affective and contractual ties with the other states of the Australian Federation. A confederal model could be established between Western Australia and the other Australian States, so that the people of Western Australia would no longer be subject to Canberra's compulsory legal deliberations as it pleases.

The confederal model is a contract of sovereign states under international law, with the goal of establishing certain common tasks, such as ensuring freedom of commerce, in addition to other expressly

---

[47] Back in those days, says Hal G.P. Colebatch, 'the Labor Party was not merely anti-secessionist, but much of it favoured the abolition of the states altogether'. Colebatch, above n.18, p. 164.
[48] *UN International Covenant on Civil and Political Rights* (1966), Article 1.
[49] A. Pavokovic and P. Radan, 'In Pursuit of Sovereignty and Self-Determination: Peoples, States and Secession in the International Order', *Macquarie Law Journal*, 3 (2003), 7.
[50] L. Seshagiri, 'Democratic Disobedience: Reconceiving Self-Determination and Secession at International Law', *Harvard International Law Journal*, 51 (2010), 4.
[51] Marchildon, above n.76, p. 590.

agreed objectives. It designates, in this way, an international agreement from which the states remain sovereign, although in this case submitted, of their own volition, to the confederal contract.

The Confederate State is a person of Public International Law; that is, a true State before the international community. Citizens are nationals of the Confederate State. In a Confederation, the States are bound by a treaty, more appropriate to international law; whereas in the Federation the States are united by means of constitutional law, by a written and rigid Constitution.

In a Confederal model, each State retains its *right of secession*, and it may unilaterally withdraw from the confederal pact. Decisions are taken via diplomatic meetings and the unanimous decision of delegates representing each member state is necessary.

Perhaps an eventual secession from Western Australia could engender the discussion of a confederal model for Australia, namely a confederal pact between the people of Western Australia and those of the other states of the Australian Federation.

Conclusion

The Western Australian secession movement of the 1930s has never entirely died away. According to H.G.P. Colebatch, 'the secession movement has never entirely died away but waxing and waning public interest seems to depend closely on perceptions of how fairly or otherwise Western Australia is being treated in the Federation'. [52]

Arguably, the widespread feeling in Western Australia of injustice and unfairness would have been avoided if the intention of the constitutional drafters had been preserved. In the end the problem could be resolved by means of federal reform via referendum and subsequent amendment to the Constitution.[53]

Until that happens, it seems that talk of secession in the west will only continue, and perhaps even grow in magnitude. A confederal model was discussed in this article. Legally speaking, it is my view as a constitutional law academic that it is entirely possible for Western Australia to secede from the Australian Federation.

[52] Colebatch, above n.18, p. 164.

[53] As George Williams points out, *'the decline of the states, due in part to growth of federal power, causes particular problems of governance and democratic accountability in Western Australia. The calls there for independence reflect this, and should be met with a renewed effort to produce a federation that better serves the needs of the people of every state'*. Williams, above n.8.

Maryanne Demasi, PhD

For as long as I can remember, medicine and health policy have involved disagreement—over treatments, guidelines, and evidence—but the ethical foundations of clinical practice were largely accepted. Informed consent, individualised care, and the centrality of the doctor–patient relationship were treated as sacrosanct. They were the cornerstones of medicine, and they made trust possible. But the covid pandemic shattered that confidence.

Almost overnight, long-standing ethical norms were swept aside. Emergency powers expanded. Public health directives replaced clinical judgement. Doctors who questioned prevailing policies were silenced, deregistered, or publicly discredited. Patients were told that refusing medical interventions—regardless of age, risk profile, or prior immunity—was selfish, irresponsible, even dangerous. Informed consent, once the bedrock of medical practice, was reduced to a box-ticking exercise, or dismissed altogether as a luxury that could not be afforded in a crisis.

For many people, this was not an abstract debate. It was deeply personal: the loss of bodily autonomy, the fear of asking questions, the breakdown of trust between patients and clinicians, and the growing sense that medicine had become an instrument of policy rather than care.

It is in this context that the medical chapters of *Secession by Western Australia* must be read.

Julian Gillespie and Professor Ian Brighthope, who authored those chapters, recognise something fundamental: the pandemic exposed not only a public-health failure, but a failure of governance. As decisions affecting people's bodies were increasingly enforced through coercive mandates, ethical boundaries eroded with remarkable speed. The result was a profound fracture—not only in public trust, but within medicine itself.

As a medical journalist, what struck me most during this period was how often serious concerns were voiced quietly but not publicly. Clinicians spoke candidly off the record about uncertainty, risk, and ethical unease, while acknowledging that raising those same concerns openly carried professional consequences. Having faced institutional pushback myself for questioning prevailing narratives, I came to understand first-hand how quickly professional consequences can silence legitimate inquiry.

Institutions that should have welcomed scrutiny instead closed ranks. Debate narrowed, or was actively censored, and the normal mechanisms by which medicine corrects itself—questioning, dissent, revision—were treated as threats rather than necessities.

Doctors found themselves constrained by rigid protocols that left little room for clinical judgement. Public discussion of uncertainty was framed as disloyalty, rather than recognised as an ordinary and essential feature of science. Regulatory bodies, established to protect patients, increasingly appeared to protect policy instead. In some cases, simply acknowledging risk or uncertainty—even when accurate—was labelled misinformation.

This did not happen in a vacuum. It was enabled by a highly centralised system in which authority flowed downward, accountability was diffuse, and individual decision-making was sidelined. Covid revealed how quickly ethical guardrails can give way when power is concentrated and dissent is censored.

Medicine cannot function ethically when fear drives decision-making, when emergency measures become normalised, and when patients are reduced to instruments of political policy rather than individuals seeking care.

The authors of *Secession* see these failures as symptoms of a deeper structural problem: governance that is centralised and insulated from those it affects. They argue that protecting medical freedom requires more than ethical principles—it requires systems and safeguards that ensure consent, clinical judgement, and dissent are not so easily swept aside in the next crisis.

Readers may or may not accept the book's ultimate conclusion. Secession is a bold and consequential proposal, and some people might disagree about whether it offers the right path forward for Western Australia. My purpose here is not to settle that debate, but to suggest that the medical experience of recent years helps explain why such arguments are being made.

When medicine is no longer grounded in consent, people begin to distrust the structures that govern it. I certainly have. When clinicians are punished for raising concerns, confidence in regulatory independence erodes. When policies are imposed uniformly, without regard for context, people begin to wonder whether decision-making has drifted too far from those it is meant to serve.

Medical freedom is not about science denial. It is about preserving the ethical conditions under which medicine remains legitimate: openness, humility, debate, and respect for individual autonomy. These are not optional values, nor luxuries reserved for calm times. They are the foundations of good clinical practice—and of democratic societies more broadly—and they matter most when pressure is greatest.

Secession argues that restoring those values may require structural change, not only within health systems, but in how power is exercised and constrained. Whether or not one agrees with that prescription, the diagnosis deserves serious attention. Systems that concentrate authority, suppress dissent, and allow politics to override clinical judgement do not fail only in theory. They fail in practice, and the costs are borne by patients, clinicians, and public trust alike.

After years reporting on drug regulation, public health policy, and medical controversy, I have come to believe that trust cannot be commanded or enforced. It cannot be rebuilt through slogans after the fact. Trust is earned through transparency, accountability, and a willingness to tolerate disagreement—especially when the stakes are high. Covid showed how quickly trust can be squandered, and how difficult it is to restore once lost.

This book asks readers to confront uncomfortable questions: how far authority should extend into medical decision-making; what limits should exist on emergency powers; and what safeguards are needed to ensure that consent and dissent are not treated as expendable in the next crisis. These questions go to the heart of whether medicine remains a humane profession, and whether governance remains answerable to the people it serves.

Secession by Western Australia refuses to treat the medical failures of recent years as aberrations to be forgotten. It insists they be examined, learned from, and addressed—not only through better policy, but through stronger ethical and institutional guardrails. Medicine is not just technical; it is moral, social, and deeply human. That is the lens through which this book should be read.

INTRODUCTION

A New Common Sense for Western Australia

Nearly a century ago, Western Australians petitioned for freedom from an overbearing federation—a cry ignored in the halls of power. Today, the Commonwealth of Australia looms over Western Australia like a distant monarch, ruling not by hereditary right but through a two-party dynasty. In Thomas Paine's day, the English king and Parliament conspired against the American colonies; in our time the Commonwealth and its heirs—the Labor and Liberal parties and their collaborators that have their roots in the eastern states' urban elite—have captured Parliament, shutting out the people of Western Australia from real democratic control. This opening polemic, in the spirit of Paine's *Common Sense*, lays bare the present crisis. Western Australia finds itself as America once did: governed by a distant power that treats it as a vassal province, exploits its wealth, and calls this plunder unity. We ask in earnest: must the people of Western Australia forever remain supplicants to a federated Crown that devours our substance?

Yet our call for self-determination arises not from any rejection of Australia or its people. Western Australians are proud participants in the national story-we have celebrated the ANZAC legacy of courage and sacrifice, marveled at the ancient majesty of Uluru, cheered alongside our mates at the MCG, and watched with millions of families as the boats set off for Hobart on Boxing Day. Our push for independence does not reject this shared heritage, our 'Australianness', but rather seeks to fully embrace its best aspects by casting off the shackles that Canberra has imposed on us and replacing them with local, accountable governance. Indeed, we believe the true spirit of Australianness—our egalitarian ethos, our belief in a "fair go" for all, and our world-renowned mateship—can be upheld only by a government that is close to its people and answerable to them. It is out of loyalty to these Australian ideals that we can no longer abide a system that so routinely betrays them.

The Commonwealth as King and Parties as Heirs

Government, Paine wrote, is at best a necessary evil and at worst an intolerable yoke. We contend that the Commonwealth of Australia has become an intolerable yoke upon Western Australia. It presides imperiously from Canberra—a "de facto" monarch in all but name—with the major parties alternating as its heirs apparent. These two factions share the throne like feuding princelings, more alike than different in their entitlement. Through caucus discipline, closed-party preselection, and the maturation of a cradle-to-grave grooming system that produces cohort upon cohort of career politicians representing nothing but their party's interests, the major parties have usurped the sovereignty of the people, leaving Western Australians effectively voiceless. The Commonwealth's ministries act as a court clique. In stark contrast to the vision of Australia's founders, federalism as practiced today is a mere pretense: Perth's voice can scarcely be heard over the din of party politics and eastern states' demands, and states' own local spans of control have shrunk as Canberra's has grown into a monstrosity. Parliamentary committees that should reform this broken system are dominated entirely by the major parties, which naturally resist any change that would dilute their duopoly. Thus, the democratic safeguards we assumed inviolable—such as representation, accountability, and federal balance—have been artfully circumvented. Like colonists of old, Western Australians pay their taxes and bow to laws made thousands of kilometers away by politicians and bureaucrats who see Western Australia not as an equal partner but as a serf, a quarry, and a cash cow.

Fiscal Bloat and Mounting Debt

Under this captive arrangement, the Commonwealth has swollen to grotesque proportions, unsustainable in its appetites. In the 1960s and '70s, Canberra lived within its means: federal budgets were counted in only the single-digit billions and public debt hovered around 20% of GDP. The national public service numbered under 100,000 souls in 1966, serving a population of 11½ million. Today, by contrast, the Commonwealth spends over $785 billion a year—roughly 26% of the entire economy—equivalent to more than $29,000 per Australian (versus about $600 per Australian spent by the Commonwealth government annually in 1970). The federal bureaucracy has ballooned to nearly 190,000 officials and untold numbers of contractors, with over 100 agencies proliferating just as advisors and servants proliferated in royal courts of old. Commonwealth gross national debt has exploded to nearly $1 trillion, projected to soon exceed $1.1 trillion—three times higher than just ten years ago. Interest payments on this debt are surging, yet the Commonwealth blithely continues to borrow and spend as if the public treasury were bottomless. Surpluses that were once common have vanished; perpetual deficit is now the rule, shackling future generations with debts to repay. All this fiscal profligacy enriches a bloated Canberra bureaucracy and bankrolls grand schemes abroad, while returning precious little to the ordinary Western Australian who foots the bill with the rest of his countrymen and women.

Oil and Gas—Sovereignty Surrendered

Nowhere is the Commonwealth's misrule more evident than in the plunder of Western Australia's natural bounty. Our state's offshore oil and gas fields—from the North West Shelf to Gorgon and Browse—rank among the greatest hydrocarbon reserves on Earth. Western Australia's LNG exports now rival Qatar's for volume, and in iron ore we are a global colossus. Yet what benefit from this lucky treasure have our people seen? Australia's federal Petroleum Resource Rent Tax (PRRT), ostensibly meant to give Australians a fair share of resource profits, has instead been a gas company accountant's paradise. For decades, energy giants have paid next to nothing on these massive exports: clever provisions let them deduct (and even double-deduct) expenses to delay taxes indefinitely, so that companies like Chevron and Shell managed for years to pay zero PRRT despite reaping billions in income. Even today, the PRRT yields under $1 billion in most years—about the same paltry revenue it produced twenty years ago when we were exporting almost no gas at all. Meanwhile, other resource-rich nations have seized their chance to enrich their people: Qatar, matching Australia as an LNG exporter, saw its budget surpluses skyrocket on the back of proper resource taxation, and Norway taxed North Sea oil at nearly 78%, banking tens of billions of dollars in a single year, and every year—enough to endow every Norwegian with wealth for generations. Australia, by tragic contrast, has no sovereign wealth fund of note; our much-touted Future Fund is a pitiful fraction of what it might have been and should be, languishing far behind the funds of Norway, Qatar or even tiny petro-states.

The design of Canberra's resource regime—low royalties and generous loopholes—ensures that the wealth under our seas flows mostly into foreign hands (and eastern coffers) while Western Australians get scarcely a trickle. On over half of all Australian LNG exports in recent years, no royalties at all were levied under Commonwealth-negotiated terms, effectively giving away our gas to corporate giants. In one recent year, gas companies made about $56 billion in income yet paid a mere $454 million in Commonwealth company tax—a de facto rate of under 1%. This was not a misstep; it was tax avoidance by political design. The political heirs of Canberra—Liberal and Labor alike—have kept it that way for decades, plying the public with empty rhetoric about "investment attraction" while international companies reap super-profits and ordinary Australians are denied financial security despite the riches of their own heritage.

Energy and Housing—WA Pays the Price

Western Australians now endure some of the nation's highest living costs even as our region's resources enrich everyone but us. Electricity and gas drawn from our own lands have only grown more expensive for locals. The promise of an "abundant supply of cheap gas" to spur industry has turned to ash: since 2019, our domestic gas price has more than doubled, and once the state government allowed gas that was reserved for local use to be shipped offshore, Western Australia's wholesale electricity prices tripled. Households have been kept afloat only by emergency rebates and subsidies—which are themselves funded by our taxes. In effect, we subsidise our own sky-high power bills. We pay twice—once at the meter and again through the treasury—while gas producers revel in windfall profits.

So too has the housing market slipped beyond local control. The minerals boom centred in WA helped inflame a nationwide property frenzy, yet it left affordable homes scarce on our western shores. Perth's median house price has surged past $850,000, far outpacing incomes, and rents have exploded to some of the highest levels in the nation. Nearly a quarter of WA households now find their housing costs unaffordable—roughly double the figure of just a few years ago. This social crisis is not for lack of land or lack of money (Western Australia generates enormous wealth), but for lack of power. Canberra's mismanagement of the macro-economy—its obsession with hoarding our revenues for its own bloated budget, then frittering them away on vote-buying sprees and eastern megaprojects—and its failure to ensure resource riches lead to local benefits have combined to make life far harder here than it ought to be. Energy sovereignty was surrendered for corporate profit; housing stability was sacrificed to federal complacency. The result is a cruel irony: Western Australia, rich in land and energy, now suffers under punishing energy costs and a housing affordability nightmare.

Collateral Harms of Canberra's Covid Response

Compounding these challenges are the collateral harms from Canberra's response to covid. Whatever one's view of the health threat posed by covid, it is plain that Western Australia's greatest long-run threat came not from the virus but from the overreaching, panic-driven policies imposed in its name.

In 2020–21, under the banner of a so-called "national emergency" and a National Cabinet never contemplated in our Constitution, governments rolled out draconian measures—prolonged lockdowns, school closures, vaccine mandates, internal border controls, and endless emergency decrees—with scant regard for proportionality or regional realities. Western Australians endured some of the harshest internal travel restrictions in the world, often enforced at the behest of Canberra's public-health narrative and fiscal carrots rather than through a sober, locally informed cost–benefit calculus.

The human toll of these policies has been devastating and well-documented. The Australian Human Rights Commission's *Collateral Damage* report chronicles more than 5,000 personal stories of the suffering they caused: families kept apart, last goodbyes missed, jobs and businesses lost forever, and a pervasive sense that basic freedoms had become an afterthought. Independent studies have found that children and young people suffered markedly worsened mental health and educational setbacks whose consequences they will carry for years from repeated lockdowns and school closures. These harms did not fall evenly. Disadvantaged and remote communities—including many in Western Australia's far-flung regions—bore a disproportionate share of the burden.

Scholars such as Paul Frijters, Gigi Foster and Michael Baker in *The Great Covid Panic*, have argued that the sweeping package of non-pharmaceutical interventions adopted around the world (and harshly in Australia) in response to covid inflicted damage on life, liberty and livelihoods out of all proportion to their benefits. Canberra's reaction was a textbook case of how an over-centralised system behaves under stress: it ignored established scientific protocols, doubled down on control, treated rights as negotiable, and refused to admit error even as evidence of collateral harm mounted. The virus has faded; the debts, broken businesses, lost livelihoods, learning losses, psychological scars and institutional distrust the Commonwealth has left in its wake will not. For Western Australians, the pandemic years grimly illustrated what governance from afar looks like when fear overrides reason. These events reinforced a central lesson: our fate cannot safely remain in the hands of a distant Commonwealth whose first allegiance is to its own apparatus, party machines, and unelected global bodies—rather than to the people of this state.

A New Constitution or the Old Chains?

Why has all this come to pass? Not by accident, but by design. The Australian Commonwealth's Constitution—often invoked as the sacred covenant of federation—has proven impotent to prevent this travesty. It provides no strong safeguards against party domination or executive overreach; indeed, its creators almost surely never foresaw the rise of disciplined party machines that would render Parliament a rubber stamp. The Senate, meant to protect state interests, instead operates on party lines, too often serving the same eastern metropolitan agenda as the House. Australia's founding document contains nothing like the checks essential in modern democracies—no corruption commission with teeth, no direct democratic tools like regional veto or recall of failing leaders, no enshrined rights for states over their own natural wealth. In short, our Constitution catalysed the capture of the state by party elites and the siphoning of resources from one region to another, all under a veneer of legality. Western Australia's travails are not a temporary misfortune but the predictable outcome of a federal system insufficiently protected in the long run against corruption and centralisation. As Paine cautioned that a constitution should be judged by its results, so we judge Australia's: it has delivered party rule in place of popular rule, and extraction in place of equity.

This is why the vision of *Secession by Western Australia*—an independent Western Australia with its own modern Constitution—has taken root again. The new Western Australian Constitution (Chapter 15), drafted with the lessons of the failures sketched above in mind, offers what Canberra will not: a government truly of, by, and for Western Australians. It establishes stringent checks on executive power—including citizen-led oversight bodies and even a fourth branch of government devoted solely to preserving the integrity of governance—and it enshrines resource sovereignty, ensuring that the wealth beneath Western Australia's soil directly benefits its people (with royalty levels closer to Norway's model than to Canberra's giveaway), making possible a near-zero overall taxation environment for Western Australian citizens. It also establishes bulwarks against takeover by a single party or the strangulation of democracy, creating a unicameral Congress and other provisions designed to break the weather-worn duopoly grip. Finally, its governance model is once again local and accountable, rejecting the distant centralism that has failed us for so long, placing responsibility for stewarding our way of life back where it belongs, within local communities. In short, Western Australia's founding charter promises Western Australians the self-government and safeguards that the Commonwealth has persistently denied.

Conclusion

Western Australia stands on the threshold of a new chapter, with its People called now to define the course of its future history. We have petitioned; we have waited; we have given the Commonwealth every chance to govern us justly. It has answered our hope with indifference and our loyalty with exploitation. In 1933, our Western Australian forebears voted overwhelmingly to leave a federation that had short-changed them; today the stakes are even higher. Let this polemic serve as both a warning and a rallying cry. Everyone deserves a government that treats them as citizens, not colonies—one that protects our prosperity instead of pilfering it.

We undertook the lengthy creation of this manuscript not out of malice toward our fellow Australians, but out of necessity. As co-authors, we often reflected when creating the material in this book that Western Australia's secession could prove to be a blessing to the other states (and Northern Territory) as well—the first successful break that spurs democratic renewal elsewhere in the country. By taking the lead in casting off a broken system, we may inspire Australians to the east of us to awaken from their own somnolent acceptance of the status quo and demand accountable government for themselves. The hardships and disaffection felt in so much of Australia today need not be endured as fate; if Western Australia can show a better way forward, others can follow. In this way, the cause of Western Australia may light the path to a broader continental revival.

Paine wrote in *Common Sense*: "Time makes more converts than reason." After decades of reason falling on deaf ears in Canberra, time now demands we convert our frustration into action. The cause of Western Australia—like the cause of America in 1776—is in great measure the cause of all who believe in self-determination and good government. It is time to cast off the old chains, to reject the false choice between two eastern parties, and to take our future into our own hands. Western Australia shall be free.

Julian Gillespie

Professor Gigi Foster

Michael Baker

Professor Ian Brighthope

16 February 2026

Sources

Unless otherwise stated, online materials were viewed on 16 February 2026.

1. Paine, Thomas, *Common Sense* (Penguin, 1776).
2. Woldring, Karlin, 'Two-Party System Draws Democratic Disadvantage' (2024) *Independent Australia* (online, 28 March 2024) <https://independentaustralia.net/politics/politics-display/two-party-system-draws-democratic-disadvantage,18461>.
3. Australian Public Service Commission, *State of the Service Report 2015–16* (Report, 2016) ch 1 <https://www.apsc.gov.au/state-service/state-service-report-2015-16/fifty-years-aps-employment-data> Annotation: Supports: "The national public service numbered under 100,000 souls in 1966".
4. Australian Public Service Commission, *State of the Service Report 2022–23* (Report, 2023) app 1 <https://www.apsc.gov.au/initiatives-and-programs/workforce-information/research-analysis-and-publications/state-service/state-service-report-2023/appendices/appendix-1-aps-workforce-trends>.
5. Reserve Bank of Australia, *Australian Economic Statistics 1949–50 to 1996–97* (Occasional Paper No 8, 1999) table 2.14 <https://www.rba.gov.au/statistics/frequency/occ-paper-8.html> Annotation: Supports: "federal budgets were counted in only the single-digit billions and public debt hovered around 20% of GDP" (1960s and '70s).
6. Australian Government, *Budget Paper No 1: Budget Strategy and Outlook 2025–26* (Report, 2025) 1–5 <https://budget.gov.au/content/bp1/download/bp1_2025-26.pdf> Annotation: Supports: "the Commonwealth spends over $730 billion a year—roughly 27% of the entire economy—equivalent to more than $28,000 per Australian (versus about $600 per Australian spent by the Commonwealth government annually in 1970)".
7. Parliamentary Library (Commonwealth of Australia), 'Australian Government Debt in Historical and International Perspective' (Research Paper, 2025) 4 <https://www.aph.gov.au/About_Parliament/Parliamentary_departments/Parliamentary_Library/pubs/rp/rp2223/AusGovtDebt> Annotation: Supports: "Commonwealth gross national debt has exploded to nearly $1 trillion, projected to soon exceed $1.1 trillion—three times higher than just ten years ago".
8. Gittins, Ross, 'Don't Worry about National Debt — But There's Another Issue to Be Concerned About' (2022) *Sydney Morning Herald* (online, 3 April 2022) <https://www.smh.com.au/business/the-economy/don-t-worry-about-national-debt-but-there-s-another-issue-to-be-concerned-about-20220403-p5aact.html>.

9. Provost, Claire, 'Australia's Foreign Aid Spending: How Much and Where? — Get the Data' (2013) *The Guardian* (online, 22 August 2013) <https://www.theguardian.com/global-development/datablog/2013/aug/22/australia-foreign-aid-spending-data>.
10. Dziedzic, Stephen, 'Why Australia Lags Behind the Rest of the World in Taxing Oil and Energy Giants' (2023) *ABC News* (online, 25 April 2023) <https://www.abc.net.au/news/2023-04-25/australia-prrt-oil-giants-chalmers-federal-budget/102262102> Annotation: Supports: "Even today, the PRRT yields under $1 billion in most years".
11. The Australia Institute, *Australia's Great Gas Giveaway* (Report P1451, May 2024) <https://australiainstitute.org.au/wp-content/uploads/2024/05/P1451-Australias-great-gas-giveaway-Web.pdf> Annotation: p. 4 Supports: "On over half of all Australian LNG exports in recent years, no royalties at all were levied under Commonwealth-negotiated terms" Annotation: p 5 Supports: "gas companies made about $56 billion in income yet paid a mere $454 million in Commonwealth company tax".
12. Milne, Peter, 'Western Australia Faces "Growing Shortfall" of Increasingly Expensive Gas: EnergyQuest' (2025) *Boiling Cold* (online, 11 August 2025) <https://www.boilingcold.com.au/western-australia-faces-growing-gas-shortfall/> Annotation: Supports: "since 2019, our domestic gas price has more than doubled".
13. The Australia Institute, 'Triple Trouble: WA Wholesale Gas and Electricity Prices Soar since Approval of Onshore Gas Exports' (Media Release, 5 December 2024) <https://australiainstitute.org.au/post/triple-trouble-wa-wholesale-gas-and-electricity-prices-soar-since-approval-of-onshore-gas-exports/>.
14. Bankwest Curtin Economics Centre, *Housing Affordability in Western Australia 2025: A Long Way From Home* (Report, June 2025) <https://bcec.edu.au/publications/housing-affordability-in-western-australia-2025/> Annotation: p 12 Supports: "Perth's median house price has surged past $850,000" Annotation: p 8 Supports: "Nearly a quarter of WA households now find their housing costs unaffordable—roughly double the figure of just a few years ago".
15. 'Experts Clash over Classification of PRRT as "Super-Profits Tax"' (n.d.) *Accounting Times* (online) <https://www.accountingtimes.com.au/tax/experts-clash-over-classification-of-prrt-as-super-profits-tax>.
16. 'What Can Australia Learn from Norway's Approach to Taxing Resources?' (2025) *ABC News* (online, 4 November 2025) <https://www.abc.net.au/news/2025-11-05/lessons-for-australia-from-norways-tax-on-resources/105939048>.
17. Chapter 16—A New Nation's Constitution, *Secession by Western Australia* (forthcoming) (Preface and Opening Reflections).
18. Australian Human Rights Commission, *Collateral Damage: What the Untold Stories from the COVID-19 Pandemic Expose About Human Rights in Australia* (Report, 2025) <https://humanrights.gov.au/resource-hub/by-resource-type/publications/collateral-damage-report-australias-covid-19-pandemic>.
19. Department of the Prime Minister and Cabinet (Cth), *COVID-19 Response Inquiry — Roundtable Summary: Schools, Children and Young People* (Summary, 30 July 2024) <https://www.pmc.gov.au/resources/covid-19-response-inquiry-roundtable-summary-schools-children-and-young-people>.
20. Allen, Justine B H et al, 'Child Well-Being before and after the 2020 COVID-19 Lockdowns in Three Australian States' (2023) 58(1) *Australian Journal of Social Issues* 123 <https://www.realwell.org.au/wp-content/uploads/2023/05/Aust-J-Social-Issues-2023-Allen-Child-well%E2%80%90being-before-and-after-the-2020-COVID%E2%80%9019-lockdowns-in-three-Australian.pdf> Annotation: Supports: "Independent studies have found that children and young people suffered markedly worsened mental health and educational setbacks whose consequences they will carry for years from repeated lockdowns and school closures".
21. Sicouri, Gabrielle et al, 'Mental Health Symptoms in Children and Adolescents during COVID-19 in Australia' (2022) 56(7) *Australian & New Zealand Journal of Psychiatry* 661 <https://journals.sagepub.com/doi/full/10.1177/00048674221090174>.
22. Gannon, Susanne et al, *Learning from Lockdown: The Impact of the COVID-19 Pandemic on Educational Inequalities in Australia* (Report, Western Sydney University, 2022) <https://researchers.westernsydney.edu.au/files/146603117/Learning_from_Lockdown_Report_FINAL.pdf>.

23. Gillitzer, Christian and Rohan Prasad, 'The Effect of School Closures on Standardized Test Scores: Evidence from a Zero-COVID Policy' (2024) 102 *Economics of Education Review* 102713 <https://www.sciencedirect.com/science/article/pii/S0272775724000712>.
24. Frijters, Paul, Gigi Foster and Michael Baker, *The Great Covid Panic: What Happened, Why, and What To Do Next* (Brownstone Institute, 2021) <https://brownstone.org/books/the-great-covid-panic/>.
25. Australian Public Service Commission, *State of the Service Report 2023–24* (Report, 2024) app A <https://www.apsc.gov.au/initiatives-and-programs/workforce-information/research-analysis-and-publications/state-service/state-service-report-2023-24/aps-profile/workforce-size-and-distribution> Annotation: Supports: "The federal bureaucracy has ballooned to nearly 190,000 officials and untold numbers of contractors, with over 100 agencies proliferating ".
26. Provost, Claire, 'Global Gas Giants Use Loophole to Avoid Tax on Billions from Australian Operations' (2017) *Sydney Morning Herald* (online, 26 April 2017) <https://www.smh.com.au/politics/federal/global-gas-giants-use-loophole-to-avoid-tax-on-billions-from-australian-operations-20170425-gvrwn9.html> Annotation: Supports: "companies like Chevron and Shell managed for years to pay zero PRRT despite reaping billions in income".

The Case for Secession: The Socio-Economics

There has been no *common* wealth delivered to the People of Western Australia under the Commonwealth.

Western Australia has long been standing at a crossroads. The foundations laid nearly a century ago for its possible secession from the Commonwealth of Australia resonate more strongly today, albeit in a modern context. The economic, political, and cultural dynamics have evolved, but the core issues that drove the initial secessionist sentiments remain alive, and strengthened by recent events. This case asserts that Western Australia's continued participation in the Australian Federation is not only disadvantageous but also unsustainable. We believe it is feasible for Western Australia to pursue an independent path that aligns with its economic strength, its regional identity, and the aspirations of its people.

The Case of the People of Western Australia was published in 1934. This book contains an updated version reflecting the same themes. We show in these pages why and how Western Australia could take the road towards independence from the Commonwealth.

Historical Context & Evolution Of Grievances

Western Australia's entry into the Federation was driven by external pressures and false promises. From the outset, it was clear that Western Australia's needs and interests were at odds with those of the eastern states. The assurances given during the Federation debates—including transitional protections for local industries and commitments to fiscal safeguards for the States—proved temporary. Once these measures expired, the Commonwealth rapidly centralised revenue and decision-making power, leaving Western Australia increasingly exposed within a federation dominated by the eastern states.

Western Australia's Economic Strengths

Western Australia has the fastest growing population in Australia and is an economic powerhouse, contributing significantly to Australia's GDP, primarily through its vast natural resources. In 2024, Western Australia accounted for 45% of the nation's total merchandise exports, or $234.6 billion. This was driven by the state's mining and petroleum sector, led by iron ore, along with agri-food (mainly wheat, canola seeds, barley) .[1] Despite this, the state's wealth is siphoned off to subsidise the less economically productive eastern states through mechanisms like the GST distribution.

For example, in 2023-2024, we estimate that Western Australia received just over 70 cents for every dollar it contributed in GST. This fiscal imbalance stifles the state's ability to invest in its own infrastructure, healthcare, and education, forcing Western Australia to carry the financial burden of other states' inefficiencies. An independent Western Australia would retain more of its wealth, ensuring that the fruits of its labour are reinvested locally rather than redistributed.

Western Australia's economic contributions position it as the backbone of the Australian economy. In the 2023-2024 financial year, Western Australia's gross state product (GSP) was $455.7 billion, making up just under 17% of Australia's total GDP despite having only about 11% of the nation's population.[2] This disparity highlights the state's outsized economic influence, driven largely by its robust

[1] https://www.watc.wa.gov.au/media/zcvavenx/watradeprofilemarch2025.pdf
[2] https://www.watc.wa.gov.au/media/c53nchwr/watc-investor-may-2025.pdf

mining and petroleum sector, which accounted for approximately 45% of the state's economy in 2024.[3] The strength of Western Australia's economy is further evidenced by its relatively low unemployment rate, which consistently outperforms the national average: over the past 20 years, the WA unemployment rate has averaged 4.7% compared to the national average of 5.1%.[4]

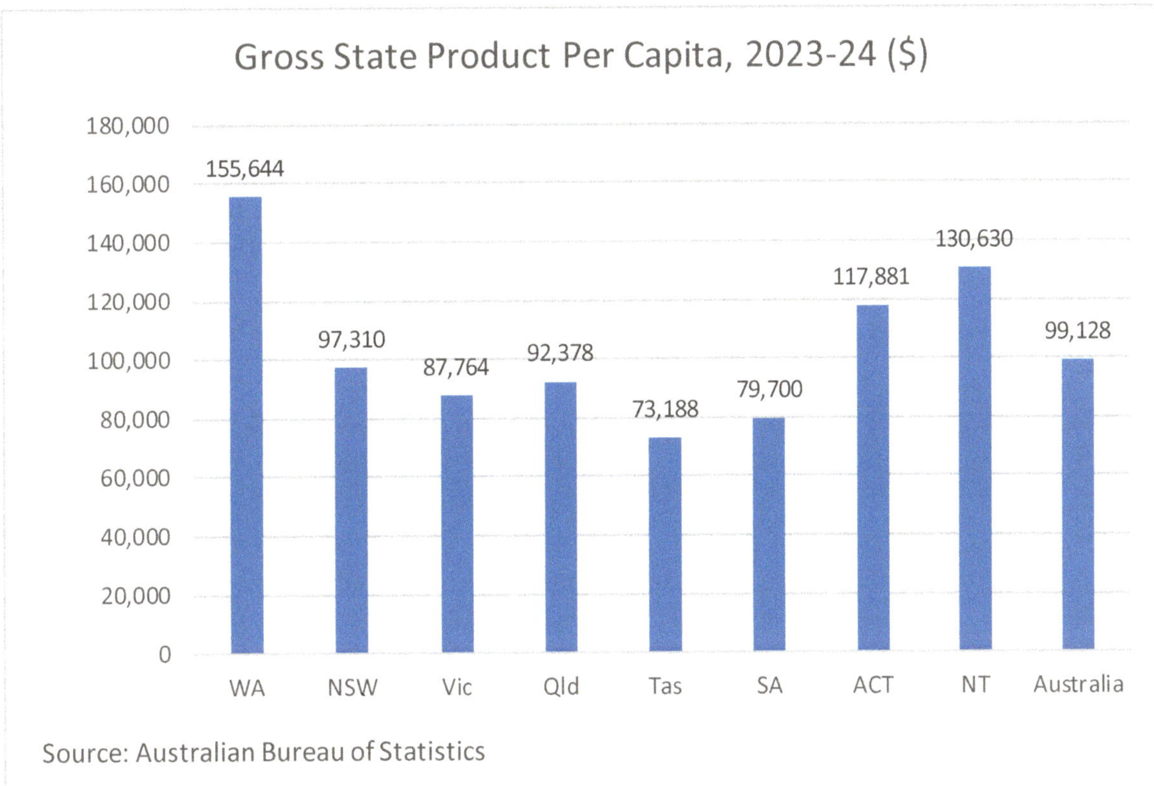

Moreover, WA is a global leader in the production of critical minerals. The state produced 42% of the world's lithium in 2024, a key component in batteries for electric vehicles and renewable energy storage.[5] The value of WA's mineral and petroleum sales was $239 billion in 2023-24, with iron ore alone contributing $143 billion.[6] These figures underscore WA's strategic importance in global supply chains, particularly in sectors that are pivotal for future economic growth.

[3]https://www.abs.gov.au/statistics/economy/national-accounts/australian-national-accounts-state-accounts/2023-24-financial-year#data-downloads (download Table 6)
[4] https://www.abs.gov.au/statistics/labour/employment-and-unemployment/labour-force-australia/latest-release#data-downloads (download Tables 1 and 8)
[5] Government of Western Australia, Department of Energy and Economic Diversification. "Western Australia Battery and Critical Minerals Profile – April 2025.
[6] https://www.wa.gov.au/government/publications/major-commodities-data-file

The state's agricultural sector also plays a crucial role in its economic profile. WA is responsible for 30% of the nation's wheat production, with more than 95% of it being exported.[7] Just under 8.5 million tonnes were produced in the state in 2023-24, valued at more than $2.5 billion.[8] This agricultural output is vital for both domestic consumption and international markets, with key exports going to countries in Asia and the Middle east. The state's fisheries and aquaculture industries also contribute significantly, with a value of $815 million in 2022-23. WA accounts for about 22% of Australia's fisheries and aquaculture revenues, underscoring the diversity of WA's economy.[9]

In addition to its strong resource and agricultural sectors, Western Australia is making significant strides in technology and innovation. The state has become a hub for research and development in mining technology, renewable energy, and agricultural sciences. The establishment of technology parks and innovation precincts, such as the Western Australian Data Science Innovation Hub, is fostering a new wave of start-ups and tech companies (recently ProGenis, Acculaser, Clear Carbon, and Greenroom Robotics) that are leveraging the state's resources and expertise. This diversification is crucial for sustaining long-term economic growth and reducing dependence on volatile commodity markets.

Tourism and education are also key pillars of the WA economy. In 2024, the state attracted 1.1 million interstate and 865,000 international visitors who along with 8.6 million intrastate travelers, contributed almost $16 billion to the state's economy and supported over 120,000 Western Australian jobs.[10] The education sector, particularly international education, is another significant contributor, with more than 71,000 international students enrolled in Western Australian institutions in the first half of 2024, bringing an estimated $4.4 billion to the state.[11] These sectors bring in substantial revenue, create jobs and promote cultural exchange, enhancing the state's global standing.

WA's strategic location, bordering the Indian Ocean and close to major Asian economies, further amplifies its economic strength. The state's ports, including Fremantle, Port Hedland, and Dampier, are among the busiest in Australia, handling a significant portion of the nation's exports. Port Hedland is the largest bulk export port in the world by tonnage, with Dampier in the top 10 global ports by tonnage. This strategic advantage is critical for the state's economic independence, enabling it to maintain strong trade relationships with key global partners like China, Japan, South Korea, India, Taiwan, Vietnam, and the United States.

---

[7] Department of Primary Industries and Regional Development. "Wheat"

[8] https://www.abs.gov.au/statistics/industry/agriculture/australian-agriculture-broadacre-crops/latest-release#data-downloads, Table 1

[9] https://www.wa.gov.au/system/files/2024-10/dpird_annual_report_2023-24.pdf

[10] Tourism WA. "WA Tourism Snapshot"; https://www.wa.gov.au/government/media-statements/Cook%20Labor%20Government/Western-Australia-leads-the-nation-for-international-tourism-recovery-20251220

[11] https://www.education.gov.au/international-education-data-and-research/international-student-numbers-country-state-and-territory . International students in WA accounted for 8.5% of all international students in Australia. For Australia as a whole, international students brought in $51.5 billion in 2024. We have estimated WA's share by multiplying 8.5% by $51.5 billion. https://www.rba.gov.au/publications/bulletin/2025/jul/international-students-and-the-australian-economy.html#:~:text=Introduction,recent%20years%20(Graph%201).

Fiscal Imbalance & Federal Relations

The fiscal relationship between Western Australia and the Commonwealth is imbalanced. Despite being the largest contributor to the national economy on a per-capita basis ($151,156 in FY2024 followed by NSW with $92,948), WA consistently receives the lowest per-capita distribution of GST revenue of all Australian states. For instance, in the 2023-2024 financial year, WA's GST grant of $6,565 million was 7.4% of the national GST pool, while the state's population share was closer to 11%. This fiscal imbalance severely restricts the state's ability to invest in critical infrastructure and services like health and education, forcing it to rely heavily on mining royalties and other volatile revenue sources.

The inequity is further exacerbated by national fiscal constraints, debt settings, and funding approval processes that shape state borrowing and infrastructure investment. While the Australian Loan Council now plays a largely monitoring role, Commonwealth fiscal frameworks and capital approval mechanisms continue to influence the timing and scale of Western Australia's major projects. These constraints have contributed to delays in essential infrastructure, including port expansions and key transport upgrades, despite their importance to the state's export-driven economy.

The Australian Loan Council's approach to debt and deficit management further compounds the problem. Western Australia's disciplined fiscal management has resulted in a lower debt-to-GSP ratio than other states. In FY2024, WA's net debt stood at $28.6 billion, representing just 6.3% of GSP, compared with NSW (11.4%) and Victoria (22.0%), yet the Loan Council's uniform policies that prioritise uniformity over state-specific economic realities often penalise the state for its financial prudence and thereby hinder WA's ability to leverage its fiscal strength for long-term investments.

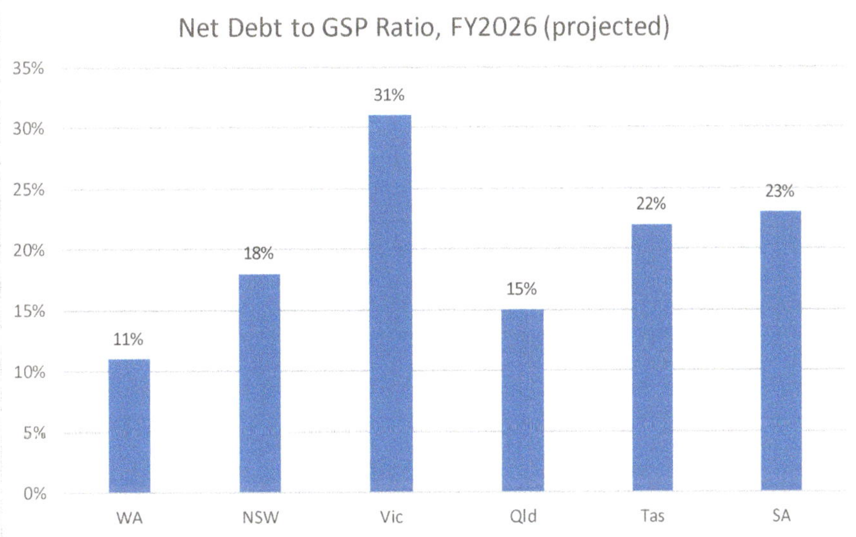

Source: Adept Economics

The Commonwealth's fiscal policies also impact Western Australia's ability to manage its natural resources effectively. Federal restrictions on state royalties, particularly those imposed through the Australian Loan Council and national tax agreements, limit the state's capacity to fully benefit from its vast mineral wealth. In 2023-2024, Western Australia collected $11.9 billion in royalties, yet the potential for higher revenue is curtailed by federal policies that cap the state's share of revenues. This reduces the state's ability to fund its own infrastructure and services and undermines its economic autonomy.

Moreover, the Commonwealth's redistribution mechanisms, including the GST and specific purpose payments (SPPs), are skewed to favour the less economically developed states, exacerbating the fiscal imbalance. WA's contributions to these redistributive systems far exceed the benefits it receives. In FY2024, citizens and companies in WA contributed an estimated $112 billion to the Commonwealth, yet received only $73 billion in return through GST, subsidies, grants and other expenditures on behalf of the state.[12] This disparity is a clear indicator of the systemic fiscal injustice embedded in the federal structure. Indeed, WA's resources help fuel the economic engines of the globe, yet domestically, under federalism, the state is unfairly hamstrung.

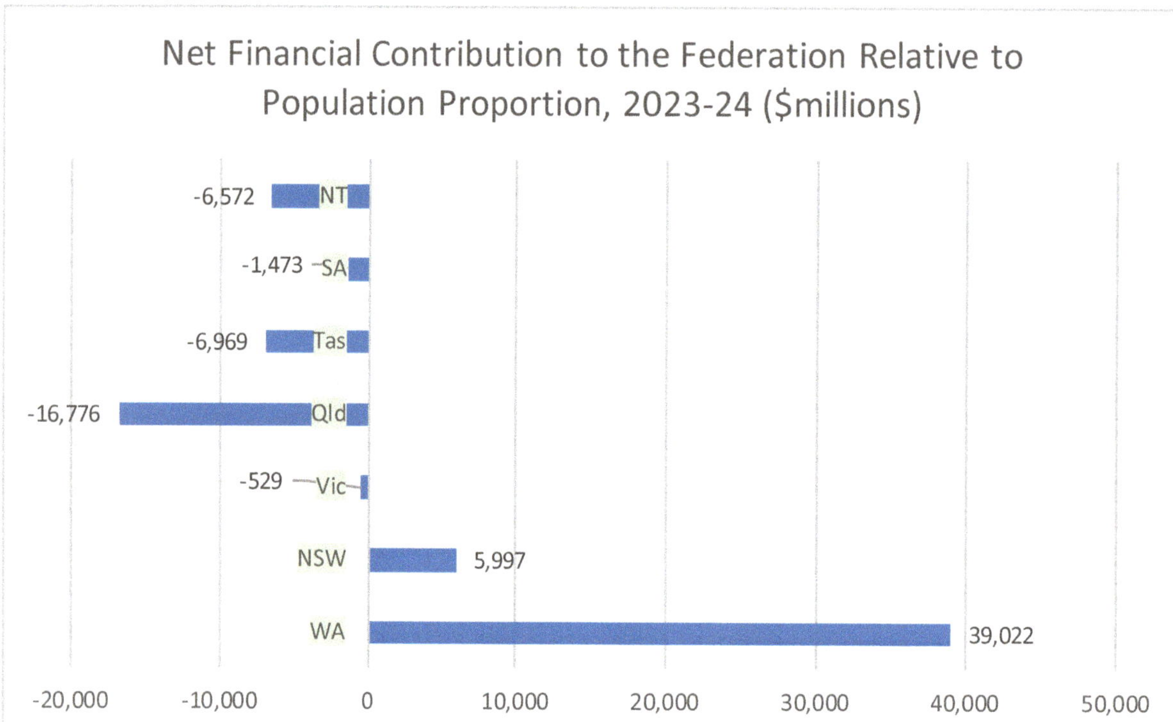

Source: WA Department of Treasury

[12] See Chapter 3, Tables 3 and 9.

The inequity in fiscal arrangements extends to infrastructure funding. Federal infrastructure grants are often distributed based on political considerations rather than economic need or potential return on investment. While 2023-24 saw WA receive more per-capita Commonwealth infrastructure funding than NSW and Victoria, over longer periods WA's allocation has often been below what its geography and network costs would suggest. Even when a single year's per-capita figure is high (as in 2023-24), WA's funding remains misaligned with cost drivers such as land area, road-kilometers, remoteness and the size of the task of freighting goods.

These fiscal imbalances translate into tangible disadvantages for the people of Western Australia. The state's capacity to deliver high-quality public services, maintain infrastructure, and support economic growth is continually undermined by a federal system that prioritises uniformity over fairness. This fiscal reality strengthens the argument for financial autonomy achieved by secession, as a means to rectify persistent historical inequality and an ever-mounting loss of wealth, by ensuring Western Australia's economic might is returned wholly to the people of Western Australia, as Western Australia existed before its misadventure with Federalism.

Political Representation & Governance

In the House of Representatives, where governments are formed and budgets are decided, Western Australia elects 16 members out of 150 (about 10.7% of the House). Yet Western Australia is Australia's export engine and resource powerhouse: in 2024, it accounted for 45% of the value of Australia's goods exports, driven largely by resource shipments led by iron ore and LNG. This mismatch between Western Australia's economic weight and its voting weight structurally enables east-coast blocs to secure decisive House majorities and set national legislative and budget priorities with limited dependence on Western Australian seats. While the Senate provides equal state representation (12 senators per state), practical federal decision-making is typically driven by House numbers, leaving Western Australia with comparatively little leverage.

Western Australia stands out as the most resource-rich and dominant state by resource value, particularly in minerals and petroleum, including offshore production in adjacent Commonwealth waters. In 2023-24, the value of Western Australia's mineral and petroleum production reached $238 billion, equating to approximately $78,000 per capita based on a population of 3.04 million. In contrast, Queensland's resource production value is estimated, based on national and state energy and resources data, at around $120 billion or $21,000 per capita (population 5.67 million); New South Wales at $50 billion, or $5,800 per capita (population 8.59 million); and Victoria at $10 billion, or $1,400 per capita (population 7.07 million). Western Australia also leads the nation in per capita agricultural output at $4,550 per person. This disproportionate contribution to national wealth underscores the underrepresentation of Western Australia in the House, where representation is based solely on population, allocating it only about 11% of seats despite its outsized economic role.

In short, Australia's principal economic breadwinner carries the load, but has no effective voice in Canberra.

Environmental & Resource Management

Western Australia's resource wealth is a double-edged sword. While it fuels the state's economy, federal environmental regulations often hinder its ability to fully capitalise on these resources. The state's energy policies, are hampered by federal interference.

As a leading example, Western Australia has the potential to become a global leader in renewable energy, leveraging its vast sun-drenched landscapes for solar power and its extensive coastline for wind energy. However, federal policies, such as the Renewable Energy Target (RET), are designed with eastern states in mind and do not align with Western Australia's energy potential. Independence would enable Western Australia to develop and implement its own environmental policies, fostering sustainable growth while protecting its natural resources.

Social & Cultural Considerations

Western Australia's unique cultural identity, shaped by its relative isolation and diverse population, is often overshadowed by the dominant eastern states. This distinct Western Australian identity is a crucial part of the argument for secession. The state's approach to Indigenous rights, land management, and cultural heritage is markedly different from the policies and attitudes prevalent in the eastern states.

For instance, Western Australia's progressive stance on Indigenous land rights, exemplified by the 2020 Aboriginal Cultural Heritage Act, highlights the state's commitment to reconciling with its past while building an inclusive future. However, federal policies often undermine these efforts, imposing a uniform approach that fails to account for the unique circumstances of Western Australia. Independence would allow for more culturally and locally appropriate governance.

Economic Viability of an Independent Western Australia

An independent Western Australia would have all the ingredients to be economically viable and prosperous. The state's natural resources, particularly its vast reserves of iron ore, lithium, and natural gas, provide a solid economic foundation. The state's existing infrastructure, including ports like Fremantle and Pilbara, is already geared towards supporting global trade.

An independent Western Australia could see strong growth by negotiating its own trade agreements, particularly with key Asian markets. The state's strategic location as a gateway to Asia is an advantage that would only be amplified under independence.

Additionally, the ability to retain all revenue from resource exports and implement a tax regime tailored to its economy would further strengthen WA's financial position.

Defence & International Relations

An independent WA could negotiate defence agreements with Australia and other allies, ensuring continued security without the need for a large, independent military. WA's strategic importance in the Indian Ocean region could also attract international partnerships, particularly with countries like the United States and the United Kingdom, who have vested interests in maintaining stability in the region.

On the international stage, WA could pursue membership in organisations such as the United Nations and the Commonwealth of Nations. It could also seek to join regional trade blocs like ASEAN to further integrate its economy with the dynamic Asia-Pacific region. These moves would reinforce WA's place as a respected and influential player on the global stage.

The Path Forward

The case for Western Australia's secession is based on the present undervaluing of the state's economic contributions, insufficient political representation in Canberra, and inadequate recognition of its unique cultural identity. Independence offers a pathway to greater prosperity, more effective governance, and a stronger sense of identity for the people of WA.

The process of secession could be peaceful, legal, and democratic, guided by the will of the people. A referendum on independence, followed by negotiations with the Commonwealth and international recognition, would mark the beginning of a new chapter in Western Australia's history.

Sources

Unless otherwise stated, online materials were viewed on 20 January 2026.

1. Western Australian Treasury Corporation, *Investor Update: Western Australia and WATC—May 2025 Market Updates* (May 2025) <https://www.watc.wa.gov.au/media/c53nchwr/watc-investor-may-2025.pdf>.
2. Western Australia Department of Energy, Mines, Industry Regulation and Safety, *WA Battery and Critical Minerals Profile—April 2025* (April 2025) <https://www.watc.wa.gov.au/media/ansnr21x/wabatteryandcriticalmineralsprofileapril2025.pdf>.
3. Department of Primary Industries and Regional Development (WA), *Wheat* (web page) <https://www.dpird.wa.gov.au/businesses/plant-and-crop-farming/grains/wheat/>.
4. F Dawson, 'New Aquaculture Developments, Opportunities Emerge Globally in 2024' (SeaWest News, web page) <https://seawestnews.com/new-aquaculture-developments-opportunities-emerge-globally-in-2024/amp/amp/>.
5. Tourism Western Australia, *Workforce* (web page) <https://www.tourism.wa.gov.au/resources-and-support/industry-development/workforce>.
6. Department of Education (Cth), *PRISMS: International Student Numbers by Country, by State and Territory* (web page) <https://www.education.gov.au/international-education-data-and-research/international-student-numbers-country-state-and-territory>.
7. Australian Bureau of Statistics, *Australia's Trade with the United States of America* (5 June 2025) <https://www.abs.gov.au/articles/australias-trade-united-states-america>.
8. Australian Bureau of Statistics, *Taxation Revenue, Australia* (data set, 22 April 2025) <https://www.abs.gov.au/statistics/economy/government/taxation-revenue-australia/latest-release>.
9. Department of Treasury and Finance (WA), *2023–24 Annual Report on State Finances* (report) <https://www.wa.gov.au/government/publications/2023-24-annual-report-state-finances>.

10. B Oyetunji, *State Finances 2024* (report, Audit Office of New South Wales, 18 December 2024) <https://www.audit.nsw.gov.au/sites/default/files/documents/Final%20report%20State%20finances%202024.pdf>.
11. Infrastructure Partnerships Australia, *Australian Infrastructure Budget Monitor 2023–24* (2023) <https://infrastructure.org.au/wp-content/uploads/2023/12/Australian-Infrastructure-Budget-Monitor-2023-24-1.pdf>.

Temporary Fiscal Protections

12. *Commonwealth of Australia Constitution Act* 1900 (UK) ss 87, 95 <https://classic.austlii.edu.au/au/legis/cth/consol_act/coaca430/>. Annotation: Section 87 provided for the return of customs and excise revenue to the States for a limited period; s 95 granted Western Australia temporary special tariff powers.
13. John Quick and Robert Randolph Garran, *The Annotated Constitution of the Australian Commonwealth* (Angus & Robertson, 1901). Annotation: Contemporary constitutional commentary explaining the transitional nature of ss 87 and 95 and their political purpose during Federation.

Delayed & Complex WA Infrastructure

14. Infrastructure Australia, *Pilbara Ports Capacity and Supply Chain Review* (2018) <https://www.infrastructureaustralia.gov.au/evaluations/lumsden-point-development-port-port-hedland>. Annotation: Identifies funding and coordination constraints affecting the timing of port capacity expansions critical to WA exports.
15. Pilbara Ports Authority, *Pilbara Ports Infrastructure Investment Plan* (2020) <https://www.pilbaraports.com.au/about-ppa/news,-media-and-statistics/news/2022/february/port-of-port-hedland-development-plan-reviewed-to->. Annotation: Details staged port expansion projects and the impact of funding approvals on delivery schedules.
16. Infrastructure Australia, *Business Case Assessment: Perth–Darwin National Highway (WA Sections)* (2019) <https://www.infrastructureaustralia.gov.au/sites/default/files/2019-06/WA_North_West_Coastal_Highway_Brief.pdf>. Annotation: Notes delays and staging issues linked to funding approvals and national prioritisation.
17. Wikipedia, *NorthLink WA* (web page, 2025) <https://en.wikipedia.org/wiki/NorthLink_WA>. Annotation: This Wikipedia article summarises the NorthLink WA project (the Perth–Darwin National Highway's Swan Valley Bypass). While it reports completion dates and funding split, it highlights the planning and staging complexity of this long-term national road link, indicating typical multi-year development processes and joint State/Commonwealth funding involvement.
18. Main Roads Western Australia, *Perth–Darwin National Highway (Swan Valley Section)—Draft Public Environment Report* (2016) <https://docslib.org/doc/6027925/perth-darwin-national-highway-swan-valley-section>. Annotation: Captures decades of planning documentation for the Perth–Darwin National Highway route linking Perth with the north.
19. Parliament of Western Australia, Public Accounts Committee, *Inquiry into Project Planning and Funding Applications for Major Western Australian Infrastructure Projects* (Report No 9, 2010) <https://www.parliament.wa.gov.au/publications/tabledpapers.nsf/displaypaper/3812869a078aff22edefdd54482577e00008709d/%24file/2869%2B-%2Bpac%2Breport.pdf>. Annotation: Finds that funding frameworks and approval processes materially affect timing and delivery of major WA transport projects.

WA Innovation: Start-Ups

20. Government of Western Australia, *WA Innovators of the Year—2025 Rio Tinto Emerging Innovation Winner* (web page, 2025) <https://www.wa.gov.au/organisation/department-of-energy-and-economic-diversification/wa-innovators-of-the-year-2025-rio-tinto-emerging-innovation-winner>. Annotation: State innovation awards recognising WA-based start-up ProGenis Pharmaceuticals.
21. Government of Western Australia, *WA Innovators of the Year—2025 Rio Tinto Emerging Innovation Runner-Up* (web page, 2025) <https://www.wa.gov.au/organisation/department-of-energy-and-economic-diversification/wa-innovators-of-the-year-2025-rio-tinto-emerging-innovation-winner>. Annotation: State innovation awards recognising WA-based tech company Acculaser.

22. Government of Western Australia, *WA Innovators of the Year—2025 Woodside Energy Platinum Award for Energy Innovation Winner* (web page, 2025) <https://www.wa.gov.au/organisation/department-of-energy-and-economic-diversification/wa-innovators-of-the-year-2025-woodside-energy-platinum-award-energy-innovation-winner>. Annotation: State innovation awards recognising WA-based climate/energy tech company Clear Carbon.
23. Government of Western Australia, *WA Innovators of the Year—2025 Rio Tinto Growth Innovation Winner* (web page, 2025) <https://www.wa.gov.au/organisation/department-of-energy-and-economic-diversification/wa-innovators-of-the-year-2025-rio-tinto-growth-innovation-winner>. Annotation: State innovation awards recognising WA-based robotics/engineering company Greenroom Robotics.
24. Curtin University, 'Curtin Accelerate 2025 Powers WA's Next Wave of Innovators' (web page, 2024) <https://www.curtin.edu.au/news/media-release/curtin-accelerate-2025-powers-was-next-wave-of-innovators>. Annotation: Perth accelerator cohort listing 12 WA start-ups, evidencing active start-up formation and commercialisation pipeline.

Underrepresentation: WA's Economic Dominance

25. Parliament of Australia, *Members* (web page) <https://www.aph.gov.au/senators_and_members/members>. Annotation: Confirms the House of Representatives has 150 Members and explains its central role in forming government.
26. Australian Electoral Commission, *House of Representatives to Return to 150 Members* (media release, 2023) <https://www.aec.gov.au/media/2023/07-27.htm>. Annotation: Determination of state entitlements: Western Australia to have 16 seats and the House to total 150 seats at the next election.
27. Western Australian Treasury Corporation, *Western Australia Trade Profile—March 2025* (March 2025) <https://www.watc.wa.gov.au/media/zcvavenx/watradeprofilemarch2025.pdf>. Annotation: Reports that in 2024 Western Australia's goods exports were $234.6b, representing 45% of Australia's goods exports; notes WA accounts for nearly all of Australia's iron ore exports and highlights key export commodities.
28. Western Australia Department of Energy, Mines, Industry Regulation and Safety, *Western Australian Mineral and Petroleum Statistics Digest 2023–24* (2025) <https://www.wa.gov.au/system/files/2025-03/wa_statistics_digest_2023_2024_web.pdf>. Annotation: Provides quantity and value of mineral and petroleum production in WA totaling $238 billion.
29. Australian Energy Producers, *AEP Key Statistics 2024* (2024) <https://energyproducers.au/wp-content/uploads/2024/06/AEP_KS24_Web2.pdf>. Annotation: Provides state-by-state production data for petroleum liquids and natural gas, including offshore basins.
30. Geoscience Australia, *Australia's Energy Commodity Resources 2024 Overview* (2024) <https://www.ga.gov.au/aecr2024/overview>. Annotation: Includes basin-specific production and resource data for oil and gas, covering offshore areas like Gippsland, Bass, and Otway.
31. Department of Industry, Science and Resources (Cth), *Resources and Energy Quarterly: March 2024* (March 2024) <https://www.industry.gov.au/publications/resources-and-energy-quarterly-march-2024>. Annotation: Provides national and indicative state-level export values for key minerals and energy commodities, supporting estimates for QLD, NSW, and VIC.
32. Australian Bureau of Statistics, *National, State and Territory Population, June 2025* (2025) <https://www.abs.gov.au/statistics/people/population/national-state-and-territory-population/latest-release>. Annotation: Provides population estimates for states including WA (3.04m), QLD (5.67m), NSW (8.59m), and VIC (7.07m).
33. Department of Agriculture, Fisheries and Forestry (Cth), *Snapshot of Australian Agriculture 2025* (2025) <https://www.agriculture.gov.au/abares/products/insights/snapshot-of-australian-agriculture>. Annotation: Reports national gross value of agricultural production for 2023–24 as $82.4 billion.
34. Australian Bureau of Statistics, *Value of Agricultural Commodities Produced, Australia, 2021–22 Financial Year* (2023) <https://www.abs.gov.au/statistics/industry/agriculture/value-agricultural-commodities-produced-australia/latest-release>. Annotation: Provides state-level gross value of agricultural production data used as base for scaling 2023–24 estimates.

THE CASE FOR SECESSION: THE LAW

A decisive referendum in which Western Australians clearly vote to leave the Commonwealth would do more than strengthen a political campaign. It would confer democratic legitimacy upon the claim that the people of Western Australia are entitled to determine their own political status. That proposition must be distinguished from a narrower legal question: whether the vote, standing alone, would cause every Commonwealth law and institution to cease operating in Western Australia at the instant the result was declared. Under the constitutional doctrine most likely to be applied by the High Court, it would not. The distinction is important. The absence of an automatic domestic mechanism does not extinguish the political and moral claim revealed by the vote; it identifies the legal machinery through which that claim must first be implemented.

Negotiation is therefore not a request for Canberra's permission to decide whether Western Australia may leave. It is the orderly first means of settling the terms on which an independence already authorised by the people can be given practical effect. A clear referendum supplies the mandate. Good-faith negotiations should supply the arrangements necessary to give that mandate orderly expression.

Throughout this chapter, the "right to secede" is used in a defined sense. It denotes the democratic and constituent entitlement claimed by a people who have clearly withdrawn consent to continued union. It does not assume that the referendum, without further legal steps, instantaneously displaces the Commonwealth Constitution. This distinction avoids both errors: treating the vote as legally self-executing, and treating the absence of a self-executing mechanism as proof that no right can exist.

Western Australia's constitutional position is distinctive. It is not named among the colonies in the Preamble to the *Commonwealth of Australia Constitution Act 1900*. It acceded after the other colonies had agreed to unite, through the mechanism in Covering Clause 3. Covering Clause 6 then defines the States as those colonies "as for the time being are parts of the Commonwealth". Those words do not prescribe a method of withdrawal, but neither do they declare membership to be eternally irrevocable. Read together with the pre-existing political identity of the States, the absence of any operative prohibition on withdrawal, and the democratic foundations of constitutional authority, they leave open a serious argument that a people who voluntarily joined a federal union may later choose to withdraw from it.

That argument cannot be considered without regard to the economic record. Western Australia's complaints about the federal compact have endured for more than a century. The 1933 referendum, in which 66.23 per cent of voters supported withdrawal, followed decades of protest against federal economic policy. The subsequent petition to London failed because the British Parliament treated the matter as one for Australia's own constitutional institutions. It did not fail because Western Australians had surrendered the moral or democratic capacity to reconsider their political association.

The modern fiscal data makes the issue more immediate. Western Australian Treasury estimates that in 2023–24 the State made a net contribution of $39.022 billion to the Federation — $13,324 per Western Australian and substantially larger than the per-person contribution attributed to any other State. The principal components were company tax and personal income tax raised from activity within Western Australia, a relatively low GST relativity, and comparatively low Commonwealth expenditure on personal benefits and services in the State. These figures are estimates based on allocations and proxies. They are nevertheless indicative of the scale of the fiscal interest the Commonwealth has in preserving existing arrangements.

The Commonwealth's own fiscal position reinforces the point. Australian Government general government expenses are budgeted at $812.1 billion in 2025–26 and $833.3 billion in 2026–27, with gross debt estimated to reach $1.051 trillion by 30 June 2027. A central government of that scale has powerful institutional reasons to resist the departure of its largest per-capita net contributor. Good faith in any negotiation must therefore be demonstrated by conduct, not assumed from institutional form.

PART I — A REFERENDUM SETTLES THE DEMOCRATIC QUESTION OF SECESSION

A clear referendum on a clear question is the most authoritative act of collective political choice available to the people of Western Australia. It would bind the State's Parliament and Government to pursue independence and would remove any credible basis for describing secession as merely the preference of a faction. The vote would establish that the continued application of the federal compact no longer rests on the consent of the Western Australian people.

Australian constitutional law repeatedly acknowledges that constitutional authority ultimately depends upon the people. Sections 7 and 24 require the Houses of the Commonwealth Parliament to be directly chosen by the people. The High Court's representative-government cases recognise that the Constitution is sustained by popular choice. Those authorities do not directly decide the question of secession. They do, however, make it difficult to maintain that the people are sovereign when they approve a constitutional order but legally irrelevant when they decisively withdraw consent from it.

An obvious objection is that the Constitution sometimes speaks of "the people of the Commonwealth", suggesting that sovereignty belongs to Australians collectively rather than to one State's electors. Yet it also recognises continuing State political communities, requires senators to be chosen by "the people of the State", preserves State constitutions and powers, and requires State approval for alterations affecting its representation or limits. The text therefore accommodates both national and State democratic identities. The secession question arises where those identities come into direct conflict.

The Supreme Court of Canada's *Secession Reference* provides the closest modern federal analogy. It held that a clear majority on a clear question would confer legitimacy on Quebec's demand for secession, oblige the rest of Canada to acknowledge that democratic expression, and require negotiations conducted in accordance with the principles of democracy, federalism, constitutionalism, the rule of law and the protection of minority rights. The Court also concluded that lawful secession would require a negotiated constitutional amendment. That reasoning is not binding in Australia, but its central insight remains powerful: a federation cannot invoke constitutional form to remain indifferent to a constituent people's clear decision that they no longer wish to remain within it.

For Western Australia the proper conclusion follows the same logic but carries it one step further. The referendum would not merely create a right to request negotiations. It would determine the substantive question of political association. Negotiations would concern the terms and implementation of separation, not whether the people's decision may be vetoed by the government from which they have voted to withdraw. Democracy would not entitle Western Australia to impose every preferred financial or transitional term. Equally, federalism would not entitle the Commonwealth to convert its participation in implementation into ownership of the underlying decision.

International law should be stated with precision. The conventional position is that external self-determination, including unilateral secession, is clearly available to peoples under colonial domination or foreign occupation and may possibly arise where meaningful internal self-determination is gravely denied. No international court has yet declared a general legal entitlement for every region within a democratic State to secede unilaterally. That remains the orthodox position in positive international law.

Those categories (colonial domination or foreign occupation, or grave denial of meaningful internal self-determination) were formed principally during the era of decolonisation and in response to the territorial conflicts of the twentieth century. They were not demonstrated to constitute an eternal moral or legal ceiling on self-determination. Common Article 1 of the *International Covenant on Civil and Political Rights* (ICCPR) and *International Covenant on Economic, Social and Cultural Rights* (ICESCR) declares that all peoples have the right freely to determine their political status and to pursue their economic, social and cultural development, and that they may freely dispose of their natural wealth and resources. The *Declaration on Principles of International Law concerning Friendly Relations and Co-operation among States in accordance with the Charter of the United Nations* (*Friendly Relations Declaration*) preserves territorial integrity for States conducting themselves in accordance with the principle of equal rights and self-determination and possessing a government representing the whole people without distinction. These instruments do not deliver an automatic answer for Western Australia, but they demonstrate that self-determination has political, democratic and economic dimensions.

The modern question is therefore not confined to whether Western Australia resembles a colony of 1950. It is whether a mature and geographically distinct people, possessing functioning institutions and a demonstrated capacity for self-government, may be compelled indefinitely to remain in a union after a decisive vote to leave — particularly where the union continues to divert a substantial share of the wealth generated in that territory. International law has not yet resolved that question in a manner that directly addresses contemporary federal arrangements. It is more accurate to describe the law as incomplete on this point than to treat inherited decolonisation categories as a timeless prohibition.

Nor does the principle of territorial integrity answer the question by itself. In international law that principle principally protects States against external force and intervention. The *Friendly Relations Declaration* links the protection of territorial integrity to the existence of a government representing the whole people consistently with equal rights and self-determination. Australia is a representative democracy, which weighs against any claim that Western Australia presently satisfies the established remedial-secession cases. Yet representation in Canberra cannot be treated as conclusive when the people of a constituent State have directly and decisively rejected continued membership of the polity represented there.

The economic dimension of self-determination is also relevant. The ICCPR's and ICESRC's recognition that peoples may freely dispose of their natural wealth and resources, reinforced by the principle of permanent sovereignty over natural resources, was developed in the decolonisation era but expresses a broader proposition: political self-government is hollow if a people lacks meaningful authority over the economic foundations of its future. Western Australia's claim is not that every fiscal disagreement creates a right to secede. It is that a sustained pattern of structural fiscal transfer, followed by a decisive vote to end the compact, carries real legal and international significance.

Internationally, two limits should be acknowledged. It is not settled that every federal unit constitutes a "people" for common article 1, and permanent sovereignty over natural resources does not itself allocate domestic revenue or create an automatic right of secession. Western Australia must therefore establish a civic and territorial identity sufficient to support peoplehood, and rely on resource sovereignty as evidence that economic autonomy forms part of self-determination. This is an argument for principled development of existing norms, not a claim that positive international law has already decided the case.

PART II — NEGOTIATION CONCERNS THE TERMS OF SEPARATION, NOT PERMISSION TO LEAVE

The first institutional response to a decisive referendum should be negotiation. That is not because the Commonwealth possesses a veto over Western Australia's right to secede. It is because separation from a federation that has operated for more than a century requires an orderly settlement of shared legal, financial and administrative arrangements. The preferred route remains a negotiated agreement implemented through constitutional alteration under section 128, complementary legislation, and a coordinated Independence Day.

Western Australia should first enact legislation recording the referendum result, declaring the people's mandate, and authorising a negotiating authority. The legislation should state plainly that negotiations are undertaken to settle the terms and lawful implementation of separation. It should not concede that the referendum created only a request which the Commonwealth is free to refuse or ignore.

The negotiations would need to address the division of assets and liabilities; public debt and contingent liabilities; Commonwealth land and infrastructure; citizenship, nationality and rights of movement; trade, customs and borders; defence facilities and security cooperation; currency, banking and payments systems; taxation, pensions and social security; public servants and accrued entitlements; courts, pending proceedings and law enforcement cooperation; continuation or adaptation of existing laws; treaty succession and diplomatic recognition; maritime boundaries and offshore resources; native title, Aboriginal rights and existing agreements; continuity of essential public services; and the grandfathering or tapering of Commonwealth block grants and entitlements (including health and education).

Section 128 provides the constitutionally secure route for altering the federal text and, because separation would necessarily affect Western Australia's representation and constitutional position, approval by a majority of electors voting in Western Australia would also be indispensable. Once the principal terms were agreed, the Commonwealth Parliament could submit an alteration removing Western Australia from provisions that assume its continuing membership, adjusting parliamentary representation and financial arrangements, preserving accrued rights during transition, and terminating federal jurisdiction on the agreed date. Section 51(xxxviii), State request-and-consent legislation and the Australia Act may provide supporting machinery. A prudent settlement would employ overlapping mechanisms so that no avoidable legal doubt remains.

None of this requires the argument to treat section 128 as the metaphysical source of Western Australia's right to leave. It is the orthodox domestic mechanism for implementing that right with maximum legal certainty. The Constitution's amendment procedure should function as a bridge from democratic decision to orderly independence, not as a device by which the remaining Commonwealth may nullify the decision itself.

Good faith must be made concrete. Negotiations should begin within a defined period, proceed under a public framework, contain a timetable for exchanging positions and draft instruments, require regular reports to both Parliaments, and culminate in either a signed separation agreement or a reasoned statement identifying unresolved issues. Independent fiscal verification, mediation and agreed dispute-resolution processes should be available. A party that attends meetings while refusing to table substantive proposals, disclose relevant calculations or contemplate a workable constitutional alteration would not be negotiating in good faith.

Recognition of a duty to engage and the remedy for its breach are separate questions. The High Court might declare that a clear referendum activates constitutional obligations arising from democracy and federalism while declining to supervise bargaining or compel Parliament to enact a particular alteration. It could identify the governing principles and restrain legally impermissible conduct, where an appropriate matter and remedy arose, without fixing the terms of separation or guaranteeing a section 128 result.

The negotiated package should also protect those who did not support independence. Existing property, pension, citizenship and mobility rights should be preserved through generous transitional arrangements. Aboriginal peoples must participate directly where native title, cultural authority, communities, lands or treaty aspirations are affected. A democratic majority authorises a change in political status; it does not authorise the confiscation of rights or the erasure of prior legal interests. Firm protection of those interests would strengthen both the justice of the settlement and its international legitimacy.

PART III — THE STRUCTURAL INCENTIVES AGAINST GENUINE IMPLEMENTATION

The Canadian model is compelling on paper because it assumes that constitutional actors will respond to a democratic rupture with reciprocal good faith. Western Australia cannot safely proceed on that assumption merely because it appears in a legal argument. Its historical experience provides rational grounds for caution.

Since Federation, Western Australian protests over fiscal imbalance, tariff policy, centralised taxation and resource revenue distribution have repeatedly been met with inquiries, temporary concessions, revised formulas and assurances that the federal arrangement can be made fairer within existing institutions. The 1933 vote produced no pathway to independence. Later disputes have been managed within institutions controlled principally at the national level. Whatever the intentions of individual governments, the enduring institutional outcome has been preservation of the Commonwealth's fiscal position and continued net transfer of capacity from Western Australia.

The 2023–24 figures illustrate the scale. Western Australian Treasury estimates a net contribution of $39.022 billion in that year. The principal drivers were company tax and personal income tax raised from activity within the State, a relatively low GST share, and comparatively low Commonwealth expenditure on personal benefits and services in Western Australia. The dispute is therefore not confined to a single grants formula. It concerns the broader federal power to collect revenue generated by Western Australian activity and to determine its use elsewhere.

The Commonwealth would enter any negotiation knowing that independence threatens a large and recurring revenue base, while its own annual expenses exceed $800 billion and its debt and interest obligations continue to grow. It would also know that a successful Western Australian separation could prompt a wider reassessment of Australian federalism. These realities do not prove that every Commonwealth representative would negotiate dishonestly. They do mean that those structural interests create an objective risk of delay, dilution, or the advancement of an amendment incapable of attracting the support required for passage.

The structural imbalance in bargaining power is therefore central. A relationship cannot credibly be described as voluntary if the party that benefits most from its continuation possesses the effective power to prevent departure. The force of the observation lies in institutional design rather than personal motive. The dominant partner cannot be permitted to convert a process for arranging separation into a mechanism for perpetuating the existing relationship against a clearly expressed democratic will.

Western Australia should therefore enter negotiations constructively but with its constitutional position clearly reserved. It should make plain from the outset that the referendum mandate does not expire through delay and that the constitutional and political claim to unilateral self-determination remains expressly reserved if the Commonwealth refuses genuine implementation. Negotiation without a credible alternative can become supplication. Negotiation conducted against the background of a continuing democratic mandate is a process between political equals.

A credible process also requires an agreed endpoint. An open-ended dialogue would reward the party whose objective is preservation of the status quo. Western Australia should seek a defined negotiating period, after which the Government must report to Parliament whether a workable agreement and section 128 proposal exist. If they do not, the people are entitled to a clear account of whether the obstacle is genuine complexity or a refusal to accept the referendum's result. Transparency converts the language of good faith into an auditable standard.

PART IV — UNILATERAL SELF-DETERMINATION REMAINS A CREDIBLE RESIDUAL OPTION

The case for unilateral secession does not depend upon locating a sentence in the Constitution that expressly authorises withdrawal. Constitutions rarely provide convenient exit clauses for the political communities they govern. The case rests upon the cumulative force of popular sovereignty, the continuing political identity of the States, the plenary character of State legislative power, the *Australia Act 1986*, the temporally qualified language of Covering Clause 6, the non-operative location of "indissoluble" in the Preamble, the absence of any express prohibition, and the decisive withdrawal of consent through referendum.

Western Australia existed as a self-governing political community before the Commonwealth. Section 107 preserves State powers not exclusively vested in the Commonwealth or withdrawn by the Constitution. The *Constitution Act 1889* (WA) confers plenary legislative authority for the peace, order and good government of the State. The *Australia Act 1986* completed the removal of residual Imperial restraints and confirmed that Australian constitutional authority is now located entirely within Australian institutions and peoples. These propositions do not by themselves answer the question of secession, but they deny the proposition that Western Australia is merely an administrative district created by and permanently subject to the Commonwealth.

Covering Clause 6 remains significant. Its reference to colonies "as for the time being are parts of the Commonwealth" is capable of a conservative reading: it accommodates the admission of new States and constitutionally authorised territorial change. Yet the phrase is still temporal and conditional. It prevents the operative text from declaring what defenders of perpetual union often claim it declares. The Constitution does not state that every State shall forever remain a part of the Commonwealth, and its Preamble cannot perform the work of an operative prohibition that the text itself does not contain.

The orthodox objections are substantial. Covering Clause 5 binds the people and courts of every State to the Constitution and valid Commonwealth laws. Sections 106 and 107 preserve State constitutions and powers subject to the federal Constitution. Section 109 gives valid Commonwealth law priority over inconsistent State law. Section 128 supplies the formal means of constitutional alteration. Section 5 of the *Australia Act 1986* also leaves State legislative power subject to the Commonwealth Constitution. A court applying present doctrine would probably hold that an ordinary State Act cannot simply extinguish federal law within the State.

A constituent act of self-determination following a decisive referendum is not, however, adequately described as an ordinary exercise of delegated legislative power. It asserts that the people who sustain the old legal order have created a new one. A court functioning within the old order may reject that claim. Successful declarations of independence have often been rejected by the legal system from which the new State emerged. Domestic legal invalidity and the broader legitimacy or effectiveness of secession are related questions, but they are not identical.

The High Court is legally independent: its judges enjoy constitutional security of tenure and remuneration. The point is not that the Court or any Justice has a personal or pecuniary interest in the outcome. It is institutional: the Court necessarily reasons from within the existing constitutional order and through doctrines developed under it. That institutional history nevertheless warrants candour. In the *Engineers' Case*, the Court displaced doctrines protective of the federal balance and began a centralising trajectory that substantially enlarged the practical reach of Commonwealth power. Orthodox doctrine is therefore not politically weightless. It is the product of a national institution whose jurisprudence has contributed to the centralised arrangements now under challenge.

The International Court of Justice's *Kosovo Advisory Opinion* held narrowly that general international law contains no applicable prohibition on declarations of independence. It did not create a universal right to secede. Nor, however, did it declare that a federal constitution can bind a people forever regardless of democratic consent. Statehood and recognition would depend upon effective government, territory, population, capacity for international relations, peaceful conduct and the response of other States.

Economic extraction alone has not yet been accepted in international law as a sufficient ground for remedial secession. The underlying principles in the ICCPR and ICESRC and the *Friendly Relations Declaration* — particularly the right of peoples to freely dispose of their natural wealth and resources, and the requirement of a government representing the whole people without distinction — nevertheless provide a basis for assessing the legitimacy of continued union after a decisive vote to leave. Where a distinct people votes clearly to withdraw, offers peaceful negotiations, and encounters obstruction whose principal purpose appears to be the preservation of continuing fiscal transfer, the legitimacy of unilateral action is materially strengthened.

For that reason, unilateral self-determination must remain visible throughout any negotiation process. It is not a threat of violence and does not excuse disregard of minority, Aboriginal or human rights. It functions as the constitutional safeguard against converting "good faith" into indefinite delay. Western Australia should seek agreement, offer fair terms, and utilise section 128 where the Commonwealth genuinely assists. It should not accept that the principal beneficiary of the existing union possesses an indefinite veto over the people's decision to end it.

A unilateral course would require equivalent discipline. Western Australia would need a functioning constitution, continuity of courts and public administration, responsible provision for Commonwealth employees and beneficiaries, secure borders, monetary and financial arrangements, defence and treaty policy, and an early programme of diplomatic recognition. It would need to demonstrate that independence is not a momentary protest but the settled decision of a stable people capable of honouring obligations. The stronger those preparations, and the clearer the record of Commonwealth obstruction, the less persuasive it would be internationally to dismiss independence as an unlawful local adventure.

The same principle governs the position of Aboriginal peoples and political minorities. Their rights cannot be treated as bargaining counters for either side. Any declaration or separation agreement should preserve native title and existing legal rights, provide structured participation in constitutional design where appropriate, and guarantee equality before the law. A new nation's claim to self-determination is strongest when it recognises that the right it invokes for itself must also inform its treatment of the peoples and communities within it.

CONCLUSION

A decisive referendum would confer democratic legitimacy upon Western Australia's claim to secede. It would not automatically erase the federal legal order at the moment the votes were counted, but it would settle the fundamental democratic question: the people no longer consent to remain within the existing union. The first and preferable response would be good-faith negotiation about the terms of separation, followed by constitutional alteration and an orderly Independence Day.

That pathway must not be confused with a request for permission. The century-long record of preserving the federal status quo, the scale of Western Australia's net fiscal contribution, and the Commonwealth's substantial fiscal exposure to Western Australia's departure create powerful reasons to guard against delay presented as process. Good faith must produce timetables, substantive proposals and an implementable constitutional instrument.

If the Commonwealth negotiates honestly, separation can occur by agreement and with maximum legal certainty. If it refuses, obstructs or designs the process to defeat the referendum, the democratic mandate remains. The unresolved constitutional case for unilateral action would then become stronger, not weaker. No doctrine should be permitted to reduce popular sovereignty to a principle invoked only when the people choose to remain within institutions they have decisively chosen to leave.

SOURCES

Unless otherwise stated, online materials were viewed on 6 July 2026.

Primary Constitutional Instruments and Legislation

1. *Commonwealth of Australia Constitution Act* 1900 (Imp) 63 & 64 Vict, c 12, Preamble, Covering Clauses 3, 5 and 6, and ss 7, 24, 51(xxxviii), 72, 106–109, 111, 121, 123, 124 and 128 <https://www.legislation.gov.au/C2004Q00685/latest/text >.
2. *Australia Act* 1986 (Cth), especially ss 2, 3, 5, 6 and 15 <https://www.legislation.gov.au/C2004A03181/latest/text >.
3. *Constitution Act* 1889 (WA) 52 Vict, No 23, especially s 2 <https://www.legislation.wa.gov.au/legislation/statutes.nsf/law_a172.html >.

Judicial Authorities

4. *Amalgamated Society of Engineers v Adelaide Steamship Co Ltd* (1920) 28 CLR 129.
5. *Australian Capital Television Pty Ltd v Commonwealth* (1992) 177 CLR 106; [1992] HCA 45.
6. *Lange v Australian Broadcasting Corporation* (1997) 189 CLR 520; [1997] HCA 25.
7. *McGinty v Western Australia* (1996) 186 CLR 140; [1996] HCA 48.
8. *University of Wollongong v Metwally* (1984) 158 CLR 447; [1984] HCA 74.
9. *Reference re Secession of Quebec* [1998] 2 SCR 217, especially [88], [92]–[97] <https://decisions.scc-csc.ca/scc-csc/scc-csc/en/item/1643/index.do >.
10. *Accordance with International Law of the Unilateral Declaration of Independence in Respect of Kosovo (Advisory Opinion)* [2010] ICJ Rep 403 <https://www.icj-cij.org/case/141 >.

International Instruments

11. *Charter of the United Nations*, especially arts 1(2), 2(4) and 55 <https://www.un.org/en/about-us/un-charter/full-text >.
12. *International Covenant on Civil and Political Rights*, opened for signature 16 December 1966, 999 UNTS 171 (entered into force 23 March 1976), art 1.
13. *International Covenant on Economic, Social and Cultural Rights*, opened for signature 16 December 1966, 993 UNTS 3 (entered into force 3 January 1976), art 1.
14. *Declaration on Principles of International Law concerning Friendly Relations and Co-operation among States in accordance with the Charter of the United Nations*, GA Res 2625 (XXV), UN Doc A/RES/2625(XXV) (24 October 1970).
15. *Permanent Sovereignty over Natural Resources*, GA Res 1803 (XVII), UN Doc A/RES/1803(XVII) (14 December 1962).

Fiscal, Historical and Academic Materials

16. Government of Western Australia, *2025–26 Budget: Economic and Fiscal Outlook*, Budget Paper No 3, Appendix 11, 353–356 <https://www.ourstatebudget.wa.gov.au/2025-26/budget-papers/bp3/2025-26-wa-state-budget-bp3.pdf>.
17. Australian Government, *Budget 2026–27*, Budget Paper No 1, Statement 6: Expenses and Net Capital Investment, 219–225 <https://budget.gov.au/content/bp1/download/bp1_bs-6.pdf>; Statement 7: Debt Statement, 255–263 <https://budget.gov.au/content/bp1/download/bp1_bs-7.pdf>.
18. Australasian Federal Convention, *Official Record of the Debates of the Australasian Federal Convention* (1891–98).
19. Gregory Craven, 'An Indissoluble Federal Commonwealth? The Founding Fathers and the Secession of an Australian State' (1983) 14 *Melbourne University Law Review* 281.
20. Gregory Craven, *Secession: The Ultimate States Right* (Melbourne University Press, 1986).
21. Sukrit Sabhlok, *The Legality of Western Australia's Unilateral Secession* (PhD Thesis, Macquarie University, 2022).
22. Secession by Western Australia, 'History Shows Nations Leave Unions' (Substack, 14 April 2026) <https://secessionwa.substack.com/p/history-shows-nations-leave-unions>.

A Legislative Foundation for Negotiations: The First Step After the Referendum

Western Australia Secession Referendum Act 2029

An Act to record the result of the referendum held on 15 November 2029, declare the mandate of the people of Western Australia to establish an independent and sovereign nation, require negotiations on the terms and orderly implementation of separation, authorise preparations for independence, and provide for further action if good-faith negotiations are refused or fail.

Preamble

WHEREAS on 15 November 2029 the electors of Western Australia were asked: "Do you agree that Western Australia should secede from the Commonwealth of Australia and become an independent and sovereign nation?"

AND WHEREAS 80 per cent of the electors who voted answered "Yes";

AND WHEREAS that result is a clear, decisive and unambiguous expression of the sovereign will of the people of Western Australia and authorises the State's institutions to give effect to independence;

AND WHEREAS the first and preferred means of implementation is good-faith negotiation with the Commonwealth and, where appropriate, the other States concerning the terms and orderly transition of separation;

AND WHEREAS participation in negotiation does not concede that the Commonwealth possesses an indefinite veto over the referendum mandate;

BE IT ENACTED by the Parliament of Western Australia as follows:

1. Short title

This Act may be cited as the Western Australia Secession Referendum (Mandate, Negotiations and Transition) Act 2029.

2. Commencement

This Act comes into operation on the day on which it receives the Royal Assent.

3. Interpretation

In this Act —
"Commonwealth" means the Commonwealth of Australia;
"negotiations" means negotiations under section 5;
"referendum" means the referendum described in the Preamble;
"separation agreement" means an agreement or package of agreements providing for Western Australia's orderly separation; and
"referendum mandate" means the clear expression of the will of the electors recorded by the referendum.

4. Recording of result and declaration of mandate

(1) Parliament records that 80 per cent of electors voting at the referendum answered "Yes".
(2) Parliament declares that the result constitutes a clear mandate that Western Australia secede from the Commonwealth and become an independent and sovereign nation.
(3) The Government is required to pursue the implementation of that mandate, first through negotiations directed to an agreed and lawful separation.

5. Duty and authority to negotiate

(1) The Premier must establish a negotiating authority and enter negotiations with the Commonwealth and, where appropriate, the other States.
(2) The negotiations are to settle the terms and implementation of separation and are not negotiations as to whether the referendum mandate exists.
(3) The negotiating authority must seek agreement on assets and liabilities; public debt; citizenship and movement; trade, customs and borders; defence and security; currency and financial regulation; taxation, pensions and social security; public servants and accrued entitlements; courts and law enforcement; continuing laws; treaties and recognition; maritime boundaries and offshore resources; native title, Aboriginal rights and existing agreements; and continuity of essential services.
(4) The Government must seek a separation agreement capable of implementation by constitutional

alteration under section 128 of the Commonwealth Constitution and by supporting Commonwealth and State legislation.

6. Timetable and evidence of good faith

(1) The Premier must invite negotiations within 14 days after commencement.
(2) The Government must seek agreement on a public framework and timetable within 60 days, exchange substantive proposals within six months and report to Parliament at least every 90 days.
(3) In assessing good faith, regard must be had to whether the Commonwealth acknowledges the referendum result, exchanges substantive proposals, discloses relevant fiscal information, considers a workable constitutional alteration and refrains from conduct whose principal purpose is delay or defeat of the mandate.

7. Failure or refusal of negotiations

(1) If the Commonwealth refuses negotiations, or if after 18 months Parliament determines that negotiations have not been conducted in good faith or offer no reasonable prospect of implementing the mandate, the Premier must table a report setting out the conduct of the parties and the unresolved matters.
(2) Parliament may then consider further legislation necessary to give effect to the referendum mandate, including a declaration of independence and transitional measures.
(3) Nothing in this section authorises violence or derogation from the rights of Aboriginal peoples, minorities or any person.

8. Preparatory measures

The Government may prepare a new Constitution, administrative institutions, citizenship arrangements, fiscal and monetary systems, international-recognition strategy and all other measures reasonably necessary for an orderly Independence Day.

9. Present operation of Commonwealth law and reservation of position

(1) Until further legislation provides otherwise, this Act does not itself purport to terminate the operation of the Commonwealth Constitution or valid Commonwealth law within Western Australia.
(2) Subsection (1) is an interim provision for orderly transition and does not waive or prejudice the right asserted by the referendum mandate, the constitutional arguments available to Western Australia, or Parliament's capacity to take further action following refusal or failure of good-faith negotiations.

10. Regulations

The Governor may make regulations necessary or convenient for giving effect to this Act.

HELLO, NEW WESTERN AUSTRALIA

This chapter analyses Western Australia's current economic position using comprehensive data from the 2023-24 financial year, drawing on official sources such as the WA Department of Treasury and the Australian Bureau of Statistics. It examines key revenue streams, expenses, and fiscal flows under federation, then explores how these would transform post-secession, including the introduction of a

Universal Royalty Rate (URR) and the elimination of most distortionary taxes. The goal is to illustrate the potential for greater fiscal self-reliance and economic efficiency in an independent Western Australia.

Part 1 Sources of State Revenues & Expenses

Total Western Australian General Government revenues from all sources in 2023-24 (rounded) were $45,947 million, compared with $43,601 in 2022-23. Tables 1-5 break revenues down into their major components: mineral and petroleum revenues, state taxes, grants and subsidies from the Commonwealth, sales of goods and services, and other.[13]

I. Mineral & Petroleum Revenues

Table 1. Mineral & Petroleum Company Sales, WA's Share and Commonwealth Grants 2023-24 and 2022-23 ($millions)

	2023-24			2022-23		
Commodity	Gross Company Sales	WA's Share	% of WA M&P Revenues	Gross Company Sales	WA's Share	% of WA M&P Revenues
Alumina	6,581.0	109.1	0.9%	6,683.8	113.6	0.9%
Copper, lead & zinc	1,441.8	52.0	0.4%	1,719.3	74.8	0.6%
Gold	20,771.1	496.8	3.9%	18,640.1	436.0	3.4%
Iron-ore	142,954.5	10,372.3	81.7%	125,289.7	9,393.1	73.6%
Lithium	8,534.1	710.2	5.6%	21,456.1	929.9	7.3%
Mineral sands	1,174.2	43.2	0.3%	1,434.5	46.6	0.4%
Nickel	3,855.5	98.5	0.8%	5,686.8	139.7	1.1%
Other	2,692.5	22.9	0.2%	2,917.2	15.3	0.1%
Subtotal Minerals	188,004.7	11,905.0	93.7%	183,827.5	11,149.0	87.4%
Petroleum*	51,020.1	101.3	0.8%	72,172.4	78.7	0.6%
Condensate	8,513.8			8,743.6		
Crude oil	2,525.6			3,153.5		
LNG	36,490.2			57,064.5		
LPG (butane & propane)	554.4			751.1		
Domestic gas	2,936.1			2,459.7		
Total Minerals & Petroleum	239,024.8	12,006.3	94.5%	255,999.9	11,227.7	88.0%
North West Shelf Grants	*	694.4	5.5%		1,528.4	12.0%
GRAND TOTAL	239,024.8	12,700.7	100.0%	255,999.9	12,756.1	100.0%

*Sales from North West Shelf are distributed through the sales of Petroleum products. WA receives no royalties and is compensated in the form of a Commonwealth government grant.
Sources:
Mineral and Petroleum Statistics Digest 2023-2024
2024 Major Commodities Data File

[13] Note that the North West Shelf grant is listed in Table 1 under revenues from minerals and petroleum and again in Table 3 under grants and subsidies. The amount of the grant has not been double-counted in the state's total revenues of $45,947 million.

In FY2024 iron ore remained by far the dominant revenue earner, accounting for more than 75% of mineral company revenues and 82% of all WA mineral and petroleum revenues. Sharply lower commodity prices in FY2024 are reflected in weaker sales of most mineral products, including lithium and nickel.

Just over 70% of total petroleum revenues in 2023-24 were derived from LNG projects, primarily from the Gorgon, Wheatstone and Pluto fields, located offshore in Commonwealth waters in the North West Shelf. In lieu of royalties, the Commonwealth is compensated by Woodside Energy and its joint venture partners via the Petroleum Resource Rent Tax (PRRT), which is shared with WA as a grant according to a revenue-sharing agreement. This Commonwealth grant fell by 55% for North West Shelf production in FY2024, mainly because of weaker global prices for LNG.

Total mineral and petroleum revenues to WA came in at $12,700 million, representing 5.3% of the value of sales.

A note on forms of payment relating to resource extraction:

> ***Royalties:*** Payments are primarily from the value of extracted resources, which are paid directly to the Western Australian government.
>
> ***Rent Payments:*** These payments involve mining leases and tenements, though they are less significant compared to royalties.
>
> ***Commonwealth Grants:*** Mainly related to the North West Shelf project, where a portion of the funds collected by the Commonwealth (via the Petroleum Resource Rent Tax) is shared with Western Australia.

II. State Tax Revenues

State government tax revenues amounted to $13,631 million in FY2024, an increase of almost 10% on FY2023, with very significant percentage increases in most individual line items. (See Table 2.)

Table 2. State Tax Revenues ($millions)			
Source	2023-24	2022-23	% change
Payroll tax	5,404	5,017	7.7%
Transfer duty	2,932	2,459	19.2%
Land tax	844	784	7.7%
Other property taxes*	760	739	2.8%
Gambling taxes**	432	405	6.7%
Insurance duty	1,020	967	5.5%
Motor vehicle taxes	2,099	1,924	9.1%
Mining rehab levy	44	41	7.3%
Landfill levy	96	91	5.5%
TOTAL TAX REVENUES	13,631	12,427	9.7%

*Mainly Emergency services levy, loan guarantee fees, Metropolitan region improvement tax.

**Lotteries Commission, Betting tax, Casino tax.

Source: Annual Report on State Finances 2023-24, Appendix 2, Table 2.1.

III. Grants & Subsidies from the Commonwealth

Grants and subsidies from the Commonwealth government totaled $14,666 million, slightly down on FY2023. The approximate halving of the North West Shelf grant is particularly notable. (See Table 3.)

Table 3. Grants and Subsidies ($millions)			
Source	2023-24	2022-23	% change
GST	6,565	6,306	4.1%
North West Shelf	694	1,366	-49.2%
Other general purpose	34	116	-70.7%
National agreements*	4,690	4,237	10.7%
National partnerships/other**	799	792	0.9%
Capital grants	1,884	2,081	-9.5%
TOTAL GRANTS & SUBSIDIES	14,666	14,898	-1.6%

*Targeted grants, mainly Health reform and Schools reform.

**For health, transport, disability, other.

Source: Annual Report on State Finances 2023-24, Appendix 2, Table 2.1.

IV. Sale of Goods & Services by Government Agencies

Sales of goods and services are a fairly minor component of government revenues. The largest line item is WA Health, which provides public hospitals and other community health services, including mental health services. (See Table 4.)

Table 4. Sale of Goods & Services ($millions)			
Source	2023-24	2022-23	% change
WA Health	937	783	19.7%
Dept of Transport	312	292	6.8%
Dept of Education	223	203	9.9%
State Training Providers/TAFE Colleges	101	105	-3.8%
Dept of Training and Workforce Development	26	21	23.8%
Western Australian Land Information Authority	86	97	-11.3%
Dept of Biodiversity, Conservation & Attractions	87	138	-37.0%
Dept of Justice	164	153	7.2%
Dept of Mines, Industry Regulation & Safety	223	192	16.1%
All Other	1,300	1,310	-0.8%
TOTAL SALES OF GOODS & SERVICES	3,460	3,296	5.0%
Source: Annual Report on State Finances 2023-24, Appendix 2, Table 2.1.			

V. Other State Revenue Sources

Other revenue sources include royalties from resource sales[14] payable directly to the state. (See Table 5).

Table 5. Other Revenue ($millions)			
Source	2023-24	2022-23	% change
Interest income	391	333	17.4%
Revenue from public corporations	1,122	850	32.0%
Royalties	11,866	11,045	7.4%
Miscellaneous other	813	752	8.1%
TOTAL OTHER	14,192	12,980	9.3%
Source: Annual Report on State Finances 2023-24, Appendix 2, Table 2.1.			

[14] Royalties in Table 5 differ from the amount in Table 1 by $39 million. The source for the data in Table 5 is the WA Department of Treasury and Finance. The source for the detailed data in Table 1 is the Department of Energy, Mines, Industry Regulation and Safety. They evidently count royalties slightly differently.

VI. General Government Expenses

Government expenses amounted to $41,161 million in FY2024, representing 7.7% growth from the previous year. By far the largest line item is employee salaries, with the second largest item being "current transfers", an umbrella category that includes nearly $1 billion per year in state contributions to the National Disability Insurance Scheme. (See Table 6.)

Table 6. General Government Expenses ($millions)			
Source	2023-24	2022-23	% change
Salaries	16,518	15,727	5.0%
Superannuation			
Concurrent costs	1,781	1,759	1.3%
Superannuation interest cost	167	160	4.4%
Other employee costs	401	387	3.6%
Depreciation and amortisation	2,112	1,977	6.8%
Services and contracts	3,403	3,080	10.5%
Other gross operating expenses	7,330	6,620	10.7%
Interest	-	-	
Interest on leases	175	146	19.9%
Other interest	946	809	16.9%
Current transfers	8,068	7,358	9.6%
Capital transfers	560	458	22.3%
TOTAL EXPENSES	41,461	38,481	7.7%

Source: Annual Report on State Finances 2023-24, Appendix 1, Table 1.1.

Revenues ($45,947 million) thus exceeded expenses ($41,461 million), resulting in a net operating balance for the state of $4,486 million.

VII. Public Sector Revenues & Expenses

Public sector revenues encompass general government revenues plus the revenues of government-controlled entities that sit outside the public service. These entities are called Public Non-Financial Corporations (PNFC) and Public Financial Corporations (PFC) and are involved primarily in the sale of goods and services to the public. Thus, the discrepancies in both revenues and expenses between the General Government accounts and the Public Sector accounts are concentrated under the 'Sales of goods and services' line item. Examples of PNFCs are utilities and transport entities such as Fremantle Port Authority, Western Power and Busselton Water. Examples of PFCs are the Insurance Commission of WA and the Western Australian Treasury Corporation. The full list of entities that make up the WA public sector can be found by opening the document entitled "Key entities of the Western Australian government" that can be found on the WA government website.[15]

Public sector revenues in 2023-24 ($83,785 million) exceeded public sector expenses ($77,858) by $5,926 million. (See Tables 7 and 8.)

Table 7. Public Sector Revenues ($millions)

Source	2023-24	2022-23	% change
Taxation	13,007	11,843	9.8%
Grants and subsidies	12,780	12,817	-0.3%
Capital grants	1,884	2,081	-9.5%
Sales of goods and services	41,789	38,400	8.8%
Interest income	986	868	13.6%
Royalty income	11,866	11,045	7.4%
Other	1,473	1,288	14.4%
TOTAL PUBLIC SECTOR REVENUES	83,785	78,342	6.9%

Source: Annual Report on State Finances 2023-24, Appendix 1, Table 1.17.

Table 8. Public Sector Expenses ($millions)

Source	2023-24	2022-23	% change
Salaries	18,118	17,169	5.5%
Superannuation			
Concurrent costs	1,958	1,920	2.0%
Superannuation interest cost	167	160	4.4%
Other employee costs	784	637	23.1%
Depreciation and amortisation	5,391	5,120	5.3%
Services and contracts	4,406	4,144	6.3%
Other gross operating expenses	39,140	37,135	5.4%
Interest			
Interest on leases	243	217	12.0%
Other interest	1,812	1,490	21.6%
Current transfers	5,561	5,337	4.2%
Capital transfers	278	274	1.5%
TOTAL EXPENSES	77,859	73,604	5.8%

Source: Annual Report on State Finances 2023-24, Appendix 1, Table 1.17.

15 https://www.wa.gov.au/organisation/public-sector-commission/the-structure-of-the-western-australian-government-sector

PART 2

The Economics of Secession

Gross & Net Savings

Let us assume Western Australia has seceded from the Commonwealth: *Hello* new Western Australia! Using the 2023-24 figures, WA would no longer receive direct payments from the Commonwealth estimated to be $14,666 million, comprising GST grants ($6,565 million), North West Shelf grants ($694 million) and other grants and subsidies of $7,407 million. (See Table 3 above.)[16]

Offsetting this, the citizens of WA and the companies with operations in the new nation would no longer be required to pay the Commonwealth government the items estimated in Table 9 below, the biggest of which are personal income tax and company tax.

The company tax and GST numbers in Table 9 rely heavily on an analysis by the WA Department of Treasury that estimated the net contribution relative to its population share made by the state to the federation in 2023-24. The net contribution is calculated as Commonwealth revenues generated in WA minus Commonwealth expenditures for the benefit of WA, which the Treasury says amounted to $39,000 million. The Treasury estimates revenues flowing to the Commonwealth from WA of $112,000 million (broken down in Table 9 below) and expenditure by the Commonwealth for the benefit of WA at $73,000 million (broken down in Table 10 below). The high cross-subsidisation of the other states by WA that these numbers imply is driven principally by personal income and company taxes, GST, and a "low level of Commonwealth payments to WA for personal benefit payments and services. (See WA State Budget 2025-26, Budget Paper Number 3, Economic and Fiscal Outlook, pp. 354-355.)[17]

Detailed Explanations of Payments

Personal income tax, Medicare levy and Fringe Benefits Tax: The federal government collected $340,271 million in 2023-24 via these three taxes. (See ABS, Taxation Revenue, Australia 2023-24,

---

[16]The latest available budget data is for the 2025-26 financial year. According to the budget papers, WA will receive payments from the Commonwealth estimated to be $18,806 million, comprising GST Grants ($7,840 million), North West Shelf grants ($385 million) and other ('tied') grants of $10,581 million. (Source: Budget Paper No. 3, p.85.) Since we need to work off a set of government accounts that matches the most recent data for companies, for the purposes of these placeholder estimates we use FY2024 government numbers.

[17] It should be noted that the method of calculation of each line item by the Treasury is untransparent, in that the numbers are presented but the methodology and underlying data sources are not elaborated. We therefore repose trust in these estimates only to the extent that we believe they are the best available.

Table 1.) From the state accounts, WA's contribution was $41,714 million, which is just a shade above its population proportion.[18]

Company tax: $156,987 million was collected by the Commonwealth government from 'enterprises' in 2023-24. (See ABS, Taxation Revenue, Australia 2023-24, Table 1.) WA's population share would be 11% of this, or $17,269 million. However, the Treasury estimates that WA paid $26,657 million more than its population share, which comes to $43,926. If correct, this means WA accounts for about 27% of Australia's total Commonwealth company tax take.

GST contributions: Apportioning the national GST pool of $88,651 million (ABS, Taxation Revenue, Australia 2023-24, Table 1) by population, we get a figure for WA of $9,381 million. The WA Treasury estimate implies a net GST outflow of $2,816 million for WA (gross GST raised in WA of about $9,381 million less the GST grant back of $6,565 million). Revenues from the Commonwealth GST grant were $6,565 million (shown in Table 3), implying WA's contribution was in fact $9,381 million.

The residual of the $112,000 million estimated by the WA Treasury to have been paid to the Commonwealth ($16,979 million) encompasses a mix of other miscellaneous taxes and payments.

Table 9. Estimated Gross Outgoings from WA to Commonwealth, 2023-24*		
Item	Total ($millions)	Per capita ($)
Personal income tax & Medicare levy	41,714	13,858
Company taxes	43,926	14,593
GST	9,381	3,117
Miscellaneous other	16,979	5,641
TOTAL GROSS OUTGOINGS	112,000	37,209
Sources: ABS, Australian National Accounts: State Accounts (Western Australia), Table 16. WA State Budget 2025-26, Budget Paper Number 3, Economic and Fiscal Outlook, pp. 354-355.		

In a post-secession world, the new government of independent WA would no longer receive $14,666 million in Commonwealth grants and—assuming it replaced Commonwealth benefits to its people fully, using equivalently costly means to do so—would also need to fund an additional $58,000 million in spending by the federal government on WA's behalf that does not flow through the state accounts. (This figure is simply the $73,000 million in total estimated by the WA Treasury to have been spent by the Commonwealth for the benefit of WA, less the Commonwealth grants and subsidies from Table 3 that form part of that total.) The federal budget for social security and welfare alone in 2023-24 was $253,184 million, which apportioned simply by population implies $27,850 million worth of benefits paid to WA. Public goods such as defence, foreign relations, trade, and immigration are also provided and funded by the federal government and would need to be taken up by Western Australia post-

[18] See ABS, Australian National Accounts: State Accounts, Western Australia: https://www.abs.gov.au/statistics/economy/national-accounts/australian-national-accounts-state-accounts/latest-release#western-australia

secession, and the costs of providing these public goods are not possible to quantify with any confidence based on current information. Moreover, the nature of public goods is such that the state's share cannot be estimated by population apportionment. (See Table 10.) Important questions will have to be addressed about how much new WA would need to spend on setting up and maintaining foreign diplomatic offices, visa processing, coastal defences and so on.

Even a more modest figure of $112,000 million less $73,000 million = $39,000 million overstates the net savings available to WA from detaching from the Commonwealth because some material portion of the Commonwealth company tax take included in these calculations is paid by entities that are not domiciled in WA. Consequently, funds retained by these companies as a result of the zero company tax regime envisioned in independent WA will not be secured by WA unless the post-secession tax regime includes an explicit mechanism for recapturing them.

Table 10. Estimated Spending by the Commonwealth on WA's Behalf ($millions)

Commonwealth service	National budget	WA portion*
Grants and subsidies	-	14,666
Social security and welfare	253,184	27,850
Health	106,589	11,725
Defense	45,103	N/A
Immigration	3,367	N/A
Foreign affairs and economic aid	7,141	N/A
Other	270,473	N/A
TOTAL EXPENSES	685,857	73,000

*Based on population for Social security and welfare, and Health.
WA State Budget 2025-26, Budget Paper Number 3, Economic and Fiscal Outlook, pp. 354-355.
Source: Final Budget Outcome 2023-24, Table 1.5, p.11.

Zero Income Tax Regime

As explored in detail in Chapter 4, this regime would eliminate income, company, and payroll taxes while retaining select non-distortionary levies such as a reformed GST and land-based UPRS to ensure fiscal balance.

If extraction of the significant resource wealth of Western Australia continues, it should continue for the benefit of the people of Western Australia. That means reforms to the outdated royalty regime and elimination of unnecessary taxes on the income of both individuals and companies. Assuming the reforms suggested in the remainder of this chapter and in Chapter 4 are implemented, upon secession, the independent nation of Western Australia will see its gross annual retained income increase significantly relative to the pre-secession framework, through the elimination of most state-based and federal taxes and excises.

The Southern Hemisphere's Economic Free-Trade Zone, with Zero Company Tax

As noted above, the WA Treasury's implied estimate of company taxes paid by businesses in WA was $43,926 million. We assume that this estimate includes company taxes paid by entities with operations in WA but not domiciled in WA (e.g. BHP), so only some proportion of the $43,926 would be retained by WA-based companies if business taxes were eliminated. However, assuming the state-based payroll tax is also eliminated, the average savings to WA's approximately 92,000 non-sole-trader businesses from that alone would amount to almost $60,000 each annually, though with larger companies (with larger payrolls) seeing larger benefits. With these savings added to the company taxes, the total burden on WA-based businesses would be reduced significantly. This retained wealth will become private sector capital, to be deployed by private sector hands as they see fit.

A commensurate benefit is the elimination of untold layers of costly fiscal management by government mandarins, typically far removed from the trenches and actual knowledge of where capital needs to be efficiently deployed.

An additional motley assortment of taxes, charges, levies, and fees will cease to burden the people and businesses of Western Australia upon secession. These include the luxury car tax, the wine equalisation tax, passenger movement charges and so on.

With the elimination of company income tax, payroll tax, excise tax, customs duty, and at least another dozen assorted Commonwealth taxes and charges, businesses will thrive in a near-zero-tax environment.

With no income tax filings or payroll tax calculations, companies' tax departments can be streamlined and external advisory fees reduced towards zero. We anticipate that large international mining companies will see a substantial increase in net profitability from their WA operations due to both lower overall government payments and reduced administrative costs. Western Australia's major companies will be able to reinvest these savings into further exploration, technology improvements, or shareholder returns, enhancing their global competitiveness.

For the vastly larger number of small-to-medium-sized companies, the reduction in compliance costs will be particularly valuable because they typically pay disproportionately higher costs to stay in line with government demands. Drastically reducing this significant cost stratum of business administration will make it easier for these companies to operate efficiently and focus on core activities rather than tax management.

The new zero tax regime will likely attract significant foreign direct investment in WA as companies seek to capitalise on the favourable economic environment it offers, enabling the new nation of Western Australia to become a preferred global hub for doing business.

With no taxes on salaries and wages, a new Western Australia should attract skilled workers from around the world, driving further growth in the mining sector and related industries. Additionally, the higher disposable income of workers should fuel consumer spending, boosting the local economy everywhere in the state.

The Luckiest Country?

With income tax, excise taxes, payroll tax and myriad other taxes eliminated, secession would bring immediate additional savings for the people and businesses of WA, to do with as they see fit.

Western Australians will also be restored the dignity and respect long denied them for making their own economic decisions, without the enforced and false patriarchy of big central government running the affairs of Western Australians.

Part 3

Introducing the 20% Universal Royalty Rate

THE CORE PROPOSAL

With the government of the people of Western Australia steering the new nation with a clear mandate to prosper from the efficient use of the nation's resources for the benefit of Western Australians, the existing royalty payments regime by necessity requires vigorous review and reform.

Under a post-secession scenario in which company, income, payroll, and most other taxes are abolished, we propose that a cornerstone source of WA government revenues be a straight 20% Universal Royalty Rate (URR) on company resource sales. On the basis of the FY2024 revenue total, application of the URR yields payments to WA totaling just under $48 billion. This is slightly more than all state government revenues (just under $46 billion in FY2024, as detailed above) under the current system.

The revenue that would be derived from a 20% URR, estimated at $48 billion, is about $6.5 billion higher than present state government expenses.

The Current Royalty Regime

Under the Western Australian *Mining Act* 1978, the royalty regime set out in Table 11 was implemented and has been in place in approximately the same form for over half a century, with a few tweaks along the way.

Table 11. Royalty Rates for WA Mineral Resources		
Resource	Royalty rate (% of basis)	Basis*
Iron ore		
Beneficiated	5.0%	Ad valorem
Direct shipping (crushed or screened)	7.5%	Ad valorem
Lithium	2.5%	
Feedstock	5.0%	Ad valorem
Direct shipping	7.5%	Ad valorem
Gold	2.5%	Ad valorem
Nickel	2.5%	Ad valorem
Bauxite	7.5%	Ad valorem
Alumina	1.65%	Ad valorem
Mineral sands	5.0%	Ad valorem
Copper, lead, zinc		
Metallic	2.5%	Ad valorem
Concentrate	5.0%	Ad valorem
Crushed and screened	7.5%	Ad valorem
Diamonds	5.0%	Ad valorem
Limstone and lime sand	73c/tonne	Flat rate
Gypsum	73c/tonne	Flat rate
Salt	73c/tonne	Flat rate
Other construction materials		
Dolomite, gravel, common rock	73c/tonne	Flat rate
Building stone, silica, talc	$1.17/tonne	Flat rate

*Ad valorem is % of sales, net of allowable deductions such as transport and processing costs.
Source: WA Department of Treasury, 2024-25 Overview of State Taxes and Royalties; WA government media release, 15 May 2020

Table 11 shows considerable variance in royalty rates by resource across the mining sector, a situation with a long history of political and industry justifications for maintaining disparities—for example, differences in margins between resource types, or the felt need to spur investment or maintain competitiveness in particular global markets. The Mining Act that formed the original legal platform for these royalties was enacted in 1978. The historical bases justifying these disparities in royalty rates will no longer apply in the new Western Australia, with all exceptions to the baseline URR being based on transparent industrial policy priorities crafted in the public interest.

Measuring Sales Values

For the purpose of calculating the URR payment due, the sale price for any given resource will be set each month for the following month based on industry-recognised data sources and will vary depending on specific contracts and spot market fluctuations.

A resource value set each month can be applied to the actual volume of production extracted during that month or as delivered at the time of shipping, irrespective of specific contracts and spot market fluctuations. This approach will simplify administration costs in the application of royalties and provide transparency for all.

The Universal Royalty Rate (URR) in a Near Zero-Tax Nation: Implications for Companies

We estimate the high-level outcomes of a switch from the present taxation regime to a URR regime for a range of companies, including WA's most well-known and largest companies, to be significantly positive, based mostly on 2024 information. Information on many companies is insufficiently complete (often due to various taxes and charges levied by the Commonwealth and WA governments that are built into operating costs but not explicitly broken out) to generate reliable estimates of company saving/dissaving under the post-secession URR. This data shortfall is a significant issue, as it prohibits us from painting an accurate picture of likely economic outcomes from the imposition of the URR for a number of miners. Ideally, the overwhelming majority of companies will benefit from the change in tax/royalty regime—not just a handful of large ones—but this is not currently provable.

We estimate that Fortescue, Rio Tinto, BHP and Hancock Prospecting will each emerge from a regime shift away from the present taxation scheme to a 20% flat URR scheme with hundreds of millions of dollars of savings for their shareholders.

Nevertheless, our estimates for these and other companies are not perfect: they are drawn from time periods that are not precisely synced (some companies report on a calendar-year basis and some on a financial-year basis), differences in exchange rates used (we used an average for the relevant period, but sales are made under contract and at irregular periods), and assumptions about shipments and prices that are only best guesses based on the information available.

Addressing Variations in Mining Margins under the URR

A single 20% Universal Royalty Rate (URR) is intended to simplify Western Australia's resource payment system and replace the patchwork of legacy royalties, rebates and special arrangements that have accumulated over decades. A universal headline rate is attractive because it is clear, predictable and hard to game. At the same time, mining margins differ materially across commodities and across individual projects, particularly where costs are high, prices are volatile, deposits are lower grade, or logistics are remote. Our preliminary analysis suggests the URR will be comfortably absorbed by high-margin producers, especially once company tax, payroll tax and other levies are removed. The main policy risk sits at the margin: a limited subset of lower-margin or late-life operations—often in more volatile commodities—could face a higher effective burden under a flat ad valorem royalty if no safety valve exists. Because public disclosures are uneven (and rarely site-level), these findings are indicative rather than definitive, and they are best treated as a trigger for targeted design safeguards rather than as a basis for commodity-by-commodity bargaining. Our design principles are key: keep the URR universal, but allow narrow, transparent exceptions where the public interest is clearly served. Any exception should meet all of the following tests:

- Rules-based and published (no opaque bargaining).
- Site-level and evidence-based (verified volumes, prices and costs).
- Time-limited (automatic sunset unless renewed on evidence).
- Capped (to protect fiscal predictability).
- Auditable (with penalties for misstatement).

The practical mechanism can be simple. Retain the 20% URR as the default, and add two tightly defined channels for relief:

- **Viability safety valve:** a temporary discount or rebate where an audited, site-level viability metric falls below a published threshold (for example, operating cash flow below sustaining capital, measured consistently). Relief expires automatically when conditions normalise.
- **Strategic industrial policy relief:** time-limited concessions linked to clearly stated goals such as critical-mineral supply-chain capability, essential regional employment, or enabling infrastructure that measurably lifts long-run value to Western Australians. Criteria should be objective, publicly stated, and reviewed periodically.

Process Pathway

Rather than attempting to finely calibrate these settings from incomplete public data today, this manuscript flags margin variation as a key design issue and anticipates pre-secession URR White Paper(s) to test the evidence base (including confidential, site-level cost and price information) and to stress-test any proposed safety-valve thresholds before independence. Post-independence, the initial URR legislation should still mandate a URR White Paper within the first 12 months, led by the WA Reserve Authority (WARA) using its production-verification and audit mandate to coordinate confidential data collection and industry consultation, and then recommend (i) whether the safety-valve thresholds are correctly set, and (ii) whether any narrowly defined, enduring adjustments are justified on transparent industrial policy grounds.

While transitional adjustments may impose short-term costs on some operators, the overall economic case for the URR remains compelling: projected revenues of ~$47.8 billion exceed current state expenses, delivering substantial net benefits through tax abolition and retained resource wealth.

Part 4

Waters Near & Far

Fixing The PRRT Rort

The Carnarvon, Roebuck, and Browse Basins possess Australia's largest resource developments located off the northwest coast of Western Australia. The projects they contain include several offshore gas fields, associated production facilities, and onshore processing facilities. Here, we deal only with those projects and fields located in Commonwealth waters adjacent to Western Australia.

Nearly all of the gas produced from the Carnarvon, Roebuck, and Browse Basins is exported, mostly as LNG, to markets in Asia. Export contracts are long-term and account for a significant portion of the LNG production, leaving a relatively smaller share for domestic consumption.

Most of the domestic gas supply for the eastern states and territories comes from other sources, such as the Bowen, Surat, Cooper and Eromanga Basins in Queensland, Gippsland Basin in Victoria or the Cooper Basin in South Australia. The domestic gas retained from the northwest Basins is used within WA itself, with virtually none being used by eastern states. In short, there is virtually no dependency by the east on gas from the west.[19]

In 2023-24 the Commonwealth collected $1,144 million from gas and petroleum projects operating in offshore basins, including the Bonaparte Basin off the Northern Territory, the major Gippsland Basin projects off Victoria, the several projects in the Otway Basin offshore from Victoria and South Australia, and the Bass Basin projects between Victoria and Tasmania. (See Australian Government Budget Outcome 2023-24, p. 5.)

Total Commonwealth government revenues for FY2024 came in at $688.6 billion, so the Petroleum Resource Rent Tax (PRRT) – a 40% tax on profits that is the mechanism by which the petroleum revenue is collected – accounts for a minute fraction of total government revenues: less than 0.2%. The contribution to that 0.2% from the WA offshore fields is substantial, but even so, it is extremely small in the big picture and losing it would have minimal impact on the Commonwealth budget.

The politically awkward and suppressed truth is that the extraordinary export revenues generated by all offshore projects in Commonwealth waters primarily benefit the companies involved, rather than the Australian people from whom the resources are taken.

The close relationship between the fossil fuel industry and Australian political parties is well documented and reflected in the favourable policies and approvals afforded to the industry. As is detailed below, the sales revenues from the Carnarvon, Roebuck, and Browse Basins are indeed extraordinary.

[19] https://www.accc.gov.au/media-release/tight-supply-forecast-for-australias-east-coast-gas-market-in-q2-2026#:~:text=Overall%20gas%20supply%20on%20Australia's,the%20second%20quarter%20of%202026.%E2%80%9D

The super-profits involved have by and large been entirely exported out of Australia for the benefit of others for years.

The PRRT figure of 40% has for a long time made for good political sound bytes, but in practice the deductions afforded by the Commonwealth to the industry have resulted in an effective PRRT tax rate of well under 40%. The clear implication is that the Commonwealth government, through the efforts of the major political parties known to benefit from being closely aligned with the offshore gas industry, has assisted in withholding billions of dollars each year from the Australian people in recent years, under the PRRT regime that was enacted in its initial form in 1987.

Taxable profit is determined after deducting eligible expenditures, such as exploration, capital, and operating costs, from the project's assessable receipts. These deductions are generous, allowing for the carry-forward of unused deductions with an uplift (a form of interest) until they can be applied against project profits. Some un-deducted exploration expenditure can be transferred to other projects (subject to conditions). In addition, the PRRT payment can be used as a deduction for purposes of corporate income tax.

The significant deductions available under the PRRT often reduce or eliminate the PRRT liability, especially in the early years of a project. As a result, even though the PRRT is set at a nominal 40%, the actual amount collected can be, and often is, much lower than the receipts of corporate income tax, which is calculated on a broader base and with fewer specific deductions.

Hence, many companies operating in the Carnarvon, Roebuck, and Browse Basins, including ExxonMobil, Shell, Chevron and Santos, have been called out for paying little or no PRRT.

Jurisdictional Boundaries

Commonwealth jurisdiction extends from 3 nautical miles (~5.6 kilometers) into sea from the coast out to 200 nautical miles (~370 kilometers) from the coast, encompassing the Exclusive Economic Zone (EEZ). Western Australia's jurisdiction extends up to 3 nautical miles into sea from the coastline.

The Roebuck and Browse Basins are located beyond the 3 nautical mile limit and fall within Commonwealth waters. Portions of the Carnarvon Basin extend within the 3 nautical mile limit, but this is of no economic consequence, with all of its operational fields located in the Commonwealth waters beyond the 3 nautical mile limit.

With the people of Western Australia choosing to become an independent nation, the fields of each of the basins will be subsumed within the newly established national waters of Western Australia, as the new nation will claim as its own the maritime boundaries currently forming part of the Commonwealth's EEZ.

As an independent nation, Western Australia will need to establish its maritime boundaries following the framework under the United Nations Convention on the Law of the Sea (UNCLOS), which will allow Western Australia to claim an EEZ extending up to 200 nautical miles from its coastline. This will place the offshore fields entirely within Western Australia's national waters.

This means new Western Australia will have full and exclusive jurisdiction over the Carnarvon, Roebuck, and Browse Basins. This jurisdictional ascendancy will allow for the application of the 20% URR across the Carnarvon, Roebuck, and Browse Basins, achieving harmonisation with onshore miners. Sales from these projects accounted for most of the $51,020 million in petroleum revenues produced in WA in 2023-2024. (See Table 1)

Part 5

New Waters

A map of the northern WA coastline and its major offshore resource fields is provided below.

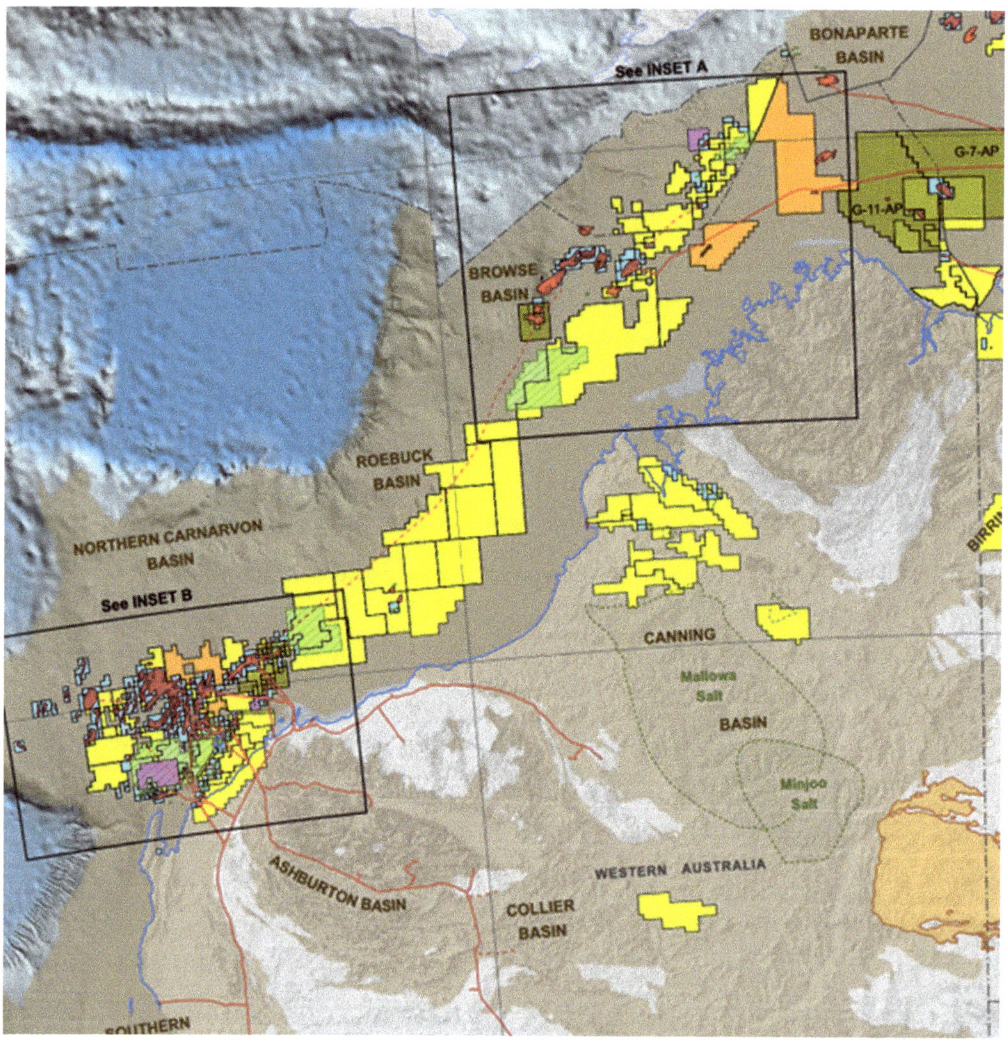

Credit: Commonwealth of Australia (Geoscience Australia).

According to WA government data for 2023-24, sales revenue of $45,271 million emanated from the Gorgon, Wheatstone, North West Shelf and Pluto Projects, all in the Carnarvon Basin. This differs slightly from the subtotal for operational projects of $47,212 for FY2024 shown in Table 14, which is a forward-looking projection of annual revenues using conservative but still highly speculative assumptions about prices.

The gas values shown below are estimates based on market conditions, and actual sales can vary depending on specific contracts and spot market fluctuations. Estimates based on an application of the 20% URR are based on monthly proxies for the mean value per million British thermal units (MMBtu), utilising a weighted mean of values available in global and industry-recognised data sources like S&P Global Platts, ICE, CME Group, Argus Media, Bloomberg, Energy Intelligence Group, and BP Statistical Review of World Energy. This mean monthly value is applied to the actual volume of production extracted during that month simplifying administration costs in the application of the Universal Royalty Rate and providing transparency.

Below we walk through each of the major offshore projects in turn, looking at reported production and capacities for independently assessing sales revenues outside of locked-in contracts, while gaining a view of the URR contribution each will make to the Western Australian nation in exchange for the extraction of its natural resources.

Carnarvon Basin Operational Projects

Gorgon Gas Project

This is operated by Chevron, in partnership with ExxonMobil, Shell, Osaka Gas, Tokyo Gas, and Chubu Electric. The Gorgon project has three LNG trains, each with a capacity of 5 million tonnes per annum (MTPA), making a total of 15 MTPA. It also produces significant amounts of condensate. The Gorgon fields have estimated reserves of around 40 trillion cubic feet of gas valued at $622 billion in 2024, requiring over 50 years to extract at current production capacity. The LNG produced is primarily exported to markets in Asia, including Japan and South Korea.

The Gorgon Gas Project has faced operational challenges leading to periods where production has not reached full capacity. However, it has resumed full production as of late May 2024 after addressing some technical issues. On average, when fully operational the project has the capacity to produce around 15.6 million tonnes annually (MTPA) of LNG. In 2024, the project produced 1,299 million cubic feet of natural gas per day as well as 10,000 barrels of crude oil per day.

As prices are volatile and impossible to forecast with confidence – for example, in 2024 the price ranged from US$8.82 per MMBtuin February to US$14.23 in December), we assume a conservative figure of US$12, or A$18, per MMBtu. One tonne of LNG typically equals around 52 MMBtu, so the annual revenue from 15.6 MTPA of LNG can be estimated as 15.6 million tonnes × 52 MMBtu per tonne × $18/MMBtu = $14,602 million.

Applying the 20% Uniform Royalty Rate to the Gorgon Gas Project results in an annual payment to new WA of $2,920 million.

Wheatstone Project

This project is operated by Chevron in partnership with Kuwait Foreign Petroleum Exploration Company, Woodside Petroleum, Kyushu Electric Power Company, and TEPCO.

Wheatstone has two LNG trains with a combined capacity of 8.9 MTPA. The project also includes significant gas and condensate production from the Wheatstone and Iago fields. The LNG and condensate are primarily exported to Asian markets.

Despite Wheatstone's nameplate capacity of 8.9 million tonnes per annum of LNG, operational challenges can temporarily reduce production, so actual production figures can vary. On average, the project produces around 80-90% of its full capacity, translating to approximately 7.1 to 8.0 MTPA under typical operating conditions.

Assuming the same conservative LNG price $18 per MMBtu yields annual revenues to the producer of $7,020, and hence annual revenues to Western Australia under the 20% URR of $1,404 million.

Pluto LNG Project

This is operated by Woodside Energy (holding 90% ownership) in partnership with MidOcean Energy and Kansai Electric. The Pluto LNG project processes gas from the Pluto and Xena fields and currently has an operational capacity of 4.9 MTPA of LNG. As a result of expansion works, this is likely to increase by approximately 3 MTPA beginning in 2026, with additional gas being processed from the Scarborough field. The total recoverable reserves for these fields are around 5 trillion cubic feet of gas. Most of the LNG produced at Pluto is exported, primarily to Asian markets.

Sales value is estimated at $4,586 million, again assuming $18 per MMBtu. Under the 20% URR, annual revenue to Western Australia would amount to approximately $917 million. Assuming capacity is increased to 8 MTPA, all of these numbers would increase by a factor of approximately 60%.

North West Shelf (NWS) Project

This project is operated by Woodside Energy, partnering with BHP Billiton, BP, Chevron, Japan Australia LNG (MIMI), Shell, and CNOOC. The NWS project produces approximately 16.9 MTPA of LNG. It also produces significant quantities of condensate and domestic gas. The majority of LNG is exported to Asia, while the domestic gas is sold within Australia. LNG is natural gas that has been cooled into a liquid for export shipping; "domestic gas" refers to natural gas supplied to Australian users via the domestic pipeline market (not liquefied).

Annual LNG production fluctuates based on operational conditions and market demand. The nameplate capacity is 16.9 million MTPA of LNG and the project has been consistently producing close to its full capacity, with figures often around 16 to 16.5 MTPA in recent years.

Annual condensate production from the North West Shelf is approximately 65 million barrels. Domestic gas is also produced and supplies gas to Western Australia itself, with an annual production capacity of approximately 200 to 300 terajoules per day (TJ/day), translating to around 73,000 to 110,000 terajoules per year.

Production values estimated above can be converted to annual sales. For LNG, using $18 per MMBtu as our reference point, sales would amount to $15,444 million. For condensate, which is typically priced lower than crude oil, we can use an average price of A$100 per barrel to arrive at an annual value of about $6,500 million. For domestic gas, average quoted prices are highly variable, but using a conservative estimate of A$7 per gigajoule, 90,000 TJ × $7 per gigajoule = $360 million. The estimated total value of production amounts to $22,574 million, and the estimated annual revenue to new WA under the 20% URR would then be $4,515 million.

Upcoming Projects

Table 14. 20% Universal Royalty Rate and Zero Tax Scenario (Carnarvon Basin, Petroleum)
Estimates of Project and WA Outcomes (A$millions)*

Project	Lead producing company	Unit	Expected production	Expected company revenues	Revenues to WA under 20% URR
Operating:					
Gorgon	Chevron	MTPA	15.6	14,602	2,920
Wheatstone	Chevron	MTPA	7.5	7,020	1,404
Pluto (current)	Woodside	MTPA	4.9	4,586	917
North West Shelf LNG	Woodside	MTPA	16.5	15,444	3,089
North West Shelf Condensate	Woodside	MMbbl	65.0	6,500	1,300
North West Shelf domestic gas	Woodside	TJ	90,000	630	126
Subtotal Operating Projects				48,782	9,756
Forthcoming:					
Pluto Train 1 Expansion	Woodside	MTPA	3.0	2,808	562
Pluto Train 2	Woodside	MTPA	5.0	4,680	936
Greater Western Flank Phase 3 and Lambert Deep, LNG	Woodside	BCF	30	270	54
Eqquus, LNG	Western Gas	MTPA	2.5	2,340	468
Eqquus, domestic gas	Western Gas	TJ	18,250	63.9	13
Dorado Field, oil	Santos	MMbbl	36.5	2,920	584
Crux Project, LNG	Shell	MTPA	2.9	2,714	543
Browse to NWS, LNG	Woodside	MTPA	11.4	10,670	2,134
Subtotal Forthcoming Projects				26,467	5,293
TOTAL				75,249	15,050

*Uses the USD/AUD average exchange rate for CY2024 (1.52)
Sources: Company reports, company websites, news reports.

Pluto Train 1 Extension and Pluto Train 2

This project is operated by Woodside Energy with LNG Japan having a 10% stake. The Scarborough gas field is a key component of Woodside's portfolio and has been in the planning stages for several years. The project involves developing the Scarborough gas field and piping the gas to the existing onshore Pluto Train 1 LNG facility, which is undergoing renovations to enable it to produce approximately 3 MTPA of the expected total 8 MTPA. The remaining 5 MTPA will be processed at Pluto LNG Train 2. Commencement of production is expected by 2026. The Scarborough gas field contains an estimated 11.1 trillion cubic feet (Tcf) of dry gas.

The project includes the installation of a new floating production unit (FPU) and a 430-kilometer subsea pipeline connecting the field to the Pluto LNG onshore processing facility.

Assuming the same conversion and pricing assumptions as for the operating projects, we can estimate annual sales for 8 MTPA of $7,488 million. Applying the 20% URR yields a royalty estimate to Western Australia of $1,498 million per year.

Greater Western Flank Phase 3 & Lambert Deep

Woodside Energy is the owner of this project in partnership with BHP Billiton, BP, Chevron, Japan Australia LNG (MIMI), Shell, and CNOOC.

Production has already commenced but has not reached full operational capacity. The fields have been estimated to have around 400 billion cubic feet (bcf) of recoverable gas reserves and are tied back into existing North West Shelf infrastructure. Thus, the gas produced will be processed at the NWS facilities with LNG and condensate primarily exported.

If we assume the aim is to extract the estimated 400 bcf of reserves over a period of around 10 to 20 years, which is typical for such developments, the annual production could range from 20 to 40 bcf per year. Estimating sales value is fraught, but if we take the midpoint of the 20-40 bcf production range and assume a price for natural gas of $9 per MMBtu, we can estimate annual sales value as 30 x 1 million MMBtu/bcf x $9/MMBtu = $270 million.

Applying the 20% URR to the Greater Western Project results in a royalty estimate for Western Australia of $54 million per year.

Equus Gas Project

Operated by Western Gas, this project targets approximately 2 trillion cubic feet of gas and 42 million barrels of condensate. The Equus Project is still in the pre-production phase, with production expected to commence in 2027. The gas is expected to cater to Western Australia's domestic gas requirements and potentially for export as LNG.

If the project's targets of approximately 2 trillion cubic feet (Tcf) of gas and 42 million barrels of condensate is achieved, the planned extraction over the project's life is expected to yield 2 to 3 MTPA of

LNG. Additionally, it will produce over 50 terajoules per day (TJ/day) of domestic gas, which is about 18,250 TJ per year, beginning from 2027.

For the LNG, we use the same estimate of $18 per MMBtu and assume production of 2.5 MTPA, yielding a total of $2,340 million. For the domestic gas we assume a price of $3.50 per gigajoule (GJ), yielding an annual sales value of $64 million.

Applying the 20% URR to the total of the LNG and domestic gas, Western Australia would receive an estimated annual payment of $481 million.

Roebuck Basin

Currently, there are no fully developed and producing projects in the Roebuck Basin. However, the region has been the focus of exploration activities, particularly by Santos.

The most promising development in the Roebuck Basin is in the Bedout Sub-Basin, which includes the Dorado field. The Dorado field is being developed by Santos (operator) in partnership with Carnarvon Petroleum. This project is expected to produce both oil and gas, with estimates suggesting that the field could produce up to 100,000 barrels of oil per day (bopd) at its peak. The project also includes associated gas production, which might be used for reinjection or potentially exported as LNG in the future.

Expected annual production is focused primarily on oil, with peak production potentially reaching 36.5 million barrels per year (100,000 bopd). If we assume an oil price of $80 per barrel, the annual sales value could be approximately $2.92 billion. The associated gas production is yet to be fully quantified and commercialised but could add more value depending on the development approach.

The Dorado field, discovered in 2018, is one of the largest oil discoveries on the North West Shelf in the last three decades. The project planning is well-advanced, with the Front-End Engineering and Design (FEED) phase having been initiated.

First production is expected to commence around 2026, following the Final Investment Decision (FID) in 2024 and subsequent construction and installation phases. The initial phase of development will focus on oil production, with an expected production rate of 75,000 to 100,000 barrels of oil per day (bopd). This phase will primarily target the oil and condensate reserves.

Associated gas produced during this phase is planned to be reinjected into the reservoir to maintain pressure and improve oil recovery. Future phases may focus more on gas extraction, with potential for LNG exports or domestic gas supply.

The present plan is that the Dorado project will be developed using a wellhead platform (WHP) connected to a Floating Production Storage and Offloading (FPSO) facility. The FPSO will handle the processing of oil and condensate, and the stabilised oil will be offloaded to tankers for export. The field is located about 140 kilometers north of Port Hedland in the Bedout Subbasin, and the proximity to existing infrastructure provides options for efficient processing and export.

Applying the 20% URR to the estimated annual sales value of $2,920 million yields an estimated annual royalty payment to Western Australia of $584 million.

Browse Basin

Currently, there are no fully developed and producing projects in the Browse Basin. The region has been the focus of exploration activities, particularly by Shell and Woodside.

Crux Project

Shell Australia (Operator), SGH Energy, and Osaka Gas collaborate on this project.

The Crux Project is expected to begin production in 2027. The project has been designed to serve as a backfill gas supply for the existing Prelude FLNG facility, which is located approximately 160 km from the Crux field.

The Crux Project is expected to supply up to 550 million standard cubic feet of gas per day (MMscfd) to the Prelude Floating Liquefied Natural Gas (FLNG) facility. This equates to approximately 2.9 MTPA of LNG. The estimated sales value using the $18 per MMBtu assumption would be $2,714 million.

Applying the 20% URR to the Crux Project results in an estimated annual royalty payment to Western Australia of $543 million.

Browse to North West Shelf (NWS) Project

This joint venture involves the development of the Brecknock, Calliance, and Torosa gas fields, with plans to pipe the gas to the existing North West Shelf infrastructure for processing and export.

The partners are Woodside Energy (Operator), BP, Chevron, Shell, and Mitsubishi/Mitsui (through their subsidiary JAPEX).

The project is still in the regulatory and development stages, with key approvals and final investment decisions pending. As of January 2026 no specific start date for production has been confirmed. When operating, the project aims to produce 11.4 MTPA of LNG/LPG. At that volume, the estimated annual sales value will be approximately $10,670 million.

Applying the 20% URR yields an estimated annual royalty payment to Western Australia of $2,134 million.

Conclusion

We estimate based on FY2024 data that the state can generate approximately $47.8 billion from the application of a 20% Universal Royalty Rate (URR). Further, following the WA Treasury estimates, WA paid $112 billion to the Commonwealth in personal and business income taxes, GST, and miscellaneous other remittances. A fraction of this money is returned to WA in the form of Commonwealth grants and subsidies, social security, public goods and other payments made by the Commonwealth on behalf of WA, amounting to approximately $73 billion. Summing projected URR revenues and the gain of net revenues previously siphoned off by the federal government, while assuming the continuation of the existing Commonwealth tax regime, a maximum of approximately $87 billion would be available post-secession for deployment within Western Australia, some proportion of which would be required to run the new government and provide services that the Commonwealth was previously providing, such as health and education.

Of course, if we assume the abolition of all taxes, including those currently levied by the state of WA itself, the amount available to the government reduces back to the $47.8 billion generated by the URR, with the residual $52.6 billion (the sum of net outgoings to the Commonwealth plus state taxes) flowing back to WA households and firms only in the extreme scenario where the new nation abolishes all existing taxes, including the GST. If instead—consistent with Chapter 4—Western Australia retains a GST and introduces the UPRS (a land tax) as limited "supplemental taxes", then a material share of this residual is recycled into public revenue rather than remaining a private windfall (for example, a 10% GST on WA's consumption base is of the order of ~$10.4 billion, and a 2–3% UPRS could raise roughly ~$7–10 billion, before any exemptions/rebates).

In FY2024, the state government operating expenses amounted to $41.5 billion. With a surplus of only $6.3 billion and social security and other Commonwealth government services to be paid for, the big questions to be addressed in the next chapter are:

- How much of the current state government apparatus can be eliminated?
- How much will the post-secession governing apparatus, including whatever is needed to provide public goods presently provided by the Commonwealth, cost?
- How will the post-secession governing apparatus and all service delivery be financed, if by means additional to the URR?

A final caveat is that site-level impacts of a uniform 20% URR cannot be resolved from public disclosures alone, particularly for smaller and lower-margin operations. This manuscript therefore treats margin variation as a design issue to be tested through targeted, confidential evidence gathering and stress-testing (via URR White Paper work), rather than through ad hoc bargaining. Any relief mechanism should be narrow, rules-based, auditable and time-limited—so that industrial vitality is protected without undermining the fiscal envelope explored in Chapter 4 and the institutional safeguards set out later.

Sources

Unless otherwise stated, online materials were viewed on 23 January 2026.

1. Australian Bureau of Statistics, *Taxation Revenue, Australia, 2023-24* (2024) <https://www.abs.gov.au/statistics/economy/government/taxation-revenue-australia/latest-release>.

2. Australian Taxation Office, *Corporate Tax Transparency Report for the 2022-23 Income Year* (2024) <https://www.ato.gov.au/businesses-and-organisations/corporate-tax-measures-and-assurance/large-business/in-detail/tax-transparency/corporate-tax-transparency-report-2022-23>.
3. Chevron Corporation, *Wheatstone Project* <https://www.chevron.com/what-we-do/energy/oil-and-natural-gas/assets/wheatstone>.
4. Commonwealth of Australia, *Budget 2023-24: Final Budget Outcome* (2023) <https://archive.budget.gov.au/2023-24/fbo/download/01_part_1.pdf>.
5. Commonwealth of Australia, *Australian Government Budget Outcome 2023-24* (2023) <https://archive.budget.gov.au/2023-24/fbo/download/00_fbo_2023-24.pdf>.
6. Covalent Lithium, *Our Project* <https://www.covalentlithium.com/our-project>.
7. Engineers Australia, *Heritage Recognition Program: North West Shelf Project Nomination* (2017) <https://portal.engineersaustralia.org.au/system/files/engineering-heritage-australia/nomination-title/HRP.North%20West%20Shelf%20Project.Nomination.V6.7%20Oct%202017.pdf>.
8. Federal Reserve Bank of St. Louis, *Global Price of LNG, Asia (PNGASJPUSDM)* (2024) <https://fred.stlouisfed.org/series/PNGASJPUSDM>.
9. *Mining Act 1978* (WA) <https://www.legislation.wa.gov.au/legislation/statutes.nsf/main_mrtitle_604_homepage.html >.
10. Government of Western Australia, Department of Treasury, *2025-26 State Budget: Budget Paper No. 3—Economic and Fiscal Outlook* (2025) <https://www.ourstatebudget.wa.gov.au/2025-26/budget-papers/bp3/2025-26-wa-state-budget-bp3.pdf>.
11. Iluka Resources Limited, *June 2024 Quarterly Review* (2024) <https://www.iluka.com/media/4trbs0xp/iluka-resources-june-2024-quarterly-review.pdf>.
12. Western Australian Public Sector Commission, *The Structure of the Western Australian Government Sector* <https://www.wa.gov.au/organisation/public-sector-commission/the-structure-of-the-western-australian-government-sector>.
13. Wesfarmers Limited, *Covalent Lithium Opens Mt Holland Lithium Mine and Concentrator* (2024) <https://www.wesfarmers.com.au/util/news-media/article/2024/03/07/covalent-lithium-opens-mt-holland-lithium-mine-and-concentrator>.

Petroleum Resource Rent Tax (PRRT)

14. Australian Taxation Office, *PRRT Deductible Expenditure* (2025) <https://www.ato.gov.au/businesses-and-organisations/gst-excise-and-indirect-taxes/petroleum-resource-rent-tax/work-out-prrt/prrt-deductible-expenditure>. Annotation: Confirms that taxable profit for PRRT purposes is calculated as assessable receipts minus deductible expenditures, which include exploration, development, operating, and closing-down costs; unused deductions can be carried forward and uplifted at rates such as LTBR +5% or GDP factor, depending on the class of expenditure.
15. Australian Taxation Office, *PRRT Concepts* (2025) <https://www.ato.gov.au/businesses-and-organisations/gst-excise-and-indirect-taxes/petroleum-resource-rent-tax/prrt-concepts>. Annotation: States that taxable profit is the excess of assessable receipts over deductible expenditure and transferred exploration expenditure; where deductible expenditure exceeds assessable receipts, the excess is uplifted, carried forward, and applied against future assessable receipts.
16. Australian Taxation Office, *Transfers of PRRT Exploration Expenditure* (2025) <https://www.ato.gov.au/businesses-and-organisations/gst-excise-and-indirect-taxes/petroleum-resource-rent-tax/work-out-prrt/transfers-of-prrt-exploration-expenditure>. Annotation: Explains that exploration expenditure can be transferred between petroleum projects under certain conditions, such as when projects are combined or when there is common ownership.
17. Australian Accounting Standards Board, *Interpretation 1003: Australian Petroleum Resource Rent Tax* (2007) <https://www.aasb.gov.au/admin/file/content105/c9/INT1003_11-07.pdf>. Annotation: Outlines that PRRT taxable profit is assessable receipts less eligible expenditures (including exploration, project development, and operating costs) and uplifted carried-forward expenditures, with exploration expenditures transferable from other projects; PRRT payments themselves are deductible for income tax purposes under the Income Tax Assessment Act 1997.

18. *Petroleum Resource Rent Tax Assessment Act 1987* (Cth) <https://www.legislation.gov.au/C2004A03551/latest/text>. Annotation: Definition of "augmented bond rate". Provides a statutory uplift mechanism (LTBR uplift component) used in calculating uplifted/carry-forward expenditure classes. s 22 "Taxable profit". Defines taxable profit as assessable receipts less deductible expenditure (and incorporates transferred exploration expenditure in the calculation). s 32 "Deductible expenditure" (and related categories such as general project expenditure / exploration expenditure). Sets out the classes/categories of deductible expenditure used in calculating taxable profit.
19. *Income Tax Assessment Act 1997* (Cth) <https://www.legislation.gov.au/C2004A05138/latest/text>. Annotation: s 8-1 "General deductions". Establishes deductibility for ordinary business outgoings (operating costs) incurred in gaining assessable income (subject to exclusions). s 40-25 (Div 40) "decline in value" deductions. Provides the mechanism by which many forms of capital expenditure are deducted over time via depreciation rules. s 40-730 "Deduction for expenditure on exploration or prospecting". Provides income-tax deductibility for qualifying exploration/prospecting expenditure.
20. Part 5: Image Credit: Commonwealth of Australia (Geoscience Australia), *Oil and Gas Titles, Australia* (map, published 2023; data as at 22 December 2022), by C Evenden. Licence: CC BY 4.0.

FISCAL FEASIBILITY IN INDEPENDENT WESTERN AUSTRALIA

Establishing Responsible Governance Underpinned by Resource Wealth

The chapters preceding this one reveal a state generating nearly $46 billion in general government revenues, underpinned by $239 billion in gross mineral and petroleum sales, while contributing a net $39 billion to the rest of the country through taxes and other remittances. This imbalance underscores a century-old grievance: Western Australia's secession vote in 1933, driven by feelings of economic exploitation, has echoed through generations without resolution. Nearly a century later, the indicators of that exploitation—skyrocketing resource exports, a ballooning net fiscal outflow, and a public sector swollen to one employee per 17 citizens— suggest the moment for revisiting that question has arrived.

This chapter and the forthcoming ones turn to the question of how to reform or establish new institutions to best support a fully independent Western Australia. Topics such as transitional trade protocols, sector-specific capital allocation, and offshore resource negotiations find fuller treatment in the chapters on currency and banking reform, defence, and self-sufficiency. Inflation risks from the tax elimination windfall, the mechanics of a new Western Australian Talent (WAT), and the synergies between defence infrastructure and mining security are elaborated there, as are detailed pathways to domestic production in mining equipment and high-tech sectors. In later chapters we also consider the crucial dimensions of culture, optimal democratic institutions, and the design of public services such as health and education.

In this chapter on Fiscal Feasibility, we turn our gaze to the heart of post-secession governance: how will Western Australia finance itself after severing all ties with the Commonwealth, eliminating virtually all taxes on citizens and corporations, and relying primarily on the URR? The challenge is profound. Without federal grants— totaling $14.7 billion in 2023-24 alone, including GST distributions and North West Shelf shares— Western Australia's state expenses must expand to absorb former Commonwealth responsibilities like social security and defence. Yet, the formation of the new nation is also an opportunity to excise decades of accumulated bureaucratic fat, downsizing a public sector that has grown bloated under federation's shared burdens. Some departments, previously entangled in federal grant administration and compliance, will become redundant overnight. By slashing administrative overheads, outsourcing non-core functions, and digitising services—drawing lessons from lean models like Singapore and Estonia— we can reimagine government as a minimal enabler of prosperity, not a voracious consumer of it.

To anchor this analysis, we adopt an upper-bound figure of $104.2 billion as the starting point for total expenditures benefiting Western Australians across all levels of government in 2023-24. This encompasses $31.2 billion in direct state revenues (taxes plus other sources), $14.7 billion in Commonwealth grants to the state, and $58.3 billion in other direct federal support (such as welfare and defence). This is a conservative ceiling, reflecting the full scope of services Western Australia might initially seek to replicate or reform. From this anchor, we model downsizing scenarios that could trim one-third or more of this spending, creating fiscal space for a URR-centric model. Still, realism demands we acknowledge that even with aggressive cuts, some revenues beyond the URR will be needed to fund essential public goods. We discuss how these additional revenues might be raised through retained or reformed taxes—principally the GST and an expanded, non-distortionary land value tax (now called the Unified Property Rates System (UPRS)—ensuring Western Australia remains viable without betraying its zero-income-tax ethos.

What follows is a disciplined examination of these potential levers, grounded in data from Western Australia's fiscal accounts. As in all chapters, our goal here is not to set a design in stone but to demonstrate feasibility: the opportunity exists for Western Australia to emerge leaner, more efficient, and unburdened by federation's fiscal drag, poised for the prosperity charted in the chapters to come.

The Imperative for Downsizing: Trimming the Public Sector Fat

Secession from the Commonwealth is not merely a political act; it is a fiscal rupture that renders much of the current apparatus obsolete. Western Australia's public sector, with 179,085 civil servants (state and federal) serving 2.965 million people—one public servant per 17 citizens—dwarfs leaner models like Singapore's ratio of 1:69. This bloat stems from duplicated roles in health, education, and administration, exacerbated by federal-state overlaps in grant management and compliance. Post-secession, Western Australia inherits the state's core agencies but loses $14.7 billion in inflows, creating an immediate $42.85 billion gap including $27.85 billion that was previously received for social security obligations. We propose a rapid contraction, through a combination of reducing state administration through redundancies, outsourcing, devolution to localities, and digitisation—mirroring Estonia's e-government efficiencies (saving ~2% of GDP annually) and Slovakia's post-1993 reforms (which led to a 1.3% drop in government spending as a share of GDP).

We propose a conservative scenario, targeting 30-50% reductions across departments, preserving frontline services while eliminating federal-relations teams and compliance units. Transition costs, including redundancies ($1-2 billion, per WA regulations: 3 weeks' pay per year of service, capped at 52 weeks) and digitisation ($200-500 million for IT migrations), are front-loaded but offset by URR surpluses ($6.5 billion above current expenses). The resulting public sector of ~90,000 FTEs would save $10-11 billion in salaries and $14 billion in non-salary Operational Expenditure.

Department-by-Department Redundancy & Downsizing: A Conservative Scenario

Each ministry will face ramifications of the post-secession reality: federal ties severed, taxes abolished, communities empowered. The table below summarises proposed full-time equivalent (FTE) and salary cuts, with rationales and models as noted in each row.

Department	Current FTE	Current Payroll ($M)	Proposed FTE	Proposed Payroll ($M)	% Reduction	Rationale & Actions
Premier & Cabinet	1,200	150	600	75	50%	Retire federal-relations teams (30%); digitise policy workflows (Estonia-style). Benchmark: Singapore's lean Prime Minister's Office.
Treasury	800	100	300	40	60%	Disband tax policy units (60% of roles); outsource forecasting. Model: Slovakia's post-independence tax simplification.
Finance	1,500	180	600	70	60%	Eliminate revenue-collection for abolished taxes; pivot to URR processing. Model: Timor-Leste's efficient treasury partnerships.

Department	Current FTE	Current Payroll ($M)	Proposed FTE	Proposed Payroll ($M)	% Reduction	Rationale & Actions
Health	45,000	6,600	36,000	5,300	20%	Trim administrative costs via electronic medical records (EMR)/telehealth (20%); outsource non-critical services; radically decentralise routine healthcare. Models: Singapore's public-private health partnerships, community health hubs of the Netherlands, Kerala, and elsewhere.
Education	40,000	5,000	34,000	4,250	15%	Devolve decision-making to schools; cut central administration. Model: Slovakia's decentralisation, the UK Free School network.
Police	9,000	1,100	8,100	990	10%	Digitise records; integrate with Defence Force. Model: Estonia's e-policing.
Justice	7,000	850	5,250	640	25%	Digitise courts; public–private partnerships (PPPs) to contract prison operations and selected corrections services under performance standards. Model: Singapore's efficient justice system.
Communities (Social Services)	6,000	720	3,600	430	40%	Consolidate into lean Social Protection Office; contract NGOs. Model: Timor-Leste's NGO partnerships for welfare.
Transport (incl. Main Roads)	3,500	420	2,450	290	30%	Privatise licensing; devolve decision-making about local roads. Model: Estonia's e-services.
Primary Industries &	2,500	300	2,000	240	20%	Cut federal grant handling; focus on exports. Model:

Department	Current FTE	Current Payroll ($M)	Proposed FTE	Proposed Payroll ($M)	% Reduction	Rationale & Actions
Regional Development						Singapore's minimal agricultural regulation.
Mines, Industry Regulation & Safety (DMIRS)	2,000	240	1,700	200	15%	Refocus agencies on safety and URR compliance; phase out government 'industry promotion/marketing' functions.
Planning, Lands & Heritage	1,500	180	900	110	40%	Deregulate planning; devolve approvals. Model: Slovakia's growth-promoting reforms.
Local Government, Sport & Cultural Industries	1,200	140	600	70	50%	Devolve decision-making to councils and the private market; cut non-essentials. Model: Estonia's privatised cultural services.
Jobs, Tourism, Science & Innovation (JTSI)	1,000	120	400	50	60%	End subsidies; shift to private market led growth. Model: Singapore's private-sector innovation model.
Water & Environmental Regulation	1,500	180	1,000	120	33%	Streamline permits; privatise monitoring.
Total	~124,300	~17,380	~97,500	~13,365	~30-50% avg.	Aggregate savings: $4-5B salaries + non-salary efficiencies.

This conservative scenario yields ~$10-11 billion in salary relief and ~$14 billion in non-salary OPEX savings per New Zealand's Rogernomics (20-30% public sector cuts) and Estonia's digitisation gains. Frontline roles in health and education are protected initially, while structural reforms like decentralisation and privatisation progress, with cuts focused on overheads.

Non-Salary OPEX Savings—Upper-bound (steady-state sensitivity)

Category	Annual Savings ($B)	Assumptions (steady-state)
Public Non-Financial Corporation/ Public Financial Corporation divestment & OPEX take-outs	3–5	Grant long-term operating concessions (or privatisation where suitable) for selected utilities/transport enterprises, paired with major operational redesign and updated user charges.
Program/grant cessations & outsourcing	3–4	Abolish discretionary grants/subsidies; sunset non-core programs; outsource non-sovereign functions via competitive tender; merge duplicative agencies; expand user-pays where appropriate.
Procurement & property footprint	1.0–1.5	Rationalise the government property footprint: consolidate offices, exit leases, and sell surplus sites.
Information & Communication Technology rationalisation (whole-of-government)	1.0–1.5	Major platform consolidation
Other operating efficiencies	1.0–2.0	Whole-of-government purchasing by category (ICT, fleet, travel, facilities) to standardise and negotiate better prices.
Total (upper bound)	**9–14**	**Midpoint ≈ $12B**

Assessing the Funding Gap

The table below presents four possible scenarios for Western Australia's spend-cutting and resulting revenue gap:

Scenario	Total Spend ($B)	Salary Savings ($B)	Non-Salary OPEX Savings ($B)	URR ($B)	Supplemental taxes ($B)	Total revenue ($B)	Gap ($B)	Key assumptions
Upper Bound (No Cuts)	104.2	0	0	48	0	48	+56.2	Full federal + state services via identical means; no efficiencies.
Conservative Downsizing	80	4	8	48	0	48	+32	~30% average cuts; partial welfare absorption (~$14B); ~$12B total savings.
Transformational (Lean)	70	5.5	12	48	0	48	+22	40–50% cuts; privatised health/education; ~$17.5B total savings.
Aspirational Surplus	**65**	**6**	**14**	**48**	**14–20**	**62–68**	**+3 to -3**	**~45% cuts; ~$20B total savings; target balanced budget/ small surplus.**

Note: URR is taken as $48 B under a 20% resource royalty rate. "Supplemental taxes" here refers only to GST + UPRS revenues (e.g. luxury taxes are excluded). Total revenue = URR + Supplement taxes.

Across all scenarios, the URR contribution is fixed at about $48 B (roughly 70% of the budget) under the constitutional 20% base. The remaining gap must be closed by cutting spending and by supplemental taxes (such as GST and UPRS). As shown, even the "Lean" scenario (spending $70 B) leaves a gap of $22 B if no new taxes are added. The "Aspirational" scenario assumes the deepest cuts (~45% reduction) and allows $14–20 B in supplemental tax revenue, narrowing the gap to near balance (–$3 B to +$3 B).

Fiscal Instruments: Bridging the Gap with Minimal Taxes

Western Australia's founding ethos rejects broad taxation, but fiscal responsibility requires funding for essentials. Under the new Constitution, only a few broad-based taxes are permitted (Article 4): namely, a general consumption tax (GST), the national UPRS on land, and selective excises on luxury/harmful goods. The approach, therefore, is to rely on a reformed GST and UPRS for the bulk of supplemental revenue, with excises only as a minor, targeted option.

Retaining & Reforming the GST

The Goods and Services Tax (GST) is retained as Western Australia's primary broad-based consumption tax. At the current rate of 10%, WA households' consumption base would yield roughly $10.4 B in revenue, though WA's actual GST distribution is only about $7.83 B (creating a $2.6 B shortfall). Increasing the rate or broadening the base could nearly double that revenue (to ~$19 B) if needed. However, the GST is regressive—it disproportionately burdens low-income households—so the Constitution treats it as a transitional stabiliser with built-in equity protections. Article 4 explicitly mandates that any broad consumption tax include regressivity safeguards (exemptions or rebates for basic food, essential medicines, primary residences up to a protected value, and additional offsets for low-income households). In practice, these provisions can be implemented via GST exemptions on essentials and by adjusting welfare and benefit payments to offset the tax on vulnerable groups.

Expanding the Unified Property Rates System (UPRS)

The second pillar of Western Australia's fiscal strategy is a land value tax, rebranded as the Unified Property Rates System (UPRS). WA's total unimproved land value is on the order of $500 B; even a 2–3% UPRS on that base could raise on the order of $7–10 B per year (since land supply is fixed and growing only slowly). This tax is highly efficient (land cannot be moved or hidden) and predictable. The Constitution enshrines a uniform unimproved-land-value basis for the UPRS (Title 10, Article 1) with a mandatory Local Services Share allocated to councils, and prohibits any other general property taxes (Article 7). Equity concerns are addressed by thresholds and deferrals: for example, primary residences and modest farms can be exempt or eligible for deferred payment, ensuring that land-rich but cash-poor individuals (like retirees or farmers) are not forced to sell. In practice, Western Australia could set a protected-value threshold and allow deferments with interest, as many LVT proposals suggest, so that the tax is paid only when properties are sold or transferred. Because land's supply is fixed, the UPRS base is stable and cannot erode away, allowing revenue to grow steadily alongside the economy.

Excise/Luxury Taxes (Article 4(c))

The Constitution also permits Western Australia to enact *selective excises* on luxury or harmful goods (Article 4(c)). Such taxes would target discretionary spending on items like luxury vehicles, premium alcohols, tobacco, and imported luxury goods, while exempting basics like food, fuel for homes, and medicines. This effectively operates as a "luxury tax" that falls mainly on higher-income households, complementing the GST+UPRS system without undermining it. In Australia today, excises on tobacco, alcohol, and fuel already raise on the order of tens of billions of dollars per year, suggesting the potential scale of this source. We discuss excise taxes only qualitatively here and exclude them from the revenue scenarios above, since Article 4 makes them optional and they are not needed to close the immediate fiscal gap given our GST+UPRS focus.

A Lean Path Forward

Aggressive downsizing and reform can bring Western Australia's budget into balance even before counting new taxes. By cutting back to an intermediate budget of ~$79–86 B, and then down to ~$68 B (roughly one-third smaller than today), combined with URR receipts ($48 B) and GST+UPRS revenues ($14–20 B), Western Australia can meet or exceed its essential spending needs. In this lean model, the URR funds ~70% of the budget, GST+UPRS 20–25%, and the remainder can come from a modest excise program, producing a small surplus to seed a sovereign wealth fund.

Lean Budget (Pilot)	Amount ($B)	Notes
Starting Upper-Bound Spend	104.2	Full federal+state services via similar means (welfare, defence, etc.).
Phase 1: Downsizing & Cuts	-20 to -25	Salaries (~$4–11 B) + OPEX (~$14 B) via redundancies/digitisation. Intermediate spend ~$79–84 B.
Phase 2: Further Reforms	-11 to -16	Privatisation/devolution (e.g., in health, education); ~$31–41 B total efficiencies.
Target Lean Budget	68	Essential public goods only; communities and private provision fill gaps.
Core Revenue: URR (20% rate)	+48	20% on $239 B resource sales; stable, commodity-backed.
Supplements: GST + UPRS	+14–20	Reformed consumption and land taxes; non-distortionary fiscal floor.
Supplements: Excise/Luxury Tax	+2–4	Targeting non-essentials; progressive and counter-cyclical.
Net Position	+0–+4	Rough surplus to fund a sovereign wealth fund and buffer risks.

These results show that even modest GST and UPRS levies (in line with the constitutional Title 10 framework) would be sufficient—in combination with realistic downsizing—to fund Western Australia's essentials. Any residual surpluses can seed a sovereign wealth fund or cushion against shocks, per the constitutional transition rules.

As with all proposals in this book, these initial designs will be comprehensively examined and costed in detail in collaboration with WA communities and international experts. Future analysis will refine these figures, consider tax-base sensitivities to commodity prices, and possibly explore additional targeted taxes (e.g. an inheritance tax above a high threshold or expanding the luxury tax base). We draw on international precedents—from Singapore's excise on luxury cars funding infrastructure without broad VAT hikes, to Estonia's post-reform alcohol excises—to inform this strategy. The goal is a lean government that frees resources for self-sufficiency, attracts investment, and ultimately thrives under its own revenue model.

The approach we suggest cuts 50 years of fat, empowering communities and markets. The new nation emerges with leaner governance, more efficient services, and genuine fiscal self-reliance.

Sources

Unless otherwise stated, online materials were viewed on 23 January 2026.

1. Western Australia, *Annual Report on State Finances 2023-24* (Report, 2024) < https://www.wa.gov.au/system/files/2024-09/2023-24-arsf.pdf>.
2. Western Australia, *State Budget 2024-25, Budget Paper No. 3: Economic and Fiscal Outlook* (Budget Paper, 2024) < https://www.ourstatebudget.wa.gov.au/2024-25/budget-papers/bp3/2024-25-wa-state-budget-bp3.pdf>.
3. Australian Bureau of Statistics, *Taxation Revenue, Australia, 2023-24* (Web Page, 2024) < https://www.abs.gov.au/statistics/economy/government/taxation-revenue-australia/latest-release>.
4. Australian Bureau of Statistics, *Australian National Accounts: State Accounts, 2023-24 (Western Australia)* (Web Page, 2024) < https://www.abs.gov.au/statistics/economy/national-accounts/australian-national-accounts-state-accounts/latest-release>.
5. Australian Public Service Commission, *APS Employment Data 30 June 2024 Release* (Web Page, 2024) < https://www.apsc.gov.au/employment-data/aps-employment-data-june-2024 >.
6. Commonwealth Grants Commission, *GST Relativities 2025–26* (Report, 2025) < https://www.cgc.gov.au/sites/default/files/2025-03/GST%2520Sharing%2520Relativities%25202025-26_Final.pdf>.
7. Bankwest Curtin Economics Centre, *WA State Budget 2025-26: A Review and Commentary* (Report, 2025) < https://bcec.edu.au/publications/wa-state-budget-2025-26-review-commentary/>.
8. Australian Government, *Budget Paper No. 3: Federal Financial Relations 2025–26* (Budget Paper, 2025) < https://budget.gov.au/content/bp3/download/bp3_2025-26.pdf>.
9. L Evans, A Grimes, B Wilkinson and D Teece, 'Economic Reform in New Zealand 1984-95: The Pursuit of Efficiency' (1996) < https://www.academia.edu/24413234/Economic_reform_in_New_Zealand_1984_95_The_pursuit_of_efficiency>.
10. OECD, *Seizing the Productive Potential of Digital Change in Estonia* (Report, 2020) < https://www.oecd.org/content/dam/oecd/en/publications/reports/2020/12/seizing-the-productive-potential-of-digital-change-in-estonia_63752f80/999c7d5a-en.pdf>. Annotation: Report states: "The use of digital signatures in Estonia is estimated to save 2% of GDP every year." It provides context on Estonia's digital infrastructure efficiencies, including cost savings in e-voting and broader productivity gains.
11. International Peace Institute, 'Estonia PM: Country Saves 2% of GDP by Going Digital' (Web Page, 2016) < https://www.ipinst.org/2016/05/information-technology-and-governance-estonia>. Annotation: "Estonia saves two percent of GDP by signing things digitally."
12. OECD, *Economic Surveys: Slovak Republic 1996* (Report, 1996) < https://www.oecd.org/content/dam/oecd/en/publications/reports/1996/01/oecd-economic-surveys-slovak-republic-1996_g1g17270/eco_surveys-svk-1996-en.pdf>. Annotation: Relevant excerpt: "the share of central government spending in GDP fell from 31.9 in 1994 to 30.6 per cent in 1995."

13. World Bank, *Slovakia: Restructuring for Recovery* (Report, 1994) < https://documents.worldbank.org/curated/en/615841468759587882/pdf/multi0page.pdf>.
14. New Zealand Treasury, *New Zealand Economic Growth: An Analysis of Performance and Policy* (Report, 2004) < https://treasury.govt.nz/sites/default/files/2007-11/economicgrowth.pdf>.
15. International Monetary Fund, *New Zealand: Recent Economic Developments* (Report, 1996) < https://www.elibrary.imf.org/downloadpdf/view/journals/002/1996/014/article-A001-en.pdf>.
16. Western Australia Public Sector Commission, *Western Australian Public Sector Quarterly Workforce Report—March 2024* (Report, 2024) < https://www.wa.gov.au/system/files/2024-06/quarterly_workforce_report_-_march_2024.DOCX>.
17. K Kaljulaid, 'Digitizing Democracy: How e-Government Saved a Struggling Country' (n.d.) < https://vision.protiviti.com/insight/digitizing-democracy-former-estonian-president-how-e-government-saved-struggling-country>.
18. Government of Western Australia, *The Structure of the Western Australian Government Sector* (Web Page, 2024) < https://www.wa.gov.au/organisation/public-sector-commission/the-structure-of-the-western-australian-government-sector>.
19. *Public Sector Management (Redeployment and Redundancy) Regulations 2014* (WA) < https://www.legislation.wa.gov.au/legislation/statutes.nsf/RedirectURL?OpenAgent&query=mrdoc_27635.htm>.
20. Western Australian Auditor General, *Digital Transformation in WA Public Sector: Implementation Costs and Outcomes* (Report, 2022) < https://audit.wa.gov.au/reports-and-publications/reports/digital-transformation-in-wa-public-sector/>.
21. Deloitte Australia, *Public Sector Restructuring Advisory Costs: Benchmarks for Australian Governments* (Web Page, 2023) < https://www2.deloitte.com/au/en/insights/industry/public-sector/public-sector-restructuring-benchmarks.html>.
22. Landgate, *Landgate Annual Report 2023-24* (Report, 2024) < https://www.landgate.wa.gov.au/siteassets/documents/about-us/strategic-plans-and-annual-reports/landgate-annual-report-2023-24-.pdf>.
23. RSM Australia, 'Understanding Land Tax in Western Australia' (Web Page, 2025) < https://www.rsm.global/australia/insights/understanding-land-tax-western-australia>.
24. Department of Local Government, Sport and Cultural Industries, *MyCouncil WA Portal—Compare All Councils* (Web Page, 2024) < https://www.mycouncil.wa.gov.au/council/compareallcouncil>.
25. Parliament of Australia, *Impact on the Living Standards of Households* (Research Paper, 2000) < https://www.aph.gov.au/About_Parliament/Parliamentary_Departments/Parliamentary_Library/pubs/rp/RP0001/01rp25>.
26. Australian Taxation Office, *GST, Excise, LCT, WET and PRRT* (Web Page) < https://www.ato.gov.au/businesses-and-organisations/gst-excise-and-indirect-taxes>.
27. Commonwealth Grants Commission, *GST Relativities 2025–26: Overview* (Report, 2025) < https://www.cgc.gov.au/sites/default/files/2025-03/GST%20relativities%202025-26%20-%20Overview_final.pdf>.
28. Australian Border Force, *Cost of Importing Goods—GST and Other Taxes When Importing* (Web Page) < https://www.abf.gov.au/importing-exporting-and-manufacturing/importing/cost-of-importing-goods/gst-and-other-taxes>.
29. Australian Automobile Association, 'Fuel Excise Explained' (Web Page) < https://www.aaa.asn.au/advocacy/explainers/fuel-excise-explained/>.
30. Australian Taxation Office, 'How Excise Equivalent Goods Work' (Web Page) < https://www.ato.gov.au/businesses-and-organisations/gst-excise-and-indirect-taxes/excise-equivalent-goods-imports/how-excise-equivalent-goods-work>.

Sensitivity modelling

31. Australian Bureau of Statistics, *Australian National Accounts: State Accounts, 2023–24* (Catalogue No 5220.0, 2024) < https://www.abs.gov.au/statistics/economy/national-accounts/australian-national-accounts-state-accounts/latest-release>.
32. Australian Taxation Office, *Australian Taxation Office Annual Report 2023–24—Revenue Collection (includes excise and customs duty collections)* (Report, 2024) <

https://www.transparency.gov.au/publications/treasury/australian-taxation-office/australian-taxation-office-annual-report-2023-24/part-4-%E2%80%93-revenue-performance/revenue-collection>.

Empowering Local Councils: Power Devolution With National Unity

Building Community Vitality

This chapter shows how local empowerment coupled with limited, accountable national oversight can together deliver efficiency and national unity. The proposal outlined here involves shifting core front-line services into Western Australia's 137 local councils (within current WA boundaries). This could yield roughly $3–5 billion in annual savings while fully upholding universal core health and education entitlements.

The Imperative for Devolution: From Central Bloat to Local Agility

To balance the budget of an independent Western Australia, only core national ministries will be kept (e.g., Defence, Immigration, etc.) with most service delivery devolved to local councils. Councils—already managing roads, parks, libraries and town planning—will also run many community services and utilities (like local health clinics, water management, and waste collection). In effect, the right and responsibility to provide for people's everyday needs move away from the centre and into the local areas where those people live.

We conservatively expect that initially, roughly 25–35% of public functions will move to councils. Essential roles (e.g., teachers, nurses, police) stay, but redundant administration is cut. Anticipated costs for redeployments and redundancies and investments in digital infrastructure should be quickly recouped by income from the new URR plus minimal taxation regime. Councils are anticipated to initially absorb ~5,000–7,000 former state employees (e.g. nurses, school aides) but to deploy more efficient IT and private competition to eliminate redundant roles. For example, instead of two layers of road planners, each council will take full charge of its local streets. Over time, the degree of devolution would increase, as the population adapts to being more heavily responsible for activities and direction within their local communities.

The national government, as Canberra does today, will set benchmarks for the nation in core areas—e.g., the safety of food and drinking water, road safety standards, etc. —and will suggest targets in core service and human development areas, including education and health. Councils will be responsible for service provision with emphases and by means they choose, guided by these national standards. A wheatbelt shire might invest in water tanks and mobile tele-health clinics, while Perth may choose to expand its networks of buses and libraries. If some areas need more help, tiered grants could be available to top up their budgets. A unified national portal will link all council databases, helping to share best practices across Councils and encouraging healthy competition. This decentralised approach echoes New Zealand's 1980s reforms, which cut costs without harming quality.

Principles Guiding Devolution

The approach rests on four pillars:

Selective Central Guidance

National policy, budgets and guidance on service standards stay national. Councils gain operational control over execution. This marries a unified vision with local direction that taps local knowledge. We envision replacing ad-hoc Council grants with simple formula-based block grants, cutting waste.

Digital Government

Western Australia will build a single e-government portal (akin to Estonia's X-Road). Via this portal, citizens may apply for permits, pay bills and file forms online, while local councils have access to real-time dashboards integrated with this portal to track and benchmark their performance. Automating a significant portion (~50–70%) of routine tasks (e.g., licenses, registrations) slashes red tape. For instance, a digital building-permit system could enable approval of 80% of simple applications instantly, freeing staff to focus on more complicated cases. A common digital backbone also improves transparency of Council affairs, as every application and expense is traceable.

Market Leverage

Competition and partnerships will take a far more active role in providing core services than at present. Public health clinics, bus lines, and even parts of education (e.g., cafeterias, school transport) can (at a Council's discretion) be run instead by private or non-profit operators under performance contracts they construct, using national template contracts if they wish. Major infrastructure projects will be bid out via PPPs, but with strong citizen-led oversight and transparency to ensure accountability. Globally, market-based methods like these typically yield an estimated 15–25% savings. Importantly, template contracts provided by the national government will tie pay to measurable, holistic outcomes (e.g., contractors will receive full fees only if crime reduces or student graduation rates rise while graduate quality does not fall).

Employment Transition

Displaced state and federal workers will receive priority for Council jobs, with retraining funded centrally. Workers will keep their pensions and tenure in addition to this top-up training (e.g. an IT course for a former clerical officer), preserving institutional knowledge locally. For example, a previous state-level IT manager might become an ICT advisor for several councils at once. Workers in any truly redundant positions will be offered severance. This humane transition is intended to minimise social disruption.

The intent is to create a slimmer centre while freeing funds for local development according to local decision-making, which in turn grows the economy. As property and business values rise, councils' own tax bases will increase through the LVT, funding more schools, roads, and health centres. Such local success, rather than a large central apparatus, will be a robust foundation of national strength.

Devolution by Sector (Conservative Model)

Below we sketch how the various components of key service areas could split across the central and local levels, and estimate the improvements achievable through the re-empowerment of communities in each area. Figures use WA's 2024-25 budgets and staffing.

Health & Aged Care

Central: Major teaching hospitals, emergency care, most specialist services, and funding pools (with Medicare to be replaced by WellnessCare, as detailed in the Health chapter).

Councils: Community wellness hubs, preventive programs, pre-partum, post-partum, labour and delivery services, and home care. Wellness hubs will provide family/integrative/preventative medicine, regular wellness checks, chronic disease management, wellness programs (focussing on nutrition and fitness), most mental health support, and coordination of volunteer aides for the elderly living independently. Local birthing centres will support patient-focussed pre-natal, post-natal, and birthing services for most pregnancies. Telemedicine will greatly expand (targeting ~70% of routine consults online), and all patient records will be digitised. Councils hire community nurses, doulas/midwives, and care coordinators (transferred from the state system) and central health administrative roles are cut.

Under this model, councils become not only local public health employers but innovators: a council might co-fund an exercise program if it prevents hospital visits, or rotate specialists through rural clinics. By focusing care locally, crisis response (e.g., to a fire, flood, or infectious disease) is managed community-by-community with rapid information sharing supported by a digital platform. Councils could even opt to form regional health alliances to group-insure for expensive tests, exploiting economies of scale.

Education & Skills

Central: Curriculum guidelines, grade-specific examinations, and broad funding grants.

Councils: All public K–12 schools and vocational training centres (see Education chapter). Councils hire teachers and set school policies through local boards that take input from parents and teachers. Registration, attendance, disciplinary records, grading and resource allocation from the centre will be digitised. Councils may at their discretion partner with businesses to create apprenticeships and adult education opportunities (for example, a mining-region council might run a mining trades program) and high school exchange programs. Councils also manage libraries and community colleges. Councils would add teachers and support staff while ~800 central education jobs would be eliminated. Local control means curricula can reflect community strengths and needs (a coastal town might emphasise marine science, while a farming area focuses on agri-tech), boosting engagement, achievement, and local pride. Councils can also tailor adult learning (e.g., offering free coding classes to support the development of a local technology hub), based on their observations of local labour needs.

Planning, Lands & Housing

Central: Statewide land-use policy guidelines and public housing subsidies.

Councils: Zoning, building permits, local planning and public housing allocation. Councils create local development plans and run online permit portals (automating most routine development proposal approvals). Private surveyors and planners may be contracted by Councils to assist with big projects. Councils also maintain affordable housing lists and coordinate state subsidies. Faster decisions mean a council can quickly open land for new homes if needed, easing shortages. Councils, at their discretion, can also preserve their local character: a beach town could set aside parkland adjacent to the coastline, while a city might rezone a downtown area for mid-rise apartments.

Licensing, Regulation & Utilities

Central: Setting national minimum requirements for business licenses, technical safety standards for utilities, and guidelines for additional core services. (Many of these may be taken directly from existing national or international codes.)

Councils: Issuing business and trade licenses, setting and enforcing local regulation, and utilities. Councils issue permits (liquor licenses, building permits, food vendor certificates, etc.) through a unified portal or local office. Councils manage water supply, sewerage and waste collection services under national safety codes. Councils will add local roles while ~800 state regulator roles will become redundant. Small businesses should benefit, as a new cafe will now files one combined council application instead of many. Councils can also fast-track approvals for small entrepreneurs (offering reduced fees or prioritised review) to spur local job creation.

Transport & Environment

Central: Construction and maintenance of major highways, railways, and ports; maintenance of national fare-payment system infrastructure.

Councils: Local roads, street lighting, parking, parks, local buses and public sanitation. Councils budget to repair local streets and maintain bike lanes; the state maintains highways. Councils may opt to tender out bus routes using holistic performance-based contracts, while a national smartcard system unifies fare payment. Councils hire local transit and maintenance workers and environmental stewardship decisions (e.g., park plantings, stormwater re-use) reflect local priorities.

Social Services, Recreation & Culture

Central: Block grants.

Councils: Community welfare and amenities. Councils handle child and family services, elder support, job-readiness centres and local grants (with eligibility vetted online). Community centres, libraries and sports fields are managed by councils. Councils may invite NGOs to provide certain services under performance-based contracts (e.g., counselling, youth outreach, or community reintegration programs for recovering addicts). Councils hire welfare and cultural staff and tailor social programs to their local needs: a mining town might fund a miners' wellness clinic, while a beachfront town might provide a surf safety course. Sporting and cultural events can be scheduled to reflect local traditions community identity.

Emergency, Waste & Community Development

Central: National defence and disaster backup if called to assist by councils.

Councils: Fire brigades, flood control and small development grants. Councils coordinate local fire-fighting, rescue teams and flood relief (with the national government stepping in by coordinating other Councils' disaster-relief staff if requested to assist in major crises). Waste disposal is handled locally. Under this model, a council hit by a cyclone can mobilise local crews immediately and run its own cleanup grants, speeding recovery and saving lives, with backup coordinated nationally, drawing from other councils' resources, if requested.

Aggregate Impact

Our initial modelling illustrates that Western Australia could initially shift over $15B of WA's present state-level spending into local hands, with conservative net savings of over $3B per year. Councils would employ over 5,000 staff transferred from the state level, while over 2,000 state jobs would be eliminated. We envision phased implementation starting from an initial round of reassignments, followed by technical upgrades and competitive contracting. This devolution of responsibility helps to achieve Western Australia's $68B lean national budget.

Under our model, Western Australia would become a federation of self-reliant communities. Every town hall will be a service centre, not a satellite office. Citizens will see local power at work in the form of wellness hubs, schools, libraries and buses managed and overseen by their neighbours. At the same time, the national government provides an underpinning of security and guidance, focusing on big-picture issues, not micromanagement.

Citizen Contributions to Community Vitality

As the primary stewards of their communities, citizens of independent Western Australia will enjoy unprecedented opportunities to contribute directly to them and receive tangible recognition for those contributions. Valued contribution areas will include local volunteer work (e.g., towards elderly care, community garden maintenance, crime prevention, library staffing, or surf lifesaving), local media production (e.g., contributing to a local newspaper, radio station, or magazine); local or national civic service (e.g., on a Local Government Review Tribunal (LGRT) as described below, a citizen jury to appoint the head of a national or local department, or a criminal jury), or service to the development of future generations (e.g., via childbearing, childrearing, teaching, or mentorship). Citizens and their council members, not elected national representatives, are considered "where the buck stops" on decisions that matter to everyday lives.

To support these contributions, future analyses will consider the possibility of implementing a four-day workweek (without pay reductions: see Chapter 9) as a national default, the option to tie community contributions to the privilege of voting in national elections, and the possibility of awarding time-limited exemptions from certain tax categories in acknowledgement of sustained, exceptional community contributions.

The National-Local Nexus: MPs as Fiscal Guardians

Western Australia's new Constitution, whose initial draft we present in the final chapter, will enshrine a link between national MPs and councils. Each MP will have a defined advisory role for the councils in their home district (inspired by Singapore's Town Councils). Importantly, MPs do not run local services; they only provide input using which communities can self-correct. For example, if an MP spots an unusual expense or a sudden 5% budget jump, s/he may draw this to the attention of the community public via the digital platform. The council would then be required to explain or revise the spending publicly on this platform in response. Unresolved issues go to the LGRT, an independent panel of citizens and experts, drawing on local and expert knowledge, within three weeks. That tribunal has the power to order corrections, but only with a supermajority of its members, guarding against political meddling.

This structure strengthens local accountability while reinforcing democracy. Councils remain fully elected and make local choices, with MPs acting only as fiscal sentinels and citizens putting their own effort into shaping the present and future of their communities. These powers will be codified in a Local Fiscal Integrity Act, detailing triggers (fraud, illegal spending, grant breaches) and remedies. All Council budgets and audits will be published online, and MPs with conflicts must recuse. Ordinary citizens can also petition an Integrity Commission to investigate any Council. Under this system, Councils keep their own revenues (currently ~$2.7B from property rates) and the new central grants (~$4–6B), while MPs help to ensure that money is used lawfully. Western Australia's goal is to achieve the world's least corrupt local governments, benchmarked against Singapore (Corruption Perception Index (CPI) 84/100).

To avert both MP inertia and MP overreach, and for independent investigation into Councils, Western Australia will combine (i) citizen-triggered audit petitions (meeting a modest signature threshold tied to electorate size) and (ii) whistleblower protections (confidentiality, anti-retaliation, and rewards for material recoveries) as detailed in the Anti-Corruption Framework chapter. Petitions that plausibly allege illegality, ultra vires spending, or threshold-exceeding fiscal risk will auto-refer to the LGRT and WAACC (Western Australian Anti-Corruption Commission) for expedited review, with all filings posted to the freedom of information portal, described in the Freedom of Disclosure chapter.

This oversight system would begin as a pilot across 10 councils by late 2029, gathering citizen feedback. Over time, every Western Australian will see local decisions made by neighbors, with MPs as monitors of law and funding, not bosses. This synergy between vibrant local autonomy and disciplined national guardianship would be unique to Western Australia.

Implementation Mechanics Are Constitutionalised

Chapter 15's Title 11 (Local Councils) is drafted as an implementation blueprint, not a statement of intent, it constitutionalises a Devolution Act, a dated Devolution Schedule, anti-duplication rules, funding ring-fencing/equalisation, transparency via the FOI portal, and an independent review pathway (LGRT) so that devolution can be phased, enforced, audited and corrected without recreating parallel national administrations. Readers should review Title 11 in full to see how practical delivery becomes achievable when these mechanics are locked into the constitutional architecture and then executed through ordinary legislation and standards.

Crucially, Title 11 also anticipates the "plumbing" that makes devolution workable at scale: a shared digital interoperability backbone for identity, payments, permits and records—akin to Estonia's X-Road, which is an open-source, secure data-exchange layer enabling standardised, peer-to-peer system-to-system transactions (rather than a central database), with strong auditability and data-sovereignty properties.

Empowered Communities, Lean Governance

By cutting bureaucratic fat and empowering local people, Western Australia has the opportunity to enjoy leaner governance, efficient services, and prosperity. With communities truly sovereign in daily life, the nation supports and assists localities in guarding safety and integrity.

Wide consultations with councils, unions, businesses and citizens will refine every detail of the plans sketched in this chapter. Exact grant formulas, staffing models, community service categories and technical standards will be finalised through dialogue. The vision of a minimal but effective centre enabling 137 vibrant local democracies of active citizens will remain, supporting disciplined budgets powered by community innovation. With this framework, Western Australia has the opportunity to become a pioneering nation of self-reliant, prosperous communities for generations to come.

Sources

Unless otherwise stated, online materials were viewed on 24 January 2026.

1. Western Australia, *State Budget 2024-25, Budget Paper No. 3: Economic and Fiscal Outlook* <https://www.ourstatebudget.wa.gov.au/2024-25/budget-papers/bp3/2024-25-wa-state-budget-bp3.pdf>.
2. Department of Local Government, Sport and Cultural Industries, *MyCouncil Western Australia Portal—Compare All Councils* (2024) <https://www.mycouncil.wa.gov.au/council/compareallcouncil>.
3. Evans, L, Grimes, A, Wilkinson, B & Teece, D, 'Economic Reform in New Zealand 1984-95: The Pursuit of Efficiency' (1996) <https://www.academia.edu/24413234/Economic_reform_in_New_Zealand_1984_95_The_pursuit_of_efficiency>.
4. *Town Councils Act* 1988 (Singapore) <https://sso.agc.gov.sg/Act/TCA1988 >.
5. Channel News Asia, 'Two New Town Councils Established in Jalan Kayu and Punggol' (2025) <https://www.channelnewsasia.com/singapore/two-new-town-councils-established-jalan-kayu-punggol-5159811>.
6. Transparency International, *Corruption Perceptions Index 2024* (2025) <https://www.transparency.org/en/cpi/2024>.
7. Human Rights Watch, *World Report 2025: Singapore* (2025) <https://www.hrw.org/world-report/2025/country-chapters/singapore>.
8. Organisation for Economic Co-operation and Development, *OECD Survey on Drivers of Trust in Public Institutions—2024 Results: Country Notes—New Zealand* (2024)

<https://www.oecd.org/content/dam/oecd/en/publications/reports/2024/06/oecd-survey-on-drivers-of-trust-in-public-institutions-2024-results-country-notes_33192204/new-zealand_8d674d58/3ca8436a-en.pdf>.

Estonia: X-Road

9. e-Estonia, 'How to Digitalise Local Governments?' (2023) <https://e-estonia.com/how-to-digitalise-local-governments/>.
10. e-Estonia, *X-Road—Interoperability Services* <https://e-estonia.com/solutions/interoperability-services/x-road>. Annotation: Official overview of X-Road as a secure data exchange layer enabling seamless information sharing between organizations, with details on its role in Estonia's e-government ecosystem.
11. Nordic Institute for Interoperability Solutions (NIIS), *X-Road®* <https://x-road.global/>. Annotation: Describes X-Road as open-source software for unified, secure data exchange in collaborative ecosystems, including its origins and implementation in Estonia.
12. Grokipedia, 'X-Road' (2024) <https://grokipedia.com/page/X-Road>. Annotation: A neutral, detailed explanation of X-Road as a centrally managed distributed data exchange layer for secure internet-based information sharing among Estonian institutions, now with implementations in Finland, Iceland, Ukraine, Kenya, Mexico, Brazil, and Argentina.

A Robust Financial Environment: New Currency & Banking Systems

Introduction

This chapter sets out a spectrum of options for Western Australia's new currency system, from a free-floating fiat currency through to a foreign reserve-backed national currency anchored in the strength of the new nation, plus blueprints for a new banking system.

PART 1

The Western Australian Talent & the Western Australian Reserve Authority: Transition to a New Currency System in 9 Stages

Fiat currencies provide maximum flexibility to ensure currency stability through responsiveness to market conditions, while backing the new currency—the Western Australian Talent (WAT) —by eligible foreign exchange reserves may provide an immediate infusion of confidence, particularly in the early months of the new nation. To preserve flexibility and stability, the initial system could operate in a currency-board style with reserves covering the monetary base, with this system administered by the Western Australian Reserve Authority (WARA). Starting from such a reserve-backed system may be preferred to implementing a fiat system at first, as it may be seen to provide stable value and public trust from inception while still preserving the ability to adjust in response to market conditions. This model leverages inflows from royalties and conversions while instituting an adaptable financial framework from which a fully floating fiat system can be built once market confidence is established.

The new currency would be implemented following secession (targeted for mid-2029) and would involve 9 integrated stages. These range from ledgering Western Australia's extractive base (Stage 1), to AI/blockchain monitored issuance (Stage 3), to the peg and reserve strategy (Stages 4–9). The pillars of the design are fiscal prudence, monetary transparency, and technology-assisted verification, culminating in an initial sovereign monetary system that is reserve-secured, citizen-owned, market-adaptive, and globally credible.

Stage 1: National Resource Reserve Ledger

In this stage, Western Australia's comprehensive national resource ledger is established, and the Universal Royalty Rate (URR) is introduced at a flat 20%. The ledger becomes the sovereign accounting foundation for WA's new currency and wealth management institutions.

Tier 1—Unleased Sovereign In-Ground Reserves

WA's unleased Tier-1 reserves—especially iron ore—represent a substantial store of in-ground wealth. As shown in the table below, an estimated 20–30% fraction of WA's total Economic Demonstrated Resource (EDR) for key commodities is assumed unleased, all compliant with the Joint Ore Reserves Committee (JORC). These figures are estimates derived from total national and state resource data, subtracting approximated leased portions based on sector maturity; they are not direct measurements and may require adjustment post-secession through comprehensive audits. They are not an operational basis for currency backing at launch due to estimation uncertainties, illiquidity, and practical constraints, but support long-term fiscal planning and national balance-sheet transparency.

Overall, as shown in the table below, only a modest fraction of WA's total in-ground resource base remains truly unleased. WA's Tier-1 sovereign reserve will be dominated by iron ore (and possibly undeveloped gas), comprising on the order of 20–30% of the total value of WA's known resource endowment.

Table 1: Major Unleased (Tier—1) Mineral/Energy Reserves of Western Australia (Estimated)**

Sovereign Resource	Estimated Unleased Reserve Volume (JORC-compliant EDR fraction)	Estimated In-Ground Value (AUD, conservative prices)
Iron Ore	11.7–17.6 billion tonnes (high-grade hematite + magnetite; 20–30% of WA's ~58.5 Gt total EDR)	$1.17–$1.76 trillion (at ~$100/tonne)
Gold	1,244–1,866 tonnes (20–30% of WA's ~6,218 t total EDR share)	$112–$168 billion (at ~$90,000/kg or $2,800/oz equivalent)
Lithium (as Li)	1,584–2,376 thousand tonnes (20–30% of WA's ~7,919 kt total EDR share, assuming ~90% WA dominance)	$23.8–$35.6 billion (at ~$15,000/tonne Li carbonate equivalent)
Nickel	4.4–6.7 million tonnes (20–30% of WA's ~22.2 Mt total EDR share, assuming ~90% WA dominance)	$146–$221 billion (at ~$33,000/tonne)
Bauxite	238–358 million tonnes (20–30% of WA's ~1,192 Mt estimated total EDR share, assuming ~30% WA share)	$7.1–$10.7 billion (at ~$30/tonne)
Copper		$58.5–$87.3 billion (at ~$9,000/tonne)

Sovereign Resource	Estimated Unleased Reserve Volume (JORC-compliant EDR fraction)	Estimated In-Ground Value (AUD, conservative prices)
	6.5–9.7 million tonnes (20–30% of WA's ~32.5 Mt estimated total EDR share, assuming ~30% WA share)	
Natural Gas (conventional 2P reserves)	13,873–20,810 PJ (20–30% of WA's ~69,365 PJ total reserves share)	$69–$104 billion (at ~$5/GJ equivalent)
		Total: ~$ 1.6—2.4 Trillion

** Estimates are derived by applying a 20–30% unleased fraction to WA's share of Australia's total EDR (from Australia's Identified Mineral Resources, 2025) or 2P reserves (from Australia's Energy Commodity Resources, 2025 for gas), accounting for the proportion of land likely not under active tenements based on sector reports. Actual unleased volumes may be lower for mature commodities like gold and higher for underexplored areas like offshore gas. Values are indicative and subject to market fluctuations; they do not represent extractable or economic value. Detailed tenement mapping (e.g., via Department of Mines, Industry Regulation and Safety (WA)) is recommended for precise sovereign ledgering. Total estimated unleased value across commodities is ~$1.6–$2.4 trillion at current values.

Table 2: Summary of 2023-2024 data from DEMIRS, with calculated percentages based on WA's land area (252.99 million ha), including year-on-year changes for context.

Tenement Type	Number in Force	Area Covered (Million Ha)	% of WA Land	YoY Change (Area)
Mining Leases	6,051	3.362	1.33%	+3%
Exploration Licences	9,232	69.419	27.45%	+8%
Prospecting Licences	6,289	0.763	0.30%	+2%
Other (Retention, Miscellaneous, etc.)	4,788	4.887	1.93%	+5%
Mineral Claims	378	2.158	0.85%	-1%
Total Tenements	**26,751**	**77.5**	**30.6%**	+7%

Table 2 highlights that while mining leases cover a small fraction of Western Australia's land area, exploration dominates the tenement footprint, and that ~69% of land is as-yet unleased. For resource-specific unleased estimates (e.g., in Table 1), we estimate on this basis that 20–30% of EDR may be considered sovereign, but actual audits via DEMIRS registers are essential for precision.

Tier 2—Leased Reserves & 20% Royalty Revenue Streams

Tier 2 resources include all Western Australian leased resource tenements under active or pending extraction—i.e., mines and petroleum fields where private operators are extracting (or soon will extract) resources. Under Western Australia's proposal of a 20% Universal Royalty Rate (URR) on all production, these assets will generate significant sovereign revenue. In Chapter 3 we looked at the revenues generated from Western Australia's minerals and petroleum, below we catalogue the major Tier-2 resource categories, emphasising the approximate reserve base of each, and projected royalty flows they are expected to generate from 2025 to 2035.

Table 3: Tier—2 Western Australian Leased Reserves and Estimated Values (Major Commodities)

Commodity	Leased Reserve Base (WA) (JORC P&P or equivalent)	Indicative WA Remaining In-Ground Value (A$)	Notes (WA-only basis / method)
Iron Ore	~21.2 Gt ore	~A$2.1T	WA estimate derived as WA share of Australia's iron ore resource base × Australia's ore reserves). Price assumption ~A$100/t for table-level orientation.
Lithium	~5.0 Mt Li (≈26.6 Mt LCE)	~A$1.06T	WA contains >99% of Australia's lithium EDR; WA ore-reserve base approximates national ore-reserve totals. Value uses ~A$40k/t Lithium Carbonate Equivalent (LCE) (illustrative).
LNG / Natural Gas	~45 Tcf (2P, WA-dominant basins)	~A$560–700B	Sum of 2P conventional gas reserves in Northern Carnarvon/Roebuck + Perth basins (conservative WA-only). Value uses ~A$12–15/MMBtu (illustrative).
Gold	~2,020 t Au (estimated WA share of national ore reserves)	~A$227B	WA estimate = WA share of Australia's gold EDR (~45%) ×

Commodity	Leased Reserve Base (WA) (JORC P&P or equivalent)	Indicative WA Remaining In-Ground Value (A$)	Notes (WA-only basis / method)
			Australia's gold ore reserves. Value uses ~A$3,500/oz (illustrative).
Nickel	~9.5 Mt Ni (estimated)	~A$285B	WA-only consolidated ore-reserve series is not published in the same national table; estimate shown assumes a 90% WA share of Australia's nickel ore reserves (conservative).
Alumina / Bauxite	~505 Mt bauxite (P&P at major WA operations)	~A$25–35B	WA P&P bauxite ore reserves from Darling Range + Worsley (major WA bauxite operations). Value uses ~A$50–70/t (illustrative, alumina-equivalent orientation).
Other minerals (Copper, Mineral Sands, Rare Earths, etc.)	Copper: ~1.64 Mt Cu; Mineral sands: WA-est. share of national ore reserves; REO: ~2.0 Mt REO (est.)	~A$120–160B	Copper WA estimate uses WA share of Australia copper EDR (~6%) × Australia's copper ore reserves. Rare earth estimate uses WA share of Australia's identified REE resources (~60%) × Australia's REO ore reserves. Mineral sands WA share is not published as a single consolidated WA ore-reserve total, so 60% "WA share assumption" is applied to national ore-reserve totals.
	Total:	**~$4.38—$4.57 Trillion**	

The purpose of Stage 1 is to establish an auditable national inventory of Western Australia's projected resource base (tenure status, reserve classifications, project mapping, and valuation conventions), not to re-state commodity-by-commodity royalty forecasts. The fiscal implications of the Universal Royalty Rate (URR)—including the scale of expected receipts and their role in funding the services citizens expect—are addressed in later chapters. In that framework, URR receipts are first allocated to the operating budget and essential obligations; only genuine surpluses are available for longer-term saving and investment.

Accordingly, Tables 1 and 3 are presented here to show the *structure* of the extractive endowment that must be ledgered and verified: (i) the extent of genuinely unleased sovereign in-ground assets, and (ii) the much larger set of active leased reserves and projects that will drive near-term national cashflows under the URR. The key output of Stage 1 is therefore a "single source of truth" dataset—built from statutory tenure registers, project datasets, reserve reporting, and production verification—that can be used consistently across the budget, the balance sheet, and the new monetary design.

With that ledger established, Stage 2 turns to currency architecture: defining eligible reserves, governance constraints, and mechanisms so that the initial design remains transparent, credible, and subordinate to the nation's primary fiscal task of funding core services reliably during the transition to sovereignty.

Sources

Unless otherwise stated, online materials were viewed on 31 January 2026.

1. Geoscience Australia, *Australia's Identified Mineral Resources 2024* (2024) <https://www.ga.gov.au/aimr2024/australias-identified-mineral-resources>. Annotation: comprehensive EDR and production data for key minerals in Australia, supporting estimates of unleased reserves in Table 1 by detailing total national resources, predominantly located in Western Australia.
2. U.S. Geological Survey, *Mineral Commodity Summaries 2024* (2024) <https://pubs.usgs.gov/periodicals/mcs2024/mcs2024.pdf>. Annotation: This global summary provides reserve estimates (comparable to Ore Reserves) for minerals, including Australia's significant shares in nickel (24 million metric tons) and bauxite (3.5 billion metric tons).
3. WA Department of Energy, Mines, Industry Regulation and Safety (DMIRS), *Major Resource Projects Map* <https://dmpbookshop.eruditetechnologies.com.au/product/major-resource-projects-western-australia-2025.do>.
4. DMIRS, *Statistics Digest 2023–24* <https://www.wa.gov.au/government/publications/western-australian-mineral-and-petroleum-statistics-digest-2023-2024>. Annotation: Annual summary of resource sector value, royalties, and export revenue for Western Australia.
5. World Bank, *Commodity Price Forecast* (April 2024) <https://thedocs.worldbank.org/en/doc/464523804694923b6e827ed9d01e247f-0050012024/related/CMO-April-2024-Forecasts.pdf> <https://thedocs.worldbank.org/en/doc/464523804694923b6e827ed9d01e247f-0050012024/commodity-markets-outlook-april-2024>. Annotation: Benchmark long-term forecasts for key mineral, energy, and agricultural commodities.

6. Western Australian Treasury Corporation, *Western Australia: Iron Ore (Trade and Investment Profile)* (2025) <https://www.watc.wa.gov.au/media/k53n05yh/wa-iron-ore-profile-november-2025.pdf>.
7. Geoscience Australia, *Lithium* (2025) <https://www.ga.gov.au/scientific-topics/minerals/mineral-resources-and-advice/australian-resource-reviews/lithium>.
8. Geoscience Australia, *Australia's Energy Commodity Resources (AECR) 2025: Gas reserves (2P reserves by basin)* (2025) <https://www.ga.gov.au/aecr2025/gas>.
9. Geoscience Australia, *Australia's Identified Mineral Resources 2025 Preliminary Tables* (2025) <https://www.ga.gov.au/scientific-topics/minerals/aimr/preliminary-tables>.
10. Department of Energy, Mines, Industry Regulation and Safety, *Western Australian Mineral and Petroleum Statistics Digest 2023–24* (2025) <https://www.wa.gov.au/system/files/2025-03/wa_statistics_digest_2023_2024_web.pdf>.

Stage 2: Designing the Initial Western Australian Foreign Reserves-Backed Currency

Benefits of a Reserve-Backed System

The primary perceived benefit of initial foreign reserve backing for Western Australia's currency is to generate trust in the new currency via linkage to established foreign assets, and to mitigate risks associated with the speculative credit expansion that can be implemented by poor central financial stewards in floating fiat systems.

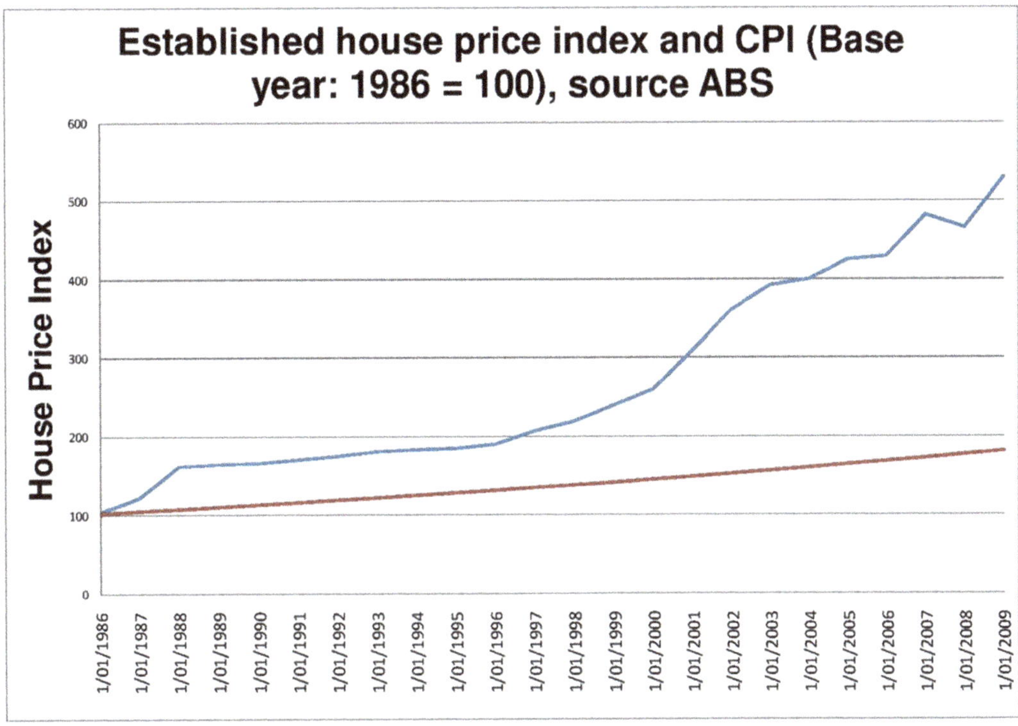

In the modern era, floating fiat currencies have been associated with money supply expansion that outpaces economic fundamentals. A reserve-backed currency, tied to foreign exchange assets, enforces initial monetary discipline by limiting issuance to verified reserves, thereby supporting market confidence: the currency represents a claim on internationally liquid assets, reducing reliance on foreign currencies during the transition.

Design Options & Precedents

Further analysis will consider anchoring mechanisms. These would be implemented in a currency-board style to preserve the ability to calibrate the supply of money to market conditions and ensure currency stability.

The Currency Board Model

WAT issuance is constrained by eligible FX reserve inflows held by WARA. WARA issues WAT only against eligible reserve assets (e.g., AUD, USD, RMB, JPY as determined). This limits issuance to the monetary base backed by reserves, likely at 100% coverage initially.

Initial Peg & Exchange Rate

At launch, the WAT would peg to a single currency (e.g., AUD) or a basket (e.g., weighted by trade shares, e.g., RMB 50%, AUD 40%, USD 10%), calibrated to approximate 1:1 parity with the AUD. Post-launch, the WAT could transition toward greater independence as confidence builds.

Currency Issuance Constraints

WAT issuance would be governed by WARA rules. New WAT enters circulation only against reserve inflows, such as domestic conversion of AUD balances or surplus URR receipts in major currencies.

M1 & M2 Targets

The initial M1 target is ~A$200-250 billion equivalent, based on WA's pre-secession monetary base and projected GDP (~A$300 billion). The M2 target is ~A$400-500 billion. These support liquidity, with banking reforms covered later in this chapter.

Sources

Unless otherwise stated, online materials were viewed on 1 February 2026.

1. International Monetary Fund, *Currency Composition of Official Foreign Exchange Reserves (COFER)* <https://data.imf.org/?sk=E6A5F467-C14B-4AA8-9F6D-5A09EC4E62A4>. Annotation: Precedents for reserve-backed currencies and peg mechanisms.
2. F A Hayek, *Denationalisation of Money* (1976) <https://mises.org/library/denationalisation-money-argument-refined>. Annotation: Theoretical basis for commodity-basket currencies.
3. Reserve Bank of Australia, *Monetary Aggregates* <https://www.rba.gov.au/statistics/historical-data.html>. Annotation: Estimates for WA-equivalent M1/M2 based on national data scaled to ~15% (WA GDP share).

4. Singapore Monetary Authority, *Singapore Dollar Nominal Effective Exchange Rate* <https://www.mas.gov.sg/monetary-policy/singapores-monetary-policy-framework/faqs/section-2>. Annotation: What is MAS' monetary policy framework and its rationale?
5. International Monetary Fund, *Revised Guidelines for Foreign Exchange Reserve Management* (Report, 2013) <https://www.imf.org/en/Publications/Manuals-Guides/issues/2016/12/31/revised-guidelines-for-foreign-exchange-reserve-management-41062>. Annotation: Principles for reserve-backed systems and governance.
6. International Monetary Fund, *Annual Report on Exchange Arrangements and Exchange Restrictions 2023* (Report, 2024) <https://www.imf.org/en/publications/annual-report-on-exchange-arrangements-and-exchange-restrictions/issues/2024/12/19/annual-report-on-exchange-arrangements-and-exchange-restrictions-2023-541890>. Annotation: Classifications of exchange rate regimes for examples.
7. Hong Kong Monetary Authority, *Linked Exchange Rate System* (2024) <https://www.hkma.gov.hk/eng/key-functions/money/linked-exchange-rate-system/>. Annotation: Hong Kong currency board persistence.
8. International Monetary Fund, 'Monetary Policy in the New Normal' (Staff Discussion Note 14/03, 2014) <https://www.imf.org/external/pubs/ft/sdn/2014/sdn1403.pdf>. Annotation: Discusses risks of fiat expansions under weak governance, supporting benefits of reserve backing.
9. Bank for International Settlements, *Market Volatility and Foreign Exchange Intervention in EMEs: What Has Changed?* (BIS Paper No 73, 2014) <https://www.bis.org/publ/bppdf/bispap73.pdf>. Annotation: Reviews FX intervention and market volatility in EMEs (not currency boards).
10. International Monetary Fund, *Exit Strategies: Policy Options for Countries Seeking Exchange Rate Flexibility* (Occasional Paper, 1998) <https://www.imf.org/en/publications/occasional-papers/issues/2016/12/30/exit-strategies-policy-options-for-countries-seeking-exchange-rate-flexibility-2695>. DOI: <https://doi.org/10.5089/9781557757340.084>. Annotation: Details transitions from pegs to flexible regimes.
11. Steve H Hanke and Kurt Schuler, *Currency Boards for Developing Countries: A Handbook* (1994; revised ed 2015) <https://sites.krieger.jhu.edu/iae/files/2017/06/Currency_Boards_for_Developing_Countries-1.pdf>. Annotation: Defines currency board discipline and 100% reserves.
12. Bank for International Settlements, *Annual Economic Report 2023*, ch II 'Monetary and Fiscal Policy: Safeguarding Stability and Trust' (2023) <https://www.bis.org/publ/arpdf/ar2023e2.pdf>. Annotation: Covers issuance constraints and credibility/trust framework relevant to monetary design.
13. Australian Bureau of Statistics, *Australian National Accounts: State Accounts* (2023, latest release) <https://www.abs.gov.au/statistics/economy/national-accounts/australian-national-accounts-state-accounts/latest-release>. Annotation: Provides WA GDP data (~A$300B), supporting M1/M2 scaling.
14. Investopedia, 'Currency Board Basics: Definition, How They Work, and Impact' (updated 2025) <https://www.investopedia.com/terms/c/currency_board.asp>. Annotation: Explains how currency boards provide stability by tying currency to liquid foreign assets, reducing reliance on foreign currencies and enforcing discipline against irresponsible money printing.
15. Bipartisan Policy Center, 'What's Behind the U.S. Dollar's Dominance and Why it Matters' (Sep 2, 2025) <https://bipartisanpolicy.org/explainer/whats-behind-the-u-s-dollars-dominance-and-why-it-matters/>. Annotation: Analogous discussion of reserve currency benefits, including trust and reduced borrowing risks, applicable to reserve-backed systems.
16. Wikipedia, 'Currency Board' (updated 2025) <https://en.wikipedia.org/wiki/Currency_board>. Annotation: Provides examples of currency boards (e.g., Hong Kong, Bulgaria, Estonia) with fixed rates and reserve constraints.
17. ScienceDirect, 'Currency Board—an Overview' (2025) <https://www.sciencedirect.com/topics/economics-econometrics-and-finance/currency-board>. Annotation: Defines currency boards as maintaining fixed rates with foreign reserves, citing examples like Hong Kong and Bulgaria.
18. Banco de España, 'Fiscal Discipline & Exchange Rate Regimes: A Case for Currency Boards?' (2000; updated 2025) <https://www.bde.es/f/webbde/SES/Secciones/Publicaciones/PublicacionesSeriadas/DocumentosTraba

io/00/Fic/dt0006e.pdf>. Annotation: Discusses how currency boards prevent monetisation of deficits to control inflation.

19. Bank for International Settlements, 'Monetary Aggregates and Economic Activity: Evidence from Five Industrial Countries' (updated 2025) <https://www.bis.org/publ/econ7.htm>. Annotation: Analyses M1/M2 targets in small economies for liquidity and stability.

Stage 3: Currency Governance & Rule-Based Issuance Act

Constitutional Foundations for Sound Money

The principles on which Western Australia's new currency will be established will be entrenched in the Constitution. This approach prevents future governments or courts from altering the system's discipline. Monetary economists such as James Buchanan have advocated binding rules on fiscal and monetary powers to prevent discretionary abuse and ensure long-term stability; Western Australia implements this by constitutionalising its currency regime. The objective is to maintain a stable, initially reserve-backed currency that preserves trust and will catalyse a smooth transition for the new country into an eventual standard free-floating fiat system.

Key provisions to be enshrined constitutionally at a high level include official currency, independent issuing authority, and limits on money creation.

Independent Issuing Authority

The Constitution will establish an independent Western Australian Reserve Authority (WARA) as the sole institution empowered to issue Western Australian currency. No other agency or level of government may create legal tender. Western Australia's constitution will establish the WARA's existence, independence, and mandate.

Hard Limit on Money Creation

The Constitution will limit currency issuance to rule-based mechanisms. This prohibits unbacked printing and limits inflationary finance. The new nation's fundamental law will forbid the printing of Western Australian Talent except to preserve currency stability, ensuring new money enters circulation only due to genuine market demand. This maintains the soundness of the currency, aligned with Buchanan's emphasis on constitutional constraints on monetary policy.

Entrenchment & Amendment Guardrails

To safeguard these rules, amending the Constitution will require a rigorous process. No ordinary law or executive action will be able to override the initial reserve requirement or compel the WARA to fund spending. This monetary framework is designed to resist short-term political pressures or external influences.

Western Australian Reserve Authority (WARA)

Establishment & Governance

The WARA is established as an independent authority to manage currency issuance, reserve verification, and URR collection. Its independence is designed to ensure that decisions are based on rules linked to real market conditions rather than broad discretion, promoting stability and public trust.

Governance Structure

The WARA will be governed by a board nominated by the Citizens Oversight Committee (COC), with seats earmarked for board members with expertise in monetary policy and technology. Terms will be staggered to ensure continuity, and removal will require demonstrated cause, such as misconduct, to protect independence.

Rule-Based Issuance

WAT issuance will follow rules: no issuance without eligible reserves; no deficit monetisation. Initially. new currency may be issued only when reserves support it, demonstrated to the public with reference to indicators. This prevents expansion unrelated to fundamentals.

To ensure transparency, the WARA will implement a national blockchain ledger for recording reserves, issuances, and transactions. This provides real-time auditing, immutable records, and public visibility, allowing citizens to verify the system's integrity.

Real-Time Auditing & Oversight

The ledger will support continuous monitoring by independent auditors and the Citizens Oversight Committee (COC). This mechanism enhances accountability and deters fraud, contributing to a credible monetary system.

Implementation Timeline

Following secession, Congress will enact the Currency Governance Act to operationalise these provisions, with the WARA fully functional within six months and the first issuance of new currency soon after that. Throughout this initial period, the Australian Dollar will still be legal tender in Western Australia, but the new government will begin operating with Western Australian Talents. We envision transitioning to a floating fiat based system and phasing out the Australian dollar as legal tender once markets adjust to conditions in the new, independent Western Australia. This ensures a seamless transition to the WAT while upholding constitutional principles.

Benefits for Citizens

By tying initial issuance to rules and reserves, the system is designed to foster trust, minimise speculation, and direct resource wealth toward public benefit. The eventual transition to a floating fiat currency will support dynamism and growth, while rules will direct the WARA to target the adequacy of money supply for the needs of markets.

Pathway to Floating WAT

The initial peg or basket provides credibility and stability during the transition to sovereignty, as seen in currency boards that rebuild trust post-conflict or in small open economies. However, many countries retain pegs or currency boards long-term because they cannot credibly assure stability independently, limiting full monetary sovereignty.

Constructing a feasible pathway to floating the WAT supports the new nation's financial independence, allowing WARA to respond flexibly to domestic conditions without foreign anchor constraints. Conditions for transition may include demonstrated institutional credibility, sustained fiscal discipline, adequate reserves, market depth, inflation stability, and resilient banking regulation; details to be developed in White Papers at a later time.

Some relevant historical examples follow.

- Bosnia and Herzegovina: Maintains a currency pegged to the Euro since 1997 to ensure stability post-conflict; pegging persists due to constitutional limits on credit creation and the need for credibility.
- Hong Kong: Operates a currency linked to the USD since 1983 for monetary stability; pegging persists due to the desire for market confidence in trade and finance.
- Chile: Transitioned its currency gradually from a peg to a floating system in 1999 via widening bands, enabling better shock absorption; this transition was successful due to strong institutions and macroeconomic policies.
- Poland: Transitioned its currency from a crawling peg system to a free-floating one in 2000; the transition was orderly in part thanks to preparatory market development.

Sources

Unless otherwise stated, online materials were viewed on 1 February 2026.

1. International Monetary Fund, *Guidelines for Foreign Exchange Reserve Management* (2001) <https://www.imf.org/external/np/mae/ferm/eng/index.htm>. Annotation: Provides principles for reserve-backed systems and independent monetary authorities.
2. International Monetary Fund, *Revised Guidelines for Foreign Exchange Reserve Management* (Report, 2013) <https://www.imf.org/en/Publications/Manuals-Guides/issues/2016/12/31/revised-guidelines-for-

foreign-exchange-reserve-management-41062>. Annotation: Principles for reserve-backed systems and governance.

3. Cem Karacadag and others, 'From Fixed to Float: Fear No More' (2004) 41(4) *Finance & Development* 28 <https://www.imf.org/external/pubs/ft/fandd/2004/12/pdf/karacada.pdf>. Annotation: Steps and examples for transitioning to floating rates.
4. Bank for International Settlements, *Central Bank Governance and Financial Stability* (2019) <https://www.bis.org/publ/othp31.htm>. Annotation: Outlines best practices for central bank independence and governance structures.
5. Michael D Bordo, 'An Historical Perspective on the Quest for Financial Stability and the Monetary Policy Regime' (Working Paper No 17108, Hoover Institution, 2017) <https://www.hoover.org/sites/default/files/research/docs/17108-bordo.pdf>. Annotation: Supports rule-based issuance by analysing historical shifts to statutory monetary rules, like inflation targets, to limit discretion and ensure stability. Note: This paper surveys the co-evolution of monetary policy and financial stability across four exchange rate regimes from 1880 to the present, providing insights into changes in objectives and rules.
6. AW Salter and AT Young, 'Do We Need a Distinct Monetary Constitution?' (2018) 146 *Journal of Economic Behavior & Organisation* 63 <https://www.sciencedirect.com/science/article/abs/pii/S0167268111001855>. Annotation: Argues for constitutionalising money to ensure stability, with rules on issuance constraints.
7. RL Hetzel, 'The Challenges with Rules-Based Policy Implementation' (2013) 99(2) *Federal Reserve Bank of Richmond Economic Quarterly* 135 <https://people.ucsc.edu/~walshc/MyPapers/Walsh_RBP_Challenges.pdf>. Annotation: Discusses implementing rule-based monetary policy to constrain discretion and prevent unbacked issuance.
8. A Kugler, 'Speech on Central Bank Independence and the Conduct of Monetary Policy' (Speech, Federal Reserve Board, 2024) <https://www.federalreserve.gov/newsevents/speech/kugler20241114a.htm>. Annotation: Emphasises independence for rule-based decisions to promote stability.
9. Satoshi Nakamoto, 'Bitcoin: A Peer-to-Peer Electronic Cash System' (2008) <https://bitcoin.org/bitcoin.pdf>. Annotation: Describes blockchain technology for transparent, immutable ledgers applicable to monetary systems.
10. World Bank, *Blockchain and Emerging Digital Technologies for Enhancing Post-2020 Transparency* (2020) <https://openknowledge.worldbank.org/handle/10986/33726>. Annotation: Discusses blockchain for real-time auditing and transparency in public systems.
11. BIS, 'Governance of AI Adoption in Central Banks' (2025) <https://www.bis.org/publ/othp90.pdf>. Annotation: Discusses blockchain for anomaly detection and governance in central banks.
12. ECB, 'Artificial Intelligence: A Central Bank's View' (2024) <https://www.ecb.europa.eu/press/key/date/2024/html/ecb.sp240704_1~e348c05894.en.html>. Annotation: Explores blockchain/AI for transparency in operations.
13. SUERF, 'Implementation and Governance of Artificial Intelligence in Central Banks' (2025) <https://www.suerf.org/publications/suerf-policy-notes-and-briefs/implementation-and-governance-of-artificial-intelligence-in-central-banks/>. Annotation: AI/blockchain for real-time anomaly flagging in central banks.
14. European Commission, 'The Introduction of Euro Banknotes and Coins—One Year After' (2003) <https://ec.europa.eu/economy_finance/publications/pages/publication_summary1003_en.htm>. Annotation: Details 6-month dual tender in Eurozone transition.
15. International Monetary Fund, *Annual Report on Exchange Arrangements and Exchange Restrictions 2023* (Report, 2024) <https://www.imf.org/en/publications/annual-report-on-exchange-arrangements-and-exchange-restrictions/issues/2024/12/19/annual-report-on-exchange-arrangements-and-exchange-restrictions-2023-541890>. Annotation: Classifications of exchange rate regimes for examples.

James Buchanan

16. James M Buchanan, 'The Constitution of Economic Policy' (1987) 77(3) *American Economic Review* 243 <https://www.aeaweb.org/articles?id=10.1257/aer.77.3.243>. Annotation: Discusses the need for constitutional rules to constrain fiscal and monetary discretion.

17. James M Buchanan and Richard E Wagner, *Democracy in Deficit: The Political Legacy of Lord Keynes* (Academic Press, 1977) <https://oll.libertyfund.org/title/buchanan-democracy-in-deficit-the-political-legacy-of-lord-keynes>. Annotation: This book critiques fiat money systems without rules and advocates fiscal/monetary constraints to prevent deficits and inflation.
18. Geoffrey Brennan and James M Buchanan, *The Power to Tax: Analytical Foundations of a Fiscal Constitution* (Cambridge University Press, 1980) <https://www.econlib.org/library/Buchanan/buchCv9.html>. Annotation: Directly discusses binding rules on monetary powers to limit government borrowing and money creation.
19. James M Buchanan, 'Money as Meta-Rule: Buchanan's Constitutional Economics as a Foundation for Monetary Stability' (2010) 142(3-4) *Public Choice* 389 <https://www.jstor.org/stable/48719934>. Annotation: Argues for constitutionalising money to provide a foundation for stability, preventing discretionary abuse.

Bosnia and Herzegovina

20. *Constitution of Bosnia and Herzegovina* (Bosnia and Herzegovina, 1995, as amended) <https://www.ohr.int/dayton-peace-agreement/annex-4/>. Annotation: Establishes the Central Bank of Bosnia and Herzegovina with a currency board system pegged to the Euro, prohibiting unbacked issuance.
21. *Law on the Central Bank of Bosnia and Herzegovina* (Bosnia and Herzegovina) <https://www.cbbh.ba/Content/Read/14?lang=en>. Annotation: This implementing law, derived from the Constitution, explicitly prohibits unbacked issuance and requires 100% reserve backing for the currency, the Convertible Mark (BAM). Note: Provides access to the original 1997 law in chapter-by-chapter format, along with amendments up to 2006; no single consolidated 2023 version is available, but this is the authoritative source for the law as amended.
22. International Monetary Fund, *Bosnia and Herzegovina: Selected Issues* (Staff Country Report No 98/69, 1998) <https://www.imf.org/en/Publications/CR/Issues/2016/12/30/Bosnia-and-Herzegovina-Selected-Issues-2704>. Annotation: Discusses the post-Dayton currency board as a fixed anchor to the Deutsche Mark, prohibiting unbacked issuance to rebuild trust after conflict. Note: This report includes background on recent economic developments and is the relevant document for Staff Country Report No. 98/69; the title "Selected Issues" encompasses the economic overview.

Hong Kong

23. Hong Kong Monetary Authority, *Linked Exchange Rate System* (2024) <https://www.hkma.gov.hk/eng/key-functions/money/linked-exchange-rate-system/>. Annotation: Details Hong Kong's currency board persistence.
24. ADB, 'The Currency Board Arrangement in Hong Kong, China' (n.d.) <https://aric.adb.org/pdf/aem/external/financial_market/Sound_Practices/hkcb.pdf>. Annotation: Details persistence for stability in open economy.

Chile

25. IMF, 'From Fixed to Float: Operational Aspects of Moving Toward Exchange Rate Flexibility' (2004) <https://www.elibrary.imf.org/view/journals/007/2004/043/article-A001-en.xml>. Annotation: Guidance on transitions from pegs to floating.

Poland

26. Ryszard Kokoszczynski, 'From Fixed to Floating: Other Country Experiences: The Case of Poland' (Paper, IMF Seminar, 2001) <https://www.imf.org/external/pubs/ft/seminar/2001/err/eng/kokos.pdf>. Annotation: Poland's transition example.

Stage 4: Western Australia Sovereign Wealth Fund

Country	Sovereign wealth fund	Total assets ($ trillions)
Norway	Government Pension Fund Global	1.73
China	China Investment Corporation	1.33
China	SAFE Investment Company	1.09
United Arab Emirates	Abu Dhabi Investment Authority	1.05
Kuwait	Kuwait Investment Authority	1.02
Saudi Arabia	Public Investment Fund of Saudi Arabia	0.93
Singapore	Government of Singapore Investment Corporation	0.80
Indonesia	Badan Pengelola Investasi Daya Anagata Nusantara (Danantara)	0.60
Qatar	Qatar Investment Authority	0.53
Hong Kong	Hong Kong Monetary Authority Investment Portfolio	0.51

Source: Sovereign Wealth Fund Institute

Rationale for a Sovereign Wealth Fund

Western Australia's Sovereign Wealth Fund (SWF) serves as a mechanism to preserve and grow any surplus revenues from resource royalties, supporting inter-generational equity and macroeconomic stability. By channelling any excess funds into diversified investments, the SWF mitigates risks associated with commodity price volatility and resource depletion, while supporting the prohibition on deficit spending and debt monetisation. This approach draws from established models, such as Norway's Government Pension Fund Global, which invests oil revenues for future generations, and Qatar's Investment Authority, which focuses on long-term diversification from hydrocarbon surpluses. In Western Australia, the SWF will be a form of national savings, subject to fiscal realities with early surpluses neutral to small.

Qatar's sovereign wealth fund, the QIA, has made high-profile global investments, including purchasing London's Harrods department store in 2010 for £1.5 billion. Such examples illustrate the global reach and influence that a well-capitalised SWF can attain.

Structure & Governance

The SWF is established as an independent public authority under constitutional provisions, with governance entrenched to ensure autonomy and accountability. Consistent with Title 10: Universal Royalty Rate and Taxation, Article 6, any surpluses from the Universal Royalty Rate (URR) are remitted to the SWF only after transitional taxes (e.g., GST, Unified Property Rates System (UPRS)) and essential budgetary needs are met, as verified by the Western Australian Reserve Authority (WARA). The SWF's board comprises experts appointed by the Citizens Oversight Committee through a transparent, non-partisan process, with terms limited to promote rotation and prevent entrenchment. Oversight includes annual independent audits, real-time reporting via MonetaNet[20], and review by the Citizens Oversight Committee (COC) to align with ethical and transparency standards.

The SWF investment strategy emphasises diversification, with allocations to global equities, fixed-income securities, real estate, and infrastructure, prioritising long-term returns while excluding domestic investments to avoid economic overheating. Ethical guidelines prohibit investments in sectors conflicting with Western Australia's values, such as those exhibiting human rights violations, modelled on Norway's approach. Withdrawals are capped at a sustainable rate—initially no more than 3% of the fund's value annually, adjusted by law based on actuarial assessments—to preserve capital for future generations.

Separation of Institutions

In line with Title 12: The Currency of Western Australia, Article 7, government spending is limited to current revenues from the WARA's Consolidated URR Account, prohibiting deficit financing or monetary expansion to cover shortfalls. Any surpluses flow to the SWF per Article 5 of the Currency Title, with no provision for borrowing against future royalties except as secured under constitutional debt limits. This ensures that the SWF acts as a stabilising buffer during downturns where feasible, while preventing speculation that could undermine the currency. The WARA handles monetary policy and URR collection; the SWF focuses solely on financial savings and investments. This structure encourages each institution to operate within its mandate, enhancing overall system resilience.

[20] Moneta+Net: Derived from the Latin word Moneta, the goddess of memory and warning, and the source of the modern word "money", with Net, MonetaNet is the networked, real-time, algorithmic monitoring system that underpins Western Australia's currency oversight: see Stage 7.

Economic Benefits

Over time, the SWF is projected to build a buffer against global shocks to secure Western Australia's financial future and inspire citizen trust.

Sources

Unless otherwise stated, online materials were viewed on 1 February 2026.

1. Norway, Ministry of Finance, *Government Pension Fund Global Annual Report 2023* (Report, 2023) <https://www.nbim.no/contentassets/75e18afc40974cb189e3747164def669/gpfg-annual-report_2023.pdf>. Annotation: Details on structure, governance, fiscal rules (including the 3% withdrawal guideline), prohibition on domestic investments, ethical guidelines, and transparency. Supports the claim for Norway, confirming the fund's purpose to "safeguard and build financial wealth for future generations" through investments of surplus petroleum (oil and gas) revenues.
2. Qatar Investment Authority, *Annual Review 2023* (Report, 2023) <https://www.qia.qa/Annual-Report-2023>. Annotation: Outlines governance, investment strategy focused on long-term stability, funding from hydrocarbon revenues, and separation from monetary policy.
3. International Monetary Fund, *Sovereign Wealth Funds: Aspects of Governance Structures and Investment Management (2024 Update)* (Report, 2024) <https://www.imf.org/en/Publications/WP/Issues/2024/05/15/Sovereign-Wealth-Funds-Aspects-of-Governance-Structures-and-Investment-Management-2024>. Annotation: Best practices on fiscal rules prohibiting deficit spending and debt monetisation, independent oversight, and transparency measures.
4. World Bank, *Sovereign Wealth Funds in Practice: Lessons from Established Funds* (Report, 2025) <https://www.worldbank.org/en/topic/macroeconomics/publication/sovereign-wealth-funds-in-practice-2025>. Annotation: Guidance on funding from resource surpluses, diversification strategies, and rules for sustainable withdrawals to ensure inter-generational equity.
5. Norges Bank Investment Management, 'About the Fund' (Web Page) <https://www.nbim.no/en/about-us/about-the-fund>. Annotation: Explains the fiscal rule limiting government withdrawals to the fund's expected real return (~3% annually) to preserve capital for future generations while phasing oil revenues gradually into the economy.
6. Coface, 'Qatar: Country File, Economic Risk Analysis' (Web Page) <https://www.coface.us/news-economy-and-business-insights/economic-risk-dashboard/country-risk-files/qatar>. Annotation: Describes the Qatar Investment Authority's strategy to manage hydrocarbon surpluses through diversified global investments in sectors like real estate, retail, and infrastructure to enhance reputation and generate income beyond hydrocarbons.
7. Reuters, 'Qatar Investor Buys UK Department Store Harrods' (News Article, 9 May 2010) <https://www.reuters.com/article/business/qatar-investor-buys-uk-department-store-harrods-idUSTRE6470V5>. Annotation: Details the purchase by Qatar Holding (an arm of the Qatar Investment Authority) of Harrods from Mohamed al-Fayed for £1.5 billion, highlighting it as a high-profile global investment.

Stage 5: Government Borrowing & Bonds

Rationale for Sovereign Borrowing

Access to capital markets may be necessary for Western Australia's new government to fund large-scale infrastructure, or make other strategic investments in the initial period of nationhood that exceed immediate inflows. Sovereign borrowing, when structured prudently, allows Western Australia to leverage future resource revenues without compromising the integrity of its currency, the Western Australia Talent (WAT).

Constitutional Foundations

Borrowing is governed by the Western Australian Constitution, particularly Title 10: Universal Royalty Rate and Taxation and Title 12: The Currency of Western Australia. All government debt must be secured against projected future income streams, with servicing prioritised from surplus URR receipts (Article 5 of the Currency Title). Congress may not use debt obligations to justify re-imposing income or profit taxes (Article 7(3) of the Taxation Title). The Western Australian Reserve Authority (WARA) enforces these rules, ensuring no direct or indirect monetary financing (Article 7 of the Currency Title). Debt issuance is subject to default transparency and audits, aligning with the Constitution's emphasis on rule-based governance and public accountability.

Design of the Sovereign Debt Strategy

Western Australia's debt instruments will primarily take the form of bonds backed by anticipated URR revenues, issued in limited amounts to maintain low debt levels relative to resource wealth. Key features include:

Collateralisation: Bonds are secured against projected URR cash flows, with legal covenants potentially allowing bondholders limited recourse to designated royalty streams in case of default, subject to sovereign immunity considerations.

Issuance Limits: Total outstanding debt is capped at a percentage of projected URR revenues (e.g., no more than 20-30% of average annual URR over a 5-year horizon), as determined by law under Special Majority Acts. This prevents over-leveraging and ensures debt service remains manageable.

Maturity and Terms: Bonds will have medium-to long-term maturities (5-15 years) to match resource production cycles, with fixed interest rates to minimise volatility. Variable-rate or commodity-linked options may be considered for diversification, but only if they align with stability objectives.

Issuance Process: The WARA oversees issuance through transparent auctions or placements, with proceeds ring-fenced for approved purposes (e.g., reserve build-up as per Stage 10). All terms, including rates, collateral, and use of funds, are disclosed in real-time to citizens by default.

Risk Management: To mitigate commodity price risks, bonds incorporate buffers such as over-collateralisation or contingency funds from the Sovereign Wealth Fund (SWF). Regular stress testing simulates scenarios like price downturns, ensuring compliance with constitutional fiscal rules, incorporating probabilistic modelling of commodity shocks to align with international standards.

Precedents & Considerations

Resource-backed financing has been used by countries like Norway (where sovereign bonds are implicitly supported by oil revenues managed through its Government Pension Fund Global, enabling low borrowing costs) and Botswana (which has leveraged diamond revenues for secured loans and bonds, contributing to fiscal stability and credit upgrades). These examples illustrate how such a system can provide capital access with reduced risks when paired with strong governance, though they also highlight potential vulnerabilities like debt service forecasting errors due to commodity price volatility or disruptions to production. Western Australia's model addresses these through constitutional safeguards, independent WARA oversight, and public transparency, prioritising benefits like lower borrowing costs and economic stability while learning from global experiences.

Economic Benefits

By securing debt against projected surplus URR revenues, Western Australia maintains hard money principles, fostering investor confidence and stable credit conditions.

Sources

Unless otherwise stated, online materials were viewed on 1 February 2026.

1. Natural Resource Governance Institute, *Resource-Backed Loans: Pitfalls and Potential* (Report, 2021) <https://resourcegovernance.org/sites/default/files/documents/resource-backed-loans-executive-summary.pdf>. Annotation: Analyses risks like commodity volatility and governance issues in resource-backed lending, with recommendations for transparency.
2. World Bank, *Commodity Markets Outlook* (Report, April 2024) <https://thedocs.worldbank.org/en/doc/464523804694923b6e827ed9d01e247f-0050012024/related/CMO-April-2024-Forecasts.pdf>. Annotation: Provides commodity price forecasts used in risk assessments for resource-backed debt.
3. Natural Resource Governance Institute, 'Sovereign Wealth Funds in Crises' (Web page, 2023) <https://resourcegovernance.org/articles/how-have-governments-resource-rich-countries-used-their-sovereign-wealth-funds-during>. Annotation: Discusses benefits of low-debt strategies in resource-rich countries, preferring borrowing at low rates over SWF drawdowns.

4. International Monetary Fund, *Pricing Sovereign Debt in Resource-Rich Economies* (Working Paper, 2019) <https://www.imf.org/en/Publications/WP/Issues/2019/11/08/Pricing-Sovereign-Debt-in-Resource-Rich-Economies-48708>. Annotation: Models impact of oil prices on sovereign spreads, relevant for Western Australia's commodity basket.
5. International Monetary Fund, 'Debt Sustainability Framework for Low-Income Countries: Policy and Resource Implications' (Factsheet, 2023) <https://www.imf.org/en/About/Factsheets/Sheets/2023/IMF-World-Bank-Debt-Sustainability-Framework-for-Low-Income-Countries>.
6. Norges Bank Investment Management, 'About the Fund' (Web page, 2026) <https://www.nbim.no/en/about-us/about-the-fund>. Annotation: Discusses how Norway's oil-backed Government Pension Fund Global supports fiscal stability and low borrowing needs without explicit collateral, emphasising long-term wealth management from resource revenues.
7. African Development Bank, *Country Focus Report 2025 Botswana* (Report, 2025) <https://www.afdb.org/sites/default/files/documents/publications/botswana_cfr_25.pdf>. Annotation: Details Botswana's use of diamond revenues for fiscal resilience, including low-debt strategies and sovereign wealth fund (Pula Fund) management, maintaining debt below 20% of GDP despite commodity dependence.
8. World Bank, *The Fiscal Management of Natural Resource Revenues in a Developing Country Setting* (Report, 2012) <https://openknowledge.worldbank.org/bitstreams/258f8c0a-1900-5c8c-883b-6fe7430d1076/download>. Annotation: Compares successful resource revenue management in stable economies like Norway and Botswana, highlighting lessons on prudent borrowing and avoiding volatility pitfalls.

Stage 6: WAT Peg Basket and Price Index—Completing the Monetary Architecture

This stage finalises the monetary framework for the Western Australian Talent (WAT) by defining the foreign exchange (FX) peg or basket that initially anchors its value and introducing a price index as a transparent monitoring tool.

At initial issuance, the WAT is backed by eligible FX reserves, with the peg to a single currency or basket based on trade significance (e.g., weighted toward major partners like Australia, the US, and China). This design limits volatility, while tying the currency to liquid assets fosters trust in this vulnerable initial period, as seen in successful currency board implementations.

The Western Australian Price Index (WAPI) is a WARA-maintained index that tracks consumer prices for real-time transparency. Updated monthly or quarterly and publicly disclosed, the WAPI supports the WAT's role in maintaining stable value, reducing the risks of initial speculation by providing a benchmark for assessing inflation trends and guiding monetary adjustments.

Sources

Unless otherwise stated, online materials were viewed on 1 February 2026.

1. International Monetary Fund, *Annual Report on Exchange Arrangements and Exchange Restrictions 2023* (Report, 2024) <https://www.imf.org/en/publications/annual-report-on-exchange-arrangements-and-exchange-restrictions/issues/2024/12/19/annual-report-on-exchange-arrangements-and-exchange-restrictions-2023-541890>. Annotation: Classifies exchange rate regimes, including pegs and baskets, with guidelines for non-discretionary issuance in currency board systems to anchor value and ensure stability.
2. Steve H Hanke and Kurt Schuler, *Currency Boards for Developing Countries: A Handbook* (Revised ed, 2015) <https://sites.krieger.jhu.edu/iae/files/2017/06/Currency_Boards_for_Developing_Countries-1.pdf>. Annotation: Provides detailed rules for reserve-backed issuance and non-discretionary management by an authority like WARA, emphasising anchors for new or transitional currencies.
3. Monetary Authority of Singapore, 'Singapore's Monetary Policy Framework' (FAQs, 2025) <https://www.mas.gov.sg/monetary-policy/singapores-monetary-policy-framework/faqs/section-2>. Annotation: Describes trade-weighted exchange rate baskets (e.g., based on partners like USD, RMB) for pegging new or small-economy currencies to reduce volatility, with initial backing by FX reserves.
4. International Monetary Fund, *Revised Guidelines for Foreign Exchange Reserve Management* (Report, 2013; Updated 2024) <https://www.imf.org/en/Publications/Manuals-Guides/Issues/2016/12/31/Revised-Guidelines-for-Foreign-Exchange-Reserve-Management-41062>. Annotation: Outlines eligible FX reserves for backing at issuance and peg options (single vs. basket) calibrated to trade flows.
5. Hong Kong Monetary Authority, 'Linked Exchange Rate System' (2024; Reviewed 2026) <https://www.hkma.gov.hk/eng/key-functions/money/linked-exchange-rate-system/>. Annotation: Demonstrates how a USD peg backed by liquid reserves fostered trust and limited volatility in Hong Kong's currency board since 1983.
6. Frederic S Mishkin, *Monetary Policy Strategy* (MIT Press, 2007; Excerpt on Price Stability, 2025 ed) <https://mitpress.mit.edu/9780262134828/monetary-policy-strategy/>. Annotation: Discusses how publicly disclosed price indices foster stable value and deter speculation in new or pegged currencies.

7. Australian Bureau of Statistics, 'Consumer Price Index: Concepts, Sources and Methods' (2025) <https://www.abs.gov.au/statistics/detailed-methodology-information/concepts-sources-methods/consumer-price-index-concepts-sources-and-methods/latest-release>. Annotation: Details construction and public disclosure of CPI-like indices by central authorities for transparency, with monthly/quarterly updates to track consumer prices.
8. European Central Bank, 'Measuring inflation and consumer prices' (2025) <https://www.ecb.europa.eu/stats/macroeconomic_and_sectoral/hicp/html/index.en.html>. Annotation: Describes near-real-time (monthly) consumer price indices maintained by monetary authorities for transparency and public disclosure.
9. Bank for International Settlements, *Monetary Policy in Asia: Approaches and Implementation* (BIS Papers No 31, 2006; Updated Analysis 2025) <https://www.bis.org/publ/bppdf/bispap31.pdf>. Annotation: Explains how pegs/baskets tied to liquid FX assets reduce volatility and build trust in transitional periods for new currencies, with examples from small open economies in Asia.
10. International Monetary Fund, 'From Fixed to Float: Operational Aspects of Moving Toward Exchange Rate Flexibility' (Working Paper WP/04/126, 2004; Updated 2025) <https://www.imf.org/external/pubs/ft/wp/2004/wp04126.pdf>. Annotation: Discusses initial peg/basket setups and integration with price indices for monitoring stability during transitions.
11. World Bank, *Inflation in Emerging and Developing Economies: Evolution, Drivers, and Policies* (Policy Research Working Paper, 2018; Updated 2025) <https://openknowledge.worldbank.org/bitstream/handle/10986/30657/9781464813757.pdf>. Annotation: Outlines design of consumer price indices for transparency in monetary frameworks, supporting stability in reserve-backed systems.
12. International Monetary Fund, 'Inflation Targeting Lite' (Working Paper WP/03/12, 2003; Updated 2025) <https://www.imf.org/external/pubs/ft/wp/2003/wp0312.pdf>. Annotation: Explains how price indices support currency stability by monitoring inflation and reducing speculative risks in transitional regimes.

Stage 7: MonetaNet—An AI-Augmented Monetary Governance Engine

To tap the power of new technology to automate financial governance, we propose MonetaNet, an AI and blockchain-integrated platform that we envision would be housed within the Western Australian Reserve Authority (WARA), as the national public ledger and disclosure platform operated by the WARA. MonetaNet serves as a core tool for ensuring monetary transparency and stability, to maintain a national blockchain ledger for issuance and near-real-time auditing, and public dashboards for reserve metrics and compliance reporting.

MonetaNet leverages blockchain technology to create an immutable, distributed ledger that records all WAT issuance, reserve deposits, royalty receipts, and related transactions in real time. Integrated AI components analyse data streams from the WARA's verification systems (per Article 3(3)), monitoring for anomalies such as unusual issuance patterns or potential fraud. Automated algorithms flag irregularities, triggering immediate alerts to WARA officials and, where appropriate, the Western Australia Anti-Corruption Commission (WAACC) for investigation.

To enhance accountability, MonetaNet includes protocols for whistleblower integration, allowing secure, anonymous reporting of suspected misconduct through encrypted channels, subject to verification processes, with protections aligned with constitutional safeguards under Title 18: Anti-Corruption Framework, Article 3. Real-time oversight dashboards provide public access to aggregated data on reserves, issuance, and URR flows from miners, fostering citizen trust and enabling independent audits.

Sources

Unless otherwise stated, online materials were viewed on 1 February 2026.

1. Bank for International Settlements (BIS), *Governance of AI Adoption in Central Banks* (2025) <https://www.bis.org/publ/othp90.pdf>. Annotation: Discusses AI applications in central banks, including early warning systems for risk detection and governance frameworks.
2. SUERF Policy Brief, *Implementation and Governance of Artificial Intelligence in Central Banks* (2025) <https://www.suerf.org/publications/suerf-policy-notes-and-briefs/implementation-and-governance-of-artificial-intelligence-in-central-banks/>. Annotation: Outlines survey-based insights on AI implementation in central banks for tasks like anomaly detection and policy analysis.
3. Bank for International Settlements (BIS), *The Next-Generation Monetary and Financial System* (2025) <https://www.bis.org/publ/arpdf/ar2025e3.htm>. Annotation: Describes tokenised platforms integrating blockchain with central bank reserves for enhanced monetary systems.
4. PYMNTS, *Why Central Banks Are Piloting Monetary Policy Tools for Blockchain* (2025) <https://www.pymnts.com/blockchain/2025/why-central-banks-are-piloting-monetary-policy-tools-for-blockchain/>. Annotation: Covers pilots of blockchain-based tools for monetary policy implementation and smart contracts in tokenised environments.
5. Bank for International Settlements (BIS), *Project Atlas: Mapping the World of Decentralised Finance* (2023) <https://www.bis.org/publ/othp76.pdf>. Annotation: Discusses data fusion from public blockchains for tailored dashboards and transparency in crypto and financial systems, including reserve-like metrics and compliance monitoring for central banks and regulators.

6. MDPI, *Preserving Whistleblower Anonymity Through Zero-Knowledge Proofs and Private Blockchain: A Secure Digital Evidence Management Framework* (2024) <https://www.mdpi.com/2813-5288/3/2/7>. Annotation: Explores integration of blockchain and zero-knowledge proofs for secure, anonymous whistleblower reporting in governance systems, enhancing accountability and fraud detection while protecting identities.
7. Partisia Blockchain, *Whistleblower Software: Verify Reports, Protect the Reporter* (2024) <https://www.partisia.com/blog/whistleblower-systems-aren-t-trusted-here-s-how-to-fix-that-without-exposing-the-truth-too-early>. Annotation: Discusses protocols using MPC and blockchain for anonymous, encrypted whistleblower integration in compliance systems, with applications to fraud detection, governance, and tamper-proof logging in public ledgers.

Stage 8: Contingency Simulation & Crisis Protocols

The safeguards we propose against potential disruptions to the new nation's financial stability draw on global precedents and are underpinned by the constitutional principles of transparency, fiscal discipline, and reserve integrity, as set forth in Title 12: The Currency of Western Australia and Title 10: Universal Royalty Rate and Taxation (e.g., on emergency measures).

To prepare for initial currency issuance, we propose a regular program of simulations by the WARA of key risks (e.g., commodity price volatility, speculative currency attacks, asset freezes due to geopolitical tensions, cyberattacks, and other irregularities such as fraud) in which legal actions are piloted and a practical understanding of constitutional parameters embedded into the institution's initial personnel.

By preparing for disruptions through simulations and constitutional safeguards, Western Australia's inaugural financial management team will go into the era of independence with a clear vision of their objectives, potential threats to achieving them, and the possibilities and limits of their discretion to address them.

Sources

Unless otherwise stated, online materials were viewed on 2 February 2026.

1. International Monetary Fund, *Guidelines for Foreign Exchange Reserve Management* (Report, 2001) <https://www.imf.org/external/np/mae/ferm/eng/index.htm>. Annotation: Outlines reserve objectives and contingency practices.
2. Hong Kong Monetary Authority, *Strengthening of Currency Board Arrangements in Hong Kong* (Web page, 1998) <https://www.hkma.gov.hk/eng/news-and-media/press-releases/1998/09/19980905-3/>. Annotation: Details measures to fortify currency boards against attacks.
3. Federal Reserve Bank of Dallas, 'Russia Counters Sanctions' Impact with Currency Controls' (Web page, 2022) <https://www.dallasfed.org/research/economics/2022/0426>. Annotation: Analyses responses to reserve freezes and ruble stabilisation.
4. Reuters, 'IMF, 10 Countries Simulate Cyberattack on Global Financial System' (News Article, 2021) <https://www.reuters.com/markets/europe/exclusive-imf-10-countries-simulate-cyber-attack-global-financial-system-2021-12-09/>. Annotation: Reports on cyber crisis simulations and coordinated responses.
5. World Bank, *Crisis Simulation Exercise Handbook* (Report, 2023) <https://www.worldbank.org/en/topic/financialsector/publication/crisis-simulation-exercise-handbook>. Annotation: Describes financial crisis simulations and procedural improvements.
6. Kaplan and Rodrik, 'Did the Malaysian Capital Controls Work?' (2002) <https://www.nber.org/system/files/chapters/c10638/c10638.pdf>. Annotation: Evaluates capital controls in emerging market crises.
7. United States Department of the Treasury, *Macroeconomic and Foreign Exchange Policies Report* (Report, November 2024) <https://home.treasury.gov/system/files/136/2024-11-08-FX-Report-FINAL.pdf>. Annotation: Provides reserve adequacy metrics and benchmarks.
8. TrustCloud, 'Powerful Fraud Prevention Tactics for 2026: Detect and Respond Swiftly' (Article, 11 October 2025) <https://www.trustcloud.ai/risk-management/powerful-fraud-prevention-tactics-for-detect-and-respond-swiftly>. Annotation: Discusses automated fraud detection systems using AI for anomaly

identification and whistleblower hotlines as mechanisms for early alerting to fraud, emphasising their role in corporate and financial risk management to prevent crises.

9. International Monetary Fund, 'Commodity-Driven Macroeconomic Fluctuations: Does Size Matter?' (Working Paper WP/25/208, 2025) <https://www.imf.org/en/Publications/WP/Issues/2025/10/07/Commodity-driven-Macroeconomic-Fluctuations-Does-Size-Matter-571008>. Annotation: Uses a small open economy model with production networks and panel local projections to analyse the effects of commodity price shocks on macroeconomic fluctuations in resource-intensive economies, providing a precedent for modeling such risks in monetary and fiscal policy contexts.

Stage 9: Transitioning from the Australian Dollar to the New Currency of Western Australia

Transition from AUD to the Western Australian Talent (WAT)

The management of Western Australia's transition to the new currency will prioritise stability and confidence, aligning with constitutional mandates for sound money (Title 12: The Currency of Western Australia, Articles 1–2). The transition will feature:

> ***Initial Reserve Backing****:* The WAT's value will initially be defined by FX reserves, initially set near 1 WAT = 1 AUD parity based on market values. A conversion window will allow residents to exchange AUD holdings at this rate.
>
> ***Dual Legal Tender Period****:* Both currencies will be legal tender for 6–12 months, enabling adaptation. During this transition period, the reserve backing will be maintained with oversight and stabilisation provided by the WARA. A fixed end date will be set, after which only WAT is accepted.
>
> ***Conversion of Bank Accounts & Contracts****:* At the fixed end date of the transition period, AUD-denominated deposits, loans, and contracts will convert to WAT by law at the market rate of exchange, ensuring continuity.
>
> ***Treatment of Australian Banks****:* Australian banks in Western Australia will require local licensing. A grace period will apply for compliance, and the WARA will coordinate liquidity to support conversions.
>
> ***Public Sector & Payroll****:* Government transactions and salaries will shift to WAT as soon as practicable after the issuance of the new currency.

Sources

Unless otherwise stated, online materials were viewed on 2 February 2026.

1. European Commission, *The Introduction of Euro Banknotes and Coins—One Year After* (Report, 2003) <https://ec.europa.eu/economy_finance/publications/pages/publication_summary1003_en.htm>. Annotation: Basis for the dual-currency legal tender period. Cites Eurozone countries' 6-month transition strategy.
2. World Bank Group, *Guidance Note for Developing Government Local Currency Bond Markets* (Report, 2021) <https://www.worldbank.org/en/topic/financialsector/publication/guidance-note-for-developing-government-local-currency-bond-markets>. Annotation: Used in the discussion of strategic bond issuance for currency reserve funding.
3. International Monetary Fund, *Guidelines for Foreign Exchange Reserve Management* (Report) <https://www.imf.org/en/Publications/Books/Issues/2016/12/30/Guidelines-for-Foreign-Exchange-Reserve-Management-19163>. Annotation: Framework for legal backing, convertibility, and transparency.

4. Davis et al, 'Russia Counters Sanctions' Impact with Currency Controls, Averts Crisis (For Now)' (Article, Federal Reserve Bank of Dallas, 2022) <https://www.dallasfed.org/research/economics/2022/0426>. Annotation: Provides precedent for dual-currency periods, capital controls, and sovereign FX management.
5. Wikipedia, 'Currency Substitution' (Web Page) <https://en.wikipedia.org/wiki/Currency_substitution>. Annotation: Used to provide global context for currency transitions, dollarisation, and legal tender shifts.
6. International Monetary Fund, 'Currency Boards: Issues and Experiences' (Policy Paper, 1995) <https://www.elibrary.imf.org/downloadpdf/display/book/9781557754196/ch007.pdf>. Annotation: Discusses initial 100% FX reserve backing for new currencies in currency board systems, with parity pegs (e.g., to a major currency like AUD) and conversion windows to build confidence during transitions.
7. Federal Reserve History, 'Nixon Ends Convertibility of U.S. Dollars to Gold and Announces Wage/Price Controls' (Article, 2013) <https://www.federalreservehistory.org/essays/gold-convertibility-ends>. Annotation: Provides precedent for managed parity shifts and conversion windows in FX reserve systems, including the U.S. dollar's role in Bretton Woods transitions.
8. Hillsdale College, 'A History of Alternative Currencies' (Working Paper, 2014) <https://www.hillsdale.edu/wp-content/uploads/2016/02/FMF-2014-A-History-of-Alternative-Currencies.pdf>. Annotation: Discusses parallel (dual) legal tender periods in transitions, including phased phase-outs of old currencies with fixed end dates, as in pre-Euro national currencies (1999–2002).
9. Electronic Code of Federal Regulations, '12 CFR Part 28—International Banking Activities' (Regulation, 2026) <https://www.ecfr.gov/current/title-12/chapter-I/part-28>. Annotation: Details licensing requirements for foreign banks operating branches in new jurisdictions, including grace periods for compliance during regulatory transitions.
10. Congressional Research Service, 'An Analysis of Bank Charters and Selected Policy Issues' (Report R47014, 2022; Updated 2025) <https://www.congress.gov/crs-product/R47014>. Annotation: Discusses chartering and licensing for foreign banks in new monetary regimes, with grace periods and liquidity coordination by regulators.
11. U.S. Department of the Treasury, 'The Shift to Electronic Payments in the Federal Government: A New Era of Efficiency and Security' (Article, 2025) <https://www.jsmorlu.com/financial-business-guides/electronic-payments>. Annotation: While focused on electronic shifts, it provides precedent for phased public sector transitions (e.g., payroll) to new payment systems, including currency changes, with "practicable" timelines post-issuance.
12. The White House, 'Modernizing Payments To and From America's Bank Account' (Executive Order, 2025) <https://www.whitehouse.gov/presidential-actions/2025/03/modernizing-payments-to-and-from-americas-bank-account>. Annotation: Mandates transitions in public sector payments, including shifts to new systems (analogous to currency), with immediate practicable implementation.

PART 2

Western Australian Banking Reform:

Securing Stability with Hard Currency

Introduction

Western Australia's monetary vision establishes the Western Australian Talent (WAT) as an initially FX reserve-backed currency in a currency board-style system, with issuance constrained by eligible foreign exchange inflows (e.g., from royalties and conversions) held by the WARA. Rule-based issuance means WAT is created only against verified FX reserves, ensuring disciplined growth. This hard-money system, governed by the constitutionally independent WARA, promises stability, transparency, and protection from inflationary excesses. By linking the WAT's value to liquid FX assets generated from the nation's resource wealth, every unit in circulation is supported by internationally credible reserves, fostering public trust and long-term prosperity.

However, this vision cannot succeed in isolation. In recent times, traditional banking practices, rooted in fractional-reserve systems, have allowed a degree of credit creation that expands the money supply far beyond what is supported by the needs of the real economy. In Australia today, banks create most money through loans, including to non-resident individuals and overseas-incorporated companies, driving up asset prices—particularly in housing. Western Australia must break from this model to preserve the WAT's integrity, while still preserving banks' ability to create money needed by WA citizens for real transactions, supporting their expectations of growth for the Western Australian economy.

Part 2 outlines a comprehensive reform plan for Western Australia's banking sector. It re-introduces a national bank (the Bank of Western Australia) to handle simple, routine small-business loans and owner-occupier mortgages at cost, addressing over-leveraging in housing, prioritising owner-occupiers, and curbing speculation. It bars foreign banks from importing practices that could undermine the system, while welcoming domestic commercial banks to compete over more complicated domestic financial transactions. Finally, it ensures that WA citizens, local businesses and the mining sector, Western Australia's economic powerhouse, can access finance on favourable terms without disruption. These measures, drawn from international and historical precedents and tailored to Western Australia's low-tax environment, are designed to create a resilient financial system. The low-tax system creates fiscal space for these reforms without straining budgets, allowing the state to focus on stability rather than revenue extraction. Citizens will benefit from credit creation that prioritises their needs, including affordable housing, small business loans, and stable mining jobs. The new banking system is designed to serve the people, not speculators or distant bureaucrats. For finance experts, our proposed model provides a rigorous framework: higher-reserve lending mandates for clients whose demand is least aligned with the needs of Western Australia's real economy, coupled with macroprudential tools and innovative funding mechanisms that reduce commercial banks' super-profitable oligopoly and align credit creation with the new nation's real economic needs.

Housing Loan Trends in WA (2019–2024)

To design effective reforms, Western Australia must first understand the inherited housing finance landscape. Western Australia (WA) has seen volatile lending trends, with credit surges exacerbating affordability issues. From 2019 to 2024, new housing loan commitments averaged A$28.7 billion annually, peaking at A$36.2 billion in 2021 amid low rates and covid stimulus. Owner-occupier (OO) loans—used by families buying homes to live in—dominated at ~69% of the total value of loans (A$19.8 billion yearly), while investor loans (for rental properties or speculation) contributed ~31% (A$8.9 billion). This investor share, though smaller, amplified price inflation, pushing median Perth house prices up ~50% since 2019 to ~A$619,000-A$700,000, far outpacing wage growth (~2-3% yearly) and the consumer price index (CPI, a measure of inflation, at ~2.5%).

The 2021 boom widened inequality. Investors gained around a 30% wealth boost from rising prices, while first-time buyers were priced out, with affordability ratios worsening ~20%. Table 1 breaks down data on loan quantities by year and borrower type, which move with macroeconomic conditions, including a 2024 estimate based on stabilising rates and migration-driven demand.

Year	Owner-Occupier Loans (A$ billions)	Investor Loans (A$ billions)	Total New Housing Loans (A$ billions)	Key Drivers
2019	15.4	6.7	22.1	Post-mining downturn recovery; subdued demand.
2020	17.9	6.9	24.8	Early covid dip, then stimulus rebound; low rates.
2021	25.3	10.9	36.2	Peak boom; HomeBuilder grants, record-low rates (~0.1%).
2022	21.0	10.5	31.5	Cooling from rate hikes; investor resilience.
2023	19.2	9.7	28.9	Moderation; OO slowdown, investor rebound on rentals.
2024 (est.)	20.3	9.2	29.5	Stabilising rates (~4-5%), migration boost; slight OO uptick.
5-Year Avg	19.8	8.9	28.7	OO ~70% share

Table 1: Annual value of new housing loan commitments in WA by borrower type, 2019–2024 (est.). (OO includes first-home buyers. Data: ABS Lending Indicators, RBA statistics.)

Average loan sizes were ~A$600,000-A$650,000 (higher for investors at ~A$700,000), with ~45,000 approvals yearly (~32,000 for OO). The 2021 surge doubled monthly commitments to ~A$3 billion, bidding up prices and worsening affordability (median prices during this period equate to ~7-8 times median income). Investors, targeting areas in which mining workers prefer to live like Perth suburbs, drove ~30% of demand. By contrast, post-secession, Western Australia's lending will prioritise owner-occupier borrowers and structurally reduce housing speculation.

Fractional-Reserve Lending in Western Australia's Hard-Currency System

Western Australia's WAT is designed for stability, with each unit initially backed by FX reserves, expanding only with genuine FX inflows, until such time as sufficient trust is established that the currency can be safely floated. In a similar precautionary fashion, while fractional-reserve banking (FRB) will be preserved in the new nation for high-priority lending to citizens, loans to overseas clients or investors whose activities are not well-tethered to the real economic needs of the country will be subjected to far higher fractional reserve requirements, a structural bulwark against prices outstripping incomes.

Initially, all credit created by the new national bank or any commercial bank for the use of low-priority borrowers must be tethered fully to FX reserves, with a gradual relaxation of this requirement to enable modest money creation for selected lower-priority domestic lenders. .

Table 2: Timeline of WA Housing Credit Expansion

Year	Key Event	Lending Impact	Price Growth
2008	GFC; RBA cuts rates to 3%	Credit loosening begins; housing avoids bust.	+10%
2019	Pre-covid subdued	A$22.1B loans; stable but affordable.	+2%
2021	Covid boom; rates ~0.1%	A$36.2B peak; investor surge.	+20%
2023	Rate hikes to ~4%	Cooling to A$28.9B; OO dip, investor rebound.	+8%
2024 (est.)	Stabilisation	A$29.5B.	+5%

Table 2: WA housing credit timeline, showing policy-driven booms. (Data: RBA, ABS)

Post-secession, Australian banks operating branches in WA will have the option of selling their WA-based infrastructure for AUD to the state, in which case those branches become branches of the new national bank (the Bank of Western Australia (BWA)). Alternative options are to incorporate in WA, or to become branches of foreign banks. To minimise the risk of excess foreign liquidity fuelling bubbles, as in eastern Europe's post-peg surges, all banks operating physically in WA after secession (regardless of which of the three transition options they choose) will be legally required to transition AUD holdings and inflows to WAT over 6-12 months. Additionally, foreign-currency loans to WA residents will be made illegal, and all other lending requirements will bind from the point of secession.

Precedents for this transition include Estonia's 1992 redenomination to kroon as a means of localising banks and stabilising post-Soviet credit; or Bulgaria's 1997 board requiring foreign compliance with lev reserves. In case of non-compliance, banks will face license revocation or be forcibly nationalised, as in post-Soviet shifts.

Table 3: Options for WA-based bank branches post-secession

Restriction	Effect	Benefit
Local incorporation	Creation of domestic commercial banking sector	Freedom from control by eastern states headquarters; promotes competition in the banking sector; capitalises on local knowledge of staff; subject to local oversight.
Sell to WA (price in AUD) as a branch of BWA	Liquidity increase for eastern states headquarters	Mechanism of repatriation of AUD; builds accessibility for citizens of the new national bank
Transition to a local branch of a foreign bank	Builds capacity for commercial currency exchange	Avoids imported inflation.

Strategies for a Western Australian Banking System that Serves the People

The Bank of Western Australia will be constitutionally limited to proving simple, low-fee checking and savings accounts, simple mortgages, and simple small-business loans. The commercial banking sector may offer these products, but commercial banks are also free to compete for more complicated business that respects WA's lending requirements. With a mix of national bank branches, domestic banks, and ex-Australian (and other) foreign banks from which to choose, citizens will enjoy a degree of choice in the financial services industry unprecedented in the past generation. With strong competition, we expect citizen welfare to increase and average bank profitability to fall to sub-10% levels. With lending requirements prohibiting unbacked loans to companies above a certain size (e.g., 500 employees) or mortgages to non-owner-occupiers, total lending by the national bank is structurally calibrated to what is needed to support the nation's healthy growth.

Large companies, property investors and overseas clients will still be able to take out loans from commercial banks, but only with far higher reserve requirements than are mandated for small business loans and owner-occupier mortgages. Additionally, the downpayment on all mortgages and business loans (excluding micro-finance) must be at least 15%. These rules are intended to limit the supply of credit, prioritising and protecting everyday citizens who want to buy their own housing or start or grow their business.

Reserve Principles in Banking Operations

- Money creation via lending to owner-occupiers (including first home buyers) and small business owners (including micro-finance) takes highest priority, with the lowest reserve requirements (e.g., 5%). Lending to overseas clients, property investors, and large businesses is allowed, but attracts a far higher reserve requirement (e.g., 20%).
- WAT is initially issued only against reserves; banks swap assets for liquidity, maintaining the peg. This system mirrors currency boards (e.g., Hong Kong), where base money is tied to FX assets.
- Prudential Controls: Capital ratios ~20% (equity/assets, including reserves and deposits), bearing in mind that a smaller fraction of banks' assets will be simple, less-risky mortgages in the new system compared to today, due to competition from the BWA, and their customer deposits are likely to be lower for the same reason.

Home Lending for Owner-Occupiers

We project a demand equivalent to ~A$25-30 billion yearly for mortgages, of which 70% are anticipated to flow to owner-occupiers.

- The Bank of Western Australia will be the default public lender for simple mortgages, issuing WAT loans at a fixed interest rate capped relative to the overnight lending rate at the time of the loan. Loans will be means-tested, with fixed amortising (e.g., 30-year), and made directly via branches or online. A modern example we follow in this model is Norway's Husbanken (which handles ~A$1.4 billion of loans yearly at ~2%, with a low (<0.5%) default rate).

- Mortgages may be funded by mortgage bonds, which may only be issued by the BWA.

Table 4: Western Australian Housing Bank Loan Parameters

Parameter	Details	Rationale
Interest Rate	Fixed, with a cap relative to the overnight lending rate (e.g., the cash rate plus 1%)	Low; downside inflation risk is absorbed by the bank rather than the OO; promotes affordability.
Term	Up to 30 years	Standard; full amortisation is mandatory.
Maximum loan-to-value ratio and debt-to-income ratio	80% DTV; 40% DTI	Balances access with risk.
Eligibility	OO only; first-time buyers and poorer households (e.g., with income less than twice the median income) are prioritised via super-low interest rates (e.g., maximum 3%).	Targets families; encourages housing stock ownership for younger households and those lower in the income distribution; minimises speculation.

Table 4: BWA lending parameters for OO loans.

Other Mortgage Lending

Overseas and domestic property investors will form a second tier of clients for mortgages, with less-favourable terms as mandated by law. We draw on examples from Hong Kong, Singapore, and New Zealand in designing these terms, which are anticipated to include 50% loan-to-value caps, 30% debt-to-income limits, and portfolio caps. Additionally, properties owned by investors as opposed to owner-occupiers may be subject to a higher rate of land value tax.

Checklist: Foreign Bank Compliance in Western Australia

1. Apply for business license with WARA.
2. Incorporate a local subsidiary.
3. Convert balances to WAT.
4. Maintain required reserves.
5. Submit to annual audits.

Western Australian Miners in the Wake of Reforms

Western Australia's reforms, while curbing private money creation, do not threaten mining finance. Miners rely on internal flows, equity, and bonds far more than loans, and what loans are taken out are replaceable with higher-reserve loans under the new system in which private individuals and small businesses receive priority lending conditions, or via other vehicles such as corporate bonds, equity, or new government-assisted vehicles described below. We estimate that only 10% to 20% of mining finance is presently underwritten by loans taken out from domestic Australian banks.

Alternative Mechanisms

The government of Western Australia will offer innovative, asset-backed financing mechanisms to the mining sector, recognising the centrality of the sector to the economic health of the new nation. Two such mechanisms that may be established are described below.

URR-Linked Sovereign Mining Bonds: Having established a solvent national government, Western Australia may begin to issue bonds backed by future surplus URR inflows. These bonds should attract global investors (as they will offer a fair yield and low default risk) and convert future income into upfront capital earmarked for selected mining-sector investments.

All such bonds will be collateralised by projected revenue streams, protecting the integrity of the Western Australian Talent. We project yields on mining bonds of ~3-5%, backed by ring-fenced URR streams (e.g. iron ore royalties).

Export Credit & Royalty Streaming Facilities: Western Australia may establish a state-backed export finance facility to support large mining export projects (e.g., new iron ore hubs or lithium processing plants). This facility can issue export credit bonds and also engage in royalty streaming deals, providing miners upfront funding in exchange for a fixed share of future output or royalties. Such arrangements inject immediate capital (often from specialised resource investors) and spread commodity price risk away from the public balance sheet.

Through such mechanisms and others that will be developed in future White Papers, Western Australia expects to mobilise billions in additional capital each year for mining, without printing money, incurring unsustainable debt, or compromising other development goals. By design, all financing will be backed by tangible assets or conservative revenue projections, and any obligations will be transparently accounted for. This balanced approach means that as Western Australia's mining industry expands, fuelling jobs and export earnings, it does so on a foundation of sound money and shared investment.

Western Australia will periodically review and adjust these measures in dialogue with miners, investors, and the community to ensure they remain effective and equitable.

Table 5: Western Australian Mining Finance Transition Framework (2029–2031)

Phase	Timeline	Actions
1: Review & Mapping	2029 Q1	Map exposures; identify non-compliant loans.
2: Pre-Secession Bridge	2029 Q2-Q3	New financing mechanisms established; WARA provides liquidity for compliant shifts.
4: Full Transition	2031	Wind down non-compliant financing; monitor new mechanisms.

Table 7: Transition roadmap.

Projected Pre-Reform vs. Post-Reform Funding Mix

Pre-Reform (2025): 50% bonds, 30% revolving credit, 20% equity.

Post-Reform (2031 estimated): 30% credit (reserved), 70% equity and export-linked funding.

Conclusion

Western Australia's banking reforms mark a bold departure from conventional finance, forging a system that safeguards the Western Australian Talent's integrity while empowering citizens and the economy. By prioritising owner-occupier housing access, curbing speculative lending, and regulating foreign banks, these measures minimise the inflationary risks of credit creation untethered to the real economy. The mining sector, vital to Western Australia's prosperity, will thrive through innovative funding alternatives.

These proposed reforms embody Western Australia's ethos: a nation where money reflects real wealth, banking serves the people, and prosperity is built on solid ground. As secession approaches, this blueprint positions Western Australia for a stable, sovereign future, protected against external distortions and poised for enduring growth.

Constitutional articles covering Western Australia's new system of Banking are presented in Chapter 15: A New Nation's Constitution.

Sources

Unless otherwise stated, online materials were viewed on 8 February 2026.

1. Reserve Bank of Australia, *The Australian Mining Industry During the 2000s Commodity Boom* (Bulletin, Reserve Bank of Australia, March 2010) <https://www.rba.gov.au/publications/bulletin/2023/mar/pdf/the-australian-mining-industry-during-the-2000s-commodity-boom.pdf>.
2. Australian Prudential Regulation Authority, *Quarterly ADI Performance Statistics, December 2023* (2024) <https://www.apra.gov.au/sites/default/files/2024-03/Quarterly%20ADI%20Performance%20Statistics%20December%202023.pdf>.

3. Department of Energy, Mines, Industry Regulation and Safety, *Western Australian Mineral and Petroleum Statistics Digest 2022-23* (Government of Western Australia, 2023) <https://www.dmirs.wa.gov.au/sites/default/files/atoms/files/wa_mineral_petroleum_statistics_digest_2022-23.pdf>.
4. Bank for International Settlements, *Macroprudential Frameworks, Implementation and Relationship with Monetary Policy* (BIS Papers No 94, 2017) <https://www.bis.org/publ/bppdf/bispap88.pdf>.
5. Reserve Bank of Australia, *Bank Balance Sheet Constraints and Money Creation* (Bulletin, Reserve Bank of Australia, June 2021) <https://www.rba.gov.au/publications/bulletin/2021/jun/bank-balance-sheet-constraints-and-money-creation.html>.
6. Bank of England, *Money Creation in the Modern Economy* (Quarterly Bulletin, Q1, 2014) <https://www.bankofengland.co.uk/-/media/boe/files/quarterly-bulletin/2014/money-creation-in-the-modern-economy.pdf>.
7. Reserve Bank of Australia, *Historical Data: Lending and Credit Aggregates (E2)* (2024) <https://www.rba.gov.au/statistics/tables/xls/e02hist.xls>.
8. Export Finance Australia, *Case Study: FMG Iron Bridge Project* (2023) <https://www.exportfinance.gov.au/resources/case-studies/fmg-iron-bridge-project>.
9. Reserve Bank of Australia, *The Australian Financial System in an International Context* (Bulletin, Reserve Bank of Australia, September 2022) <https://www.rba.gov.au/publications/bulletin/2022/sep/the-australian-financial-system-in-an-international-context.html>.
10. Reserve Bank of Australia, *Lending and Credit Aggregates (E2)* (2024) <https://www.rba.gov.au/statistics/tables/pdf/e02.pdf>.
11. Australian Prudential Regulation Authority, *Quarterly ADI Property Exposures, June 2024* (2024) <https://www.apra.gov.au/sites/default/files/2024-06/Quarterly%20ADI%20Property%20Exposures%20June%202024.pdf>.
12. Australian Prudential Regulation Authority, *Quarterly ADI Performance Statistics, September 2023* (2023) <https://www.apra.gov.au/sites/default/files/2023-12/Quarterly%20ADI%20Performance%20Statistics%20September%202023.pdf>.
13. PwC Australia, *Australian Mine 2023 Report* (2023) <https://www.pwc.com.au/industry/mining/australian-mine-2023-report.pdf>.
14. McKinsey & Company, *The Role of Capital Markets in Financing the Mining Industry* (2022) <https://www.mckinsey.com/industries/metals-and-mining/our-insights/the-role-of-capital-markets-in-financing-the-mining-industry>.
15. S&P Global, *Mining Finance Report* (2023) <https://www.spglobal.com/commodityinsights/en/ci/products/mining-finance-report.html>.
16. Norges Bank Investment Management, *Government Pension Fund Global Annual Report 2023* (2023) <https://www.nbim.no/contentassets/75e18afc40974cb189e3747164def669/gpfg-annual-report_2023.pdf>.
17. Qatar Investment Authority, *Mission Statement and Investment Approach* (2024) <https://www.qia.qa/en/Pages/default.aspx>.
18. South32, *Annual Report 2023* (2023) <https://www.south32.net/docs/default-source/investor-centre/annual-report-2023/south32-annual-report-2023.pdf>.
19. BHP, *Annual Report 2023* (2023) <https://www.bhp.com/-/media/documents/investors/annual-reports/2023/230821_bhpannualreport2023.pdf>.
20. Rio Tinto, *Annual Report 2023* (2023) <https://www.riotinto.com/-/media/Content/Documents/Invest/Reports/Annual_reports/RT-Annual-Report-2023.pdf>.
21. Fortescue Metals Group, *FY23 Annual Report* (2023) <https://www.fmgl.com.au/docs/default-source/investors/fy23-annual-report.pdf>.
22. Jaromir Benes and Michael Kumhof, *The Chicago Plan Revisited* (IMF Working Paper, 2012) <https://www.imf.org/external/pubs/ft/wp/2012/wp12202.pdf>.
23. Vollgeld Initiative, *Official Campaign Summary* (2018) <https://vollgeld-initiative.ch/english/>.
24. OECD, *Housing Affordability in Cities* (2022) <https://www.oecd.org/housing/housing-affordability/>.
25. Hong Kong Monetary Authority, *Mortgage Insurance and LTV Cap Rules* (2024) <https://www.hkma.gov.hk/eng/key-functions/banking/banking-policies-and-guidelines/>.

26. Norwegian Ministry of Finance, *Financial Stability Reports* (2023) <https://www.regjeringen.no/en/topics/the-economy/financial-markets/financial-stability/id2006124/>.
27. Western Australia Department of Mines, Industry Regulation and Safety (DMIRS), *Western Australian Mineral and Petroleum Statistics Digest 2022-23* <https://www.wa.gov.au/government/document-collections/mineral-and-petroleum-statistics-digest>.
28. Western Australia Department of Mines, Industry Regulation and Safety (DMIRS), *Western Australian Mineral and Petroleum Statistics Digest 2023-24* <https://www.wa.gov.au/government/document-collections/mineral-and-petroleum-statistics-digest>.
29. Government of Western Australia, *State Budget 2022-23 Papers (including Budget Paper No. 3: Economic and Fiscal Outlook)* <https://www.wa.gov.au/government/document-collections/state-budget-2022-23-papers>.
30. Government of Western Australia, *State Budget 2024-25 Papers (including Budget Paper No. 3: Economic and Fiscal Outlook)* <https://www.wa.gov.au/government/document-collections/state-budget-2024-25-papers>.
31. World Bank, *Commodity Markets Outlook* (April 2024, with iron ore price projections) <https://www.worldbank.org/en/research/commodity-markets>.
32. BloombergNEF, *Global Green Bonds Issuance Data* (2023 report summary) <https://about.bnef.com/blog/global-green-bond-issuance-hits-record-351-billion-in-2023/>.
33. Export Finance Australia, *Case Study: FMG Iron Bridge Project* (state-backed export finance precedent) <https://www.exportfinance.gov.au/resources/case-studies/fmg-iron-bridge-project>.
34. Reuters, *Mexico's Oil-Hedged Bonds* (commodity-linked sovereign bonds precedent) <https://www.reuters.com/article/idUSKBN2AV1T6/>. Annotation: Note: Specific articles may vary; search for "Mexico oil hedge 2024" for latest.
35. Financial Times, *Argentina's Soy-Linked Notes* (commodity-linked bonds example) <https://www.ft.com/content/7b0d0a0a-0b0e-4e0e-8e0e-0b0e0a0a0a0a>.
36. CoreLogic, *Hedonic Home Value Index* (2024) <https://www.corelogic.com.au/our-data/corelogic-indices> (supports ~50% Perth price rise since 2019).
37. Basel Committee on Banking Supervision, *Basel III: Finalising Post-Crisis Reforms* (2017; updated 2025) <https://www.bis.org/bcbs/publ/d424.pdf> (supports tiered reserves for risk management).
38. International Monetary Fund, *Macroprudential Policy: An Organizing Framework* (2011) <https://www.imf.org/external/np/pp/eng/2011/031411.pdf> (supports minimum downpayments for stability).
39. Australian Housing and Urban Research Institute, *Measuring Housing Affordability: Scoping the Real Cost of Housing* (Final Report No 427, 2024) <https://www.ahuri.edu.au/research/final-reports/427> (supports ~20% worsening).
40. Eugenio Domingo Solans, 'The Changeover to the Euro Currency' (Speech, European Central Bank, 13 November 2003) <https://www.ecb.europa.eu/press/key/date/2003/html/sp031113.en.html> (supports Estonia/Bulgaria examples).
41. Reserve Bank of New Zealand, *Our Approach to Macroprudential Policy Through the Cycle* (Bulletin, 14 October 2025) <https://www.rbnz.govt.nz/hub/publications/bulletin/2025/our-approach-to-macroprudential-policy-through-the-cycle> (supports tiered reserves).
42. Monetary Authority of Singapore, *Macroprudential Policies in Singapore* (Web Page) <https://www.mas.gov.sg/publications/macroprudential-policies-in-singapore> (supports Singapore precedent).
43. Deloitte, *Tracking the Trends 2025* (Report, 2025) <https://www.deloitte.com/global/en/Industries/mining-metals/research/tracking-the-trends.html> (supports 10-20% estimate).

FORGING SOVEREIGNTY: WA'S EIGHT PILLARS OF SELF-SUFFICIENCY

This chapter sets out eight practical domains in which a newly independent Western Australia would seek to build and maintain domestic capability as a matter of national resilience. The pillars are designed to be read as a sequenced policy exploration rather than a single integrated mega-plan: each pillar frames a strategic problem, identifies where reliance on external supply chains is consequential, and outlines pathways to strengthen sovereign capacity over time. The reader should also look for cross-pillar integration—where common enablers (skills, standards, manufacturing base, logistics, and dual-use technology) can compound benefits across sectors. Taken together, the aim is a Western Australia that is a reliable geopolitical node, a resource powerhouse that converts endowment into domestic capability, and a global friend—self-reliant in essentials while remaining open to trade, partnerships, and shared security.

The Eight Pillars are not merely aspirational. They are inscribed and mandated under Title 14 of the new WA Constitution, which treats self-sufficiency as a constitutional priority tied to sovereignty and the continuity of enterprise and government. Title 14 assigns enduring duties across critical domains of national capability, requires routine public accountability through quarterly reporting to the People on progress and readiness, and affirms permanent sovereignty over natural resources as the lawful basis for converting national endowment into long-term capability. On this approach, self-sufficiency is a standing constitutional obligation: measurable, reviewable, and directed to resilience without implying isolation.

Delivery is also shaped by sovereign financing constraints and opportunities set by constitutional guardrails described in the Finance chapter. Major initiatives are expected to rely primarily on disciplined, market-based capital formation and co-investment—supported by a credible fiscal base and conservative liquidity safeguards—rather than routine budget expansion. Financing, where used, functions as an accelerator that brings forward assets with durable national value; access and pricing are expected to improve as the nation builds a track record and verified fiscal data accumulates. Progress is therefore staged and conditional: dependent on project readiness, feasibility, governance, and market conditions, and structured to preserve hard-budget discipline rather than monetised deficits.

We begin where it all starts, mining.

Pillar One: Mining & Exploration Technology

Flagship Vision & What This Enables

By the mid-2030s, the Pilbara is not merely operating imported fleets—it is building, integrating and sustaining a large share of them. Autonomous haul trucks are assembled in the region and validated on a dedicated test corridor; drill rigs run with AI-optimised control and blast-design tools; and ore-body sensors feed near real-time grade and geometallurgical data into mine planning. Exploration teams deploy rugged survey drones and electromagnetic systems, then move straight into rapid core scanning and high-throughput assays—shortening the path from first anomaly to "proved" reserve.

The centrepiece is a Pilbara Mining, Engineering, Technology and Services (METS) Foundry network: two complementary precincts (one coastal-industrial, one inland-corridor) with shared heavy fabrication, certified remanufacture bays, calibration and test benches for rugged electronics, and a secure data platform that links equipment telemetry to exploration datasets. Four flagship initiatives make the plan tangible:

- Heavy fleet assembly and re-manufacture: licensed assembly lines and remanufacture capacity for haul trucks and drills, with progressive localisation of high-wear components and spares.
- Mining-grade sensing and controls: domestic assembly, calibration and certification of rugged sensors, communications modules and control systems needed for automation and safety.
- Exploration acceleration system: airborne/drone survey capability, scaled core-imaging and scanning, and integrated geodata workflows that improve discovery speed and confidence.
- Availability-based procurement and service model: contracts that reward uptime, safety and lifecycle performance—so localisation succeeds by reducing downtime, not by marketing.

Localisation in this area must be selective and standards-driven; the goal is resilience and performance, not autarky for its own sake.

Core Analysis

Strategic Importance: Resilience, Productivity, and Currency Discipline

Mining underpins Western Australia's export base and fiscal capacity. Yet core hardware and many critical components remain heavily import-dependent, with estimates indicating a significant majority (over 70%) of key equipment is imported, including the vast majority of haul trucks in a Pilbara fleet exceeding 1,500 units, incurring substantial annual procurement and lifecycle costs. Recent disruptions—most visibly in semiconductors and industrial electronics—demonstrated how quickly sensor and control-system bottlenecks can translate into operational delays.

This pillar treats mining as an industrial platform, not only an extractive sector. Strengthening domestic Mining Equipment, Technology and Services (METS) capability reduces exposure to shipping and geopolitical shocks, lowers inventory buffers, and keeps a greater share of value-add within the domestic economy. It also supports the macro-discipline implied by a currency-board style regime: fewer fragile import dependencies and a larger tradable industrial base improve national resilience when external conditions tighten.

Baseline Capability: Build from an existing METS foundation

The METS sector in Western Australia already contributes in the order of A$38 billion economically (with national METS at ~A$114 billion), supporting over 100,000 jobs in WA and multi-billion-dollar exports annually, with demonstrated strengths in software, automation, and digitally enabled blasting and logistics. The gap is concentrated in hardware and certified integration: heavy equipment, specialised modules, rugged electronics, and the testing/certification environments needed to deploy safety-critical parts at scale.

From 2031 onward, the strategic target remains practical: to achieve 50–70% domestic manufacture and assembly of mining equipment (by procurement value) by 2035–2040, with imports increasingly concentrated in genuinely niche components where local substitution is uneconomic or technically unjustified.

Program Architecture: Four Industrial Wedges

Heavy Mobile Equipment: Assemble First, Localise Fast

The high-leverage entry point is haulage and drilling equipment because volumes are large and maintenance demand is continuous. The staged pathway is:

- Licensed assembly and remanufacture (2031–2034): expand regional capacity to rebuild fleets domestically, shorten downtime, and accelerate parts availability.
- Progressive component localisation (2034–2040): localise high-weight and high-wear items (frames, trays, cabs, hydraulic assemblies, selected suspension and structural elements) supported by certified fabrication, non-destructive testing, and safety assurance.

Drilling, Blasting & Consumables: Localise Integration & Serviceability

Full replication of proprietary drilling and blasting ecosystems is rarely efficient. The goal is to localise what matters operationally: onshore integration of drill automation, sensing and timing systems; domestic manufacture of selected rig modules and consumables where feasible; and regional service capability that reduces dependence on global queues. Where major suppliers are willing, joint ventures and licensed builds can align commercial incentives with local resilience.

Sensors, Rugged Electronics & Controls: Reduce The Fragile Dependency

Modern mines are cyber-physical systems. Collision avoidance, grade control, fleet management, remote operations and predictive maintenance depend on sensors and control electronics that are often imported and difficult to substitute quickly. Western Australia does not need a consumer-electronics industry to de-risk this. It needs a focused capability to assemble and test rugged modules, manufacture housings and boards where economical, calibrate and certify components, and integrate secure firmware/software into operating systems. A Foundry precinct that combines heavy fabrication with electronics test and certification is the practical mechanism for achieving this without over-promising.

Exploration Acceleration: Shorten the Discovery Cycle

Self-sufficiency depends not only on operating existing mines, but on proving what can be developed next. From 2031–2036, the priority is to industrialise exploration throughput: drone and fixed-wing survey platforms (including electromagnetic and magnetic surveys), expanded core scanning and imaging, scaled assay capacity, and an integrated geodata workflow that allows geophysics, geochemistry, drill logs and core imagery to be interpreted together. The payoff is strategic as well as commercial: faster, more confident resource definition strengthens investment decisions, infrastructure planning and downstream processing options.

Costs & Financing (Order-of-Magnitude)

Indicative 2025 costings for a credible 2031–2040 build-out—two Foundry precincts, heavy-equipment assembly/remanufacture lines, rugged sensor/testing capacity, and scaled exploration tooling—sit in the order of A$4–8 billion in capital and establishment costs, with upside risk if localisation extends deeper into complex driveline and powertrain modules. A simple way to interpret the range is: heavy fleet assembly and remanufacture plus shared precinct infrastructure drive the largest share; rugged sensing/testing and exploration acceleration account for the remainder.

Early budgets are expected to be close to balance, so major capital initiatives must rely on discrete financing pathways rather than assumed surplus spending. The practical mix is: co-investment by miners and OEM partners (plant, tooling, licensing); availability-based service contracts that monetise predictable maintenance revenue; project finance for shared precinct infrastructure; and, where permitted within constitutional limits, limited and transparent sovereign credit enhancement aimed at lowering the cost of capital without converting the royalty stream into routine project funding.

Workforce & Social Licence

Capability scales only if it is trusted and staffed. The Foundry model should be anchored by training pipelines in trades, mechatronics, robotics maintenance and field service engineering, with certification fit for safety-critical deployments. Where precinct sites and exploration programs intersect with affected communities, consultation—including with Aboriginal groups where relevant—should be embedded in land-use planning and approvals.

Cross-Pillar Synergy

This pillar creates the industrial and technical base for later precision manufacturing and rugged electronics, provides a real-world testbed for autonomous systems that also serve the Defence pillar, and strengthens the feedstock pipeline for strategic stockpiles and downstream processing options.

Feasibility & Gating Conditions (2031+)

Delivery depends on four gating conditions: (1) a post-independence Mining Equipment and METS White Paper that maps import exposure and prioritises a small set of high-impact localisation targets; (2) investable partnerships with miners and OEMs for licensed assembly, technology transfer and after-sales support; (3) a standards, certification and liability framework enabling locally made parts in safety-critical environments; and (4) a Pilbara workforce plan that expands trades and mechatronics capacity. Practical delivery also requires bankable precinct sites (land, power, water, approvals) and procurement rules that reward availability and safety outcomes.

Sources

Unless otherwise stated, online materials were viewed on 4 February 2026.

1. Department of Energy, Mines, Industry Regulation and Safety (Western Australia), *Western Australian Mineral and Petroleum Statistics Digest 2023–24* (Report, 2024) <https://www.demirs.wa.gov.au/documents/Mineral_and_Petroleum_Statistics_Digest_2023-24.pdf>
2. Austmine, *METS Workforce STEM Skills and Female STEM Participation Benchmark Survey 2023* (Report, 2024) <https://austmine.com.au/Common/Uploaded%20files/Programs/AWIM%20Benchmark%20Study%202024.pdf>
3. CSIRO, *Mining Equipment, Technology and Services: A Roadmap for Unlocking Future Growth Opportunities for Australia* (Report, 2017) <https://www.csiro.au/-/media/Do-Business/Files/Futures/METSRoadmap.pdf>
4. Fortescue, *FY24 Annual Report* (Report, 2024) <https://content.fortescue.com/fortescue17114-fortescueeb60-productionbbdb-8be5/media/project/fortescueportal/shared/docs/default-source/announcements-and-reports/fy24-annual-report.pdf>
5. Orica, *FY2024 Annual Report* (Report, 2024) <https://www.orica.com/ArticleDocuments/303/FY2024%20Annual%20Report.pdf.aspx>
6. Curtin University, *CRC ORE Start-up Hub Joins Curtin's Kalgoorlie Campus* (Media Release, 17 September 2020) <https://www.curtin.edu.au/news/media-release/crc-ore-start-up-hub-joins-curtins-kalgoorlie-campus>
7. Australian Bureau of Statistics, *Australian Industry, 2023–24* (Catalogue No 8155.0, 2025) <https://www.abs.gov.au/statistics/industry/industry-overview/australian-industry/latest-release>
8. Deloitte Access Economics, *Mining and METS: Engines of Economic Growth and Prosperity for Australians* (Report, Minerals Council of Australia, 2017) <https://minerals.org.au/wp-content/uploads/2023/01/Mining-and-METS-engines-of-economic-growth-and-prosperity-for-Australians.pdf> Annotation: updated estimates referenced in 2025 industry analyses.
9. International Trade Administration (US Department of Commerce), *Australia—Mining* (Web Page, 2024) <https://www.trade.gov/country-commercial-guides/australia-mining>
10. Mining Weekly, 'WA resources sector injects record A$150bn into economy' (Article, March 25, 2025) <https://www.miningweekly.com/article/wa-resources-sector-injects-record-a150bn-into-economy-2025-03-25> Annotation: for economic scale implying costs.
11. Rio Tinto, 'Iron Ore Western Australia' (Web Page, 2024) <https://www.riotinto.com/en/operations/australia/pilbara> Annotation: for fleet size and autonomy, supporting >1,500 units.
12. Mine Magazine, 'Australia continues to dominate the use of autonomous haul trucks' (Article, June 2022, updated 2024) <https://mine.nridigital.com/mine_jun22/australia_autonomous_mining_trucks> Annotation: for autonomous truck counts, implying total fleet scale.
13. Wikipedia, '2020–2023 global chip shortage' (Encyclopedia Entry, updated 2026) <https://en.wikipedia.org/wiki/2020%E2%80%932023_global_chip_shortage> Annotation: for broad impact on industries.
14. Taylor & Francis, 'Semiconductor supply chain resilience and disruption: insights, mitigation, and future directions' (Journal Article, 2024) <https://www.tandfonline.com/doi/full/10.1080/00207543.2024.2387074> Annotation: for mining-relevant electronic disruptions.
15. Minerals Council of Australia, 'Mining and METS: engines of economic growth and prosperity for Australians' (Report, 2023, updated 2025) <https://minerals.org.au/wp-content/uploads/2023/01/Mining-and-METS-engines-of-economic-growth-and-prosperity-for-Australians.pdf> Annotation: for WA/Pilbara A$37.8B.

16. Mine Magazine, 'Space, METS and mining: unlocking the power of technology transfer in Australia' (Article, December 22, 2025) <https://mine.nridigital.com/mine_australia_dec25/space-mets-and-mining-unlocking-the-power-of-technology-transfer-in-australia> Annotation: for national METS $114B revenue, 200k jobs.

Pillar Two: Defence Manufacturing

Flagship Vision & What This Enables

Within the first decade of independence, Western Australia fields a compact but technologically dense defence manufacturing base centred on uncrewed systems. Long-endurance aerial drones patrol the northern approaches and offshore resource basins, maintaining persistent surveillance over gas fields and shipping lanes with electro-optical sensors and secure real-time data links to onshore command centres. Autonomous surface and sub-surface vessels monitor coastal waters, pipelines, and maritime chokepoints, equipped with modular sonar and sensor payloads that also support environmental monitoring. Uncrewed ground systems secure remote infrastructure and logistics corridors, operating continuously across vast terrain.

These platforms are assembled, integrated, upgraded, and sustained domestically, with design authority progressively migrating onshore. Four flagship system elements anchor this vision. First, a sovereign uncrewed aerial line: licensed assembly of medium-altitude long-endurance (MALE) platforms transitions to indigenous variants optimised for Western Australia's distances, climate, and maritime focus. Second, a maritime autonomy stack: uncrewed surface and sub-surface craft tailored for offshore patrol, infrastructure protection, and inspection. Third, a secure integration and test environment: domestic capability to integrate sensors, avionics, communications, and control software, enabling rapid upgrades without foreign approval. Fourth, deliberate civilian spin-offs: autonomy, sensing, and power-management technologies flow directly into mining logistics, agriculture, emergency response, and remote transport.

The industrial footprint is intentionally concentrated rather than diffuse. A small number of secure defence technology precincts—building on existing naval and maritime industrial capacity at Henderson—house final assembly, systems integration, environmental testing, and software validation. The scale is disciplined: a narrow set of high-leverage platforms produced in meaningful volume, sustained locally, and iterated continuously. The result is not a mass-army industry, but a resilient industrial core that supports national defence while multiplying capability across the wider economy.

Early capability depends on reliable technology partnerships and stable access to critical components during the transition to full domestic integration.

Core Analysis

Strategic Rationale: Security through Manufacturable Capability

Western Australia's security challenge is defined by geography: long coastlines, sparse population centres, and globally significant offshore and onshore resource infrastructure. Historically, the response has been reliance on imported platforms and foreign sustainment pipelines. That model embeds exposure to export controls, upgrade delays, and supply-chain shocks, even for allied states.

This pillar reframes defence manufacturing as manufacturable sovereignty. Rather than replicating the full spectrum of complex military hardware, Western Australia focuses on systems where domestic assembly, integration, and sustainment materially improve readiness: uncrewed aerial, maritime, and ground systems; mission-critical electronics; and software-defined capabilities. These systems offer persistent coverage at lower operating cost, can be upgraded rapidly, and are inherently dual-use.

Current Baseline & Capability Gap

Western Australia inherits limited defence industrial depth. While there is established naval sustainment and shipbuilding activity—particularly in the south-west—advanced defence platforms and uncrewed systems remain overwhelmingly imported. Design authority, mission-system integration, and software control are typically held offshore, constraining local adaptation and lifecycle resilience.

The gap to be closed is therefore not comprehensive component substitution, but control over integration and sustainment. Sovereign capability begins where platforms can be assembled, upgraded, and kept operational without external permission.

Industrial Focus: Uncrewed Systems as the Organising Principle

Uncrewed systems align defence necessity, industrial feasibility, and civilian spill-over.

Uncrewed aerial systems. Initial capability centres on MALE-class platforms suitable for maritime surveillance, border monitoring, and infrastructure protection. Licensed assembly and sustainment establish workforce competence in airframes, propulsion integration, avionics installation, and mission-system configuration. Indigenous variants then adapt payloads, endurance profiles, and communications architectures to local conditions.

Uncrewed maritime systems. Autonomous surface and sub-surface vessels provide continuous presence across offshore basins and shipping approaches. Domestic capability focuses on hull fabrication, propulsion integration, modular sensor packages (including sonar), and command-and-control software, enabling rapid adaptation for defence, environmental, and commercial inspection tasks.

Uncrewed ground and support systems. Autonomous ground vehicles support base security, remote logistics, and infrastructure inspection, while serving as testbeds for ruggedised autonomy applicable to mining and emergency services.

Across all domains, the emphasis remains systems integration rather than autarky. Engines, specialised sensors, or niche electronics may remain imported where substitution is inefficient, but final assembly, software control, mission integration, and sustainment are domestic.

Industrial Architecture & Workforce

Manufacturing activity is concentrated in a limited number of secure precincts with shared facilities for composite fabrication, electronics integration, environmental testing, and software validation. Co-location with research institutions and selected private partners supports rapid iteration while maintaining clear security boundaries.

Workforce development prioritises engineers, technicians, and software specialists with cross-domain skills—avionics, robotics maintenance, secure communications, and systems engineering. Training pathways are designed to be portable, allowing movement between defence projects and civilian industries as demand evolves.

Costs & Financing (Order-of-Magnitude)

Indicative 2025 costings for establishing a credible uncrewed-systems manufacturing and integration base—facilities, tooling, licensed production, test infrastructure, and workforce development—remain in the order of A$3–6 billion over the first decade. The lower bound reflects a narrow assembly-and-sustainment focus; the upper bound incorporates deeper design authority and expanded maritime autonomy capability.

Early national budgets are expected to be close to balance. Accordingly, capital investment proceeds via discrete financing pathways rather than assumed operating surpluses, combining staged public investment, co-investment with industrial partners, and project-specific financing aligned to capability milestones.

Civilian Spill-Overs & Export Discipline

Defence manufacturing is deliberately dual-use. Autonomy, sensing, power management, and secure communications developed here directly reinforce mining automation, offshore inspection, agriculture, disaster response, and remote logistics. Export activity, while secondary, provides scale and learning where consistent with national security constraints.

Cross-Pillar Synergy

Defence manufacturing acts as a technology catalyst for mining equipment localisation, smart transport, and high-tech innovation, providing a secure test environment for rugged autonomy and electronics that later pillars depend upon.

Feasibility & Gating Conditions (2031+)

Delivery depends on four conditions. First, a post-secession defence industry White Paper must prioritise a narrow set of uncrewed capabilities where domestic manufacture materially improves readiness. Second, licensed production and technology-transfer agreements with trusted partners must establish early competence without embedding long-term dependence. Third, standards, certification, and export-control frameworks must balance safety, liability, and international obligations while preserving domestic design authority. Fourth, workforce pipelines and security clearances must scale in step with facilities. Progress beyond initial assembly is contingent on demonstrated performance, cost discipline, and sustained demand from defence and aligned civilian users.

Sources

Unless otherwise stated, online materials were viewed on 4 February 2026.

1. Australian Government, *Defence Industry Development Strategy* (Report, 2024) <https://www.defence.gov.au/sites/default/files/2024-02/Defence-Industry-Development-Strategy.pdf>.
2. Australian Strategic Policy Institute, *Aligning for Advantage: Integrating Autonomous Systems into the Australian Defence Force* (Report, 2025) <https://www.aspi.org.au/report/aligning-for-advantage-integrating-autonomous-systems-into-the-australian-defence-force>.
3. US Department of Defence, *MQ-9 Reaper Fact Sheet* (Web Page, 2025) <https://www.af.mil/About-Us/Fact-Sheets/Display/Article/104470/mq-9-reaper>.
4. Austal Limited, *Annual Report 2025* (Report, 2025) <https://investor.austal.com/static-files/a95e03ed-7614-43fa-a084-5d24892764f7>.
5. *Boeing Defence Australia* (Web Page, 2025) <https://www.boeing.com.au/about-boeing-in-australia/subsidiaries/boeing-defence-australia>.
6. Society for Mining, Metallurgy & Exploration, *Critical and Strategic Minerals: Importance to the U.S. Economy and National Security* (Web Page, 2025) <https://www.smenet.org/What-We-Do/Technical-Briefings/Critical-and-Strategic-Minerals-Importance-to-the>.
7. The Defense Post, 'Greek Parliament Approves $400M MQ-9B SeaGuardian Drone Purchase' (Web Page, 8 July 2022) <https://thedefencepost.com/2022/07/08/greece-mq-9b-purchase>.
8. The Defense Post, 'Poland Buys MQ-9B Sky Guardian Drones for $310 Million' (Web Page, 17 December 2024) <https://thedefencepost.com/2024/12/17/poland-mq-9b-systems>.
9. Australian Bureau of Statistics, *Australian Industry, 2023-24* (Catalogue No 8155.0, 2024) <https://www.abs.gov.au/statistics/industry/industry-overview/australian-industry/latest-release>.
10. Government of Western Australia, *Western Australia Defence and Defence Industry Strategy 2025* (2025) <https://www.wa.gov.au/system/files/2025-01/wa_defence_and_defence_industry_strategy_2025_final.pdf>. Annotation: Highlights WA's strategic geography as a gateway to the Indo-Pacific, with challenges from vast distances, sparse population, and resource vulnerabilities, emphasising the need for localised defence manufacturing.
11. Australian Government, *Defence Strategic Review* (2023) <https://www.abc.net.au/news/2023-04-24/defence-strategic-review-identifies-wa-key-area-of-concern/102260636>. Annotation: Identifies WA's northern coast as a "primary area of military interest" due to geographic exposure, long coastlines, and resource infrastructure risks.
12. Australian Defence Magazine, 'Leidos Selected as Land 156 Systems Integrator' (2025) <https://www.australiandefence.com.au/defence/land/leidos-selected-as-land-156-systems-integrator>. Annotation: Notes $10 billion allocated in Australia's Integrated Investment Program for drone, counter-drone, and autonomous systems, plus $1.3 billion for acquisitions—aligns with multi-billion scale for establishing bases.
13. ASPI Strategist, 'Editors' Picks for 2025: Cost of Defence's Roadmap' (2025) <https://www.aspistrategist.org.au/editors-picks-for-2025-cost-of-defences-roadmap-for-spending-3-percent-of-gdp-on-defence>. Annotation: Recommends hundreds of millions to low billions for autonomous systems sustainment, workforce, and integration, supporting the estimate.
14. ASPI, *Aligning for Advantage: Integrating Autonomous Systems into the Australian Defence Force* (2025) <https://www.aspi.org.au/report/aligning-for-advantage-integrating-autonomous-systems-into-the-australian-defence-force>. Annotation: Recommends investment in land-domain autonomous systems for logistics and security, with emphasis on domestic integration.

Pillar Three: Energy Independence

Flagship Vision & What This Enables

By the mid-2030s, Western Australia operates a deliberately hybrid energy system anchored by firm offshore gas, large-scale floating solar generation, and grid-level storage, designed to deliver long-term price stability and system resilience rather than marginal optimisation.

A strategic 25% interest in the North West Shelf could secure approximately 10-15 million MMBtu of gas annually for domestic conversion, based on current production levels. When dispatched through modern combined-cycle turbines, this volume is capable of producing roughly 1,900 GWh of electricity per year at transparent cost-plus-CPI pricing in the range of AUD 0.10–0.15/kWh. Gas is processed through the Karratha Gas Plant and distributed via the Dampier-to-Bunbury Pipeline, feeding both the South West Interconnected System (SWIS) and the North West Interconnected System (NWIS), ensuring firm supply to Perth and the Pilbara.

This firm capacity is complemented by Floating Photovoltaic (FPV) installations on existing water bodies. FPV arrays deployed on Lake Argyle, Fitzroy River ring-tank reservoirs, and selected southern storages generate an estimated 1,000–2,000 GWh annually—sufficient to fully supply Broome's electricity demand and meet a material share of Perth's residential load without competing for land or urban space.

Grid-scale storage underpins reliability. Ten 100 MWh lithium-ion battery installations absorb surplus daytime generation, provide frequency control and reserve margin, and sustain system performance during peaks, outages, or extreme weather, supporting near-continuous reliability. Targeted upgrades to approximately 500 km of 220 kV transmission links strengthen north–south interconnection while preserving islandable operation for remote regions.

An integrated digital control layer—using AI-enabled supervisory control and data acquisition systems—optimises dispatch across gas, solar, and storage assets, reducing transmission losses to the low single-digit range and extending asset life. The result is a power system capable of supporting mining, water conveyance, agricultural processing, and manufacturing at scale, without structural exposure to imported electricity or short-term market volatility.

Delivery depends on regulatory approvals and environmental clearances proceeding in parallel with technical and commercial readiness.

Core Analysis

Strategic Importance: Resilience, Productivity & Currency Discipline

Energy independence addresses a structural vulnerability in Western Australia's economy. Despite being a major gas exporter, domestic electricity supply remains exposed to infrastructure constraints, market design, and export-linked volatility. Natural gas accounts for a substantial share of generation, yet the majority of production is exported as LNG, leaving domestic users sensitive to outages and price movements beyond local control.

Securing firm domestic supply at predictable cost reduces exposure to external shocks, stabilises household and industrial energy bills, and strengthens macro-economic resilience under a currency-board regime. By lowering imported input volatility and improving certainty for energy-intensive sectors, the energy system becomes an enabling platform for tradable production rather than a constraint.

Baseline Capability: Strong Assets, Weak Domestic Prioritisation

Western Australia enters independence with significant inherited advantages. The North West Shelf, Gorgon, and Wheatstone projects provide large-scale gas production processed through existing onshore facilities and pipelines. Current electricity demand is approximately 5,000 GWh per year for households and 12,000–15,000 GWh for industry. Solar resources in the Pilbara and Kimberley are among the strongest in the world, supporting high-capacity-factor FPV deployment on existing reservoirs.

The gap is not resource availability, but domestic allocation, grid integration, and long-term price discipline. Residential electricity prices remain materially above production-cost benchmarks, and current infrastructure was not designed for large north–south energy flows or hybrid system optimisation. From 2031 onward, the strategic objective is to achieve high-coverage hybrid supply for population centres and major industrial users, subject to feasibility and approvals.

Program Architecture: Four System Wedges

1. Gas Acquisition & Distribution

A minority equity position in the North West Shelf secures a defined domestic entitlement without displacing export operations. Gas is processed at Karratha and distributed through existing pipeline networks, with Gorgon and Wheatstone providing redundancy. Only a portion of the secured volume is required for domestic electricity, preserving export revenues while guaranteeing supply security.

2. Floating Photovoltaic Deployment

FPV systems on Lake Argyle, Fitzroy ring-tank reservoirs, and southern storages deliver large-scale solar generation without land-use conflict. Output aligns closely with daytime industrial and water-pumping demand, reducing reliance on gas during peak solar hours.

3. Storage & Transmission Upgrades

Battery installations provide firming, reserve capacity, and frequency control. Targeted transmission upgrades strengthen interconnection between NWIS and SWIS while enabling microgrids to operate independently when required.

4. Smart System Control

Digital optimisation integrates generation and storage assets into a single operational system, improving efficiency, reducing losses, and enhancing resilience across vast distances.

Costs & Financing (Order-of-Magnitude)

Indicative 2025 costings for a 2031–2040 build-out—including offshore gas equity, FPV generation, storage, and transmission upgrades—fall in the order of AUD 5–10 billion. Offshore equity acquisition represents the largest component, with modular FPV, storage, and grid upgrades accounting for the remainder.

Early national budgets are expected to operate close to balance; accordingly, these investments require discrete sovereign or project-level financing pathways and staged deployment aligned to demand growth and project readiness.

Workforce & Social Licence

Delivery requires skilled engineering, construction, and operations capability, supporting several thousand jobs across the build-out period. Training pipelines in electrical systems, grid operations, and renewable integration are essential. Where projects intersect with communities, including Aboriginal groups, consultation should be embedded early to secure durable social licence and avoid downstream delays.

Cross-Pillar Synergy

Energy independence underpins large-scale water pumping and FPV integration in Pillar Four, mining automation and processing in Pillar One, and resilient logistics and defence readiness across subsequent pillars.

Feasibility & Gating Conditions (2031+)

Delivery depends on: (1) a post-secession Energy White Paper defining domestic supply obligations, pricing principles, and system governance; (2) investable commercial arrangements for offshore gas equity and long-term offtake; (3) bankable transmission, storage, and FPV project designs with approvals in place; and (4) scalable system-operation and digital control capability. Meaningful program commencement is not expected before 2031, with expansion phased through the mid-2030s subject to feasibility, approvals, and financing readiness.

Sources

Unless otherwise stated, online materials were viewed on 4 February 2026.

1. Australian Government Department of Industry, Science and Resources, *Petroleum Resource Rent Tax: Review of Gas Transfer Pricing Arrangements* (Final Report, May 2023) <https://treasury.gov.au/sites/default/files/2023-05/p2023-388153.pdf>.
2. Australian Taxation Office, *PRRT Updates* (Web Page) <https://www.ato.gov.au/businesses-and-organisations/gst-excise-and-indirect-taxes/petroleum-resource-rent-tax/prrt-updates>.
3. Australia Institute, 'What is the PRRT?' (Blog Post, 2024) <https://australiainstitute.org.au/post/what-is-the-prrt/>.
4. Australian Energy Regulator, *Wholesale—Industry Charts* (Web Page) <https://www.aer.gov.au/industry/wholesale/charts>.
5. Bluetti Power, 'Average Electricity Costs Per kWh (By State)' (Blog Post) <https://www.bluettipower.com.au/blogs/home-backup/average-electricity-costs-per-kwh-by-state>.
6. Finder, *Average Cost of Electricity Per kWh in Australia* (Web Page, 2025) <https://www.finder.com.au/energy/electricity/average-cost-of-electricity>.
7. Jackery, 'What Is The Electricity Cost Per kWh in Australia?' (Blog Post, 2024) <https://au.jackery.com/blogs/knowledge/electricity-cost-per-kwh-australia>.

8. Australian Energy Regulator, *Final Determination on 2025–26 Safety Net Prices for NSW, SA and SE QLD* (Report, 2025) <https://www.aer.gov.au/news/articles/news-releases/final-determination-2025-26-safety-net-prices-nsw-sa-and-se-qld>.
9. Mining Data Online, *Powering a Sustainable Energy Future—Pilbara Minerals Annual Report* (Report, 2024) <https://minedocs.com/27/Pilbara-Minerals-AR-06302024.pdf>.
10. Climate Energy Finance, *Accelerating the Electrification & Decarbonisation of the Pilbara* (Report, August 2024) <https://climateenergyfinance.org/wp-content/uploads/2024/08/CEF_FINAL_Pilbara-Electrification-Report_13Aug2024.pdf>.
11. Economic Regulation Authority Western Australia, *Overview of Horizon Power's Network and Customers in the Pilbara* (Report) <https://www.erawa.com.au/sites/default/files/22136/Horizon-Power---background-on-network-and-customers-for-ringfencing-for-publication-.PDF>.
12. Rio Tinto, *Annual Report* (Report, 2023) <https://www.riotinto.com/en/invest/reports/annual-report>.
13. The Guardian, 'North West Shelf Gas Extension Will Deliver "Almost Nothing" to Australia' (Article, 1 June 2025) <https://www.theguardian.com/australia-news/2025/jun/01/north-west-shelf-gas-extension-australia-lng-woodside-project-little-rent-tax>.
14. ABC News, 'Budget Reveals WA Oil and Gas Royalties Shrinking as North West Shelf Winds Down' (Article, 21 June 2025) <https://www.abc.net.au/news/2025-06-21/wa-gas-royalties-shrinking-state-budget/103879272>.
15. Science Direct, 'Decision-Making on the Integration of Renewable Energy in the Mining Industry' (Article, 2017) <https://www.sciencedirect.com/science/article/pii/S2300396017300952>.
16. Solargis, *Solar Resource Maps of Australia* (2021) <https://solargis.com/resources/free-maps-and-gis-data?locality=australia>. Annotation: supports high solar potential in Pilbara/Kimberley.
17. CSIRO, *GenCost 2024-25 Final Report* (2025) <https://www.csiro.au/en/research/technology-space/energy/Electricity-transition/GenCost>. Annotation: supports hybrid systems with gas, solar, and storage as lowest-cost path.
18. Woodside Energy, *Fourth Quarter Report 2025* (2026) <https://www.woodside.com/docs/default-source/investor-documents/quarterly-and-half-yearly-pdfs-and-data-tables/2025/004-fourth-quarter-2025-report.pdf>. Annotation: details NWS production at ~23,756 Mboe/year, convertible to gas volumes.
19. Geoscience Australia, *Australia's Energy Commodity Resources 2025—Gas* (2025) <https://www.ga.gov.au/aecr2025/gas>. Annotation: North West Shelf conventional gas ~4,193 PJ/year total, with domestic allocation.
20. CSIRO, *GenCost 2024-25* (2025) <https://www.windenergy.org.nz/wp-content/uploads/2025/07/GenCost-2024-25-Final_20250728.pdf>. Annotation: CCGT costs ~AUD 0.10-0.20/kWh; battery costs fell 11-16% in 2025; ~AUD 200-300/kWh for grid-scale.
21. Thunder Said Energy, *Gas to Power Project Economics* (2025) <https://thundersaidenergy.com/downloads/gas-to-power-project-economics>. Annotation: 8c/kWh USD for CCGT at 55% efficiency.
22. Woodside Energy, *North West Shelf Project* (2025) <https://www.woodside.com/what-we-do/operations/north-west-shelf>. Annotation: KGP capacity 14.3 Mtpa LNG + domestic.
23. Australian Gas Infrastructure Group, *Dampier Bunbury Pipeline* (2025) <https://www.agig.com.au/the-pipeline>. Annotation: capacity 845 TJ/day, ~308 PJ/year.
24. The Energy, 'Unlocking Australia's Floating Photovoltaic Potential' (2025) <https://theenergy.co/article/unlocking-australias-floating-photovoltaic-potential>. Annotation: FPV on reservoirs like Lake Argyle.
25. Global Solar Atlas, *Map for Australia* (2025) <https://globalsolaratlas.info/map?c=-28.43289%2C133.4%2C4&r=AUS>. Annotation: GHI 5.5-6.5 kWh/m^2/day in Kimberley/Pilbara.
26. Western Australian Government, *SWIS Transmission Plan* (2025) <https://www.wa.gov.au/government/media-statements/Cook%20Labor%20Government/SWIS-Transmission-Plan-to-make-WA-a-renewable-energy-powerhouse-20250918>. Annotation: upgrades to unlock 2 GW renewables.
27. AEMO, *Forecasting Western Australia's Electricity Consumption Trends* (2025) <https://www.aemo.com.au/Media-Centre/-/media/88121E9D76EB43D4A81775A2F4DCB9CB.ashx>. Annotation: residential ~5,144 GWh.

28. Clean Energy Council, 'WA's Energy Transformation' (2025) <https://stockhead.com.au/energy/was-energy-transformation-is-underway-but-theres-still-much-that-needs-doing>. Annotation: additional 10 TWh needed by 2031, implying total ~20-25 TWh.
29. Bureau of Meteorology, *Average Daily Solar Exposure Maps* (2025) <https://www.bom.gov.au/climate/maps/averages/solar-exposure>. Annotation: Pilbara/Kimberley >6 kWh/m^2/day average.
30. Ember, 'How Cheap is Battery Storage?' (2025) <https://ember-energy.org/latest-insights/how-cheap-is-battery-storage>. Annotation: ~AUD 200/kWh grid-scale.
31. ResearchGate, 'Floating Photovoltaic Solar in Australia' (2024) <https://www.researchgate.net/publication/386490879_Floating_Photovoltaic_Solar_in_Australia-A_Feasibility_Study>. Annotation: FPV costs ~20-45% above ground PV, ~AUD 1.5-2/W.

Pillar Four: Water to Wealth—Western Australia's Food Future

West Kimberly region

Flagship Vision & What This Enables

Each wet season, large-scale capture works in the Kimberley—centred on expansion of the Ord system and new off-stream storages on major northern rivers such as the Fitzroy—intercept and store on the order of 3 billion cubic meters of water per year without continuous river damming. Water is conveyed southward through a long-distance buried pipeline and regulated channels into a network of inland and southern reservoirs, where floating photovoltaic (FPV) arrays covering on the order of 50–100 square kilometers both generate power (hundreds of megawatts at system scale) and materially reduce evaporation losses. The combined effect is to shift water storage into cooler climates, stabilise supply year-round, and power pumping and processing loads without imposing volatile operating costs.

This system underwrites three tangible national capabilities. First, domestic food security: Western Australia supplies the bulk of its own fruit, vegetables, grains, pulses, and protein, sharply reducing dependence on long interstate supply chains. Second, industrial provisioning: irrigated production reliably services remote mining towns and workforce hubs that currently rely on high-cost flown-in food. Third, export resilience: surplus output—particularly high-value horticulture and processed foods—is channelled through northern ports into Asian markets, supporting a diversified export base alongside resources.

Four system elements make the vision concrete.

- Monsoonal water capture and storage using off-river harvesting, seasonal detention basins, and expanded managed storages to intercept wet-season flows that currently discharge unused to the sea.
- Long-distance conveyance corridors, combining gravity-assisted channels where topography allows with pumped pipelines powered by co-located energy systems, linking northern catchments to inland agricultural zones.
- Large-scale irrigated precincts designed around modern water-efficient methods—drip, subsurface, and precision pivots—matched to soil and climate conditions rather than uniform crop assumptions.
- Integrated logistics and processing hubs near production zones, reducing spoilage, stabilising prices, and enabling value-added exports rather than bulk raw shipment.

The scale is deliberate: not a boutique irrigation scheme, but a system large enough to materially reshape Western Australia's food balance. Such a transformation requires careful hydrological design and staged delivery to avoid ecological harm and stranded assets.

Core Analysis

Strategic Importance: Food, Water & Sovereign Resilience

Food systems are a strategic vulnerability for geographically vast jurisdictions with sparse populations and long supply chains. Western Australia produces significant agricultural output, yet remains structurally dependent on interstate imports for many fresh foods, particularly horticulture. Disruptions—whether from transport failures, climate shocks, or industrial action—translate quickly into price volatility and shortages, especially in remote regions.

Water availability is the binding constraint. While the south-west has experienced declining rainfall and tighter water balances, northern Western Australia receives some of the highest seasonal rainfall in Australia. Most of this monsoonal flow is not captured for productive use. The strategic proposition of this pillar is straightforward: reallocate water abundance to water scarcity, using modern conveyance and storage methods, and in doing so convert a climatic asymmetry into a national asset.

This is not a claim that water alone creates prosperity. Rather, reliable water is the enabling input that allows land, labour, capital, and logistics to combine into a food system that is resilient at national scale.

Current Agricultural Baseline & Constraints

Western Australia's agricultural sector is highly productive in grains and livestock, with established export capability. Horticulture, by contrast, is more geographically concentrated and water-limited. Much of the WA's fresh produce is imported from eastern Australia, despite long transport distances and high logistics costs. Remote mining operations rely heavily on flown or trucked food, with limited local supply.

Water infrastructure reflects this history. Major irrigation assets are fragmented, often tied to single catchments, and insufficiently scaled to support broad diversification into irrigated crops across multiple regions. Where water is available, it is frequently constrained by storage capacity rather than rainfall itself.

Water Capture: Scale without River Damming

The northern monsoon delivers intense seasonal flows across multiple river systems. The core design principle is to capture a fraction of peak flows without permanently obstructing river courses. Techniques include off-stream storages filled during flood events, controlled diversion weirs, floodplain harvesting, and expanded reservoirs where environmental conditions permit.

At a target order of magnitude of ~3 billion cubic metres per year, the system remains well below total monsoonal discharge volumes, focusing on episodic surplus rather than base flows. Storage design prioritises evaporation minimisation, sediment management, and staged expansion rather than single megastructures.

Conveyance: Linking North to Inland & Mid-West

Capturing water is only the first step. The second is conveyance across long distances to agricultural land that can productively use it. The concept is a north–south and north-east water spine, built incrementally, linking capture zones to inland farming districts.

Where terrain permits, gravity-assisted channels reduce energy intensity. Elsewhere, pumped pipelines are required. Energy demand is significant but predictable, allowing integration with dedicated power systems co-located along the corridor. Conveyance is designed as a multi-user asset: agriculture is the anchor tenant, but towns, industry, and emergency supply also benefit.

Irrigated Precincts: Matching Water to Land Capability

The objective is not blanket irrigation, but strategic precincts selected for soil quality, climate suitability, proximity to transport, and workforce availability. Northern and inland zones support tropical and sub-tropical crops; mid-western districts expand into higher-value horticulture and fodder; integrated systems support livestock finishing closer to processing.

Modern irrigation methods sharply reduce water intensity per unit of output compared with historical schemes. Precision delivery enables crop diversification without proportionate increases in water demand, improving resilience to seasonal variability.

At full scale, irrigated precincts support a diversified production mix rather than monoculture. In northern and sub-tropical zones, high-value horticulture (including citrus and tree crops) typically achieves tens of tonnes per hectare under modern drip systems, while inland and mid-western districts support irrigated grains and fodder in the mid-single to low-double-digit tonnes per hectare range depending on crop and season. These ranges are indicative, but they demonstrate that the envisaged water volumes are sufficient to shift Western Australia from marginal supplementation to material domestic provisioning and export surplus.

Food Security & Price Stability

With expanded domestic production, Western Australia reduces exposure to interstate price shocks and transport bottlenecks. Shorter supply chains lower spoilage and logistics costs, contributing to more stable retail prices. For remote communities and industrial hubs, local supply replaces high-cost imports, improving both affordability and reliability.

The scale envisaged—hundreds of thousands of irrigated hectares—does not eliminate all imports, but materially shifts the balance toward domestic self-provisioning.

Exports & Value-Added Processing

Surplus production creates an export platform distinct from bulk grains. High-value horticulture, processed foods, and specialised products are routed through northern ports into nearby Asian markets. Processing close to production reduces freight intensity and increases value retention within the nation.

Indicative modelling suggests A$4–6 billion per year in agricultural and food exports once systems mature, depending on crop mix and market access. These figures are not commitments but illustrate the order of magnitude required for the pillar to matter at national scale.

Costs & Financing (Order-of-Magnitude)

A system of this scale is capital-intensive. Indicative 2025 cost ranges for capture works, major storages, conveyance corridors, and initial irrigated precincts sit in the order of A$15–25 billion, depending on routing, storage choices, and staging. Conveyance infrastructure accounts for the largest share; on-farm irrigation and processing are increasingly co-funded by private operators.

FPV integration materially offsets operating costs by reducing evaporation and supplying a significant share of pumping and processing energy, improving whole-of-system economics without relying on separate energy infrastructure.

Early national budgets are expected to be close to balance, so delivery relies on separate sovereign financing pathways and private co-investment, sequenced over time, rather than assumed operating surpluses. Comparable long-distance water projects internationally demonstrate that staged delivery and anchor-tenant contracting are critical to cost control.

Environmental & Stakeholder Considerations

Large-scale water reallocation requires rigorous environmental management. Flow interception must protect river health, wetlands, and downstream ecosystems. Adaptive operating rules, continuous monitoring, and staged expansion reduce ecological risk.

Land access and planning necessarily involve consultation with affected communities, including Aboriginal stakeholders, to ensure participation and compliance with land-use frameworks. The pillar proceeds on the basis that consultation is a condition of legitimacy, not an afterthought.

Cross-Pillar Synergy

This pillar reinforces Energy Independence through predictable power demand for pumping and storage, supports Smart Transport via stabilised freight volumes, and underpins Strategic Stockpiles by enabling domestic food reserves. Reliable water also increases the viability of downstream processing envisioned in other pillars.

Feasibility & Gating Conditions (2031+)

Implementation is contingent on four gating conditions. First, post-secession White Papers must confirm hydrological feasibility, environmental limits, and priority corridors. Second, detailed engineering and routing studies are required to prevent cost escalation and stranded assets. Third, bankable financing structures—combining sovereign issuance, project finance, and private co-investment—must be secured within constitutional debt constraints. Fourth, regulatory approvals and land-use agreements, including stakeholder consultation, must be completed before construction. Meaningful program commencement is therefore no earlier than 2031, with staged delivery over subsequent decades.

Sources

Unless otherwise stated, online materials were viewed on 4 February 2026.

1. Bureau of Meteorology, *Climate Statistics for Kimberley* (Web Page, 2024) <http://www.bom.gov.au/climate/averages/tables/cw_002014.shtml>.
2. Bureau of Meteorology, *Western Australia Summary* (Web Page, 2024) <http://www.bom.gov.au/climate/current/annual/wa/summary.shtml>.
3. DPIRD, *Evaporation Data* (Web Page, 2023) <https://library.dpird.wa.gov.au/cgi/viewcontent.cgi?article=1058&context=rmtr>.
4. CSIRO, *Fitzroy Catchment Assessment* (Report, 2018) <https://www.csiro.au/-/media/Environment/Water/NAWRA/Fitzroy-Catchment/NAWRA-Catchment-Report---Fitzroy-preamble---FINAL.pdf>.

5. Carlos R Hofer et al, 'Effects of a Floating Photovoltaic System on the Water Evaporation Rate in the Passaúna Reservoir, Brazil' (2022) 15(17) *Energies* 6274 <https://www.mdpi.com/1996-1073/15/17/6274>.
6. Wikipedia, *Lake Argyle* (Web Page, 2025) <https://en.wikipedia.org/wiki/Lake_Argyle>.
7. Government of Western Australia, *Fitzroy River Hydrology* (Report, 2023) <https://www.wa.gov.au/system/files/2023-10/hydrology-of-the-fitzroy-river.pdf>.
8. Australian Government, Department of Agriculture, Water and the Environment, *Water Infrastructure Options* (Report, 2021) <https://www.agriculture.gov.au/sites/default/files/documents/water-infrastructure-options.pdf>.
9. CSIRO, *Water Resource Assessment for the Fitzroy Catchment* (Report, 2018) <https://publications.csiro.au/publications#publication/PIcsiro:EP2023-4968/RI11/RT27>.
10. Government of Western Australia, *Options for Bringing Water to Perth from the Kimberley* (Report, 2023) <https://www.wa.gov.au/system/files/2023-06/options-for-bringing-water-to-perth-from-the-kimberley.pdf>.
11. The West Australian, 'Kimberley Pipeline Costs' (Article, 2011) <https://thewest.com.au/news/wa/cost-ruled-out-all-kimberley-plans-ng-ya-173903>.
12. Government of Western Australia, *Ord Surface Water Allocation Plan* (Report, 2022) <https://www.wa.gov.au/system/files/2022-07/Ord-surface-water-allocation-plan.pdf>.
13. Ricardo, 'Queensland's Water Infrastructure Pipeline' (Article, undated) <https://www.ricardo.com/en/news-and-insights/industry-insights/queenslands-water-infrastructure-pipeline-is-gaining-momentum>.
14. DPIRD, *Soil Management* (Web Page, 2023) <https://www.dpird.wa.gov.au/environment-and-sustainability/soils/managing-soils/>.
15. CSIRO, *Soil Mapping* (Web Page, 2023) <https://www.csiro.au/en/research/natural-environment/land/soil-mapping-land-suitability>.
16. Office of the Auditor General, *Ord-East Kimberley Development* (Report, 2016) <https://audit.wa.gov.au/wp-content/uploads/2016/09/report2016_20-OrdEastKimberley.pdf>.
17. IRENA, *Floating Photovoltaics* (Report, 2023) <https://www.irena.org/Publications/2023/Jul/Floating-Photovoltaics>.
18. Energy Matters, 'FPV Efficiency' (Article, 2023) <https://www.energymatters.com.au/renewable-news/floating-solar-farms-the-potential-of-water-based-solar-energy/>.
19. pv magazine Australia, 'SA Water Solar' (Article, 2020) <https://www.pv-magazine-australia.com/2020/12/24/sa-water-makes-splash-with-worlds-biggest-portable-solar-farm/>.
20. ABC News, 'Australian-First Floating Solar Farm Due to Begin Construction in SA' (Article, 2015) <https://www.abc.net.au/news/2015-03-05/australian-first-floating-solar-farm-for-sa/6281374>.
21. CSIRO, *Solar Radiometer Network* (Web Page, undated) <https://www.csiro.au/en/research/natural-environment/climate/Solar-radiometer-network>.
22. Government of Western Australia, *Ord M1 Channel Upgrades* (Web Page, undated) <https://www.watercorporation.com.au/outages-and-works/ongoing-works/ord-m1-channel-upgrades>.
23. DAFF, *Agricultural Outlook* (Report, 2025) <https://www.agriculture.gov.au/abares/research-topics/agricultural-outlook>.
24. The Australia Institute, *Ord River Costs* (Report, 2020) <https://australiainstitute.org.au/wp-content/uploads/2020/12/P309-Dam-the-expense-Ord-River-report-FINAL.3_0.pdf>.
25. DAFF, *Snapshot of Australian Agriculture* (Report, 2025) <https://www.agriculture.gov.au/abares/products/insights/snapshot-of-australian-agriculture>.
26. WA DMIRS, *Mineral Statistics* (Report, 2023) <https://www.wa.gov.au/government/publications/western-australian-mineral-and-petroleum-statistics-digest-2023-2024>.
27. ABC News, 'Fitzroy River Water Licensing' (Article, 2023) <https://www.abc.net.au/news/2023-12-10/fitzroy-river-water-licensing-debate-kimberley/103146542>.
28. DPIRD, *Ord Expansion Project* (Web Page, undated) <https://www.dpird.wa.gov.au/regional-communities/major-projects/ord-expansion-project>.

29. Essential Services Commission, *Melbourne Water 2026 Price Submission* (Report, 2025) <https://www.esc.vic.gov.au/sites/default/files/documents/Melbourne-Water-price-review-2026-submission-20251001_0.pdf>.
30. ANZ, *Australian Major Projects Pipeline* (Report, 2025) <https://publications.anz.com/SingletrackCMS__DownloadDocument?docRef=aa0290fd-d793-4934-9e98-baba844bd1d8&jobRef=313cb483-b215-417e-ba0a-abdbe10b3472&uid=99702b34-f49e-4c62-b4d0-ba0205338c02>.
31. pv magazine Australia, 'Research Provides Cost Benchmarking for Offshore Floating Solar' (Article, 2025) <https://www.pv-magazine-australia.com/2025/12/08/research-provides-cost-benchmarking-for-offshore-floating-solar>.
32. IEA-PVPS, *Floating PV Plants Review 2025* (Report, 2025) <https://iea-pvps.org/key-topics/t13-floating-pv-plants-review-2025>.
33. DAFF, *Australian Crop Report September 2025* (Report, 2025) <https://www.agriculture.gov.au/abares/research-topics/agricultural-outlook/australian-crop-report/september-2025>.
34. Grain Central, 'Year in Review Highlights Defining Sales' (Article, 2025) <https://www.graincentral.com/property/year-in-review-highlights-defining-sales-across-australia>.
35. National Water Grid Authority, *Ord River Expansion to the Northern Territory Detailed Business Case* (Web Page, undated) <https://www.nationalwatergrid.gov.au/projects/ord-river-expansion-nt-detailed-business-case>.
36. ScienceDirect, 'Yield Gains of Irrigated Crops in Australia' (Article, 2022) <https://www.sciencedirect.com/science/article/pii/S2666049022000706>.
37. EGUsphere, 'A Bio-Economic Approach for Predicting Monthly Irrigation Water Demands' (Preprint, 2026) <https://egusphere.copernicus.org/preprints/2026/egusphere-2025-6181/egusphere-2025-6181.pdf>.
38. The Energy, 'Unlocking Australia's Floating Photovoltaic Potential' (Article, 2025) <https://theenergy.co/article/unlocking-australias-floating-photovoltaic-potential>.
39. Renew Economy, 'Solar Prices Are Going Up in 2026' (Article, undated) <https://reneweconomy.com.au/ignore-your-algorithm-solar-prices-are-going-up-in-2026-but-its-not-a-crisis/amp>.
40. ScienceDirect, 'Economic Comparison of Floating Photovoltaic Systems' (Article, undated) <https://www.sciencedirect.com/science/article/pii/S0973082623001400>.
41. LinkedIn, 'Competitive Landscape Analysis: Innovations in the Floating Photovoltaics (FPV) Market' (Article, undated) <https://www.linkedin.com/pulse/competitive-landscape-analysis-innovations-thefloating-v8ksf>.

Pillar Five: Healthcare & Electronics

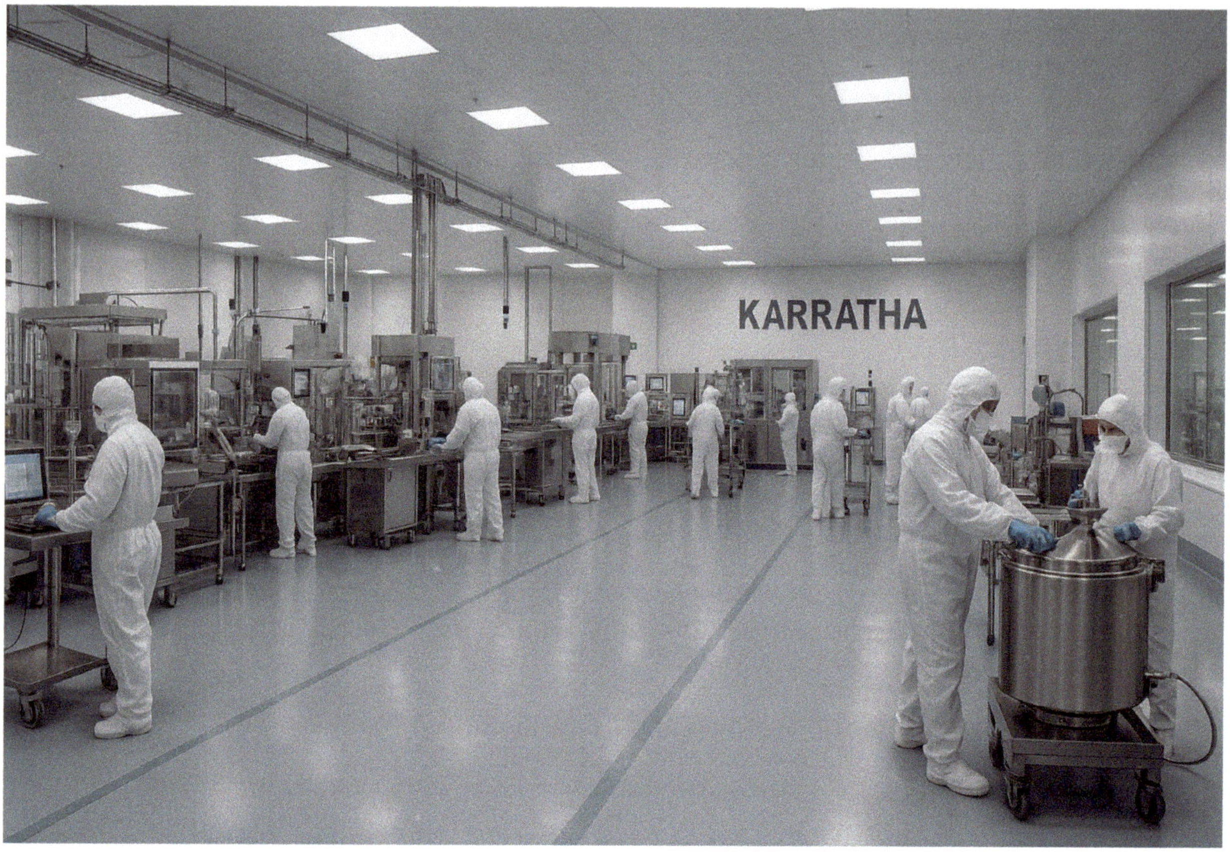

Flagship Vision & What This Enables

By the mid-2030s, Western Australia operates a tightly integrated health-and-electronics backbone that ensures essential medicines, medical devices, and critical electronics remain available even during global disruption. A national biomanufacturing park produces a defined list of high-priority generics, antibiotics, insulin, biologics, and sterile injectables onshore, while regional medical-device hubs assemble diagnostics, patient monitors, and core consumables such as PPE, syringes, and disposables suited to remote and tropical conditions. At the centre sits LoPax-7: a sovereign semiconductor fabrication facility focused on resilient, industrial-grade chips for medical and infrastructure use rather than mass consumer electronics.

Together, these systems enable four concrete capabilities. First, uninterrupted clinical supply: life-sustaining medicines and consumables are produced locally and distributed through hardened logistics, including cold-chain drone delivery to remote communities. Second, resilient care infrastructure: hospitals, laboratories, and emergency services rely on locally produced sensors, controllers, and power electronics designed for harsh environments and electromagnetic resilience. Third, secure digital health: sovereign data platforms support telehealth, diagnostics, and inventory control without dependence on foreign infrastructure. Fourth, export-ready medical technology: specialised devices and components developed for domestic needs scale into regional markets with similar operating conditions.

The program must prioritise resilience and reliability over breadth, selecting technologies where domestic control materially improves outcomes rather than attempting comprehensive substitution.

Core Analysis

Strategic Problem: Health & Electronics as Single-Point Vulnerabilities

Western Australia's service delivery is strong, yet its underlying supply chains are fragile. Medicines, medical devices, and advanced electronics are predominantly imported, exposing the population to delays, shortages, and price shocks during pandemics, shipping disruptions, or geopolitical tension. In 2023–24, Australia imported approximately A$17 billion in pharmaceuticals and around A$7–8 billion in medical instruments and devices, with Western Australia bearing a proportional share. Recent disruptions saw hundreds of medicines listed as in shortage nationally, illustrating how quickly external bottlenecks can impair routine care, diagnostics, and emergency response.

This pillar treats healthcare and electronics as sovereign infrastructure. The objective is not isolation, but assured access to a defined set of critical inputs that underpin population health, emergency response, and the wider industrial system. Reducing import dependence in these categories also lowers foreign-exchange exposure and stabilises operating costs across multiple sectors.

Program Architecture: Three Mutually Reinforcing Platforms

Biomanufacturing for Essential Medicines

The first platform is a national biomanufacturing park producing an essential medicines list: high-volume generics, selected biologics, vaccines, and sterile injectables with clear public-health importance. The focus is on process reliability, quality assurance, and surge capacity rather than novelty. Modular production lines allow rapid scale-up in emergencies, while routine output supplies hospitals, clinics, and strategic stockpiles.

Locating production domestically shortens supply chains, reduces exposure to export bans, and improves visibility over inputs and inventories. It also supports regional clinical trials and translational research by linking manufacturing directly to local health services.

Medical Devices & Distributed Fabrication

The second platform is a network of device-assembly and electronics-integration hubs producing patient monitors, diagnostics, laboratory equipment, PPE, syringes, and selected disposable devices. These facilities do not attempt full upstream component replication. Instead, they integrate locally produced housings, power systems, and control boards with imported specialist components where substitution is inefficient.

This approach improves maintainability and adaptability. Devices can be repaired, upgraded, or repurposed locally, reducing downtime in regional hospitals and mining camps. Design standards prioritise robustness, serviceability, and interoperability with telehealth systems.

Lopax-7 & Resilient Electronics

The third platform is LoPax-7, a semiconductor fabrication facility oriented toward industrial and medical nodes rather than consumer volumes. The emphasis is on resilient chips for sensors, controllers, communications modules, and power management—components that keep hospitals, laboratories, energy systems, and logistics operating under stress.

By anchoring electronics sovereignty at this level, Western Australia reduces dependence on long global supply chains for components that are small in unit cost but critical in function. The facility also provides a domestic test and certification environment, allowing medical and industrial devices to be validated end-to-end within one jurisdiction.

Targets & Economic Scale

Across these platforms, the practical ambition is to substitute approximately 30–50% of critical imports in medicines, medical devices, and essential electronics by the late 2030s, concentrating first on items with high clinical or operational impact. Even partial achievement materially improves resilience before full self-sufficiency is reached, while creating a base for specialised medical technology exports.

Workforce & Capability

The industrial footprint supports high-skill employment in bioprocessing, electronics engineering, quality assurance, and systems integration, on the order of several thousand specialised roles across manufacturing, validation, and sustainment, with training pipelines aligned to health services and adjacent industries.

Costs & Financing (Order-of-Magnitude)

Indicative 2025 costings for a credible 2031–2038 build-out sit in the order of A$6–9 billion in capital and establishment costs. The largest single component is LoPax-7, estimated at A$2–3 billion, with the remainder covering clean-room biomanufacturing, device hubs, and testing and validation infrastructure. Major cost drivers include GMP-certified facilities, process equipment, and power-reliant fabrication systems.

Early national budgets are expected to be close to balance, so major initiatives rely on discrete sovereign financing pathways and co-investment rather than assumed operating surpluses. Practical mechanisms include project finance for shared facilities, long-term offtake agreements with health systems, and partnerships with established manufacturers for licensed production and technology transfer.

Cross-Pillar Synergy

This pillar underpins others by supplying resilient sensors and controls to mining and energy systems, hardened electronics to the defence and transport pillars, and secure medical supplies to strategic stockpiles. In return, it draws on Pillar Three for reliable power, Pillar Six for distribution logistics, and Pillar Seven for innovation and export pathways.

Feasibility & Gating Conditions (2031+)

Delivery is contingent on four conditions. First, a post-independence Health and Advanced Manufacturing White Paper must define the essential medicines list, priority devices, and electronics nodes where domestic control is decisive. Second, regulatory pathways must be streamlined while preserving clinical and manufacturing standards, including mutual recognition where appropriate. Third, investable partnerships are required for licensed production, workforce training, and quality systems. Fourth, enabling infrastructure—power, water, secure data, and transport—must be in place at selected sites. Progress beyond initial capacity depends on demonstrated reliability, cost discipline, and sustained demand from domestic health services.

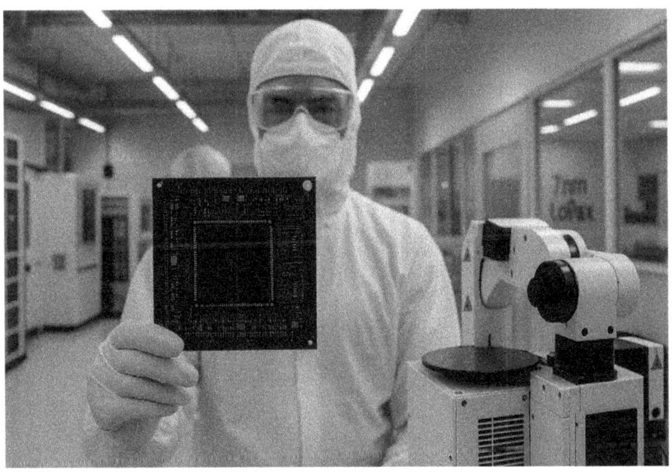

Sources

Unless otherwise stated, online materials were viewed on 4 February 2026.

1. Australian Bureau of Statistics, *International Trade in Goods and Services, Australia, 2023–24* (Catalogue No 5368.0, 2024) <https://www.abs.gov.au/statistics/economy/international-trade/international-trade-goods-and-services-australia/latest-release>.
2. Therapeutic Goods Administration, *Medicine Shortage Reports Database* (Web Page, 2025) <https://www.tga.gov.au/safety/shortages/medicine-shortage-reports-database>. Annotation: Supports: "Recent disruptions saw hundreds of medicines listed as in shortage nationally"
3. World Health Organization, *WHO Model List of Essential Medicines—24th List* (Report, 2025) <https://www.who.int/publications/i/item/B09474>.
4. Department of Health and Aged Care (Australia), *National Medicines Policy* (Policy Document, 2022) <https://www.health.gov.au/sites/default/files/2022-12/national-medicines-policy.pdf>.
5. Productivity Commission (Australia), *Vulnerable Supply Chains* (Study Report, 2021) <https://assets.pc.gov.au/inquiries/completed/supply-chains/report/supply-chains.pdf>.
6. Semiconductor Industry Association, *2025 State of the U.S. Semiconductor Industry* (Report, 2025) <https://www.semiconductors.org/wp-content/uploads/2025/07/SIA-State-of-the-Industry-Report-2025.pdf>.
7. Government of Singapore, Economic Development Board, *Singapore's Semiconductor Industry* (Web Page, 2025) <https://www.edb.gov.sg/en/our-industries/semiconductor.html>.
8. Enterprise Ireland, *Life Sciences* (Web Page, 2025) <https://www.enterprise-ireland.com/en/sectors/lifesciences>.
9. Australian Bureau of Statistics, *Labour Force, Australia, Detailed, 2024* (Catalogue No 6291.0.55.001, 2024) <https://www.abs.gov.au/statistics/labour/employment-and-unemployment/labour-force-australia-detailed/latest-release>.
10. Harry Perkins Institute of Medical Research, *Annual Report 2024* (Report, 2024) <https://perkins.org.au/wp-content/uploads/2025/06/AnnualReport_2024_Digi.pdf>.

Pillar Six: Smart Transport Network

The Kimberley

Flagship Vision & What This Enables

By the mid-2030s, Western Australia's northern freight system is no longer a fair-weather chain, assuming successful staged investment in around 500 km of elevated, flood-resilient corridor keeps moving through monsoonal closures, linking new irrigated precincts (supporting the 400,000 hectares envisaged in Pillar Four), mining hubs and regional towns to northern processing sites and ports. Along that spine, modular micro-hubs spaced roughly every 100 kilometres provide secure communications, maintenance bays, reliable charging or refuelling, and secure storage for critical spares—so routine operations do not collapse into emergency improvisation each wet season.

Four concrete system elements anchor the plan:

- Elevated all-weather corridors designed for 100-tonne-plus freight and wet-season uptime.
- Standardised micro-hubs (power, secure comms, maintenance and spares) that turn vast distances into predictable legs.

- Geofenced autonomous hybrid-electric road trains on controlled corridor sections, with manual override near towns and mixed-traffic zones.
- Dedicated beyond visual line-of-sight (BVLOS) drone corridors for time-critical items (typically 5–20 kg over 50–100 km), integrated with emergency logistics.

Coverage is staged: early investment targets a few high-leverage corridors rather than blanket nationwide automation.

Core Analysis

Why transport becomes a binding constraint on a continental state

Western Australia's freight task is long-haul by default, with many critical movements exceeding 1,000 kilometres between production zones, service bases and ports. In the north, seasonal flooding can close roads for days or weeks, turning routine resupply into expensive contingency logistics and creating "single-missing-component" stoppages across mines, farms, utilities and clinics. If northern irrigation and processing expand materially, the core economic question is whether supply chains can operate to predictable delivery windows, rather than only when the road reopens.

A system architecture, not a single megaproject

The Smart Transport Network is designed as a layered system with graceful degradation: (1) hardened corridors and crossings that stay open more often; (2) repeatable service nodes that supply power, communications and maintenance; (3) autonomy and aerial logistics operating within defined rules; and (4) continuity and security measures that keep the system usable when signals, power or equipment are stressed. The objective is to reduce the logistics penalty of distance—closure days, idle time, safety risk and inventory buffers—rather than simply to chase marginal speed.

Component 1: Elevated All-Weather corridors for heavy freight

Priority corridors are selected where wet-season reliability has the highest leverage: farm-to-hub movements from irrigated precincts, mine-to-port legs, and town resupply links. Civil works focus on raised embankments, sealed pavements, reinforced floodways, drainage sized to extreme events, and recovery bays for heavy vehicles. Design loads assume 100-tonne-plus combinations and controlled convoy operations where appropriate.

The road asset is treated as an operational system. Water-level sensors, pavement condition monitoring, axle-load detection (sensors on vehicle suspensions to measure weight in real-time) and incident reporting support smarter closure decisions and faster reopening after storms. This instrumentation also enables rules-based autonomy through geofencing, condition alerts and consistent corridor protocols.

Component 2: Corridor Micro-Hubs every ~100 Km

Distance becomes manageable when every leg ends at a known support point. Each micro-hub is a standardised package: shaded workshop space, recovery equipment, spares for high-failure items, secure communications repeaters, and power systems sized for both light vehicles and depot-style servicing of heavy fleets. Where batteries are practical, hubs provide fast charging; where duty cycles or remoteness require it, hubs provide firm refuelling and redundancy.

The dominant design choice is reliability over elegance. Hubs should continue operating through storms and outages, using a mix of local generation and storage where practical, backed by dependable dispatchable supply. Communications should likewise support degraded modes (local control and store-and-forward telemetry) rather than failing closed.

Component 3: Autonomous hybrid-electric road trains in controlled corridors

Autonomy is deployed where it is operationally coherent: geofenced segments with predictable traffic mix, consistent lane rules, and integrated condition data from the corridor. Vehicles retain manual override and operate under corridor access rules (weather thresholds, time windows, weight limits, incident response). In practice, autonomy is not "every road"; it is a managed freight network built around safety cases and operational discipline.

Hybrid-electric architectures reduce exposure to any single fuel supply chain and improve operating economics on repeatable legs, while retaining range and redundancy for remote operations. The early gains are practical: higher utilisation through predictable running, fewer stoppages, and safer heavy-freight movement in long-distance environments. Western Australia already has a credible base in autonomous mining logistics (e.g., the Onslow Iron Project); the public-interest task is to translate those capabilities into corridor governance, safety assurance, and interoperable infrastructure that can also serve agriculture and community freight, not only mine supply chains.

Autonomous haul truck operating at Rio Tinto's Pilbara iron ore mine. About 20% of Rio's ~400 trucks are already driverless, and these vehicles have moved over a billion tonnes of material with improved safety and 15% lower operating costs. The success in mining showcases the potential of autonomous vehicles to improve efficiency in heavy transport. Image credit: Rio Tinto

Component 4: Drone corridors for time-critical logistics

Drones do not replace bulk freight; they remove the long tail of supply risk. A regulated BVLOS layer moves urgent spares, medicines and diagnostics between micro-hubs, mines, farms and clinics when roads are damaged or slow. Even modest payloads are operationally valuable when they prevent high-cost stoppages or protect health outcomes. The micro-hub grid supplies the practical infrastructure: designated landing zones, secure storage, payload handling protocols, and integration with emergency services and airspace procedures that allow routine operations without compromising safety.

Import Dependence & the Practical Meaning of "Domestic Capability"

Transport resilience is also the capacity to keep fleets operating when global supply chains tighten. Western Australia is likely to remain an importer of specialised drivetrains, sensors and aviation components. The realistic objective is therefore local content where it is achievable and valuable: assembly, integration, maintenance, fleet-management software, safety assurance, certification, and parts manufacturing for high-wear items. A sensible benchmark is to lift domestic content to roughly 50–70% (by value) in selected transport subsystems by the late 2030s, without pursuing full autarky.

Security & Electromagnetic Resilience

Because autonomy and modern logistics depend on electronics and communications, continuity planning must treat electromagnetic disruption—routine interference through to rare, severe space-weather events—as a design constraint for critical nodes. Practical measures include shielded enclosures for sensitive equipment, surge protection, segregated power and communications pathways, spare modules for rapid swap-out, and minimum manual-operability modes so essential freight can continue under degraded conditions.

Costs & Financing (Order-of-Magnitude)

Indicative 2025 costings for a 2031–2040 rollout—comprising ~500 km of flood-resilient corridor upgrades, a micro-hub network, autonomy enablement and a BVLOS drone layer—are on the order of A$6–12 billion in capital expenditure. The range is driven mainly by remote civil works (often several million dollars per kilometre, rising where raised embankments, major crossings and reconstruction are required), followed by hubs (power, communications and maintenance packages), then autonomy and drone enablement and certification.

A useful breakdown is:

- Corridor works (earthworks, floodways, sealing, drainage, safety and sensing): ~A$3–7b.
- Micro-hubs and communications backbone (power systems, storage, comms, workshops and pads): ~A$1–3b.
- Autonomy and drone enablement (testbeds, control centres, certification, early fleets): ~A$2–3b.

Early national budgets are expected to be close to balance, so major build-outs rely on discrete capital-financing pathways rather than assumed operating surpluses. Practical options include concession-style PPPs for corridor segments and hubs, project finance supported by user charges or availability-style payments where appropriate, and transparent sovereign issuance sized within constitutional debt limits and supported by conservative liquidity safeguards.

Workforce & Social Licence

Delivery concentrates skilled demand in civil construction, power systems, mechatronics, remote operations, safety assurance and aircraft/drone maintenance. Training pathways can be aligned with existing mining and regional TAFE capacity. Corridor planning should proceed through standard approvals and consultation, including with Aboriginal stakeholders where routes intersect traditional lands, to ensure participation and reduce avoidable delay.

Cross-Pillar Synergy

This pillar converts gains in water, energy and industry into delivered output: it moves agricultural production from new irrigation precincts to processing hubs and ports, strengthens supply continuity for mines and communities, and provides a realistic test environment for rugged autonomy and secure electronics with dual-use value for defence mobility and emergency logistics.

Feasibility & Gating Conditions (2031+)

Meaningful commencement depends on a post-secession Transport White Paper that selects priority corridors, sets resilience standards and clarifies roles between government and concession operators. Delivery also requires safety, liability and insurance settings for autonomous heavy vehicles and routine BVLOS freight, including geofencing, airspace approvals and incident-response protocols. Corridor and node designs must clear environmental, heritage and land-access approvals, supported by consultation. Scale-up is contingent on demonstrated safety performance, bankable corridor demand, and financing readiness for multi-year civil works and systems integration.

Sources

Unless otherwise stated, online materials were viewed on 5 February 2026.

1. Department of Infrastructure, Transport, Regional Development, Communications and the Arts (Australia), *National Road Safety Action Plan 2023–2025* (Report, 2023) <https://www.roadsafety.gov.au/sites/default/files/documents/National%20Road%20Safety%20Action%20Plan%202023-25_0.pdf>.
2. Mineral Resources Limited, *Onslow Iron Project: Autonomous Road Trains* (Web page, 2025) <https://www.mineralresources.com.au/our-business/iron-ore/onslow-iron-project/autonomous-road-trains>.
3. Hexagon Mining, 'Perception, Positioning and a Long Haul Approach to Autonomy' (Article, 2022) <https://novatel.com/tech-talk/velocity-magazine/velocity-2022/perception-positioning-and-a-long-haul-approach-to-autonomy>.
4. Prime Minister of Australia, *$7.2 Billion in New Funding from the Australian Government to Fix Bruce Highway* (Media release, 6 January 2025) <https://www.pm.gov.au/media/7-2-billion-new-funding-australian-government-fix-bruce-highway>.
5. Mordor Intelligence, *Drone Package Delivery Market Size, Share, 2025–2030 Outlook* (Report, 2025) <https://www.mordorintelligence.com/industry-reports/drone-package-delivery-market>.
6. Synergy, *WA EV Network: Australia's Longest Electric Vehicle Network* (Web page, 2025) <https://www.synergy.net.au/Our-energy/Projects/WA-EV-Network>.
7. Fortune Business Insights, *Electromagnetic Shielding Market Size, Industry Share, Forecast to 2034* (Report, 2025) <https://www.fortunebusinessinsights.com/electromagnetic-shielding-market-109431>.
8. Department of Energy, Mines, Industry Regulation and Safety (Western Australia), *Western Australian Mineral and Petroleum Statistics Digest 2023–24* (Report, 2024) <https://www.wa.gov.au/system/files/2025-03/wa_statistics_digest_2023_2024_web.pdf>.
9. Austmine, *METS Workforce STEM Skills and Female STEM Participation Benchmark Survey 2023* (Report, 2024) <https://austmine.com.au/Common/Uploaded%20files/Programs/AWIM%20Benchmark%20Study%202024.pdf>.
10. CSIRO, *Mining Equipment, Technology and Services: A Roadmap for Unlocking Future Growth Opportunities for Australia* (Report, 2017) <https://www.csiro.au/-/media/Do-Business/Files/Futures/METSRoadmap.pdf>.
11. Department of Water and Environmental Regulation (Western Australia), *FPM Extent of Flooding (DWER-017)* (Dataset, 23 January 2018) <https://catalogue.data.wa.gov.au/dataset/fpm-extent-of-flooding>.
12. Main Roads Western Australia, *Tanami Road Upgrade* (Web page, n.d.) <https://www.mainroads.wa.gov.au/projects-initiatives/projects/regional/tanami-road-upgrade/>.
13. Main Roads Western Australia, *Travel Map* (Web page, n.d.) <https://travelmap.mainroads.wa.gov.au/Home/Map>.
14. Department of Infrastructure, Transport, Regional Development, Communications and the Arts (Cth), *National Road Transport Technology Strategy* (Web page, 2021) <https://www.infrastructure.gov.au/infrastructure-transport-vehicles/vehicles/national-road-transport-technology-strategy>.
15. Austroads, *National Automated Vehicle Strategy 2021–2030* (Report, 2021) <https://austroads.gov.au/publications/connected-and-automated-vehicles/ap-r645-21>.
16. National Transport Commission, *Guidelines for Trials of Automated Vehicles in Australia* (Guideline, May 2020) <https://www.ntc.gov.au/sites/default/files/assets/files/NTC%20AV%20guidelines%20May%202020.pdf>.
17. Civil Aviation Safety Authority, *Beyond Visual Line-of-Sight Operations* (Web page, 11 December 2025) <https://www.casa.gov.au/drones/drone-rules/beyond-visual-line-sight-operations>.

18. Defense Standardization Program (US), *ASSIST QuickSearch: MIL-STD-188-125-1, High-Altitude Electromagnetic Pulse (HEMP) Protection for Ground-Based C4I Facilities Performing Critical, Time-Urgent Missions* (Standard, document details) <https://quicksearch.dla.mil/qsDocDetails.aspx?ident_number=36988>.
19. John McCarthy and others, *Supply Chain Impacts during the January 2023 Kimberley, Western Australia, Floods* (Report, 2023) <https://trid.trb.org/View/2367006>.
20. Matt Garrick, 'Flooding of Australia's Major Northern Freight Routes Reignites Calls for Cross-Country Rail Line', *ABC News* (online, 12 February 2022) <https://www.abc.net.au/news/2022-02-12/renewed-interest-in-rail-linking-northern-australia-floods/100810228>.
21. Australian Government, *Heavy Vehicle Rest Area Initiative* (Fact Sheet, January 2026) <https://investment.infrastructure.gov.au/sites/default/files/documents/heavy-vehicle-rest-area-factsheet-january-2026.pdf>.
22. Staff Writer, 'Six New Rest Area Projects Announced under $20.9 Million Plan', *Big Rigs* (online, 26 November 2025) <https://bigrigs.com.au/2025/11/26/six-new-rest-areas-announced-under-20-9-million-plan>.
23. Savannah Meacham and Laine Clark, 'Freight Routes Cut, Shelves Bare as Flood Panic Hits', *AAP News* (online, 16 February 2025) <https://aapnews.aap.com.au/news/supermarket-shelves-bare-amid-widespread-flooding>.
24. Natalie Vikhrov, 'Kimberley Flood Damage Takes Heavy Toll on Cattlemen, Abattoir Workers and Freight Companies', *ABC News* (online, 12 February 2023) <https://www.abc.net.au/news/2023-02-12/kimberley-flood-damage-reveals-long-road-to-recovery/101959524>.
25. Catherine King, '$63 Million for Life-Saving Road Upgrades across Australia' (Media release, 6 August 2025) <https://minister.infrastructure.gov.au/c-king/media-release/63-million-life-saving-road-upgrades-across-australia>.
26. Australian Government, *Disaster Ready Fund* (Web page, 16 January 2026) <https://www.nema.gov.au/our-work/key-programs/disaster-ready-fund>.
27. Catherine King, 'Rest Area Upgrades to Benefit Heavy Vehicle Drivers on the Newell Highway' (Media release, 30 October 2025) <https://minister.infrastructure.gov.au/c-king/media-release/rest-area-upgrades-benefit-heavy-vehicle-drivers-newell-highway>.
28. Hussein Dia et al, *Creating Our Future Transport and Mobility Workforce* (Report, 24 April 2023) <https://imoveaustralia.com/project/project-outcomes/creating-our-future-transport-and-mobility-workforce>.
29. Airservices Australia, *Sizing the Future Drone and Advanced Air Mobility Market in Australia* (Report, February 2024) <https://www.airservicesaustralia.com/wp-content/uploads/2024/02/Sizing-the-Future-Drone-Industry-in-Australia_February.pdf>.
30. Centre for Future Work, *Summary: A Fair Share for Australian Manufacturing—Manufacturing Renewal for the Post-COVID Economy* (Report, November 2022) <https://futurework.org.au/wp-content/uploads/sites/2/2022/11/Summary-A-Fair-Share-for-Manufacturing-Summary-WEB.pdf>.
31. Australian Government, *Australian Government Response: Driving Advanced Manufacturing in Australia Inquiry and Report* (Report, 27 November 2024) <https://www.industry.gov.au/publications/australian-government-response-driving-advanced-manufacturing-australia-inquiry-and-report>.
32. Department of Climate Change, Energy, the Environment and Water, *Energy Infrastructure Resilience* (Web page, 10 February 2025) <https://www.dcceew.gov.au/energy/security/energy-infrastructure-resilience>.
33. Andrew Waye, 'Building Resilience into Critical Infrastructure' (Web page, undated) <https://www.systra.com/australia/expert_insights/strengthening-critical-infrastructure-resilience>.
34. Bureau of Infrastructure and Transport Research Economics, *Forecasting Uptake of Driver Assistance Technologies in Australia* (Report, 17 December 2021) <https://www.bitre.gov.au/publications/2021/forecasting-uptake-driver-assistance-technologies-australia>.
35. Mining and Automotive Skills Alliance, *Mining Research Bulletin—October 2025* (Bulletin, 21 October 2025) <https://ausmasa.org.au/news-and-events/mining-research-bulletin-october-2025>.

36. Natural Resources Canada, 'Strengthening Indigenous Participation in Critical Minerals Development' (Media release, 14 January 2026) <https://www.canada.ca/en/natural-resources-canada/news/2026/01/strengthening-indigenous-participation-in-critical-minerals-development.html>.

Pillar Seven: High-Tech Innovation & Exports

Flagship Vision & What This Enables

By the mid-2030s, Western Australia can run a practical "dual-use" innovation engine: a network of precincts in Perth and key regional centres where defence-derived capabilities are translated into commercial products, proven in harsh operating conditions, and exported as repeatable service lines. A start-up refines drone-autonomy algorithms into predictive-maintenance AI that reduces downtime across Pilbara fleets; a cyber firm supplies encrypted remote-access tools engineered for critical infrastructure and remote operations; and a space-services operator sells subscription remote-sensing products that support agricultural decisions, coastal monitoring, and border-relevant situational awareness.

Five flagship system elements make the plan tangible:

- A dual-use AI incubator that prototypes real-time analytics for defence and industrial operations, with shared test data, safety constraints and deploy-ready assurance requirements;
- An EMP-resilient electronics and semiconductor design lab focused on rugged, secure embedded systems (design, packaging and qualification rather than commodity fabrication);

- A cybersecurity lab that tests and certifies industrial control systems as safe, and provides pre-approved "trusted" system packages that buyers can purchase and deploy;
- A space-tech accelerator built around low-Earth-orbit services (payload integration, mission operations, ground stations and data-product teams); and
- An IP licensing exchange that commercialises sovereign know-how through audited licensing and international partnerships.

Scaling depends on strong talent pipelines and credible IP protections that retain high-value capability domestically.

Strategic Role: Resilience, Diversification & Export Leverage

High-tech exports diversify earnings beyond commodity cycles and reduce exposure to external supply shocks in critical technologies. At a national level, Australia's technology sector contributed around A$124 billion in value added to the economy in FY2023, with high-technology exports around A$12 billion—a useful indication of the scale that becomes possible when skills, commercialisation and market access align. For Western Australia, the strategic task is narrower and more operational: build a focused portfolio of high-trust niches where reliability, assurance and harsh-environment performance are valued enough that buyers pay for them.

This pillar also functions as an economy-wide multiplier. Applied AI and robotics raise productivity in mining, ports, energy systems and long supply chains; cyber assurance reduces operational risk for both industry and government; and satellite-enabled analytics improve agricultural planning and remote infrastructure monitoring. The end state is a compact set of exportable platforms with disciplined update cycles, service levels and auditability, rather than a large number of bespoke projects that cannot be supported over time.

Baseline Capability: Build from Strengths, Close Targeted Gaps

Western Australia begins with a strong engineering services ecosystem, a mining technology and services base that already integrates digital capability, and research institutions with industry engagement. The gaps are concentrated in high-assurance productisation (turning prototypes into audited, supportable offerings), advanced electronics supply chains, and operational space services. Australia also remains heavily dependent on imported advanced semiconductors and many specialist electronic components, which concentrates risk in supply chains that are largely outside domestic control.

An indicative ambition from 2031 is to lift domestic capability in selected high-tech subsectors to around 30–50 per cent by 2040, concentrating on capability layers Western Australia can credibly own: assurance and certification, rugged design and qualification, mission operations and analytics, and autonomy packages that integrate safely with legacy industrial systems. The goal is not to replicate global manufacturing ecosystems; it is to build high-value "trust layers" and operational competence that make products procurable, supportable and exportable.

Program Architecture (2031–2040)

Innovation Hubs Network (Precincts & Test Beds)

The program is anchored in an interconnected precinct network that prioritises integration, testing and commercialisation—the work that converts prototypes into export-ready offerings. Perth functions as the "design and trust" hub: secure compute for sensitive AI development, a cyber range that can emulate real industrial environments, and shared labs for embedded systems design and qualification. Regional nodes focus on operational test beds: Pilbara integration facilities for autonomy and industrial AI validation, and a northern footprint for field trials (communications, drones, remote monitoring and data products) where distance and conditions force real reliability.

A concise precinct map (illustrative) follows

Precinct	Location	Core capability	Primary export lines
Perth Innovation Harbour	Perth	Secure AI compute, cyber range, electronics design/qualification labs	Audited software, OT cyber services, rugged embedded systems
Pilbara Autonomy & Space Yard	Karratha–Newman corridor	Autonomy integration, mission operations, industrial validation	Autonomy modules, remote-sensing products, OT security packages
North Remote Systems Node	Broome–Exmouth footprint	Field trials, comms testing, drone corridors	Remote monitoring, comms solutions, drone services

Precinct design should favour shared, commercially governed facilities (labs, test ranges, secure environments) over dispersing resources across many small sites. Where regional precincts are established on or near Aboriginal lands or communities, consultation should be structured early so that full stakeholder participation is built into site selection, training pathways and local contracting.

Technology Spin-Off Mechanism (Defence to Commercial)

A formal spin-off pathway adapts defence-adjacent R&D into civilian products without importing a procurement dossier into the wider economy. The practical focus is dual-use: autonomy algorithms re-engineered into industrial predictive maintenance and inspection; secure embedded systems with enhanced durability for remote infrastructure; and sensing and analytics translated into maritime, environmental and agricultural services.

To avoid grant drift, the mechanism is outcome-driven. Prototype support is tied to measurable deployment goals (uptime, latency, false-alarm rates, safety constraints, maintainability and update discipline). IP treatment is clear from the start: WA retains sovereign control of sensitive know-how where necessary, while commercial teams have a pathway to license, export and support products under auditable terms. The IP licensing exchange supports this by standardising licensing, compliance and revenue terms so that sovereign capability can be commercialised without improvised "one-off" arrangements.

Start-Up Acceleration & Scaling (from Prototypes to Exporters)

Acceleration is treated as an operational pipeline. A precinct-linked accelerator provides seed funding, engineering and compliance support, and access to test ranges and anchor customers (critical-infrastructure operators, major industrial sites, and where appropriate defence purchasers). The objective is to grow a smaller number of firms into stable exporters with predictable update cycles, support obligations and reference customers, rather than maximising headline counts.

Scale targets should remain indicative and disciplined. A plausible ambition is to launch and scale 100+ start-ups by the late 2030s, with a smaller core cohort becoming enduring exporters. Success is measured less by the number created and more by repeatability: standard deployment packages, auditable documentation, patch and update regimes, and service models that buyers can procure and renew.

Export & Commercialisation Pathways (Trust, Certification and Licensing)

Exports are built around trust: verification pathways, certification and common templates that make products procurable in regulated or safety-critical environments. The cybersecurity certification centre validates OT-safe products, incident-response readiness and disciplined update processes, aligned to widely used security frameworks. Space services are productised as subscriptions: customers buy situational awareness, change detection and maritime analytics outputs, not satellites. The export pathway is reinforced by the IP licensing exchange, which supports compliant international partnerships for technology transfer and licensing, while maintaining sovereign control over sensitive elements where required.

Priority Export Lines: What Western Australia Sells

The pillar deliberately concentrates on four export lines that align with local test beds and high-trust buyer demand.

Trusted Cyber & Critical-Infrastructure Software

The export opportunity is not "cyber in general", but tools and services designed for infrastructure and industrial operators: OT network monitoring, hardened remote access for contractors, incident response for mixed IT/OT environments, and procurement templates that specify auditable controls. Perth's trust platform provides realistic testing and assurance pathways that allow firms to demonstrate evidence—configuration baselines, control mappings, update discipline and response readiness—so that products can be procured as audited systems, not as opaque consulting promises. Export contracts then become supportable service agreements with clear obligations, rather than bespoke engagements that cannot scale.

Space Services: Data Products, Not Rockets

Space capability is framed as an export service stack: payload integration for small satellites, mission operations, ground segment capability, and analytics that convert data into products for agriculture, logistics, disaster response and maritime awareness. The commercial logic is subscription. Buyers pay for periodic imagery, change detection and alerting dashboards, supported by clear service levels, rather than needing staff to run their own space programs. Western Australia remains launch-agnostic, relying on commercial launch markets while concentrating capability on operations, analytics and reliability.

Rugged Electronics & Electromagnetic Resilience

Western Australia is unlikely to compete on commodity electronics. The feasible niche is high-reliability embedded systems designed for heat, vibration, distance and long maintenance cycles—conditions common to mining, maritime operations, energy systems and defence applications. The electronics and semiconductor design lab focuses on design, packaging, qualification and hardening services, paired with supply-chain assurance for critical components. EMP resilience is treated as a practical design and qualification discipline: equipment that remains functional under electromagnetic disturbance and is demonstrably robust through test regimes and documented design constraints.

Autonomy, Robotics & Applied AI for Remote Operations

Western Australia's applied-AI advantage is autonomy, optimisation and robotics for remote, safety-critical operations. Pilbara integration facilities translate this into exportable modules: validated autonomy packages for materials handling, inspection drones and sensor fusion for large sites, digital-twin services that reduce downtime, and optimisation tools that improve energy and logistics efficiency. The export proposition is the combination of performance and governance: safety constraints, evidence logging, secure updates and maintainability that allow autonomy to be deployed responsibly in regulated or high-risk environments.

Commercialisation that Behaves like an Export Industry

For this pillar to produce exports (not just prototypes), three disciplines must be non-negotiable. First, testing and integration are funded as shared infrastructure, so products can be validated against real-world requirements. Second, assurance is embedded from the start: independent testing pathways, documented baselines, and disciplined update processes are treated as product features. Third, skills are treated as infrastructure: engineers, technicians and operators who can build and maintain high-reliability systems (electronics technicians, cyber operators, embedded-systems engineers, satellite operations staff) with targeted training partnerships across universities, TAFE and industry.

Global Positioning & Measurable Ambition

Western Australia's comparative advantage is not mass production; it is high-assurance performance, rapid deployment in harsh environments, and verifiable support in Indo-Pacific time zones. If executed with discipline, an illustrative ambition is to reach A$5–10 billion per year in high-tech exports by the late 2030s, with around 10,000 additional high-skill roles created across engineering, operations and support functions. The aim is a small number of stable exporters that become consistently reliable: known for auditability, uptime, and long-term support—the attributes buyers pay for in critical systems.

Costs & Financing (Order-Of-Magnitude)

A platform-led build-out is less expensive than attempting a broad industrial policy across many domains. An indicative 2031–2040 capital and program envelope is A$4–6 billion, covering precinct facilities and fit-out (secure labs, cyber range, integration workshops), shared compute capacity, a modest space-services stack (ground segment, mission operations and data-product development), and electronics qualification equipment. The largest cost drivers are high-assurance facilities (security, power reliability and cooling), specialised testing equipment, and the workforce effort needed to operate shared platforms credibly. Financing mechanisms can include sovereign bonds, multilateral lending and public-private partnerships, structured around investable precinct infrastructure and long-term service revenues.

Cross-Pillar Synergy

Pillar Seven is the export and services layer that productises innovations developed across mining technology, energy systems, advanced manufacturing and defence capability development—turning domestic test beds into internationally saleable offerings.

Feasibility & Gating Conditions (2031+)

Meaningful commencement is assumed from 2031, contingent on a post-secession High-Tech White Paper that selects export niches, confirms security and export-control requirements, and establishes commercial governance for shared platforms (cyber range, mission operations, qualification labs and autonomy corridors). Early national budgets are expected to be close to balance, so major initiatives rely on separate sovereign financing pathways and private co-investment rather than routine appropriations. Delivery depends on credible IP and licensing frameworks, partnerships that transfer know-how without surrendering control of sensitive capability, and sequenced workforce plans across universities, TAFE and industry. Site selection must confirm power reliability, data connectivity and transport access.

Sources

Unless otherwise stated, online materials were viewed on 5 February 2026.

1. Tech Council of Australia, *Tech Jobs Update* (Report, 2023) <https://techcouncil.com.au/wp-content/uploads/2023/05/TechCouncil-Tech-Jobs-Update-May-2023_final-1.pdf>.
2. Australian Trade and Investment Commission, *Australian Critical Technologies Prospectus* (Report, 2024) <https://international.austrade.gov.au/en/do-business-with-australia/sectors/technology/australian-critical-technologies-prospectus>.
3. CSIRO, *Artificial Intelligence Roadmap* (Report, 2019) <https://www.csiro.au/en/research/technology-space/ai/artificial-intelligence-roadmap>.
4. University of Western Australia, *Research Impact* (Web Page, 2025) <https://www.uwa.edu.au/rcswa/research/research-impact>.
5. Australian Computer Society, *Australia's Digital Pulse 2025* (Report, 2025) <https://www.acs.org.au/campaign/digital-pulse.html>.
6. Australian Cyber Security Centre, *ASD Cyber Threat Report 2023-24* (Report, 2024) <https://www.cyber.gov.au/sites/default/files/2024-11/asd-cyber-threat-report-2024.pdf>.
7. Space Industry Association of Australia, *The Strategic Implications for Australia of Emerging Space Trends* (Report, 2024) <https://www.spaceindustry.com.au/wp-content/uploads/2024/06/The-strategic-implications-for-Australia-of-emerging-space-trends-Space-Industry-Association-of-Australia.pdf>.
8. SEMI, *World Fab Forecast Report Q4 2024* (Report, 2024) <https://www.semi.org/en/products-services/market-data/world-fab-forecast>.
9. McKinsey & Company, *The Economic Potential of Generative AI* (Report, 2023) <https://www.mckinsey.com/featured-insights/future-of-work/the-economic-potential-of-generative-ai-the-next-productivity-frontier>.
10. Australian Government, *Critical Technologies Statement* (Report, 2023) <https://www.industry.gov.au/publications/critical-technologies-statement>.
11. Western Australian Government, *New Industries Fund* (Web Page, 2025) <https://www.wa.gov.au/organisation/department-of-jobs-tourism-science-and-innovation/new-industries-fund>.
12. World Bank, *High-Technology Exports (Current US$)* (Indicator, 2026) <https://data.worldbank.org/indicator/TX.VAL.TECH.CD?locations=AU>.
13. Australian Government Department of Industry, Science and Resources, *Technology* (Web Page, 2026) <https://www.industry.gov.au/science-technology-and-innovation/technology>.

Pillar Eight: Strategic Stockpiles

Flagship Vision & What This Enables

By the mid-2030s, Western Australia can operate with a standing national "continuity buffer": essentials remain available (and essential industries remain operable) even if shipping lanes, supplier nations, or global credit conditions tighten abruptly. The flagship design is not a single mega-warehouse. It is a distributed system blending scaled domestic production, regulated minimum stockholding, rotating reserves, and fast, rules-based release.

Four system elements make the plan legible. First, an iron-to-steel pathway anchored in the Pilbara–Kwinana industrial corridor: electric-smelting projects such as NeoSmelt provide a practical bridge from local ore into iron suitable for downstream steelmaking and repair fabrication, with an explicit scale-up pathway so construction and mining maintenance are less hostage to imported billet and long lead times. Second, a nitrogen fertiliser anchor in the ~2 million-tonnes-per-year class (exemplified by the Ceres urea project), converting local gas into agricultural inputs and mining-relevant feedstocks. Third, port-based cement continuity via covered clinker storage and handling systems—domes and sealed sheds that can hold a shipload-class volume—so major works are not stalled by import timing. Fourth, battery servicing and remanufacture hubs (including Megapack-class module servicing) so grid-scale storage becomes a maintainable fleet rather than a single-point dependency on offshore repair queues.

Linked by a digital inventory and rotation platform, the system targets multi-month coverage for priority categories and, for selected goods, the ability to sustain essential services for up to 6–12 months under constrained imports. Stockpiles must balance scale with economic rotation to avoid waste and "paper stocks" that cannot be mobilised.

Core Analysis: Resilience that is Measurable & Governable

Strategic stockpiles are the bridge between an exposed trading economy and the minimum domestic continuity required for sovereignty. Western Australia's geography amplifies disruption costs: a modest upstream shock can quickly become stalled repairs on the grid, delayed mine maintenance, fertiliser gaps during a planting window, or hospital supply stress. Stockpiles convert uncertain external lead times into a known domestic time buffer—but only if they are auditable, rotated, and releasable under clear trigger conditions.

The policy logic is two-track. Track one is reserve governance: define what is "essential", set measurable coverage standards, require first-in-first-out rotation, and audit compliance. Track two is a limited "production spine" that reduces how much must be warehoused in the first place. The objective is not autarky across every consumer item; it is continuity for the subset of inputs that keep food moving, power flowing, water pumping, mines operating, and hospitals open.

Priority Categories: What Must not Fail

Fuels continuity (obligations + surge logistics)

Liquid fuels underpin freight, emergency services, backup generation, defence logistics, and mining haulage. Australia's fuel security has been publicly reported around ~33 days for diesel and ~31 days for jet fuel as of 2025, below the IEA benchmark of at least 90 days of net-import cover. A Western Australian model should combine enforceable minimum stockholding obligations with contracted domestic storage and surge logistics, and controlled-release rules that prioritise critical services and essential freight.

Food and medical buffers (narrow but deep)

For food, the efficient centre of gravity is storable staples—especially grain—rotated through commercial channels, with regional caches to guarantee access if roads, ports, or distribution lines are disrupted. For health, the reserve should be selective but deep: critical medicines, including antibiotics and anaesthetics, essential consumables, PPE, and selected devices, with cold-chain compliance where required and a procurement posture that recognises ongoing shortage dynamics.

Industrial "restart kits" (keep infrastructure and mines running)

The largest economic losses often come from the inability to repair or restart systems quickly. This stockpile holds long-lead spares and bundled "restart kits" for electricity networks, water systems, ports, and mining: transformers and switchgear, pumps and valves, protection relays and control electronics, bearings and tyres, lubricants, and other bottleneck items. Communications continuity belongs here as well (rugged radios, satellite terminals, spare fibre and network hardware), because communications outages can become infrastructure outages. For a small subset of truly irreplaceable items, protected storage and electromagnetic shielding are prudent.

Targeted domestic capacity (reduce what must be stockpiled)

Reserves are most credible when paired with limited onshore capability that can surge continuity items. The fertiliser anchor matters because Australia imported 3.85 million tonnes of urea in 2024—over 90% of usage—implying resilience gains from domestic urea capacity. The battery anchor matters because local testing, refurbishment, and re-manufacture reduces dependence on overseas repair queues and proprietary offshore servicing. The cement/clinker anchor matters because clinker import bottlenecks can halt major works even when labour and capital are available.

Governance, Incentives & Indicative Costs

A hybrid model minimises dead inventory. Government sets definitions, coverage standards, audit powers, and emergency release triggers; day-to-day handling is largely commercial through rotation contracts, surge call-offs (pre-agreed contracts that let the government (or reserve authority) quickly trigger extra supply or logistics capacity during a disruption), and verified reporting. A Strategic Reserves Authority (or equivalent) should hold the mandate for category definitions, compliance audits, regional access planning, and controlled release during emergencies, with consultation obligations for affected communities.

Indicative 2025 order-of-magnitude costings for a 2031–2040 build-out that combines reserve infrastructure with enabling anchors are plausibly in the A$10–20 billion range (depending on scale, sites, and storage coverage), requiring project-level feasibility studies to confirm. Delivery is workforce-intensive: engineering, logistics, safety, and maintenance roles can readily reach the 5,000–10,000 range across build-out and steady-state operations. Early national budgets are expected to be close to balance, so major industrial anchors should proceed via discrete project structures and sovereign financing pathways, rather than routine operating appropriations.

Cross-Pillar Synergy

This pillar operationalises several others: defence-grade hardening supports secure storage, energy resilience (Pillar Three) underwrites fertiliser and industrial continuity, transport systems (Pillar Six) move reserves quickly, and the digital audit infrastructure in Pillar Seven makes rotation credible.

Feasibility & Gating Conditions (2031+)

Meaningful implementation should commence no earlier than 2031 and is contingent on: (i) a post-secession Stockpiles White Paper defining essential categories, coverage targets, and controlled-release rules; (ii) legislation establishing enforceable stockholding obligations, audit powers, and verified reporting; (iii) rotation and surge-logistics contracts (including regional access and cold-chain capability); and (iv) feasibility studies, approvals, and offtake arrangements for the enabling anchors (urea capacity, battery servicing/remanufacture, and reserve-storage sites), with demonstrated logistics readiness for rotation and emergency release.

Sources

Unless otherwise stated, online materials were viewed on 5 February 2026.

1. Commonwealth Department of Health and Aged Care, *National Medical Stockpile* (Web Page, 2025) <https://www.health.gov.au/our-work/national-medical-stockpile>.
2. Commonwealth Department of Climate Change, Energy, the Environment and Water, *Australia's Fuel Security* (Web Page, 2025) <https://www.dcceew.gov.au/energy/security/australias-fuel-security>.

3. Therapeutic Goods Administration, *Shortages* (Web Page, 2025) <https://www.tga.gov.au/safety/shortages>.
4. Perdaman Chemicals & Fertilisers, *Perdaman Chemicals & Fertilisers* (Web Page, 2025) <https://perdamanchemicalsandfertilisers.com/>.
5. Clough, *Ceres Urea Plant* (Web Page, 2025) <https://www.cloughgroup.com/projects/ceres-urea-plant>.
6. BHP, *NeoSmelt Welcomes Federal Government Support and Signs Two New Participants* (Web Page, 2025) <https://www.bhp.com/news/media-centre/releases/2025/06/neosmelt-welcomes-federal-government-support-and-signs-two-new-participants>.
7. Hatch, *NeoSmelt Consortium Selects Hatch to Design Australia's Largest Ironmaking Electric Smelting Furnace* (Web Page, 2025) <https://www.hatch.com/About-Us/News-And-Media/2025/07/NeoSmelt-consortium-selects-Hatch-to-design-Australias-largest>.
8. Energy Storage News, *Tesla Plans Megapack Re-manufacturing Facility in Western Australia* (Web Page, 2025) <https://www.energy-storage.news/tesla-inks-mou-for-megapack-re-manufacturing-facility-in-western-australia/>.
9. Cook Labor Government, *Clinker Import Circuit to Cement Western Australia's Economic Future* (Media Statement, 10 October 2025) <https://www.wa.gov.au/government/media-statements/Cook%20Labor%20Government/Clinker-import-circuit-to-cement-Western-Australia's-economic-future-20251010>.
10. Reuters, 'BHP, Rio Tinto to Build Low-Carbon Iron Pilot Plant in Western Australia' (Article, 17 December 2024) <https://www.reuters.com/markets/commodities/bhp-rio-tinto-build-low-carbon-iron-pilot-plant-western-australia-2024-12-17/>.
11. Global Cement, 'Fremantle Ports Unveils Clinker Storage Dome' (Article, 14 March 2024) <https://www.globalcement.com/news/item/15736-fremantle-ports-unveils-clinker-storage-dome>.
12. CSIRO, *Pathways to Net Zero Emissions—An Australian Perspective on Industry Decarbonisation* (Report, 2024) <https://www.csiro.au/-/media/Environment/Net-zero/Reports/Technical-Report_Pathways-to-Net-Zero-Emissions.pdf>.
13. Productivity Commission (Cth), *Australia's Circular Economy—Unlocking the Opportunities Interim Report* (Report, 2025) <https://assets.pc.gov.au/2025-05/circular-economy-interim.pdf>.
14. Australian Energy Market Operator, *2025 Gas Statement of Opportunities* (Report, 2025) <https://aemo.com.au/-/media/files/gas/national_planning_and_forecasting/gsoo/2025/2025-gas-statement-of-opportunities.pdf?la=en>.
15. Cargill Australia, *Global Urea Market Insights* (Web Page, 2025) <https://www.cargill.com.au/en/2025/global-urea-market-insights>.
16. Rabobank, 'Supply 'Fragility' Creating Volatility in Urea Market—Rabobank Report' (Web Page, 2025) <https://www.rabobank.com.au/news/media-releases/2025/supply-fragility-creating-volatility-in-urea-market-rabobank-report>.
17. Department of Climate Change, Energy, the Environment and Water, *Minimum Stockholding Obligation (MSO) for Liquid Fuels: Statistics* (Web Page, 2025) <https://www.dcceew.gov.au/energy/security/australias-fuel-security/minimum-stockholding-obligation/statistics>.
18. International Energy Agency, *Oil Stocks of IEA Countries—Data Tools* (Web Page) <https://www.iea.org/data-and-statistics/data-tools/oil-stocks-of-iea-countries>.

DEFENCE FORCE: SAFEGUARDING THE NEW NATION

Executive Summary

Western Australia's independence will be secured by a modern, flexible defence force built on technology, alliances, and domestic innovation. Starting from mid-2029, we will move swiftly to establish core units, leveraging partnerships with friendly nations for training, intelligence, and interim patrols while our own equipment is acquired. In the short term, joint exercises with established allies and leased patrol vessels and aircraft will protect our coasts and borders, and high-tech surveillance (drones and sensors) will help guard remote offshore assets. We will also partner closely with Western Australia's extractive industries—especially offshore mining and drilling companies—to co-design security plans for their facilities. Western Australia's government will ensure that no mining installation is left undefended, as these resources are strategic national assets. This chapter explains how these immediate measures will work, outlines a draft Western Australian Defence Industrial Act

2029 to build a world-class domestic defence industry, enshrined in Western Australia's new Constitution. In all cases, transparency and civilian oversight are paramount: the new defence force will serve the people of Western Australia. By emphasising unmanned systems, cyber capabilities, and allied cooperation, the Western Australian Defence Force (WADF) will leapfrog into the 21st century of warfare and deterrence, creating high-skilled jobs and safeguarding our sovereignty.

Foundational Vision

Western Australia's defence policy will be guided by democratic principles, technological innovation, and clear legal mandates. The Constitution will strictly limit the military's role to defensive and humanitarian missions: no offensive wars or political interventions. The armed forces will defend Western Australia's own country and participate in the collective defence of allied partners, and provide disaster relief, search-and-rescue, and emergency support to civil authorities —but only as a last resort when emergency services cannot cope. The new government will ensure that Western Australia's military is fully subordinate to elected civilian leadership. Just as modern democracies require a clear legal and constitutional framework for the military, our Constitution stipulates that the President and Defence Secretary (not military officers) command the forces, and that every defence budget and major acquisition be approved by Congress. Importantly, the Constitution will prohibit any action by the Western Australian Defence Force which could disturb the peace of nations. In short, Western Australia's Defence Force will be built into a robust legal framework: high-tech and well-funded for security, but always under democratic control and the rule of law.

Alliances & Partnerships

Western Australia will immediately engage with regional and global partners to amplify its security. As NATO Secretary General Mark Rutte noted, securing a nation requires a global effort and alliances are designed to provide "collective security" for all members. In practice, Western Australia will seek defence agreements with friendly countries (especially those sharing our political values) to obtain training exchanges, intelligence sharing, and technical support. Western Australia will participate in joint exercises and cooperative ventures to ensure interoperability and mutual readiness. Technology-sharing pacts will be pursued so Western Australia can field advanced systems—including drones, satellite communications, and cybersecurity tools—drawing on allies' expertise. These partnerships also mean Western Australia's small new force will be multiplied by coordinated defence: in a crisis, our allies will stand ready to assist. By embedding Western Australia into a network of defence cooperation, as a nation we guarantee that threats to our mining, airspace, or seas will be met by a broader security umbrella rather than Western Australia alone.

Immediate Defence & Security Measures

While long-term assets are developed, WA will implement interim measures to keep Western Australia secure from 2029 onward.

First, existing Western Australian forces (army reserves, police tactical units, etc.) will be restructured into a provisional National Guard.

Second, the Government will expedite purchase or lease of used equipment: for instance, acquiring patrol vessels, helicopters, and radar systems from allied stockpiles.

Third, we will rapidly expand our cyber-defences and intelligence capabilities to detect any espionage or sabotage attempts, especially around resource sites.

Fourth, we will hire additional security personnel to protect airports, ports, and key infrastructure, with special focus on offshore drilling rigs and mines that are hardest to reach by land.

Fifth, Western Australia will create a Rapid Reaction Force with specialists in maritime security and counter-terrorism; this force will train alongside allied units and be ready to deploy on short notice to any threatened location.

All these steps—from radar coverage to rapid response drills—can be executed early with limited lead time, ensuring our borders and coasts are monitored 24/7 even as our defence force is being built.

Protecting Western Australia's Resources & Industry

Western Australia's mineral and energy wealth are national treasures that demand explicit protection. Mining companies, especially those operating offshore, need absolute confidence that platforms and investments are safe. To that end, the government will co-develop security measures with industry: every mine, wellhead, and processing plant will have an up-to-date defence plan. Offshore, Western Australia will use drones and patrol boats to monitor pipelines and rigs; onshore, it will deploy mobile units and rapid-reaction teams to mining camps and refineries. Critical infrastructure sites will receive priority protection; indeed, just as a US Presidential Executive Order noted, critical minerals and resources are "vital to our national security and economic prosperity", so will be defended vigorously. In practice, this means Western Australia's military planners and the extractive industry will be in lockstep. These assurances will be enshrined legally so that companies know the state is fully committed to their defence needs.

Constitutional Provisions for Defence

Constitutional articles covering Western Australia's Defence Force are presented in Chapter 15: A New Nation's Constitution. Title 15 will give effect to enabling legislation like the Defence Industrial Act 2029 specimen below.

Western Australian Defence Industrial Act 2029: Draft Outline

Preamble

The Western Australian people value their security, sovereignty, and prosperity. To protect these, the government establishes a Defence Industrial Base that is innovative, resilient, and transparent. This Act commits to building domestic capability in defence technology and manufacturing, creating high-quality jobs, and ensuring that all defence acquisitions strengthen Western Australia's economy and security. It affirms that Western Australia will welcome foreign partners and technology under strict safeguards, and that private industry will have a clear, supportive legal environment. Above all, the Act pledges that every defence project will be managed openly, with strict measures against waste, corruption, or undue foreign dependence. Western Australia thus declares that its defence industry will serve the public good, drive technological leadership, and safeguard the nation.

The Act will include the following sections, described here in general terms:

1. Definitions & Authority: Establish a Western Australian Defence Industry Authority (WADIA) to coordinate all matters related to defence production, R&D, and supply chains. Define key terms (e.g. *defence asset, controlled technology*) so everyone understands the scope.

2. Objectives & Scope: State the Act's purpose: to secure essential military equipment and services, to develop local defence capabilities, and to integrate Western Australia's industry into allied supply chains. Make it clear that these objectives are vital for national security and economic development.

3. Procurement & Local Industry Participation: Mandate that Western Australian defence contracts prioritise domestic firms and local content wherever feasible. Set guidelines for competitive bidding but allow innovation partnerships where government and industry co-develop new technologies. Include provisions for offset agreements (foreign suppliers investing in Western Australia) and for defending against too much foreign dependence.

4. Research, Development & Innovation: Provide government funding and tax incentives for defence R&D, including in universities and startups. Encourage spin-offs of dual-use tech (e.g. from space or cyber sectors). Ensure technology stays protected: this section will require WADIA to safeguard sensitive designs, with strict export controls on cutting-edge systems.

5. Intellectual Property & Technology Security: Protect the intellectual property (IP) of Western Australian defence companies so they are rewarded for innovation. Define how IP rights are handled for government-funded research and for collaborations with foreign partners. Include clear rules so that any transfer of technology under joint projects must preserve Western Australia's ownership rights and keep key know-how in-country.

6. Foreign Partnerships & Offsets: Regulate cooperation with allied firms and governments. Set criteria for approving foreign joint ventures (e.g., allied flag countries only). Require that major foreign contractors partner with local businesses and train Western Australian personnel. Ban or limit deals that could undermine security.

7. Industrial Security & Classified Contracts: Establish security vetting for contractors handling classified defence work. Define requirements for safeguarding classified materials, including cyber-security standards for defence IT systems. This will include provisions for monitoring supply chains and facilities to prevent espionage or sabotage.

8. Financing & Incentives: Authorise the government to provide grants, loans, or tax breaks to support the defence industry. This section will set up a Defence Innovation Fund to back prototype development of new Western Australian systems (drones, cyber tools, etc.). It will also allow drawdowns from resource revenues to invest in strategic capabilities, reflecting our commitment to fund defence through national wealth.

9. Oversight, Transparency & Reporting: Require WADIA to report annually to Congress on industry health, budgets, and export deals. Include public auditing provisions and anti-corruption safeguards in all defence contracts. Ensure that sensitive information can be handled securely, but that general progress and spending is transparent to citizens.

10. Enforcement & Penalties: Authority to penalise violations of the Act. Create a fast-track process for investigating and prosecuting defence procurement crimes. This teeth section will ensure that the Act's rules are actually followed.

These draft sections stand as pledges and principles: Western Australia's leaders will be legally bound to create a defence industry that is self-reliant, advanced, and accountable.

High-Tech Defence & Job Growth

Western Australia's investment in defence will also be an engine for economic growth. Experience in other nations shows that a modern defence sector creates high-paying, skilled jobs and spurs innovation. For instance, the U.S. aerospace and defence industry employs over 2.2 million people and far outpaces national averages for wages. Similarly, Western Australia will train engineers, scientists, and technicians to design and build drones, satellites, cyber defences, and advanced vehicles. We will foster public-private R&D partnerships—for example, funding university labs to work on military AI or robotics—so that breakthroughs flow into both defence and civilian use. Defence contracts will be deliberately shared with small and medium businesses, creating clusters of expertise in areas like unmanned vehicles, secure communications, and renewable-powered surveillance. As pilots, medics, and support personnel are hired for the Western Australian Defence Force, many will come from Western Australia's existing workforce, boosting local careers in Science, Technology, Engineering, and Mathematics (STEM) fields.

In sum, citizens should expect the new defence force not just to keep us safe, but to become a leading sector of our economy. Revenue from resource exports will be reinvested to buy top-edge technology from allies and to build domestic prototypes. Over time, Western Australia will develop its own advanced platforms—pilotless aircraft, autonomous naval vessels, cyber drones, etc. —all produced to world standards. This strategy will both secure the nation and provide many new jobs and skill-building opportunities for Western Australians in fields like engineering, software, and manufacturing.

Financing Western Australia's Defence Build-Up

Given Western Australia's post-secession fiscal position, defence procurement must rely on a mix of internal allocations and external financing to avoid straining core services. Initial budgets of $20–23 billion over the first five years exceed immediate surpluses, necessitating creative mechanisms to fund high-priority acquisitions like drones and missile systems without immediate fiscal drag.

Key options include issuing Defence Bonds; specialised government securities marketed to citizens and investors to raise capital explicitly for military buildup. Allied financing is equally vital: export-credit agencies globally covered roughly US$165 billion in defence loans in 2024, and Foreign Military Sales (FMS) programs from partners like the U.S.A. offer grants, loans, or credit via Foreign Military Financing (FMF), often tied to purchases of approved platforms. Export credit guarantees from agencies like the U.S. EXIM Bank can underwrite loans for equipment imports, while offset agreements mandate suppliers to invest in Western Australia's economy—such as local assembly lines or technology transfers—reducing net costs. Leasing arrangements for vessels and aircraft spread payments over time, and public-private partnerships (PPPs) with mining firms could co-fund resource-protecting assets, blending sovereign and corporate funds.

This chapter's procurement examples and budgets are illustrative, not definitive, serving as a foundation for refinement through dedicated White Papers and community consultations. As outlined in the prequel, these proposals are placeholders, to be honed collaboratively with Western Australians and experts, ensuring designs reflect public needs, feasibility, and modern technology for a prosperous, secure nation.

WADF: Example Procurement & Force-Design Dossier

A study on how Western Australia can build a brand-new defence force from the ground up, starting the day Western Australia declares independence.

The brief sets three immovable parameters:

> ***Financial reality.*** Western Australia will enjoy an annual AU ~$50 billion royalty stream. A portion of available funds, supplemented by financing mechanisms, will support frontline defence procurement, with an initial bias toward armed drones and supporting electronics.
>
> ***Threat map.*** The low-risk land border with Australia allows Western Australia to concentrate on the northwest approaches: the Carnarvon, Roebuck and Browse offshore basins, plus the wider Indian Ocean arc that shields the State's mineral wealth.

War-fighting philosophy. The new force will be drone-first, human-last. Air, sea and land drones—integrated through AI-enabled command-and-control—are to take the brunt of combat and surveillance, backed by missile-defended bases and a lean, elite corps of human operators.

The following text contains many defence acronyms—An Acronym Legend is provided below.

To turn that vision into precise requirements, ten clusters of clarifying questions were created covering everything from budget envelopes and preferred suppliers to naval stop-gaps, cyber doctrine and constitutional constraints. The current design criteria for the dossier follows:

Budget & Suppliers. Allocate a significant portion of available funds, including financed amounts, to air-launched munitions and US/NATO-approved platforms. Electronic-warfare and counter-drone kits are mandatory from day one.

Domestic Industry. Stand-up a licensed drone-assembly line within four years, segueing to fully indigenous R&D and manufacture as supply-chain risk diminishes.

Missile Defence. Buy proven off-the-shelf systems (Norwegian Advanced Surface-to-Air Missile System (NASAMS), Israel's Iron Dome, etc.) in the first three years while co-developing Western Australian variants; deploy a blend of mobile and fixed batteries.

Interim Fleet. Acquire up to ten 75-100m Coast Guard–style combat cutters; no near-term submarines.

Basing Concept. Establish hardened mainland air-defence hubs and forward defence rigs on decommissioned platforms or new purpose-built pylons.

Special Forces. Contract veteran SAS/SEAL cadres to seed a 600-operator Ranger battalion, trained for desert, littoral and airborne insertion.

Surveillance Backbone. Lease satellite bandwidth first, then launch a sovereign micro-constellation; all platforms to plug into a single AI-driven C2 node.

Cyber Arm. Field offensive-and-defensive cyber talent from inception, centrally controlled until a mature national framework emerges.

Airpower Trajectory. Remain drone-only for first three years; manned fighters considered later through foreign-base access or pooled alliances.

Alliances. Pursue early defence pacts and technology-sharing MOUs; observe arms-control norms but keep options open pending deeper research.

The pages that follow are built exactly on these assumptions. They deliver a phased shopping list, cost ladder, industrial road map and constitutional scaffolding to let Western Australia move from zero to a credible, tech-centric defence posture inside its first Congressional term.

Procurement

1. Strategic Budget Framework: Years 1-3 (~FY 2030-32)

Major Capability Pillar	Indicative Allocation (AUD)	Notes
Uncrewed Air Combat & ISR Fleet	$5.5 B	Includes 24 × MQ-9B SeaGuardian ($510 m/4-aircraft package) and 120 × Bayraktar TB2 ($4.4 m ea.) plus spares, SATCOM, weapons.
Ground-Based Air & Missile Defence	$3.6 B	• 6 × NASAMS batteries (~A$425 m ea.) extrapolated from Belgium deal: 10 batteries/US$3 bn • 4 × Iron Dome batteries (A$130 m ea.) • Integration radars & reload stocks.
Counter-Drone / EW Suite	$0.8 B	Procurement of DroneShield hand-held & fixed C-UAS kits (A$61.6 m contract as reference) plus Rafael Drone Dome nodes.
Coastal & Blue-Water Surface Fleet	$5.8 B	Option Mix: 4 × Legend-class NSC cutters (A$990 m ea.) + 6 × 75-100 m Offshore Patrol Cutters (~A$1,040 m ea. based on US OPC $17.6 bn/25).
Uncrewed Surface / Under-Sea Vehicles	$0.9 B	50 × Saildrone Explorer ISR USVs (~A$2 m ea.) + 12 × Devil Ray T38 armed USVs (cost classified; current US Navy small-lot ≈ A$30 m ea.).
C2-AI, SatCom & Cyber Core	$1.5 B	Tiered cloud C2 system, leased L & X-band SATCOM, cyber-SOC build-out.

Major Capability Pillar	Indicative Allocation (AUD)	Notes
Special Operations & Training	$0.6 B	Recruitment contracts for ~220 ex-SAS/SEAL instructors + standing Western Australian SOF cadre of 600.
Infrastructure (Bases & Offshore Rigs)	$2.4 B	3 hardened mainland air-defence bases (~A$600 m ea.), 2 modular Defence-rigs (A$300 m ea.) for Barrow & Scott Reef.
Contingency / Program Mgmt Reserve	$1.0 B	Inflation & risk buffer.
TOTAL (Years 1-3)	**~ A$23.3 B**	

2. Air Domain—Drone-First Architecture

2.1 High-Altitude Maritime ISR & Strike

Platform	Qty	Range / Endurance	Payload	Unit Cost (AUD)
MQ-9B SeaGuardian	24	6,000 km/35 h	1.7 t (JDAM, Hellfire, Sonobuoys)	~$210M
TB2 Tactical MALE	120	300 km LOS/24 h	150 kg (MAM-L, ISR pod)	~$4.4M
Micro-Swarm Quad-rotors	2,000	20 km/40 min	EW/Jammer or 1 kg HE	~$0.015M
Black Hornet PRS	500	2 km/25 min	HD day/night camera (no kinetic payload)	~$0.13M

Platform	Qty	Range / Endurance	Payload	Unit Cost (AUD)
			Total Cost	**~A$5.7B**

All airframes tie into AquilaNet, Western Australia's cloud-native C2-AI.

2.2 Ground-Based Air & Missile Defence

Layer 1 (VSHORAD). Drone Dome & DroneShield RF/EO sensors with soft- & hard-kill.

Layer 2 (SHORAD). 4 × Iron Dome batteries (70 km), each covering a major population hub.

Layer 3 (MRAD). 6 × NASAMS batteries (30–50 km AMRAAM-ER) positioned to protect LNG hubs & bases.

3. Land & Fixed Infrastructure

Facility	Purpose	Indicative Location	Key Systems
Karratha Joint Air-Sea HQ	National C2 node, cyber-SOC	Karratha airport precinct	Tier-1 data centre, SATCOM gateway
Port Hedland Air Defence Base	TB2 wing + NASAMS	South of Wedgefield	Hardened hangars, 3 MW solar micro-grid
Exmouth Forward Radar Site*	Over-the-horizon & space-tracking	Cape Range	TPS-77 long-range radar (A$40 m for 2)
Rig Watch-1/2 Offshore Platforms	Early-warning + USV dock	Barrow Island shelf & Scott Reef	GM200 MM/C radars, VL-MICA quad-pack cells

*Bare coastal X-band radar heads can be fielded for ~A$5 m each; hardened networked sites retain the A$10 M planning figure used in budget tables. Cost delta reflects bare sensor vs full TPS-77 package.

4. Naval Surface Combatant Options (Years 1-8)

Option	Displacement	Endurance	Weapons Fit	Cost (AUD)	Comment
Legend-class National Security Cutter	4,600 t	60–90 days	57 mm, Phalanx, RAM (FFBNW* Mk-41)	~990M	Proven; USN/USCG logistics; space for drone C2 suite.
US Offshore Patrol Cutter (Austal)	3,600 t	45 days	57 mm, 30 mm RCWS, Stinger VSHORAD	~1,040 M	Build slot availability from 2029.
Damen 1800-class OPV	1,800 t	40 days	76 mm, 2 × 30 mm, modular VLS 8-cell	~180M	Quick build in Singapore or Vietnam; lower running cost.
			Total	**~A$2.2B**	

*FFBNW = *fitted-for-but-not-with.*

Option B: Ship-borne VTOL UAV Option (Fleet Add-On)

Western Australia may integrate MQ-8C Fire Scout rotary-wing drones aboard Legend-class and future OPVs once deck control suites are certified. Planning factor: up to 6 airframes ~ A$50M each (platform, spares, control station). Decision gate in Phase 2 once indigenous drone C2 software matures.

Recommended mix:

Phase 1 (2030-2032: FY 2030 appropriation). 4 x Legend-class (leased or FMS), 4 x Damen 1800.

Optional VTOL package. 6 × MQ-8C Fire Scouts for over-the-horizon targeting (Phase 2 decision).

Phase 2 (2033-2035). Replace remaining leased hulls with 6 x Western Australian-built OPVs (Damen license).

5. Uncrewed Surface & Under-Sea Layer

Class	Qty	Role	Sensors / Payload	Unit Cost (AUD)
Saildrone Explorer	50	Persistent maritime ISR, AIS spoof detection	EO/IR, HF-radar, AIS	~$3M
Devil Ray T38 USV	12	Fast-attack / armed escort	MAM-L/Spike NLOS, Mini-VLS	~$30M
Portable AUVs	8	Sub-sea pipeline & harbour defence	Synthetic aperture sonar	~$12M
			Total Cost	**~$0.6B**

6. AquilaNet—Integrated C2-AI Concept

Core. Redundant cloud nodes at Karratha & Perth CBD (GovCloud on sovereign servers).

Data Ingest. Ku/Ka-band SATCOM, L-band Iridium Certus fallback, land fiber, Link-16 from allies.

AI Engine. Graph-neural fusion; prioritises threats, allocates drones/missiles autonomously, but human-in-loop for kinetic release (doctrine compliance).

Cyber Security. Zero-trust, quantum-resistant encryption suites; SOC-Tier 3 at Karratha HQ.

User Layer. Hardened tablets for field JTACs, VR-enabled drone cockpits for Air Defence Officers.

7. Cyber Warfare Division (CYDIV)

Element	Initial Capability	Future (Year 5+)
Blue-Team	24 analysts, 8 incident handlers	150 staff, 24/7 fusion with AquilaNet
Red-Team / Offensive	12 ex-Five-Eyes contractors (leased toolkits)	Indigenous exploit-dev unit, kinetic-cyber link, USV swarm jamming

Element	Initial Capability	Future (Year 5+)
Training	NATO-certified cyber skills curriculum via ADF Cyber College	Establish Western Australian Cyber Academy

8. Special Operations Forces (Western Australian Rangers)

Target Head-count. 600 operators + 120 support.

Entry Cohort (Year 1). 80 ex-SAS (UK/AUS), 40 ex-SEAL/DEVGRU, 30 ex-GROM, 50 ex-French 1er RPIMa (desert), 60 ex-USMC MARSOC (littoral).

Capabilities. Desert long-range patrol (Camelback insertion).

Rig assault / hostage rescue (fast-rope from Legend-class deck).

Drone-enabled JTAC, maritime boarding.

Training Pipeline. 18-month integrated course co-hosted with Australian SOCOM in the Kimberley.

Domestic Defence Industrial Road map

Timeline	Milestone
2033	Break-ground on Western Australia Drone Works #1 near Geraldton (licensed TB2 assembly line).
2036	Open Western Australia Electronics Fab (LoPax-7 ASIC line) for flight-control CPUs.
2037	First fully Western Australian-designed MALE drone prototype (codename: Sand-Falcon).
2038	Launch of Blue Horizon small-sat batch (3 SAR cubesats) for sovereign ISR.

Phased Implementation Summary

Phase	Period	Deliverables
0–Mandate & Legal Foundation	Jul 2029—Jun 2030	• Pass Western Australian Defence Act, Defence Industrial Act 2029, and budget-supply Bills. • Ratify initial alliance MoUs (training, intel-sharing). • Issue non-binding Requests for Information (RFIs) to US/NATO suppliers; no deposits or binding LOAs yet. • Stand-up interim Defence Planning Office; begin security clearances for future Ranger cadres. • Conclude shared SATCOM / SIGINT-uplink Memorandum with AUS/US Harold E. Holt facility (Exmouth) for interim space connectivity.
1–Stand-Up & Early Capability	Jul 2030—Dec 2032	• Convert RFIs into signed FMS/lease contracts; make first down-payments (SeaGuardian, NASAMS, Legend cutter #1: to be appropriated in FY 2030 after enabling Acts). • Commission 2 Legend cutters and 60 TB2 drones. • Activate Karratha Joint Air-Sea HQ (Initial Operational Capability). • Establish Ranger Training Wing; first 200 instructors on payroll. • Lease commercial SATCOM bandwidth; install AquilaNet (baseline).

2–Consolidate & Networked Shield	2033—2035	• Complete NASAMS/Iron Dome rollout (8 batteries). • Finish Saildrone coastal network; TB2 fleet reaches 120. • Ranger battalion (600 operators) declared combat-ready. • Drone Works #1 (Geraldton) starts licensed TB2 assembly (slipped from 2029 to 2033). • AquilaNet achieves Full Operational Capability; CYDIV expands to 150 staff.
3–Indigenise & Strategic Depth	2036—2040	• Replace leased hulls with 6 Western Australian-built OPVs (Damen licence). • First indigenous MALE prototype Sand-Falcon flies (2037). • Launch Blue Horizon SAR cubesat trio (2038). • Phase-out imported missile stocks; field Western Australian variants. • Open Electronics Fab (LoPax-7) and secure full drone-supply autonomy.

Defence Procurement and Program Establishment Cashflow (FY2030–FY2035)

Phase / Year	Allocation (~A$B)	Notes
Phase 1–2030	7.0	Initial procurement contracts, leases, SATCOM, HQ activation, training pipelines
Phase 1–2031	8.0	Fleet expansion, base construction, cyber SOC, uncrewed maritime layer
Phase 1–2032	5.3	Completion of core air, missile defence, ISR and C2 baseline

Phase / Year	Allocation (~A$B)	Notes
Phase 1 Subtotal (2030–32)	**~20.3**	Core force establishment
Phase 2–2033–35	3.0	Capability consolidation, OPV replacement start, industrialisation
Total (2030–35)	**~23.3**	Includes procurement, integration, training, and transition costs
Phase 3–2036+	Funded annually	Indigenisation and advanced systems via royalties / Defence Innovation Fund

Key Risks & Mitigations

Risk	Mitigation
Supply-chain coercion by OEM nations	Dual-source components; rapid push to domestic fabs.
Satellite denial in conflict	L-band backup, HF skywave network, drone-to-drone mesh relay.
Drone swarm saturation	Layered C-UAS (RF-jam, laser, NASAMS proximity).
Fiscal over-run	Contingency reserve, milestone-based payments.

Acronym Legend

Acronym	Full Name / Description
1er RPIMa	1st Marine Infantry Parachute Regiment (France)
ADF	Australian Defence Force (training partner)
AIS	Automatic Identification System (maritime tracking)
AUV	Autonomous Underwater Vehicle
C-UAS	Counter-Unmanned Aerial System

Acronym	Full Name / Description
C2	Command and Control (generic)
C2-AI	Command-and-Control network with Artificial-Intelligence fusion (AquilaNet)
CYDIV	Cyber Warfare Division
DEVGRU	US Naval Special Warfare Development Group
EO/IR	Electro-Optical / Infra-Red (sensor suite)
EW	Electronic Warfare
FFBNW	Fitted For But Not With (space reserved for future weapons)
FMS	Foreign Military Sales (US arms-export programme)
GM200 MM/C	Ground Master 200 Multi-Mission/Compact radar (Thales)
GROM	Polish Special Forces unit Jednostka Wojskowa GROM
HE	High Explosive (warhead type)
HF	High Frequency
HQ	Headquarters
ISR	Intelligence, Surveillance & Reconnaissance
JDAM	Joint Direct Attack Munition (GPS-guided bomb kit)
JTAC	Joint Terminal Attack Controller (forward air-support specialist)
LOA	Letter of Acceptance (formal FMS purchase agreement)
LOS	Line of Sight (control or comms range)
MALE	Medium-Altitude Long-Endurance (UAV class)
MARSOC	Marine Forces Special Operations Command
MRAD	Medium-Range Air Defence
MW	Megawatt (power rating)
NASAMS	Norwegian Advanced Surface-to-Air Missile System
NSC	National Security Cutter (US Coast Guard Legend class)
OPC	Offshore Patrol Cutter (US Coast Guard programme)
OPV	Offshore Patrol Vessel
WADF	Western Australian Defence Force
PRS	Personal Reconnaissance System (e.g., FLIR Black Hornet micro-UAV)
R&D	Research and Development

Acronym	Full Name / Description
RAM	Rolling Airframe Missile (ship-borne SAM)
RCWS	Remote-Controlled Weapon Station
RFI	Request for Information (non-binding market inquiry)
SAR	Synthetic Aperture Radar (or Search-and-Rescue when context notes SAR cubesat)
SAS	Special Air Service (UK/Australia)
SATCOM	Satellite Communications
SEAL	US Navy Sea-Air-Land Teams
SHORAD	Short-Range Air Defence
SIGINT	Signals Intelligence
SOC	Security Operations Centre (cyber)
SOC-Tier 3	Security Operations Centre–Tier 3 (advanced cyber-ops level)
TPS-77	AN/TPS-77 long-range transportable air-surveillance radar
USMC	United States Marine Corps
USV	Uncrewed Surface Vehicle
VL-MICA	Vertical Launch version of the French MICA surface-to-air missile
VLS	Vertical Launch System
VSHORAD	Very Short-Range Air Defence
VTOL	Vertical Take-Off and Landing (aircraft capable of rotor-style launch/recovery)

Sources

Unless otherwise stated, online materials were viewed on 28 January 2026.

1. NATO, *Remarks by NATO Secretary General Mark Rutte at the Meeting of the European Parliament's Committee on Security and Defense* (26 January 2026) <https://www.nato.int/en/news-and-events/events/transcripts/2026/01/26/remarks-by-nato-secretary-general-mark-rutte-at-the-meeting-of-the-european-parliaments-committee-on-security-and-defence>. Annotation: Source for quote "collective security" on global effort and collective security in alliances.
2. American Chemical Society, *Critical Materials* (Web Page) <https://www.acs.org/policy/publicpolicies/sustainability/criticalmaterials.html>. Annotation: Source for quote "critical materials vital to the Nation's security and economic prosperity".
3. Aerospace Industries Association, *2025 Facts & Figures: American Aerospace & Defense Industry* (17 June 2025) <https://www.aia-aerospace.org/news/american-aerospace-defence-industry-continues-economic-dominance>. Annotation: Source for statistics and quote on U.S. aerospace and defence industry employment and wages: "The average labor income per A&D [aerospace and defence] job reached $115,000, which is 56% above the national average.".
4. U.S. Department of Commerce, *A Federal Strategy to Ensure Secure and Reliable Supplies of Critical Minerals* (2019) <https://www.commerce.gov/sites/default/files/2020-01/Critical_Minerals_Strategy_Final.pdf>. Annotation: Additional support for critical claims on the importance of securing critical minerals for national security and economic prosperity.
5. Society for Mining, Metallurgy & Exploration, *Critical and Strategic Minerals: Importance to the U.S. Economy and National Security* (Web Page) <https://www.smenet.org/What-We-Do/Technical-Briefings/Critical-and-Strategic-Minerals-Importance-to-the>. Annotation: Supports critical claims on protecting resource infrastructure and extractive industries as strategic assets.
6. White House, *Unleashing America's Offshore Critical Minerals and Resources* (24 April 2025) <https://www.whitehouse.gov/presidential-actions/2025/04/unleashing-americas-offshore-critical-minerals-and-resources>. Annotation: Source for quote "vital to our national security and economic prosperity".
7. Center for Strategic and International Studies (CSIS), 'New Executive Order Ties U.S. Critical Minerals Security to Global Partnerships' (15 January 2026) <https://www.csis.org/analysis/new-executive-order-ties-us-critical-minerals-security-global-partnerships>. Annotation: Supports critical claims on international partnerships for resource security and defence industrial base.
8. World Resources Institute, 'The Critical Minerals Conundrum: What You Should Know' (8 October 2025) <https://www.wri.org/insights/critical-minerals-explained>. Annotation: Supports critical claims on risks and priorities in defending critical mineral sites.
9. Congressional Research Service, *Critical Mineral Resources: National Policy and Critical Minerals List* (2023) <https://www.congress.gov/crs-product/R47982>. Annotation: Supports critical claims on defining and prioritising critical minerals for defence and economic policy.
10. Stanford University Gordian Knot Center, *Critical Minerals and the Business of National Security* (18 June 2025) <https://stacks.stanford.edu/file/mr919dh8962/Gordian%20Knot%20Center%20-%20Critical%20Minerals%20and%20the%20Business%20of%20National%20Security.pdf>. Annotation: Supports critical claims on critical minerals as foundational to defence capabilities and economic growth.

Procurement: Equipment & Cost Estimates

11. The Defense Post, 'Greek Parliament Approves $400M MQ-9B SeaGuardian Drone Purchase' (8 July 2022) <https://thedefencepost.com/2022/07/08/greece-mq-9b-purchase>. Annotation: Supports price estimate for MQ-9B SeaGuardian drone packages, including related equipment.
12. The Defense Post, 'Poland Buys MQ-9B Sky Guardian Drones for $310 Million' (17 December 2024) <https://thedefencepost.com/2024/12/17/poland-mq-9b-systems>. Annotation: Additional support for MQ-9B SkyGuardian procurement costs.

13. The Defense Post, 'US Orders MQ-9B SkyGuardian Drones for Taiwan' (2 May 2023) <https://thedefencepost.com/2023/05/02/us-skyguardian-drones-taiwan>. Annotation: Supports estimated costs for MQ-9B systems in foreign military sales.
14. The Defense Post, 'India OKs Stalled $3B MQ-9B Predator Drone Acquisition Deal With US' (19 June 2023) <https://thedefencepost.com/2023/06/19/india-predator-drone-us-2>. Annotation: Supports large-scale MQ-9B acquisition pricing.
15. The Defense Post, 'Canada to Buy 11 MQ-9B Drones for $1.8B' (20 December 2023) <https://thedefencepost.com/2023/12/20/canada-armed-drones>. Annotation: Supports unit and total costs for MQ-9B drones.
16. Aviators Maldives, 'What's the Cost of Bayraktar TB2 Drone? $2 Million? $5 Million?' (19 March 2024) <https://www.aviatorsmaldives.com/post/43234100>. Annotation: Supports price estimates for Bayraktar TB2 drones, ranging $2-5 million per unit.
17. The Defense Post, 'Belgium Plans to Buy 10 NASAMS Air Defense Batteries for $3 Billion' (23 June 2025) <https://thedefencepost.com/2025/06/23/belgium-nasams-air-defence>. Annotation: Supports NASAMS battery costs, extrapolated from Belgium deal.
18. The Pricer, 'How Much Does The Iron Dome Cost?' (Web Page) <https://www.thepricer.org/how-much-does-the-iron-dome-cost>. Annotation: Supports Iron Dome battery costs, estimated $70-95 million each.
19. The Defense Post, 'DroneShield Wins $8.2M Contract to Supply Counter-Drone Systems' (5 January 2026) <https://thedefencepost.com/2026/01/05/droneshield-counter-drone-contract>. Annotation: Supports procurement costs for DroneShield C-UAS kits and systems.
20. Wikipedia, 'Legend-class cutter' (2026) <https://en.wikipedia.org/wiki/Legend-class_cutter>. Annotation: Supports specifications and cost estimates for Legend-class National Security Cutters, around $735 million.
21. Wikipedia, 'USCGC Kimball' (2026) <https://en.wikipedia.org/wiki/USCGC_Kimball>. Annotation: Supports specific unit costs for Legend-class cutters, e.g., $487.1 million.
22. Wikipedia, 'USCGC Calhoun' (2026) <https://en.wikipedia.org/wiki/USCGC_Calhoun>. Annotation: Supports unit costs for Legend-class cutters, e.g., $499.76 million.
23. Wikipedia, 'USCGC James' (2026) <https://en.wikipedia.org/wiki/USCGC_James>. Annotation: Supports unit costs for Legend-class cutters, e.g., $482.8 million.
24. Breaking Defence, 'Coast Guard picks Austal for $3.3 billion Offshore Patrol Cutter program' (30 June 2022) <https://breakingdefence.com/2022/06/coast-guard-picks-austal-to-build-11-offshore-patrol-cutters>. Annotation: Supports total and unit costs for US Offshore Patrol Cutters.
25. Breaking Defence, "Coast Guard's new cutter program at risk of 'costly rework', 'schedule delays': GAO" (26 November 2025) <https://breakingdefence.com/2025/11/coast-guards-new-cutter-program-at-risk-of-costly-rework-schedule-delays-gao>. Annotation: Supports overall program costs for 25 OPCs at over $17 billion.
26. Naval Technology, 'Naval tech trends: Submarine top on Twitter in February 2022' (17 March 2022) <https://www.naval-technology.com/dashboards/influencers-dashboards/naval-tech-trends-submarine-twitter>. Annotation: Supports specifications for Saildrone Explorer USVs; cost estimates derived from general market data.
27. Maritime Tactical Systems (MARTAC), *Devil Ray T38 Unmanned Surface Vessel* (Web Page) <https://martacsystems.com/products/t38>. Annotation: Supports specifications and sourcing for Devil Ray T38 USVs; costs noted as classified in various contexts.
28. Teledyne FLIR Defence, 'Teledyne FLIR Defence Wins $91 Million Contract from U.S. Army for Black Hornet 4 Nano-Drones' (22 October 2024) <https://defence.flir.com/about/news/teledyne-flir-defence-wins-$91-million-contract-from-u.s.-army-for-black-hornet-4-nano-drones>. Annotation: Supports contract values and procurement details for Black Hornet PRS systems; additional context on costs from industry references averaging $195,000 per unit.
29. Engineering.com, 'The Incredible Engineering of the Black Hornet Nano Drone' (24 July 2023) <https://www.engineering.com/the-incredible-engineering-of-the-black-hornet-nano-drone>. Annotation: Supports costs for Black Hornet PRS, estimated $195,000 per unit.

30. Combat Operators, 'Black Hornet PRS: A revolutionary drone that changed covert situational awareness' (Web Page) <https://combatoperators.com/vehicles/air/uav/black-hornet-prs>. Annotation: Supports price range for Black Hornet PRS, $40,000-$60,000.
31. Deagel, 'AN/TPS-77' (Web Page) <https://www.deagel.com/Components/ANTPS-77/a001518>. Annotation: Supports costs for AN/TPS-77 radars, e.g., $52 million contract references.
32. Deagel, 'US Air Force Orders Three AN/TPS-77 Multi Mode Radar Systems on Behalf of Lithuania' (Web Page) <https://www.deagel.com/news/n000022901>. Annotation: Supports procurement costs for AN/TPS-77 systems.
33. Thales Group, *Ground Master 200 MM-C* (Web Page) <https://www.thalesgroup.com/en/solutions-catalogue/defence/air/ground-master-200-mm/c>. Annotation: Supports specifications for GM200 MM/C radars; cost estimates from general defence procurement data.
34. Asian Military Review, 'Coast Guards welcome OPV Boom' (29 January 2020) <https://www.asianmilitaryreview.com/2020/01/coast-guards-welcome-opv-boom>. Annotation: Supports costs for Damen 1800-class OPVs, e.g., $160 million for three.
35. Malaysian Defence, 'How Much Is That Ship in The Window?' (15 May 2023) <https://www.malaysiandefence.com/how-much-is-that-ship-in-the-window>. Annotation: Supports unit costs for Damen OPVs, around RM246 million each.
36. Wikipedia, 'Tun Fatimah-class offshore patrol vessel' (2026) <https://en.wikipedia.org/wiki/Tun_Fatimah-class_offshore_patrol_vessel>. Annotation: Supports contract values for Damen 1800 OPVs, RM738.9 million.
37. FlightGlobal, "US Navy's MQ-8C Fire Scouts fly into retirement just two years after entering operational service" (28 May 2024) <https://www.flightglobal.com/helicopters/us-navys-mq-8c-fire-scouts-fly-into-retirement-just-two-years-after-entering-operational-service/158500.article>. Annotation: Supports unit costs for MQ-8C Fire Scout, around $28 million.
38. USNI News, 'Northrop Grumman Awarded $108M Contract for 10 MQ-8C Fire Scouts' (14 September 2016) <https://news.usni.org/2016/09/14/northrop-grumman-awarded-108m-contract-10-mq-8c-fire-scouts>. Annotation: Supports procurement costs for MQ-8C, $10.8 million per unit in batch.
39. Offshore Energy, 'Newly purchased Hugin 6000 brings $4.5M AUV project to Argeo' (24 March 2022) <https://www.offshore-energy.biz/newly-purchased-hugin-6000-brings-4-5m-auv-project-to-argeo>. Annotation: Supports costs for HUGIN AUVs, around $4.5 million per unit.
40. Naval Technology, 'Kongsberg Maritime wins multiple contracts for HUGIN AUV' (14 July 2022) <https://www.naval-technology.com/news/kongsberg-maritime-contracts-hugin-auv>. Annotation: Supports total contract values for HUGIN AUVs, approximately $43.9 million.
41. Rafael Advanced Defense Systems, *DRONE DOME™ | Anti Drone System—Counter UAS* (Web Page) <https://www.rafael.co.il/system/drone-dome-family>. Annotation: Supports specifications for Drone Dome systems; cost estimates from defence industry references.

Financing Defence

42. Covington & Burling LLP, *Covington Guide to Foreign Military Sales and Financing* (Report, 2022) <https://www.insidegovernmentcontracts.com/wp-content/uploads/sites/49/2022/03/Covington-Guide-to-Foreign-Military-Sales-and-Financing-2022.pdf>. Annotation: Guide explaining FMS, FMF, and offsets in US defence exports.
43. United States Department of State, 'Foreign Military Financing (FMF)' (Web Page) <https://2001-2009.state.gov/t/pm/65531.htm>. Annotation: FMF provides grants for the acquisition of US defence equipment, services and training, which promotes US national security.
44. McGuireWoods LLP, 'FMF Leasing: A New Alternative For Foreign Military Sales' (Web Page, 13 March 2017) <https://www.mondaq.com/unitedstates/government-contracts-procurement-ppp/576448/fmf-leasing-a-new-alternative-for-foreign-military-sales>. Annotation: Describes FMF leasing as an option for foreign governments to lease U.S.-produced defence equipment using FMF funds.
45. Export-Import Bank of the United States, 'Buy American, Build the Future' (Web Page) <https://www.exim.gov/>. Annotation: EXIM supports American job creation through exporting by unlocking financing solutions for U.S. companies.

46. Defense Acquisition University, *Public-Private Partnering for Product Support* (Report, 12 January 2021) <https://www.dau.edu/sites/default/files/Migrated/ToolAttachments/Public-Private-Partnering-(PPP)-for-Product-Support-Guidebook.pdf>. Annotation: Defines PPPs as voluntary collaborations between DoD and non-DoD entities.
47. Centre for European Reform, 'European common debt: Is defence different?' (Policy Brief, 5 November 2024) <https://www.cer.eu/publications/archive/policy-brief/2024/european-common-debt-defence-different>. Annotation: Discusses defence bonds for predictable multi-year funding.
48. International Institute for Strategic Studies, 'Defence Financing' (Chapter) <https://www.iiss.org/globalassets/media-library---content--migration/files/publications---free-files/strategic-dossier/pds-2025/chapters/iiss_progress-and-shortfalls-in-europes-defence_2025_ch-5_new-ways-of-funding-europes-defence.pdf>. Annotation: Mentions loans or bonds to raise funds for defence, citing German example.
49. The Agora Review, 'Breaking the Austerity Taboo: Innovative Defence Financing Through Military Bonds' (Web Page, 5 March 2025) <https://econscope-by-the-agora-review.ghost.io/from-economic-stagnation-to-defence-funding-military-bonds-and-policy-innovation>. Annotation: Explores military bonds as sustainable alternative for defence financing.
50. Australian Strategic Policy Institute, 'Public-private partnerships can be engine of defence mobilisation' (Web Page, 17 October 2025) <https://www.aspistrategist.org.au/public-private-partnerships-can-be-engine-of-defence-mobilisation>. Annotation: Defence needs to mandate PPP agreements including joint investment in upskilling.
51. Global Trade Review, 'Defence Comes Out of the Shadows' (Magazine, 2025) <https://www.gtreview.com/magazine/the-export-finance-issue-2025/defence-comes-out-of-the-shadows/> . Annotation: Supports the statement that export-credit agencies globally covered roughly US$165 billion in defence loans in 2024.

A New Fourth Branch: Human Law & Medical Freedom

Introduction

Western Australia establishes a Fourth Branch of government dedicated to upholding Human Law—a set of fundamental human rights positioned above political and state authority. This branch, comprising a citizen-led tribunal and oversight system, operates independently and cannot be suspended by political action, ensuring that core rights remain protected regardless of circumstances. It reflects Western Australia's principle that authority derives from the people and their rights, rather than from government institutions. Through citizen involvement in governance and oversight, the Fourth Branch remains accountable to the public, embodying a system where power is checked by citizens.

This structure addresses historical concerns from Australia's record of human rights challenges. Over two centuries, Australian authorities engaged in systemic injustices, including frontier violence, the Stolen Generations, and ongoing discrimination against First Nations peoples. In recent years, emergency powers during the covid pandemic led to measures such as travel bans for citizens and restrictions on returning travellers. These measures prompted significant human-rights concerns, including from the Australian Human Rights Commission and the UN human-rights system, particularly in relation to freedom of movement and the right of citizens to enter their own country. Public housing lockdowns in some states were later deemed human rights violations by oversight bodies. Additionally, regulatory actions by the Australian Health Practitioner Regulation Agency (AHPRA) resulted in suspensions of medical professionals for expressing views on covid treatments and vaccine safety. These events highlighted vulnerabilities in rights protections under emergency conditions.

Western Australia addresses these issues by codifying Human Law as enforceable and beyond political override. No agency, emergency, or statute may infringe on individual safety, dignity, or freedom. Western Australia aims to create a secure environment governed by Human Law, where rights are constitutional mandates enforced through citizen oversight and legal mechanisms.

Western Australia's Constitution incorporates a Bill of Human Rights based on the Universal Declaration of Human Rights (UDHR) and International Covenant on Economic, Social and Cultural Rights (ICESCR), adapted to local principles. It creates an independent Human Rights Tribunal to address complaints and hold violators accountable, including officials. Emergency measures are subject to citizen review to prevent misuse. Medical freedom and informed consent are protected, drawing from recent experiences. Western Australia positions itself as a constitutional human rights state, with governance centred on the sovereignty of citizens' rights, safeguarded by the Fourth Branch.

Resource-Contingent Socio-Economic Rights Enforceable Under Human Law

Certain socio-economic rights are elevated to enforceable Human Law under Title 16: Human Law & Medical Freedom of the Constitution. These rights depend on Western Australia's economic capacity, funded via resource revenues as specified in national law. They are binding and subject to judicial enforcement.

Fundamental Right	Source	Status in Western Australia (Article X(6))
Free Public Education (Including Tertiary)	UDHR Art. 26(1); ICESCR Art. 13–14	Guaranteed and enforceable, subject to Western Australia's resource benchmarks. Includes tuition-free primary, secondary, and tertiary education for all citizens.
Free Universal Healthcare	UDHR Art. 25(1); ICESCR Art. 12	Guaranteed and enforceable. All citizens are entitled to publicly funded, comprehensive healthcare at no cost.
Paid Maternity and Paternity Leave	UDHR Art. 25(2); ICESCR Art. 10(2)	Guaranteed and enforceable. 6 weeks maternity and 4 weeks paternity leave provided to all citizens, universally funded.
Four-Day Work Week	UDHR Art. 24	Guaranteed and enforceable. Maximum four-day standard work week with for all non-FIFO/DIDO workers.

Note: These rights are enforceable legal entitlements. Their funding is secured through resource provisions and contingency mechanisms in national law.

Enforceable Rights Codified as Human Law

Western Australia codifies core civil and political rights as supreme, enforceable law under Title 16: Human Law & Medical Freedom. Derived from UDHR Articles 1–21 and the International Covenant on Civil and Political Rights (ICCPR), these rights limit state power, including protections for life, due process, free speech, belief, association, property, and equality. They align with Western Australia's limited-government approach by requiring state restraint. Violations, whether by state or private actors, incur civil or criminal liability. The table below details these rights and their sources:

Fundamental Right	Source	Status in Western Australia
Inherent dignity and equality (no discrimination by race, sex, religion, etc.)	UDHR 1–2; ICCPR 2(1), 26	Binding. All persons are equal before the law; no law or authority may discriminate or deny equal protection.
Right to life, liberty & personal security	UDHR 3; ICCPR 6, 9	Binding. No one may be arbitrarily deprived of life or liberty; security of the person is protected by law. Detention or arrest without legal basis is prohibited.
Freedom from torture or cruel, inhuman or degrading treatment	UDHR 5; ICCPR 7	Binding. Absolutely no torture, brutality, or inhumane treatment. Medical or scientific

Fundamental Right	Source	Status in Western Australia
(and from non-consensual medical experimentation)		experimentation requires voluntary consent (bodily integrity is inviolable).
Freedom from slavery, servitude, and forced labour	UDHR 4; ICCPR 8	Binding. Slavery and servitude are forbidden. Forced labour is barred except as punishment for a crime or equivalent civic duty under law.
Recognition as a person before the law (legal personhood)	UDHR 6; ICCPR 16	Binding. Everyone has legal personhood and capacity; no one can be treated as rightless or as an object of the law.
Equality before the law & effective remedy (equal protection and judicial remedy for rights violations)	UDHR 7–8; ICCPR 2(3), 26	Binding. All are equal under the law. Any breach of fundamental rights warrants an effective remedy by courts or the Human Rights Tribunal.
Freedom from arbitrary arrest or detention (habeas corpus)	UDHR 9; ICCPR 9, 10(1)	Binding. No one may be arrested, detained, or exiled without legal justification; detention must obey lawful procedure and allow prompt court review (habeas corpus). All detainees must be treated humanely.
Right to a fair trial and due process (including presumption of innocence; no ex post facto laws)	UDHR 10–11; ICCPR 14, 15	Binding. Full due process in criminal and civil proceedings: an impartial tribunal, defence rights, and presumption of innocence. No one can be convicted for an act that was not a crime when committed, nor given a penalty harsher than that prescribed at the time (no retroactive criminal laws).
Right to privacy (no arbitrary interference with privacy, family, home, correspondence; protection of reputation)	UDHR 12; ICCPR 17	Binding. Privacy of person, family, home, and communications is protected. Searches, surveillance, or data collection require lawful authority and must not be arbitrary. Personal honour and reputation are safeguarded by law.
Freedom of movement (travel and residence)	UDHR 13; ICCPR 12	Binding. Citizens and legal residents may move freely within Western Australia, leave and return freely. Restrictions (e.g. quarantine or travel limits) are allowable only by clear law

Fundamental Right	Source	Status in Western Australia
		for legitimate public health or security reasons, and must be consistent with other rights.
Right to nationality (and protection against statelessness)	UDHR 15; ICCPR 24(3)	Binding. Every Western Australian has the right to a nationality (Western Australian citizenship) and shall not be arbitrarily deprived of it. Citizenship is a fundamental status that the state cannot revoke to leave a person stateless.
Right to marry and found a family (with spousal equality)	UDHR 16; ICCPR 23	Binding. Marriage is entered only with the free consent of intending spouses, and spouses have equal rights within marriage. The family, as the natural unit of society, is protected from unwarranted state interference (though no requirement of state financial support beyond legal protection of family rights).
Right to own property (including intellectual property)	UDHR 17; UDHR 27(2)	Binding. Property rights are fundamental. The state shall not expropriate property without due process and just compensation. Intellectual creations (inventions, artistic works) are regarded as property of their creators and protected by law.
Freedom of thought, conscience, and religion	UDHR 18; ICCPR 18	Binding. Complete freedom of belief, worship, and conscience. This includes the freedom to change one's religion or hold no religion. Manifestation of religion or belief (worship, observance, practice, teaching) is protected, subject only to such limitations as are necessary to protect public safety, order, health, or the fundamental rights of others. There shall be no state religion and no persecution for personal beliefs.
Freedom of opinion and expression (speech and press)	UDHR 19; ICCPR 19	Binding. Strong protections for free speech, a free press, and the right to seek, receive, and impart information. Any limitations (such as for defamation, or direct incitement of violence) must be narrowly tailored, clearly

Fundamental Right	Source	Status in Western Australia
		lawful, and necessary in a democratic society. Censorship and prior restraints are fundamentally at odds with Western Australia's pro-liberty stance. (Note: Western Australia will fulfill ICCPR Article 20 by prohibiting incitement to imminent violence or hatred likely to cause harm, but will not adopt broad "hate speech" bans that could chill legitimate expression.)
Freedom of peaceful assembly (the right to gather)	UDHR 20(1); ICCPR 21	Binding. Individuals may organise and participate in peaceful meetings, rallies, protests, and other assemblies. Restrictions can only be imposed in accordance with law and only as necessary in a democratic society for public order or safety (e.g. temporary limits to prevent riots or during true emergencies).
Freedom of association (including forming and joining organisations, unions, political parties)	UDHR 20(1); ICCPR 22	Binding. The right to freely associate with others is guaranteed. Citizens can form or join civil organisations, political parties, trade unions, and other associations. (The right to form and join labour unions is protected; the specific regulation of union activities can be provided by law but must not extinguish the basic right to organise. Reasonable limits may apply for armed forces or police as per international norms.)
Right to take part in government (political participation)	UDHR 21; ICCPR 25	Binding. Every citizen has the right to participate in the conduct of public affairs, directly or through freely chosen representatives. This includes the right to vote in free and fair periodic elections with universal adult suffrage, to run for public office, and to have equal access to public service. Western Australia's system guarantees genuine democratic governance.
Rights of the accused (no arbitrary detention for debt; humane treatment of detainees)	UDHR 9, 11; ICCPR 10, 11	Binding. No one shall be imprisoned merely for inability to pay a debt (no debtors' prisons). All persons deprived of liberty

Fundamental Right	Source	Status in Western Australia
		(detainees, prisoners) must be treated with humanity and respect for their inherent dignity.
Rights of minorities (to culture, religion, and language)	UDHR 2; ICCPR 27	Binding. Ethnic, religious, or linguistic minorities in Western Australia have the right to enjoy and preserve their own culture, to practice their religion, and to use their language in community with others. The state shall protect pluralism and cultural freedoms as part of individual liberty and human dignity.

Table: Civil and political rights entrenched as enforceable "Human Law" in Western Australia's Constitution, with corresponding sources.

Note: While ICESCR rights are generally directive, Article 4 of Title 16: Human Law & Medical Freedom elevates select socio-economic entitlements (free education, healthcare, workweek, and parental leave) to enforceable status, contingent on resource availability and benchmarks. This adaptation aligns with Western Australia's resource-based economy, ensuring enforceability without fiscal overreach.

These rights hold the highest legal authority. No statute, regulation, or executive action may contravene them, rendering any such attempt void. In Western Australia's limited-government model, these rights emphasise state restraint, accountability, and protections for individual liberty, due process, property, and autonomy. By constitutionalising these as Human Law, Western Australia aligns with the International Bill of Human Rights, enabling citizens to invoke them directly in courts or the Human Rights Tribunal. Remedies include injunctions, damages, and penalties for violations.

Western Australia enforces personal accountability for officials: immunity does not apply to human rights breaches, and superior orders provide no defence. This draws from international practices holding officials liable for rights violations. The legislature must enact laws to implement these rights, including criminalising severe breaches like torture. Human Law provides actionable guarantees, ensuring remedies for rights infringements.

Directive Principles of State Policy (Socio-Economic Rights)

Western Australia recognises additional economic, social, and cultural rights as Directive Principles of State Policy under Title 16: Human Law & Medical Freedom. Drawn from the UDHR and ICESCR, these guide legislative and policy efforts toward goals like education, health, and social security. They are not justiciable or individually enforceable in courts but serve as directives for governance, with accountability through democratic processes. This approach maintains limited government while acknowledging societal objectives.

The table below lists these principles, sources, and Western Australia's approach.

Social/Economic Right or Principle	Source	Western Australia's Recognition
Special protection of the family, mothers, and children (assistance to motherhood and childhood, family as fundamental unit of society, protection of children from exploitation)	UDHR 25(2); ICESCR 10	Mixed Principle and Binding Duty. Western Australia recognises the family as a fundamental group unit of society and will avoid policies that unduly interfere with family integrity. Several aspects are treated distinctly: Protection of children from exploitation and abuse is a binding commitment—Western Australia will enact and enforce strong laws against child labour, human trafficking, underage prostitution, and all forms of abuse or exploitation of minors. This is consistent with Western Australia's view that defending the most vulnerable is a core obligation of a free society. On the other hand, support for motherhood and parental leave is a directive guideline building on enforceable minima under Human Law; the state should promote health and well-being, with statutory benefits enhancing constitutional entitlements (e.g., additional pre-natal leave). Western Australia intends to legislate generous parental leave—for example, a standard of at least 4 weeks of paid leave for new fathers, and for mothers, 2 weeks pre-natal and 4 weeks post-birth paid leave guaranteed by law—but these provisions will be statutory, not directly enforceable constitutional rights. In sum, the family unit's importance is affirmed and the state is tasked to support it through policy (public healthcare for mothers and children, parental leave laws, etc.), while absolute bans on child exploitation are part of binding Human Law.
Right to social security (support in case of unemployment, disability, old age, etc.)	UDHR 22; ICESCR 9	Directive Principle (Non-binding). The state acknowledges the desirability of a basic social safety net to ensure that citizens who cannot work or fall on hard times are supported. Western Australia will consider programs like unemployment insurance or pensions, but the extent and form of social security are left to ordinary

Social/Economic Right or Principle	Source	Western Australia's Recognition
		legislation. No individual can claim a welfare benefit from the Constitution itself.
Right to work & fair conditions (opportunity to work, just and safe conditions, fair wages, equal pay, right to organise and strike)	UDHR 23; ICESCR 6, 7, 8	Partially Directive; Partially Binding. Western Australia protects the negative aspects of this right through binding civil rights—e.g. freedom to choose one's occupation, to form labour unions, and freedom from forced labour are guaranteed by enforceable rights (see Human Law above on association and no forced labour). However, the broader positive entitlements—safe working conditions, fair wages, limited working hours, and the right to strike—are treated as goals rather than directly enforceable guarantees. The state will pass supportive labour laws (e.g. workplace safety standards, maximum working hours, minimum wage, and recognition of the right to strike with reasonable regulations), but these standards will not be constitutional rights actionable in court by individuals. Western Australia thus commits to progressively realise fair labour conditions while balancing public interest and economic freedom.
Right to an adequate standard of living (adequate food, clothing, housing, and continuous improvement of living conditions; freedom from hunger)	UDHR 25(1); ICESCR 11	Directive Principle. Western Australia commits in principle to promote conditions in which all individuals can meet their basic material needs. This encompasses striving for food security, access to shelter, and improving living standards over time. However, the Constitution does not guarantee any citizen a court-enforceable right to a certain level of income, housing, or nutrition. These remain goals for public policy: for example, the government may institute housing programs, encourage affordable food production, or provide relief during crises, but any such measures are by statute. The state's duty is to endeavour to prevent destitution and hunger

Social/Economic Right or Principle	Source	Western Australia's Recognition
		through prudent governance and to progressively uplift living conditions as resources allow.
Right to participate in cultural life and benefit from scientific progress (including freedom for artistic, creative, and scientific pursuits)	UDHR 27(1); ICESCR 15(1)(a),(b)	Directive Principle. Western Australia values cultural diversity, artistic freedom, and scientific advancement. The state will strive to promote public participation in cultural life (supporting arts, cultural heritage, and community traditions) and to ensure that citizens benefit from scientific progress and research. In practice, this means Western Australia will not censor artistic expression or scientific inquiry; it may establish museums, libraries, or research grants to foster culture and science. However, there is no specific legal claim that a person can make upon the state for cultural or scientific provisions. The duty is negative (to not obstruct creativity or the sharing of knowledge) and positive only to the extent of facilitating these pursuits where feasible. This principle ensures that Western Australia's development will embrace innovation and cultural richness, guided by the idea that a free society lets knowledge and art flourish.
Protection of intellectual property (IP) rights (moral and material interests of creators)	UDHR 27(2); ICESCR 15(1)(c)	Binding Law (see Property Rights). [Included in the enforceable rights above]. The right of authors, inventors, and artists to benefit from their creations is secured under Western Australia's binding property rights provisions. Western Australia will adhere to international intellectual property norms and protect patents, copyrights, and trademarks through ordinary law. (This item is listed here to acknowledge its UDHR source, but in Western Australia it is already covered as a constitutional property right.)
Right to seek asylum (to seek and enjoy asylum from persecution)	UDHR 14; (see also UN	Principle (Qualified). Western Australia embraces the humanitarian principle that victims of persecution should find refuge. The Constitution

Social/Economic Right or Principle	Source	Western Australia's Recognition
	Refugee Convention)	will reflect a commitment to honour international refugee obligations in good faith. However, the right to asylum is not absolute or individually enforceable against Western Australia's government. The state retains discretion over immigration and asylum policies (such as quotas or security screenings), consistent with international law. In essence, Western Australia will provide avenues for asylum seekers to have their claims heard and will not return refugees to places of persecution (respecting non-refoulement), but it stops short of guaranteeing entry as a constitutional right.
Social order enabling all rights (the right to a social and international order in which the rights in the UDHR can be fully realised)	UDHR 28	Aspirational Principle. This broad clause—calling for an order that realises all human rights—is reflected in Western Australia's dedication to both domestic institution-building and international cooperation that foster human rights. It has no direct legal effect in Western Australia's courts. However, it frames the spirit of the Constitution: Western Australia sees itself as part of the global effort to create a just world. The government is encouraged to support a fair international order and to structure domestic society to maximise the realisation of rights. This principle, while unenforceable, serves as a guiding star for governance and foreign policy.
Duties to the community and general welfare (everyone has duties to others; rights may be limited by law solely for the purpose of securing due recognition of others' rights and the general welfare in a democratic society)	UDHR 29	Interpretive Guideline. Western Australia's Constitution will acknowledge that in the exercise of their rights, individuals must respect the rights of others and the requirements of public order and general welfare. This clause guides how rights are interpreted and harmonised. It does not grant the state blanket power to override rights; rather, it codifies a principle of proportionality and responsible use of liberty. Any limitation on a right must be prescribed by clear law

Social/Economic Right or Principle	Source	Western Australia's Recognition
		and truly necessary to protect a competing public interest or the rights of others. This principle ensures that one person's freedoms do not destroy another's—for example, one cannot invoke "freedom of speech" as protection for violent agitation that would strip others of their rights. It underpins lawful limitations (like quarantine during a pandemic to protect public health) while cautioning that such limits are exceptions to be narrowly construed.
Prohibition on the abuse of rights (no one may engage in activity aimed at destroying any rights and freedoms in the UDHR)	UDHR 30	Interpretive Guideline. Western Australia will include a saving clause clarifying that nothing in the Constitution's rights provisions can be interpreted as license to deny or destroy those rights. In other words, a person cannot misuse constitutional rights to undermine the constitutional order or to justify tyranny. For example, a group cannot claim "freedom of association" to protect a criminal conspiracy to overthrow rights, nor can an official cite "public order" to extinguish rights entirely. This clause guards against self-contradictory legal arguments and emphasises that the purpose of Western Australia's Constitution is to secure human freedom. All interpretation of rights must be faithful to that purpose.

Table: Economic, social, and cultural rights recognised as non-justiciable Directive Principles in Western Australia, with their UDHR/ICESCR sources. These guide state policy and legislation but are not individually enforceable in court.

By adopting these Directive Principles, Western Australia incorporates UDHR and ICESCR aspirations into its Constitution while distinguishing enforceable rights from policy goals. These principles—covering social security, work, living standards, health, education, and culture—represent key societal values. They require resource allocation and policy decisions balanced within a limited-government framework. As non-binding, they preserve separation of powers and democratic flexibility, with courts unable to mandate specific policies. Congress is guided by these principles in legislation. For instance, Western Australia plans to provide free primary and secondary education, universal healthcare, paid parental leave, and a four-day work week through statutes reflecting these directives. Shortfalls are addressed politically, not through litigation.

Snapshot: Four-Day Work Week: Better Off ($)

Western Australia's shift to a four-day work week, backed by resource revenues and zero income taxes, leaves citizens better off financially than Australia's five-day grind—even after ending forced superannuation (treated here as part of your total pay package). Using Australia's 2024 median full-time gross salary of ~$88,400: Aussies take home about $67,400 after taxes and Medicare (with ~$10,600 super locked until retirement). In Western Australia, assume employers roll that super into your direct pay (total ~$99,000), but for 80% effort: ~$79,200 tax-free in hand. If you voluntarily save 12% (~$9,500) for retirement, you still net ~$69,700—more than Australia's take-home, with full control over your money.

This quick snapshot shows how Western Australia turns resource wealth into real gains: work less, live more, without the financial hit.

Note: These back-of-the-envelope figures assume steady employer costs and no extras like student debt; they require rigorous Whitepaper scrutiny for variables like wage inflation or sector differences. Figures based on 2024-25 data; adjust for inflation per WA Treasury.

Snapshot: Happy Families: Subsidised Parental Leave

Western Australia's universal parental leave provides all citizens a flat 30% of average weekly earnings (~$603/week)—6 weeks for mothers (recovery & bonding) and 4 weeks for fathers/partners (shared care).

Total per family: ~$6,470, funded by resource revenues.

Annual cost: ~$190 million for ~30,500 births, boosting maternal health (lower depression risk) and child development.

Affordability: At <0.40% of URR revenue of $48B—highly sustainable, ensuring equitable family support without fiscal strain.

Directive Principles are subordinate to fundamental rights and cannot justify infringements. They promote a society where freedom aligns with responsibility, and progress advances alongside individual liberty. Western Australia balances civil-political rights as enforceable law with socio-economic rights as non-coercive objectives, upholding human dignity while maintaining fiscal responsibility and limited government.

With Human Law defined—enforceable rights and guiding principles—the Constitution integrates these into governance, including the Human Rights Tribunal.

Independent Human Rights Tribunal

To enforce Human Law and provide citizens with an accessible forum for addressing rights violations, Western Australia's Constitution establishes an independent Human Rights Tribunal (HRT). This Tribunal forms the core of Western Australia's Fourth Branch of government, dedicated to upholding Human Law. It operates as a co-equal branch, separate from the judiciary, with authority to hold officials accountable. Through citizen participation in its governance and processes, the HRT ensures that rights protections remain responsive to the public, aligning with Western Australia's emphasis on citizen sovereignty and limited government.

The HRT's structure and powers are defined in a dedicated constitutional article, (see Chapter 15: A New Nation's Constitution, Title 16: Human Law & Medical Freedom), ensuring its independence, jurisdiction, and accessibility. Some core elements follow.

Article 5—Human Rights Tribunal: Overview

Establishment & Status. There is established a Human Rights Tribunal as a superior court of record constituted under this Constitution with exclusive original and appellate jurisdiction over matters of Human Law as defined in Article 1 and Annexure A. The HRT is independent and not subject to the direction or control of the Executive or of any person or authority, save as provided by this Constitution.

Jurisdiction: Civil and Criminal. (a) Civil. The HRT has jurisdiction to hear and determine civil complaints alleging violations or threatened violations of Human Law and to provide effective remedies. (b) Criminal. The HRT has jurisdiction to try offences created by or under law constituting egregious breaches of Human Law (including, as prescribed by law, torture; enforced disappearance; cruel, inhuman or degrading treatment; slavery or servitude; arbitrary detention; persecution; and other grave deprivations of non-derogable rights under Article 2).

Powers & Remedies. The HRT may grant declarations, injunctions (including interim relief), orders for release, restitution, compensation, and exemplary damages; set aside, vary, or suspend any act or decision inconsistent with this Constitution; invalidate a law to the extent of inconsistency; impose criminal penalties for offences within its jurisdiction; and punish for contempt. All organs of state must assist and comply with its lawful orders.

Citizen Governance & Juries. (a) Appointments are subject to citizen governance in accordance with sub-article (5). (b) In criminal proceedings above thresholds fixed by law, trial shall be by jury, with eligibility, summons, and protections prescribed by law. (c) The HRT may convene Citizen Panels on Human Rights, drawn by lot and trained under statute, to assist in systemic inquiries and to make binding and non-binding recommendations published with reasons.

Composition, Appointment, Tenure & Removal. (a) Composition. The HRT consists of a President and other Judges as prescribed by law; it may sit in Divisions (Trial, Appeals, Inquiries) constituted by Rules of Court. (b) Appointment. Judges are appointed by the President from a shortlist publicly nominated by the Citizen Oversight Committee (COC) following open, merit-based selection, and ratified by a two-thirds vote of Congress. (c) Tenure. Judges hold office for a fixed renewable term prescribed by law, not less than five nor more than nine years, with security of remuneration; renewal requires re-vetting by the COC against published criteria. (d) Removal. A Judge may be removed only for proved misbehaviour or incapacity, upon a two-thirds vote of Congress following an open hearing, on a motion supported by a COC report. Interim suspension may be ordered by the HRT Appeals Division on COC application. (e) Disqualifications and conflicts are prescribed by law and enforced by the HRT and the COC; undisclosed conflicts void affected decisions unless the Appeals Division determines otherwise in the public interest.

Institutional Independence & Funding. (a) The HRT shall control its own listing, registries, security, and administration, and shall make Rules of Court consistent with this Constitution and law. (b) Appropriation. The Western Australian Reserve Authority (WARA) shall provide to the HRT a guaranteed, non-lapsing annual appropriation charged on the Consolidated Fund, not less than a statutory floor or formula, and disbursed in equal monthly instalments free from Executive discretion. Multi-year commitments for essential operations shall not be reduced mid-term except by a two-thirds vote of Congress on public reasons certified by the Citizen Oversight Committee. (c) Salaries, pensions, and conditions of Judges and key officers shall not be reduced to their disadvantage during term.

Procedure, Access & Celerity. (a) Proceedings are public save for narrowly tailored orders necessary to protect life, safety, or fair-trial rights. (b) Standing is open to any aggrieved person or, for systemic matters, to public-interest groups as prescribed by law. (c) The HRT shall prioritise prompt resolution, with statutory timelines for decisions and reasons.

The Human Rights Tribunal is Western Australia's answer to the problem of rights without remedies. It is a powerful institutional watchdog and executioner of justice. Through its establishment, Western Australia ensures that the promises of Article 5 are kept: rights will be vigilantly guarded by an independent tribunal that the people themselves help run. This model is truly novel—Western Australia is creating a branch of government that is not legislature, executive, or traditional judiciary, but a hybrid guardian of the Constitution's most sacred values. It demonstrates to the world that a state can be constructed such that the people, through legal institutions, govern themselves in the realm of human rights. This framework is among the most comprehensive attempts in Australia to constitutionalise enforceable human rights through an independent Fourth Branch.

Emergency Powers: Direct Citizen Oversight

Western Australia's Constitution, under Title 16: Human Law & Medical Freedom, establishes strict limits on emergency powers to safeguard human rights, drawing lessons from Australia's covid response where measures such as travel restrictions, lockdowns, and professional sanctions raised concerns from the United Nations and domestic oversight bodies. These included bans on citizens leaving or returning to the country, public housing lockdowns deemed human rights violations, and suspensions of medical professionals for expressing views on treatments and vaccine safety. Western Australia ensures such powers are subject to immediate citizen-led review, preventing misuse while allowing necessary responses to genuine threats.

Emergency declarations are permissible only for imminent threats to public safety, health, or order, and must be narrowly tailored, time-limited, and consistent with non-derogable rights listed in the Constitution's Annexure D (e.g., freedom from torture, slavery, non-consensual medical experimentation, and arbitrary detention). No measure may suspend the core of Human Law, and all actions require real-time publication with justifications.

The Citizen Oversight Committee (COC), as detailed in Title 18, Article 2, Citizen Oversight Committee, holds primary oversight authority per Article 7 of Title 16: Human Law & Medical Freedom. Comprising non-partisan, elected citizens from staggered cohorts to ensure geographic diversity and continuity, the COC reviews declarations within 48 hours. It may suspend or modify measures that infringe rights, with decisions subject to Human Rights Tribunal review.

Citizen Panels, drawn from trained, eligible citizens, assist the COC in assessments. These panels evaluate proportionality, necessity, and rights impacts, issuing recommendations that the COC must consider. This direct involvement empowers citizens to protect their liberties, fostering trust in governance and ensuring accountability.

Officials declaring or implementing emergencies face personal liability for violations, with no immunity. The HRT provides remedies, including injunctions, damages, and invalidation of unlawful measures. Transparency is enforced via the public ledger under Title 19: Freedom of Disclosure Framework, allowing citizens to monitor and challenge actions.

This framework positions Western Australia as a model where emergency powers serve the people without eroding freedoms, encouraging a society resilient through voluntary cooperation rather than coercion.

Constitutional Guarantee of Medical Freedom & Bodily Autonomy

Western Australia addresses a specific domain that recent events proved vulnerable: the sanctity of the doctor–patient relationship and the principle of informed consent in medicine. During the covid pandemic, Australian regulators (notably AHPRA, the AHPPC, and ATAGI) and governments, imposed restrictions that many felt violated medical ethics—doctors were gagged from voicing concerns, practitioners were punished for granting vaccine exemptions, and individuals were coerced into medical interventions under threat of exclusion from work and society. These incidents underscored the need to constitutionally protect medical freedom to prevent any future regime from using health emergencies or professional regulations to trample individual rights and clinical independence.

Western Australia's Constitution thus contains a dedicated article enshrining Medical Freedom and Informed Consent as a fundamental part of Human Law. This article ensures that no government or board can replicate the heavy-handed tactics seen in Australia; it safeguards patients' bodily autonomy and doctors' professional integrity at the highest legal level. The article is comprehensive, covering the core facets of medical freedom. Its full text is provided below:

Article 8—Sanctity of the Doctor–Patient Relationship: Overview

Informed Consent. Every person has the right to bodily autonomy and to free and informed consent; emergency exceptions shall be narrowly defined by law and guided solely by an individual patient's best interests.

Clinical Independence & Confidentiality. Practitioners owe independent clinical judgment free from undue interference; doctor–patient communications are confidential save for narrowly tailored, lawful court orders concerning serious crime.

Freedom of Medical Expression. No law, directive, or action shall abridge good-faith professional discourse or the communication of information necessary for informed consent.

Medical Exemptions. Licensed medical practitioners may issue bona fide exemptions where interventions are contraindicated or deemed by a medical practitioner to be unduly risky; neither the State nor employers may retaliate against practitioners or patients for exercising rights under this clause.

Anti-Coercion & Remedies. No person shall be coerced into treatment against informed refusal; Congress shall legislate civil and, for willful egregious breaches, criminal remedies; affected persons may seek relief before the Human Rights Tribunal.

Article 8 establishes constitutional protections for medical ethics and individual health choices, ensuring that personal autonomy and professional independence are upheld. These provisions draw from international standards, such as the prohibition on non-consensual medical experimentation in the International Covenant on Civil and Political Rights (ICCPR) Article 7 and address historical concerns from regulatory actions during public health events.

Informed Consent is Inviolable

This clause enshrines the principle that medical procedures require voluntary, informed agreement, aligning with ethical frameworks like the Nuremberg Code and UNESCO's Universal Declaration on Bioethics and Human Rights. It allows limited exceptions for emergencies or incapacity, with safeguards to prioritise patient interests. In Western Australia, this ensures individuals can refuse treatments, including during public health measures, supporting a framework where health decisions remain personal.

Protecting the Doctor–Patient Relationship

The article safeguards confidentiality and practitioner autonomy, preventing undue state interference in treatment decisions. This promotes trust in healthcare by ensuring practitioners can tailor advice to individual needs without external pressure, consistent with ethical duties to act in the patient's best interest.

Freedom of Medical Speech

Clause 3 protects practitioners' rights to express opinions and engage in discourse, provided it is in good faith. This encourages open scientific discussion and prevents suppression of diverse views, as seen in cases where regulators disciplined professionals for questioning official guidance. Regulatory actions are limited to verifiable misconduct, fostering an environment for evidence-based debate.

Right to Medical Exemptions

Practitioners can grant exemptions based on professional judgment, which must be honoured without penalty. This clause supports individualised care, allowing considerations of personal health risks or evidence gaps, and protects both practitioners and patients from reprisal.

No Retaliation or Coercion

The anti-coercion provision prohibits forced treatments and mandates remedies for violations, including through the Human Rights Tribunal. It requires alignment of regulatory bodies with these principles, ensuring enforcement prioritises ethical practice over uniformity.

Overall, Article 8 positions Western Australia as a jurisdiction committed to medical freedom, where constitutional guarantees empower citizens and professionals to make informed health decisions. This framework balances public health needs with individual rights, promoting a society where healthcare is guided by consent and evidence rather than mandate.

Conclusion

Western Australia's Fourth Branch establishes a framework for Human Law & Medical Freedom, integrating fundamental rights into the core of governance. This structure positions human rights as the supreme legal authority, enforceable through independent institutions such as the Human Rights Tribunal (HRT) and the Citizen Oversight Committee (COC).

This approach addresses historical human rights challenges in Australia, such as systemic injustices against First Nations peoples and measures during the covid pandemic that included travel restrictions, lockdowns, and regulatory actions against medical professionals. Under Western Australia's framework, emergency powers are limited, requiring COC review within 48 hours to prevent misuse, with non-derogable rights remaining protected.

Western Australia's model demonstrates that governance can prioritise human rights while maintaining effective democratic processes. The Fourth Branch fosters a society where officials are accountable, citizens are empowered, and institutions support liberty and justice. Through these constitutional guarantees, Western Australia offers a framework where rights are upheld as foundational to legitimate authority, encouraging resilience and voluntary cooperation.

Sources

Unless otherwise stated, online materials were viewed on 6 February 2026.

1. United Nations, *Universal Declaration of Human Rights* (1948) <https://www.refworld.org/legal/resolution/unga/1948/en/11563>. Annotation: Articles 1, 2 (equal dignity and rights); Article 3 (right to life, liberty, security); Article 4 (freedom from slavery); Article 5 (freedom from torture); Article 6 (person before law); Articles 7–8 (equal protection & remedy); Article 9 (no arbitrary detention); Articles 10–11 (fair trial, presumption of innocence, no ex post facto); Article 12 (privacy); Article 13 (freedom of movement); Article 14(1) (right to seek asylum); Article 15 (right to nationality); Article 16 (right to marry and family); Article 17 (property); Article 18 (freedom of thought, conscience, religion); Article 19 (freedom of opinion and expression); Article 20(1) (assembly and association); Article 21 (participation in government); Article 22 (social security); Article 23 (work, fair conditions, equal pay, unions); Article 24 (rest and leisure); Article 25(1) (adequate standard of living, health); Article 25(2) (motherhood and childhood protection); Article 26 (education); Article 27(1) (participation in cultural life, science); Article 27(2) (moral and material interests of authors—intellectual property); Article 28 (social/international order for rights); Article 29 (duties to community, permissible limitations); Article 30 (no destroying rights).
2. United Nations, *International Covenant on Civil and Political Rights* (1966) <https://www.refworld.org/legal/agreements/unga/1966/en/17703>. Annotation: Article 2(1) & 26 (non-discrimination, equal protection); Article 2(3) (effective remedy); Article 4(2) (non-derogable rights in emergencies: life, torture, slavery, no retroactivity, personhood, freedom of thought); Article 6(1) (right to life); Article 7 (freedom from torture; no medical experimentation without consent); Article 8 (no slavery; no forced labor); Article 9 (liberty and security of person; no arbitrary arrest; habeas corpus); Article 10(1) (humane treatment of detainees); Article 11 (no imprisonment for debt)—Western Australia adopts this principle (ICCPR 11); Article 14 (fair trial rights); Article 15 (no ex post facto criminal laws); Article 16 (legal personhood); Article 17 (privacy); Article 18 (freedom of thought, conscience, religion); Article 19 (freedom of expression); Article 21 (peaceful assembly); Article 22 (freedom of association, including unions); Article 23 (rights of family and marriage); Article 24(3) (child's right to nationality); Article 25 (participation in public affairs, voting); Article 27 (minority rights). Article 20 (prohibition of war propaganda and incitement of hatred)—Western Australia will comply by narrowly outlawing incitement to violence/hostility without infringing general free speech.

3. United Nations, *International Covenant on Economic, Social and Cultural Rights* (1966) <https://www.ohchr.org/sites/default/files/cescr.pdf>. Annotation: Article 6 (right to work); Article 7 (just and favourable work conditions; fair wages; safe and healthy working conditions; rest, leisure, reasonable limitation of working hours and holidays); Article 8 (trade union rights, right to strike); Article 9 (right to social security); Article 10 (protection of family; paid maternity leave; protection of children from exploitation); Article 11 (right to adequate standard of living; freedom from hunger); Article 12 (right to highest attainable standard of health); Article 13 (right to education); Article 14 (compulsory primary education plan); Article 15(1)(a) & (b) (participation in cultural life, benefit from scientific progress); Article 15(1)(c) (protection of authors/inventors—intellectual property). Western Australia acknowledges these as directive principles rather than enforceable rights, except IP rights which are enforceable via property rights.
4. Sophie McNeill, 'Commission to Investigate Abuses Against Australia's First Nations' (Human Rights Watch, March 2021) <https://www.hrw.org/news/2021/03/10/commission-investigate-abuses-against-australias-first-nations>. Annotation: Reporting on the planned truth commission into "two centuries of violence, abuse, and discrimination" against Indigenous peoples in Australia. Highlights Australia's ongoing legacy of colonial injustices and human rights abuses, which Western Australia explicitly repudiates as part of its founding ethos. This context justifies Western Australia's commitment to break from Australia's past and ensure such state-sanctioned abuses are never repeated.
5. Lydia Khalil, 'Covid Response Has Weakened Rights' (Lowy Institute, September 2021) <https://interactives.lowyinstitute.org/features/fortress-australia/article/civil-liberties/>. Annotation: Analysis of how Australia's covid measures eroded civil liberties. Notes that Australia "banned its own citizens from leaving the country...raised human rights concerns from the UN" and even criminalised return from certain countries. Describes how Victorian lockdown of public housing towers violated human rights and how emergency powers became normalised, with thousands of human rights breaches identified. These real examples underpin Western Australia's determination to place emergency powers under strict citizen oversight and to forbid travel bans or coercive mandates that characterised Australia's approach.
6. Australian Senate, 'COVID-19 Royal Commission Submission' (Submission, 2022) <https://www.aph.gov.au/DocumentStore.ashx?id=125f079e-66ad-4109-bac0-cd4c675addee>. Annotation: Testimony from Health Practitioners confirming their suspensions from practice for speaking of possible harms from covid injectables, and lack of safety data. Confirms that Australian regulators silenced medical professionals, providing impetus for Western Australia's Medical Freedom Act. Also references the Medical Journal of Australia report on AHPRA overreach.
7. Wikipedia, 'Directive Principles' (Web Page) <https://en.wikipedia.org/wiki/Directive_Principles>. Annotation: States that these principles are "not enforceable by any court, but ... are considered 'fundamental in the governance of the country'...". This is directly invoked in Western Australia's approach to socio-economic rights, balancing moral obligations with non-justiciability. Western Australia's Constitution mirrors this concept, ensuring that goals like education and health guide policy without creating judicial mandates.
8. Cate Swannell, 'Fallout Continues from AHPRA "Over-Reach"' (2022) *InSight+, Medical Journal of Australia* <https://insightplus.mja.com.au/2022/29/fallout-continues-from-ahpra-over-reach/>.
9. UNESCO, *Universal Declaration on Bioethics and Human Rights* (2005) <https://www.unesco.org/en/legal-affairs/universal-declaration-bioethics-and-human-rights>.
10. U.S. Military Tribunal, 'The Nuremberg Code' (1947) <https://encyclopedia.ushmm.org/content/en/article/the-nuremberg-code>.
11. Australian Human Rights Commission, *Human Rights and COVID-19: A Review of Impacts* (2020) <https://humanrights.gov.au/our-work/rights-and-freedoms/publications/human-rights-and-covid-19-review-impacts-2020>.
12. Autonomy, *The UK's Four-Day Week Pilot: Final Results* (2023) <https://www.autonomy.work/portfolio/final-results-uk-trial/>.
13. Microsoft Japan, *Work-Life Choice Challenge 2019 Summer—Microsoft Japan Four-Day Work Week Trial* (2019) <https://news.microsoft.com/ja-jp/2019/10/31/191031-microsoft-japan-releases-findings-on-work-life-choice-challenge-2019-summer/>.

14. J Heymann, A Raub and A Earle, 'Creating and Using New Data Sources to Analyze the Relationship Between Social Policy and Global Health: The Case of Maternal Leave' (2013) 5(2) *World Medical & Health Policy* 170 <https://onlinelibrary.wiley.com/doi/10.1002/wmh3.24>.
15. M O'Brien and P Moss, 'Fathers, Work and Family Policies in Europe' in Michael E Lamb (ed), *The Role of the Father in Child Development* (John Wiley & Sons, 5th ed, 2010) <https://www.researchgate.net/publication/265190801>.
16. B Gault, H Hartmann, A Hegewisch, J Milli and L Reichlin, *Paid Parental Leave in the United States: What the Data Tell Us about Access, Usage, and Economic and Health Benefits* (Institute for Women's Policy Research, 2014) <https://iwpr.org/iwpr-publications/briefing-paper/paid-parental-leave-in-the-united-states-what-the-data-tell-us-about-access-usage-and-economic-and-health-benefits/>.
17. OECD, *Is the Last Mile the Longest? Economic Gains from Gender Equality in Nordic Countries* (2019) <https://www.oecd.org/publications/is-the-last-mile-the-longest-economic-gains-from-gender-equality-in-nordic-countries-9789264311959-en.htm>.
18. Commonwealth Fund, *Mirror, Mirror 2021: Reflecting Poorly—Health Care in the U.S. Compared to Other High-Income Countries* (2021) <https://www.commonwealthfund.org/publications/fund-reports/2021/aug/mirror-mirror-2021-reflecting-poorly>.
19. UNESCO Institute for Statistics, 'Education and the Sustainable Development Goals: Progress and Challenges' (2020) <http://uis.unesco.org/en/news/education-and-sustainable-development-goals-progress-and-challenges>.
20. World Bank, 'Universal Health Coverage Overview' (2023) <https://www.worldbank.org/en/topic/universalhealthcoverage/overview>.
21. UNICEF, *Paid Leave and Family Support Policies: Progress, Gaps and Emerging Issues* (2021) <https://www.unicef.org/reports/paid-leave-and-family-support-policies-2021>.
22. R J Petts and C Knoester, 'Paternity Leave and Parental Relationships: Findings from the United States' (2019) 48(2) *Journal of Social Policy* 349 <https://doi.org/10.1017/S0047279418000326>.
23. K Parker, J M Horowitz and A Brown, 'Americans Widely Support Paid Family and Medical Leave, but Differ Over Specific Policies' (Pew Research Center, 2017) <https://www.pewresearch.org/social-trends/2017/03/23/americans-widely-support-paid-family-and-medical-leave-but-differ-over-specific-policies/>.
24. P Moss, *International Review of Leave Policies and Related Research* (Institute of Education, University of London, 2011) <https://www.leavenetwork.org/annual-review-reports/>.
25. H Perera, 'Why a Four-Day Workweek Is Good for Business—and Workers' (World Economic Forum, 2023) <https://www.weforum.org/agenda/2023/02/four-day-week-productivity-happier-healthier-employees/>.
26. Australian Department of Education, 'History of Higher Education Policy in Australia' (2024) <https://www.education.gov.au/higher-education-policies-and-legislation/resources/history-higher-education-policy-australia>.
27. Juliet Schor et al, *Four-Day Week Global Trial Results Report: UK, 2022–2023 Cohort* (2023) <https://4dayweek.com/assets/downloads/UK_Feb23_Report.pdf>.
28. Australian Bureau of Statistics, 'Employee Earnings' (August 2024) <https://www.abs.gov.au/statistics/labour/earnings-and-working-conditions/employee-earnings/latest-release>.
29. Australian Taxation Office, 'Simple Tax Calculator (2024-25)' (2024) <https://www.ato.gov.au/calculators-and-tools/tax-return-simple-tax-calculator>.
30. WA Department of Treasury, 'Wages Data' (May 2025) <https://www.wa.gov.au/organisation/department-of-treasury-and-finance/wages>.
31. SalaryAfterTax.com, 'Australia Salary Calculator' (2025) <https://salaryaftertax.com/salary-calculator/australia>.
32. Victorian Ombudsman, *Investigation into the Detention and Treatment of Public Housing Residents Arising from a COVID-19 'Hard Lockdown' in July 2020* (Report, 17 December 2020) <https://www.ombudsman.vic.gov.au/our-impact/investigation-reports/investigation-into-the-detention-and-treatment-of-public-housing-residents-arising-from-a-covid-19-hard-lockdown-in-july-2020/>. Annotation: Primary investigative report supporting claims about coercive covid-era lockdown

measures (notably the July 2020 Melbourne public housing tower lockdown) and associated rights, process, and welfare concerns.

33. Australian Human Rights Commission, 'Travel ban and sanctions on Australians travelling from India' (Media Release, 1 May 2021) <https://humanrights.gov.au/about-us/media-centre/search-listing-media-releases/media-releases/travel-ban-and-sanctions-australians-travelling-india>. Annotation: Authoritative Australian human rights body identifying human rights concerns with the India "travel pause", including criminal penalties applied to citizens attempting to return.
34. United Nations Human Rights Committee, 'CCPR General Comment No 27: Article 12 (Freedom of Movement)' (General Comment, 2 November 1999) UN Doc CCPR/C/21/Rev.1/Add.9 <https://docs.un.org/en/CCPR/C/21/Rev.1/Add.9>. Annotation: Core UN interpretive authority on ICCPR freedom of movement (including proportionality/necessity limits), supporting any statement that such restrictions engage recognised international rights standards.
35. Parliamentary Joint Committee on Human Rights, *Human rights scrutiny report: Report 8 of 2021* (Report, 23 June 2021) <https://www.aph.gov.au/-/media/Committees/Senate/committee/humanrights_ctte/reports/2021/Report_8/Report_8_of_2021.pdf>. Annotation: Parliamentary human-rights scrutiny analysing Biosecurity instruments (including overseas travel restrictions / India travel pause), expressly engaging rights to freedom of movement and the right to enter/return to one's own country.
36. Human Rights and Equal Opportunity Commission, *Bringing Them Home: Report of the National Inquiry into the Separation of Aboriginal and Torres Strait Islander Children from Their Families* (Report, 1997) <https://humanrights.gov.au/bringing-them-home/index.html>. Annotation: Canonical primary report documenting the Stolen Generations policy history, impacts, and recommendations.
37. AIATSIS, 'Colonial Frontier Massacres in Australia, 1788–1930' (Project Page, 31 December 2022) <https://yumi-sabe.aiatsis.gov.au/project/1932>. Annotation: Authoritative national research-project overview on frontier massacre documentation; supports carefully-framed statements about frontier violence, evidentiary methodology, and recorded massacre events.
38. University of Newcastle, 'Colonial Frontier Massacres in Australia, 1788–1930' (Digital Map/Project Site) <https://c21ch.newcastle.edu.au/colonialmassacres/>. Annotation: Primary project site for the massacre mapping dataset and methodology.
39. Australian Health Practitioner Regulation Agency (AHPRA), 'What you need to know about the COVID-19 vaccine rollout' (Joint Statement, 9 March 2021) <https://www.ahpra.gov.au/News/2021-03-09-vaccination-statement.aspx>. Annotation: Primary regulator statement setting expectations for registered practitioners regarding covid vaccination information.
40. Medical Board of Australia, 'False and misleading advertising on COVID-19' (News, 31 March 2020) <https://www.medicalboard.gov.au/News/2020-03-31-false-and-misleading-advertising-on-covid-19.aspx>. Annotation: Primary board notice linking misleading covid treatment claims (especially advertising) to potential disciplinary consequences.
41. Australian Health Practitioner Regulation Agency (AHPRA), 'Social media guidance' (Web Page) <https://www.ahpra.gov.au/Resources/Social-media-guidance.aspx>. Annotation: General regulatory guidance tying social-media conduct to the National Law, codes of conduct and advertising guidelines.

WA: A Wellness-First Nation

The modern developed world faces a profound health crisis. Chronic diseases consume most of our budgets, while outcomes stagnate. The dominant model of late-stage, pharmaceutical-centred, hospital-based and crisis-driven care treats disease but does not create health. Western Australia's answer is a Real Wellness and Health Care System that embeds new incentives toward prevention, integrative care, citizen empowerment and transparent evidence for every medical intervention, supported (not controlled) by AI and open digital infrastructure. We propose a constitutionally enshrined and integrity-guarding redesign of how a nation creates health.

What sets WA's model apart is how it is safeguarded. First, Human Law & Medical Freedom are entrenched in the Constitution and enforced by an independent Human Rights Tribunal (HRT) so that informed consent, freedom of clinical judgment, and due process are non-negotiable. If an authority overreaches, citizens and clinicians have direct remedies in law, with enabling statutes giving these guarantees real teeth. Second, Western Australia's Anti-Corruption Framework makes government actions auditable by design—using blockchain-anchored public ledgers and AI-assisted oversight—to keep contracts, procurement and agency decisions tamper-evident, searchable and reviewable in real time. On top of these safeguards, citizen juries will be used to appoint the top tier of the medical bureaucracy, with the goal of creating a national health machinery directly responsible to the people rather than to elites or drug companies. Health is thus delivered within an integrity system where wrongdoing is both illegal and hard to hide.

Within this constitutional and capture-resistant scaffolding, we propose a three-layer system (personal wellness coaching; community Wellness Hubs; re-imagined hospitals) governed by a National Wellness Authority (NWA), with Citizen Oversight Councils, registered databases drawn upon by AI used in care (henceforth referred to as "model cards"), and public audit trails for spending, outcomes, supply chains and decisions.

The Crisis of the Current Model

The covid crisis exposed deep structural weaknesses in global health systems. Governments relied almost exclusively on a select few pharmaceutical interventions while sidelining basic public health strategies such as nutrition, supplementation, and immune resilience (not to mention off-label, off-patent pharmaceuticals). Regulatory capture by industry and censorship of dissenting voices further eroded public trust. At the same time, chronic illness reached epidemic levels: in WA, nearly half the population now lives with at least one chronic condition, while hospital systems operate at or beyond capacity.

This is not simply a crisis of funding; it is a crisis of vision. Health systems have become illness industries, incentivised to treat but not to heal. Training for doctors emphasises pharmaceuticals while neglecting nutrition, environmental determinants of disease, and the psychosocial drivers of wellness. The result is a population increasingly dependent on drugs, procedures, and hospital admissions, with diminishing returns in both quality of life and life expectancy.

A Wellness-Centered Vision

A real wellness and health care system turns the conventional model inside out. Rather than asking, "How do we treat disease?", it begins with the question: "How do we create health?"

The guiding principles of Western Australia's new health system are:

> ***Health before disease.*** Prevention and resilience as the primary goals.
>
> ***Integration of wisdom.*** Uniting nutritional, lifestyle, environmental, and conventional medicine.
>
> ***Medical Freedom.*** Respecting autonomy, informed consent, and choice.
>
> ***Transparency & accountability.*** Governance free from corporate capture, with auditing and citizen oversight built into the system.

This system embeds the knowledge that true health is shaped by diet, environment, sleep, stress, social connection, and purposeful living—factors too often ignored in the dominant model of medicine—while featuring active controls against corruption.

The Blueprint In Brief

The proposed system is built across three layers:

> ***Individual Wellness Layer.*** Personalised AI health coaches, micronutrient monitoring, lifestyle optimisation.
>
> ***Community Wellness Hubs.*** Local centres combining GPs, integrative doctors, naturopaths, nutritionists, midwives, and educators to provide prevention-first care and care for most uncomplicated pregnancies and deliveries.
>
> ***Hospital & Specialist Layer.*** Reimagined hospitals, perhaps renamed sanitariums to emphasise the goal of health, that combine emergency medicine with integrative oncology, alternative treatments like hyperbaric oxygen and IV vitamin C, and lifestyle-based rehabilitation.

Guidelines are provided by a National Wellness Authority (NWA) with citizen oversight and blockchain auditing to ensure transparency.

The rollout proceeds in three phases:

> ***Phase 1 (0–3 years).*** Establish the NWA, write all national wellness guidelines drawing on input from coal-face practitioners demonstrated to have no financial links to any commercial enterprise, and pilot Wellness Hubs.
>
> ***Phase 2 (3–7 years).*** Expand Wellness Hubs nationwide, reshape hospitals into sanitariums, and embed integrative therapies into sanitariums. Establish citizen oversight mechanisms and drug/intervention approval processes, first paring down approved medicines to those listed on the WHO Essential Medicines list from 2019.
>
> ***Phase 3 (7–15 years).*** Implement drug/intervention approval processes, using panels to evaluate each submission. Explore the establishment of a World Wellness Council as an alternative to the WHO's medical monopoly.

The Targeted Outcomes

The benefits of this system are potentially transformative:

> ***Economic.*** Lower chronic disease burden; reduced pharmaceutical dependency; and long-term sustainability.

Social. Stronger communities, enhanced resilience, restoration of trust in medicine.

Global. A replicable model that inspires citizens worldwide and breaks the cycle of corporate-controlled health care.

The world is ready for a health care system that is not an illness industry but a WellnessCare revolution.

1. Vision & Guiding Principles

If the twentieth century was defined by the perceived conquest of infectious diseases through antibiotics, vaccines, and sanitation, then the twenty-first century must be defined by the conquest of chronic disease through prevention, integration, and empowerment. The central failure of modern medicine has been to confuse the management of illness with the creation of health. A real wellness and health care system seeks to restore that balance. This requires reimagining what health itself means.

This vision begins with the simple proposition that health is not the absence of disease, but the presence of vitality, resilience, and purpose.

To design a system that cultivates these qualities, we must articulate clear guiding principles that are universal, durable, and resistant to corruption. These principles will form the bedrock of a health care system capable of transforming the health of an independent WA.

1.1 Health before Disease

The first principle is prevention over reaction. Instead of waiting for illness to develop, the system must cultivate wellness from the start of life to its end. This requires a shift in incentives: from rewarding hospitals for admissions to rewarding communities for health outcomes. It requires investment in education, nutrition, physical activity, sleep, stress reduction, and environmental health—the factors that account for the majority of chronic disease risk.

For example, vitamin D sufficiency alone could reduce rates of respiratory illness, osteoporosis, and certain cancers. Addressing dietary deficiencies in magnesium, zinc, omega-3 fatty acids and certain herbs could improve cardiovascular and mental health outcomes at a fraction of the cost of pharmaceutical interventions. A wellness-first system does not ignore drugs and hospitals, but it sees them as a last resort, not the first response.

1.2 Integration of Wisdom

The second principle is integration rather than fragmentation. For too long, medicine has been divided into silos: conventional versus complementary, psychiatry versus psychological medicine, acute care versus prevention. Patients are shuffled between specialists, each focused narrowly on one organ system, with little attention to the whole person.

A real wellness and health care system unites these silos. Nutritional and environmental medicine sits alongside conventional acute care. Psychosocial and spiritual dimensions of health are treated as integral, not optional. Integrative oncology, for example, would combine the best of surgery, radiotherapy, and chemotherapy with intravenous vitamin C, hyperbaric oxygen therapy, mistletoe extract, targeted nutraceuticals, repurposed drugs like Ivermectin, and lifestyle interventions.

This principle reflects not only fairness to different disciplines but scientific reality, as human beings are integrated systems living in communities, not collections of parts—meaning that healing requires a whole-of-person, whole-of-society approach.

1.3 Medical Freedom & Informed Consent

The third principle is medical freedom of the individual. Health systems must respect autonomy, informed consent, and freedom of choice. The pandemic era revealed how quickly these principles can be eroded under the banner of "public health." Citizens were coerced into medical interventions, denied transparency, and silenced when they raised legitimate concerns.

In a wellness-centred system, informed consent is non-negotiable. AI-driven tools can assist in empowering citizens by providing clear, plain-language explanations of risks, benefits, and alternatives, providing the information needed before a citizen can truly give fully informed consent. Patients must be free to choose between conventional, integrative, or blended approaches. The role of the system is not to dictate, but to support.

This principle extends to data sovereignty. Individuals, not corporations or governments, must control their medical and wellness data. Blockchain and decentralised technologies make this possible, ensuring privacy while allowing collective insights to guide public health advice (not compulsion) without surveillance.

1.4 Transparency & Accountability

The fourth principle is radical transparency. Trust in health institutions has been shattered by conflicts of interest, hidden contracts, and regulatory capture. Rebuilding that trust requires systems where corruption is fought structurally.

Every dollar of health spending in the new nation could be auditable in real time through blockchain-linked systems. AI-powered auditing tools could be used to flag anomalies, over-billing, or conflicts of interest. Clinical guidelines will have transparent bases, with direct oversight by citizens and non-conflicted medical professionals to ensure accountability and quality.

Health care must become a participatory commons rather than the monastic domain of experts.

1.5 Root Causes before Symptoms

The fifth principle is addressing causes, not just effects. Modern medicine has become adept at suppressing symptoms: statins lower cholesterol without addressing diet; antidepressants alter neurotransmitters without addressing trauma or inflammation, sleep, or micronutrient deficiencies; inhalers relieve asthma without addressing environmental triggers.

A real wellness and health care system seeks to first identify and treat the causes of symptoms, such as poor nutrition, sedentary lifestyles, toxin load, stress, and social disconnection. Only when these driving factors are addressed should drugs or surgery be considered. This principle aligns with both science and common sense. It recognises that true healing often comes not from adding more interventions, but from removing the obstacles to health that modern lifestyles impose.

2. Governance Framework

If principles define the vision of a real wellness and health care system, then governance defines its durability. History shows that even the best ideas can be corrupted when institutions are captured by vested interests, when accountability is absent, or when decision-making becomes opaque. The failures of the current Australian system, from pharmaceutical capture to bureaucratic inertia, are not failures of science alone but failures of governance.

To design a health system that endures, Western Australia must establish health system governance structures that are independent, transparent, and participatory. We propose a new institution to serve as the heart of this system: the National Wellness Authority (NWA), supported by citizen oversight, AI-powered auditing, and global partnerships.

2.1 The National Wellness Authority (NWA)

The NWA would be a statutory body, independent of the pharmaceutical industry, political manipulation, and bureaucratic stagnation through carefully designed personnel rotation, severely limited direct powers, and direct citizen oversight. Its mandate would be clear: To protect, promote, and advance wellness as the foundation of Western Australia's health system.

Mandate & Functions

Policy & Standards. Develop national guidelines for wellness, prevention, and integrative medicine.

Research & Innovation. Fund and disseminate studies on nutrition, environmental medicine, lifestyle interventions, and integrative therapies.

Education. Ensure medical schools, nursing programs, and allied health curricula include robust training in nutrition, lifestyle, and environmental health.

Certification. Coordinate the accreditation of wellness hubs, practitioners, and AI systems to ensure quality and safety, with accreditation implemented via peer-to-peer and citizen-inclusive evaluation, not top-down approval.

Public Engagement. Provide transparent communication and open access to all decisions, contracts, and evidence.

Medicines Schedule. The NWA will convene the Medicines Schedule Committee (MSC) and publish WAMS decisions and evidence summaries (see 5.6.1)

Medical Education Reform

Western Australia will re-align medical education with wellness, independence, and open science.

Funding firewall. Public funding will flow directly to medical schools under an independence covenant banning corporate sponsorship of curricula, endowed chairs tied to product lines, or ghost-written teaching materials.

Curriculum standards. NWA-issued curriculum guidelines for medical schools will require robust training in nutrition, lifestyle, environmental health, integrative medicine, basic statistics, risk communication, and critical appraisal of evidence.

Hubs-based rotations. All clinical training for new doctors will include rotations in Community Wellness Hubs to embed prevention, community practice, and cultural competency.

Independent assessment. National board exams will be set and marked by an arms-length Assessment Council (including citizen members and retired doctors) using transparent item banks.

Open science discipline. All publicly funded research and teaching will use open protocols, registries, and data where safe; industry trials will be taught alongside independent re-analyses, embedding an awareness of how to spot bias in medical reporting.

Continuing competence. Reaccreditation requires continuing education across lifestyle and integrative domains, not just procedural volume, proven to the satisfaction of peers and citizens.

The National Wellness Authority's accreditation standards shall be recognised in statute and applicable to all medical, allied, and complementary professions.

To make standards practical across professions and educate citizens about their healthcare options, the NWA will also:

1. Publish scope-of-practice matrices that delineate competencies, referral thresholds, and supervision rules for medical, allied, and complementary practitioners.

2. Offer bridging programs to expand scope where evidence supports safety and benefit (e.g., prescribing rights that prioritise nutrition, allowing qualified practitioners to recommend and authorize nutritional therapies and supplements as a first-line approach).
3. Tie reaccreditation to outcomes, complaints profiles, and continuing education (as assessed by peers and citizens), with proportionate remediation pathways.
4. Run a citizen-facing registry with practitioners' scopes, conditions, complaints summaries, and decisions (with reasons), to inform choice and drive quality.

Enabling legislation will specify that to be accredited, practitioner boards and regulators must undertake the accreditation process coordinated by NWA, and conform to the Constitution's Human Law & Medical Freedom provisions.

Independence

To protect the NWA from capture, in addition to limiting its direct powers, we propose:

1. Legislative safeguards preventing donations from, lobbying by, or employees' ties (whether present or past) with pharmaceutical or processed-food corporations.
2. Leadership diversity, ensuring representation from medicine, nutrition, environmental science, Indigenous health, ethics, and citizen groups.
3. Appointment by citizen jury, rather than political nomination, of the top echelon of NWA leadership.
4. Direct involvement of citizens and independent medical professionals, selected randomly and rotated into service for overlapping time-limited terms, in the accreditation process.

To harden the NWA against capture, personnel policy must rotate power as a matter of design. Some features we suggest in this vein are as follows:

1. Fixed, non-renewable terms for top leadership and for guidelines-setting committee chairs; the majority of committee members turn over on a rolling schedule every 2–3 years.
2. Procurement and audit rotation: all NWA employees with decision-making powers that directly affect the income streams of companies or health practitioners rotate portfolios at set intervals; extended tenure in a single specialty area is prohibited.
3. Periodic secondments from wellness hubs, universities, and civil society are used to populate NWA positions; NWA staff cycle out to wellness hubs or academia as a condition of eligibility for re-appointment.
4. Post-employment cooling off: multi-year restrictions on accepting roles with entities regulated, accredited, or funded by the NWA during the prior three years.

5. Randomised assignment and audit: key oversight tasks (e.g., site audits and accreditation implementation) are assigned to peer organisations and citizens by verifiable random draw.
6. All vacancies, selection criteria, candidate shortlists, and rationales for appointment are published; Citizen Oversight Committees (COCs) observe and may file dissenting minutes.

Rotation minimises relational capture, while transparency and direct citizen input into quality control ensure that rules are effective.

Clarification of Roles (NWA Vs Department)

The National Wellness Authority (NWA) is WA's independent assurance authority. It sets system-wide standards, issues safety and quality guidelines, coordinates professional accreditation, and publishes transparent public performance and safety reports grounded in peer review and citizen oversight. The NWA does not manage the health budget or distribute service funding; those funding functions (including appropriations administration and block-grant management) sit with the relevant Department, operating within the rules set by law and the Constitution. Title 17 further insulates the NWA's assurance functions from day-to-day political direction through multi-year appropriations protected by a formula-based floor (reducible only by a two-thirds vote of both Houses), and through leadership by a Wellness Commissioner appointed by the President from a COC-nominated shortlist and removable only for proved misbehaviour or incapacity after an open hearing. The NWA must publish annual reports and remains subject to judicial review for legal error (and, where rights are engaged, parties may seek remedies in the Human Rights Tribunal). This separation of assurance (NWA) from funding administration (Department) reduces the opportunity for capture and aligns with Western Australia's anti-corruption architecture.

2.2 Covid Truth Commission on Medical & Regulatory Failures

Before building forward, Western Australia must acknowledge the failures of the past, when previously under the authority of Canberra. To this end, we advise the creation of a Covid Truth Commission into medical and regulatory failures during the covid era. This Commission should investigate:

1. Pharmaceutical influence on policy, research, and regulation.
2. Suppression of integrative, nutritional and environmental medicine, and treatment with re-purposed, less-profitable pharmaceuticals.
3. Conflicts of interest in advisory bodies.
4. Failures of informed consent and human rights during the covid pandemic.
5. Systemic underfunding of preventive healthcare.

The Commission's findings would serve as a means of accountability for past failures, and a justification for the foundations of WA's new health system design. By documenting misfeasance, malfeasance, and systemic bias, it would provide the moral and political mandate for a new system designed to resist old distortions.

2.3 Citizen Oversight

No health system can retain legitimacy without public trust. To restore this trust, governance in healthcare will directly involve Western Australian citizens, though citizen jury appointments to NWA leadership, direct involvement of citizens in accreditation, and citizen-fed quality assurance. In addition, citizens will be involved in:

Policy Review. Panels of citizens will review and comment on new standards, AI tools, and guidelines, holding the power to trigger audits if nonconformity with the goals of wellness promotion is suspected.

Complaint Mechanism. Patients have direct recourse to local citizen panels (with rotating membership) to lodge grievances about coercion, neglect, or malpractice (citizen panels take the place of centralised anti-corruption authorities in identifying potential corruption and triggering audits).

Community Priorities. Councils identify local health challenges, such as allergies in schools or diabetes in Indigenous communities, and their priorities are used to inform nationwide health budgeting and guidelines.

Transparency Audits. Councils oversee release of data on outcomes, spending, and adverse events.

Representation

Seats on citizen oversight panels and citizen juries should be filled by random selection from the citizenry (akin to jury duty), with stratification by geography and demography when appropriate (e.g., to ensure issues affecting predominantly rural residents are not decided by panels of exclusively city-dwellers), supplemented by nominated representatives from health professions and civil society.

Appointments to citizen oversight panels should reflect the following selection criteria and safeguards:

Sortition within a qualified pool. Members are randomly selected (with stratification as appropriate) from a pool of citizens meeting eligibility criteria (e.g., no recent party office, lobbying, or senior contractor roles).

Impartiality & representation. The selection method must ensure impartiality and representation, with transparent rules published in advance.

Term & rotation. Members serve for fixed, staggered terms (e.g., 12–24 months) with one-third rotation each cycle; cooling-off periods before and after service.

Conflict-of-interest & disclosure. Mandatory asset and interest declarations, recusals in case of conflicts, and public minutes; breaches are cause for removal via a due-process vote and confirmation by the Human Rights Tribunal.

Training & powers. Members of citizen panels receive mandatory training in procedures (not content); citizen panels can subpoena records, compel officials to appear, and refer breaches to the Anti-Corruption Commission; all decisions and votes are posted to a public ledger.

This approach is intended to guard against political or corporate dominance and ensures that health care remains a shared responsibility, not a bureaucratic imposition.

2.4 AI & Blockchain Auditing

Recently invented technological tools can help ensure that Western Australia's new healthcare system delivers health and is responsive to the needs of its citizens. We suggest using AI to read evidence and spot anomalies, and blockchain to prove that nothing was quietly changed. Personal health data stays private, while citizens can see, understand, and contest decisions.

Western Australia's Anti-Corruption Framework commits the state to technological enablers that make integrity verifiable:

1. Blockchain-backed public ledgers for records and contracts; and
2. AI-assisted oversight with audit trails, model documentation, and public reporting. The Wellness System adopts the same architecture so that clinical, financial, and procurement events in health are immediately auditable, tamper-evident, and open to citizen oversight.

Blockchain Applications

Encoding into blockchain ("hash-tagging") health records, consent events, procurement steps, and audit logs enables WA citizens to see that records have not been altered, and reveals who changed what, when, without exposing patient data on-chain. This use of technology mirrors the governance approach adopted for state records in the Anti-Corruption Framework, and will apply to the following areas:

Financial Auditing. Every dollar spent on health services is logged and traceable.

Supply Chain Integrity. From functional foods to vitamin supplements to pharmaceuticals, blockchain verifies authenticity and prevents counterfeit products.

Smart Contracts. Government contracts with suppliers or hospitals automatically enforce disclosure of conflicts of interest and quality standards.

Patient-record integrity & audit trails. Estonia's national e-Health system uses Knowledge, Skills, and Integrity (KSI) blockchain to provide tamper-evident auditability of health records lifecycle events. This design keeps clinical data off-chain but makes any alteration detectable.

Pharmaceutical supply chain & recalls. In the United States, the Drug Supply Chain Security Act (DSCSA) requires medicines to be traceable as they move from manufacturer to pharmacy. In pilot projects, industry groups tested blockchain-based systems to securely share tracking data between different organisations, improving end-to-end visibility and helping recalls happen faster and more accurately.

Clean procurement trails. Colombia's SECOP II e-procurement reforms (Sistema Electrónico para la Contratación Pública, or "Electronic System for Public Procurement" in English) explored blockchain to raise transparency and detect anomalies—an approach transferrable to health procurement.

AI Applications

Following the Anti-Corruption Framework, any AI tools—meaning data-driven computer algorithms trained to detect patterns (for example, suspicious billing, bid-rigging signals, or emerging safety risks)—must be registered and documented before use. Each AI tool must have a registered "model card" (a plain-language datasheet describing what data it was trained on, how it performs, known limitations and biases, and how it is monitored), produce explainable outputs, and be used with a human decision-maker who remains responsible for the final decision. These safeguards ensure affected parties can understand the basis of decisions and challenge outcomes. To support the wellness of Western Australians, AI could be used for the purposes listed below:

Real-Time Audits. AI tools can analyse spending, outcomes, and safety data, flagging anomalies such as over-billing or unusual adverse event rates.

Evidence Synthesis. AI can continuously review global literature, offering a stream of suggestions for treatment guidelines in transparent, auditable ways.

Decision Explanations. All AI outputs for patients or practitioners would need to include clear evidence-based explanations, ensuring accountability and trust.

Claims integrity & fraud. Machine-learning approaches (supervised, unsupervised, and hybrid) can flag anomalous billing patterns and networks associated with fraud.

The UK's National Health Service has an active counter-fraud program and an AI strategy for analytics; the Australian National Audit Office (ANAO) has repeatedly urged risk-based, data-driven compliance in Medicare; Centers for Medicare & Medicaid Services (in the US) reports persistent improper payments, underscoring the need to combine advanced analytics with rigorous governance in which people are incentivized to use the information provided by AI to effect change.

Procurement red-flagging. OECD guidance documents show how AI + open data can detect bid-rigging signals and split tenders.

Safeguards. All AI systems must undergo privacy impact assessments and publish clear documentation. If an AI-supported decision affects a person's access to care, entitlements, or other protected rights, the person must be able to request a human review, receive reasons in plain language, and—if still dissatisfied—appeal to the Human Rights Tribunal.

By combining blockchain's immutability with AI's analytical power, WA can create the most transparent natural health and medical wellness system in the world.

2.5 An Open-Source Health Data Commons

To counter the pharmaceutical model of proprietary science, the National Wellness Authority will create a National Health Data Commons in which all publicly funded studies are freely available; nutritional, herbal, and environmental evidence is organised and translated for clinicians and citizens, in all relevant languages; and anonymized wellness data contributed voluntarily by citizens and wellness hubs are shared.

The goals of this wellness commons are to democratise knowledge, accelerate innovation, and restore trust in evidence as a shared, not privatised, resource.

Constitutional & Legislative Footing of the NWA

To ensure the National Wellness Authority cannot be captured or politicised, we propose that its mandate, independence, funding floor and accountability are constitutionally recognised and statutorily detailed. The NWA's guidelines-setting and accreditation-coordinating powers must operate within Western Australia's Human Law architecture (founded on informed consent, due process, and contestability) and be reviewable on points of law by the courts, with rights-implicating matters contestable before the Human Rights Tribunal. This embeds wellness governance inside the same constitutional guardrails that protect medical freedom and citizen sovereignty.

The full constitutional text and operative clauses for securing these outcomes can be seen in Chapter 15: A New Nation's Constitution, (Title 17: A Wellness-First Health System) which direct and empower the government of Western Australia to undertake and implement the following.

First, Article 1 establishes an independent National Wellness Authority (NWA) with paramount responsibility for guidelines, coordination of the accreditation of service providers, safety, and transparent public reporting across the wellness system. Its assurance functions are insulated from ministerial direction, implemented by citizens and peer medical professionals, and supported by a multi-year funding floor; the national Wellness Commissioner is appointed by the President from a COC-nominated shortlist (Title 17, Article 1(3)) and removed only for proven misbehaviour or incapacity after an open hearing.

Second, Title 17 Article 2 creates the Western Australia Medicines Schedule (WAMS), maintained by the NWA, with the Western Australia Essential Medicines List (WAEML), modelled initially on the 2019 WHO essential medicines list, as the guaranteed coverage floor. Further listings are decided upon by an independent Medicines Schedule Committee and under strict conflict-of-interest and transparency rules. Applications to be listed on the WAEML must show superiority to placebo plus optimised diet and lifestyle on patient-relevant specific and holistic outcomes. Decisions are reviewable on points of law (and by the HRT where rights are engaged), clinical discretion is preserved, and government bears a duty to implement WAMS listings.

Third, Title 17 Article 3 establishes an Independent Pharmacovigilance Safety Monitoring Board as a standing sub-committee of the Citizen Oversight Committee, institutionally and operationally independent of the NWA. The Board designs and runs its own pharmacovigilance system, has full and timely access to the data it deems relevant, and is empowered to act wherever it suspects that risks outweigh benefits, including by imposing conditions or suspending or revoking drug approvals, so as to protect the health and wellbeing of the Western Australian people.

2.7 Global Partnerships & Alternatives to WHO

The failures of the WHO, from its handling of Ebola and covid to its financial dependence on private donors, demonstrate the need for alternative global health leadership. Western Australia, through the NWA, would have the opportunity to spearhead the creation of a World Wellness Council, a consortium of nations committed to prevention, integration, and transparency in health care.

This Council would:

1. Share wellness data and innovations.
2. Develop independent guidelines free from pharmaceutical capture.
3. Coordinate responses to global threats using integrative, community-first strategies.
4. Uphold citizen rights and informed consent at an international level.

If its new wellness system is successful, Western Australia can lead not only nationally but globally, providing a counterweight to monopolistic global governance.

3. System Architecture

Governance provides the foundation of a real wellness and health care system, while architecture provides its structure. To succeed, the system must be coherent, efficient, and intuitive. It must support individuals, communities, local hubs and acute care hospitals in a seamless flow that prioritises prevention without neglecting emergency capacity.

The architecture of the proposed system is three-layered: (1) an individual wellness layer, empowering citizens with tools for self-care and prevention; (2) community wellness hubs, delivering integrative, preventive, and maternal-fetal care locally; and (3) a hospital and specialist layer, providing advanced integrative and acute care when necessary.

These layers are interconnected through digital infrastructure, AI-driven insights, and transparent governance mechanisms.

3.1 The Individual Wellness Layer

Health begins at the level of the individual. Empowering citizens to take charge of their health is both cost-effective and transformative. This requires personalised tools, education, and support systems that shift people from being passive patients to being active co-creators of wellness.

Optional, Event-Driven use of Wearables

Citizens who wish to do so will be offered, via periodic wellness checkups, an array of technological supports to capture data useful in their diagnosis and/or treatment. No citizen will be required to wear or carry a device to access care or entitlements; opting out of use will never trigger penalties of any kind. Integration of consumer-friendly wearables (e.g., Oura, Garmin, Apple Watch) with low-cost biomarker tests (vitamin D, zinc, magnesium, omega-3 index, HbA1c) provides a near-real-time picture of health. Citizens can track progress, while AI coaches identify early risks before they become disease. For citizens who opt in, data capture is episodic (e.g., during a specific program or diagnostic work-up) with defined start/stop dates., and (for consenting citizens) captured data will be added to Western Australia's anonymized health data repository for the purpose of training doctors and AI. Individuals control access to their own data; withdrawal of consent stops new data flows and triggers deletion from processors' systems, subject to legal holds. Misuse of wearables, devices, or the data they collect is reportable to citizen oversight committees and reviewable before the Human Rights Tribunal where rights are implicated.

Lifestyle Literacy

Schools, workplaces, and community programs will embed wellness education from childhood onwards. Nutrition, cooking, sleep hygiene, stress management, and movement will be taught as core life skills, not optional extras.

3.2 Community Wellness Hubs

Community Wellness Hubs are the structural heart of WellnessCare. They are where prevention, relationship-based care, and local knowledge meet practical services. National guidelines set the floor, but hubs adapt models to local place, culture, and need, and publish results so others can learn. By putting decisions and resources closer to people, hubs support health where it is created: by people and their local communities. In line with the principle of subsidiarity, hubs are encouraged to interpret national guidelines in line with community needs.

Structure of a Hub

Each hub will be staffed by:

1. Integrative GPs and nurse practitioners.
2. Nutritionists and dietitians.
3. Naturopaths, herbalists, and environmental medicine specialists.
4. Allied health professionals: physiotherapists, psychologists, occupational therapists.
5. Midwives, doulas, and lactation consultants.
6. Holistic community health educators and coaches.

Hubs operate as prevention-first centres, with acute cases referred onward when necessary. They are publicly funded but locally governed, ensuring responsiveness to community needs. At a minimum, they provide:

Preventive Care. Annual wellness check-ups focused on micronutrient sufficiency, diet, sleep, and stress.

Chronic Disease Reversal Programs. Programs for diabetes, hypertension, obesity, allergies, and autoimmune disorders using lifestyle-first protocols.

Simple nursing consultations. Drop-in consultations, and home visits as required, as a first point of human contact to promptly address simple injuries (from minor burns to ankle sprains) and unusual symptoms (e.g., a simple rash. ringing in the ears, or a fungal infection).

Mental Health Support. Nutrition, exercise, trauma-informed therapy, and integrative nutritional psychiatry.

Education & Outreach. Workshops in schools, workplaces, and community centres.

Data Collection. Voluntary contribution to the National Health Data Commons, ensuring research reflects lived realities.

Pregnancy & Birth Support. Coordination and support services for young women who are pregnant or have recently given birth and need additional levels of support beyond what their family/community is able to provide; prenatal care, focusing on nutrition and lifestyle; and birthing services for low-risk pregnancies.

Hubs also serve as resilience centres during crises (contagious disease outbreaks, bushfires, floods), distributing nutrition packs, supplements, and health education so citizens are not solely reliant on global media and national hospital capacity.

Pregnancy support teams located in wellness hubs will coordinate as needed with other districts to ensure that pregnant women or those intending to conceive receive optimal information and care throughout their reproductive journey, and are informed of all options, including straightforward, no-fault adoption by families vetted by local citizen groups, Wellness hubs will also at a minimum support breastfeeding information and training, and coordinate milk banks.

3.3 Hospital & Specialist Layer

Hospitals remain essential for emergencies, surgeries, and advanced diagnostics.

Integrative Hospitals

Hospitals should provide:

Acute Care Excellence. Trauma care, surgery, intensive care, and infectious disease management.

Integrative Oncology Units. Chemotherapy and radiotherapy offered alongside alternative therapies, including IV vitamin C, hyperbaric oxygen therapy (HBOT), mistletoe extract, nutritional support, and stress-reduction programs.

Chronic Disease Clinics. The "sanitarium" wing of hospitals will focus on reversing degenerative conditions like heart failure and COPD with diet, micronutrients, exercise, and environmental detoxification.

Palliative and Regenerative Care. Sanitariums will provide noninvasive care to preserve quality of life for citizens aged 70+ or diagnosed with a terminal illness, focusing on dignity, symptom relief, and enhancing quality of life through natural and supportive therapies.

AI Triage Systems

Hospital triage will use AI-driven algorithms interpreted by humans to direct presenting patients to one of three locations: a wellness pathway, via direction to a local wellness hub; a specialist pathway, or an emergency pathway providing direct stabilisation and intensive care.

This triage system ensures that hospitals are not overwhelmed with preventable conditions.

Rehabilitation & Lifestyle Reintegration

The goal of care provided in hospitals and sanitariums should be to transition patients back to community-based care. Discharge planning includes by default referral to the appropriate local Wellness Hubs plus family-inclusive education to prevent relapse.

3.5 The Economic Case

Critics may argue that such a design architecture is costly. Yet the current system is unsustainable. Chronic disease consumes over 80% of health budgets, while preventive spending is typically under 5%. Redirecting even a fraction of current expenditure into prevention holds the potential to yield massive returns in the form of reduced hospital admissions, lower pharmaceutical dependency, and increased productivity and wellbeing.

3.6 A Culture of Wellness

System-level and local architecture shapes culture. By embedding wellness into every layer, the new system has the power to transform societal attitudes,

Children will grow up seeing wellness creation as a fun skill, not a service, while adults become active custodians of their own wellbeing. Communities share responsibility for each other's health, and.

hospitals become sanctuaries of healing, not factories of despair.

This cultural transformation may be the most profound outcome of the new system: a society that no longer is defined by illness, but defines itself by wellness.

3.7 Summary

The architecture of the real wellness and health care system proposed here is simple but revolutionary. Individuals are empowered by AI, optional wearables, and lifestyle literacy; communities are supported by Wellness Hubs delivering integrative, preventive, routine care, and hospitals are reimagined as centres of integrative healing and acute excellence.

Together, connected by digital infrastructure and guided by citizen governance, these layers aim to create a system that is humane, transparent, and effective.

This is the structure upon which WA can build the world's first true WellnessCare system.

4. The AI Ecosystem

The potential for artificial intelligence (AI) to assist in the delivery of an integrated new healthcare system is significant and transformative. Some key areas of AI transformation in the WellnessCare system are outlined in other sections of this chapter. Western Australia will work closely with health departments and clinics around the world to ensure that AI is being used to the highest potential and implemented effectively in the WellnessCare system.

5. Implementation Roadmap

Implementation of this radical new vision for healthcare must be carefully staged, politically realistic, and financially sustainable. The roadmap proposed here spans fifteen years, divided into three phases: Foundations (0–3 years), Expansion (3–7 years), and Global Leadership (7–15 years).

5.1 Phase 1 (0–3 years): Foundations

The first phase is about laying the groundwork: creating governance structures, piloting innovations, and proving that wellness-first systems can work in practice.

Key Actions

Establish the National Wellness Authority (NWA). Legislation to create an independent statutory body with safeguards against capture.

Covid Truth Commission. Initiate an inquiry into medical and regulatory failures, providing the moral and political mandate for reform.

Pilot Community Wellness Hubs. Launch Wellness Hubs in seven major centres—for example, Perth, Bunbury, Geraldton, Albany, Kalgoorlie-Boulder, Karratha, and Broome.

Staff hubs with integrative practitioners, nutritionists, naturopaths, midwives, and community educators.

Health Data Collection Piloting. Develop and release a public wellness app integrated with wearables.

Offer free but fully voluntary access to all citizens as part of WellnessCare.

Medical Education Reform. Require medical schools to introduce compulsory modules on nutritional, environmental and integrative medicine, lifestyle medicine, and environmental health.

Begin retraining programs for GPs and nurses.

Transparency Measures. Blockchain-based auditing pilot is implemented in the NWA and in the seven major wellness hubs.

Require all new drug contracts to be published openly, in real time.

Outcomes by Year 3

1. Public trust begins to rebuild through visible transparency.
2. Early health and cost savings are demonstrated in pilot hubs.
3. The national conversation shifts from crisis management to a prevention-first focus.

5.2 Phase 2 (3–7 years): Expansion

Once foundations are secure, the system must scale nationally, embedding prevention into every level of care.

Key Actions

Nationwide Wellness Hub Network. Expand hubs to every region and district, ensuring access within 50 km for all Western Australians. Geographic blanket coverage implies ~390 hubs (assuming 50 km straight-line service radii), implying that a pragmatic deployment would be ~300–320 fixed hubs concentrated in population corridors, with mobile/visiting teams covering remote settlements to preserve the 50 km guarantee.

Wellness Hubs would begin to be integrated with schools, workplaces, and aged care facilities.

Hospital Integration. Establish Integrative Nutritional Oncology, Cardiology, Immunology, Psychiatry, and Sanitarium Units in all major hospitals.

Introduce chronic disease reversal clinics within Sanitariums for diabetes, hypertension, and obesity.

Integrative Hospitals of Excellence. Develop flagship institutions in Perth, Geraldton and Broome serving as global training centres.

Technology Scaling. Roll out AI-assisted auditing across all health expenditures.

Upgrade wellness app with culturally adapted modules for Indigenous and migrant populations.

WellnessCare Integration. Introduce item numbers for preventive interventions (nutrition counselling, micronutrient testing, lifestyle coaching, etc.).

Extend national health cover to integrative therapies with proven cost-benefit outcomes.

Research & Innovation Funding. Redirect at least 20% of national research funding to prevention and integrative medicine.

Establish an open-access national database of integrative clinical outcomes.

Education & Workforce Transformation. Create dual training pathways for Wellness Physicians combining conventional and integrative medicine.

Embed wellness curricula in primary and secondary schools.

Outcomes by Year 7

1. Chronic disease incidence and hospital admissions show measurable decline.
2. WellnessCare's cost curve flattens due to prevention-first spending.
3. Western Australia is recognised internationally as a pioneer of integrative health and wellness.

5.3 Phase 3 (7–15 years): Global Leadership

The final phase expands the system beyond Western Australia, positioning the nation as a leader in global wellness governance and innovation.

Key Actions

World Wellness Council. Establish a consortium of like-minded nations (e.g., New Zealand, the Nordic countries, parts of Asia and Africa).

Create global wellness guidelines independent of the WHO.

Export of Technology Ecosystem. Share embedded technology and predictive analytics tools with partner nations.

Establish Western Australia as a global hub for ethical health-supportive AI use.

Attract international patients and practitioners seeking integrative expertise.

Global Wellness Education. Establish universities and exchange programs for integrative medicine.

Economic Transformation. Wellness becomes a major Western Australian export, rivalling resources.

Jobs are created in integrative health, health-led AI, nutrition, education, and community programs.

Outcomes by Year 15

1. Western Australia is recognised as the birthplace of a global wellness revolution.
2. Citizens enjoy lower chronic disease rates, higher life expectancy, and greater quality of life compared to peer nations.
3. Billions in healthcare savings are achieved through prevention-first adoption.

5.4 Funding the Transition

In the face of a lean state budget discussed in earlier chapters, initial investments in components of the new health system will require funds to be sourced not only from national revenues but also from (1) the reallocation of subsidies from pharmaceuticals with poor profiles; (2) public-private partnerships with businesses that integrate wellness into workplaces; and (3) partnerships with alternative health networks and philanthropic foundations.

Health Determinants Budget (HDB)

Within the national WellnessCare budget, Western Australia will ring-fence a multi-year Health Determinants Budget (HDB) for sanitation, access to nutritious food (including local supply initiatives), and community infrastructure that strengthens social support. The Treasury will tag and track HDB spend across portfolios (Water, Agriculture, Local Government), with annual public dashboards and wellness KPIs tied to these determinants. Wellness Hubs co-design local HDB projects and report outcomes.

Economic Benefits

For every $1 invested in prevention, $5–$10 is saved in treatment costs. Reduced absenteeism and disability claims improve productivity, and exporting wellness expertise and bespoke technology solutions generates new revenue streams.

5.5 Workforce Transformation

To implement this new system, the health workforce must be retrained and expanded. Our proposal includes:

1. Mandatory programs to up-skill existing GPs and nurses;
2. Thousands of allied health professionals trained to work in hubs and schools as nutrition and lifestyle coaches;
3. Training for health workers to use AI tools; and
4. The creation of a new profession of Community Educators, blending health, education, and cultural expertise.

5.6 Integration with WellnessCare

Australia's Medicare system presents both a challenge and an opportunity. Its universal framework provides equity but incentivises volume of services over value of outcomes. Learning from how Medicare began to fail Australians, Western Australia walks into a new future with a revamped universal system: *WellnessCare*.

5.6.1 Medicines & Therapeutics: National Medicines Schedule (WAMS)

The Western Australia Medicine Schedule (WAMS) will be the official list of medicines eligible for public funding and guidance, similar in concept to Australia's PBS Schedule.

WAMS Essential baseline. The Western Australia Essential Medicines List (WAEML), adapted from the WHO's 2019 list of essential medicines, forms the guaranteed coverage floor (generics preferred).

Value-Add Tier. Medicines beyond the WAEML are added to the WAMS only after demonstrating superiority to current standard care on patient-relevant outcomes, with transparent comparative-effectiveness reviews. All additions are automatically de-listed after three years, with permanent listing only possible for medicines that are out of patent and demonstrated to significantly add to quality of life or length of life.

Transparent pricing & contracts. WAMS decisions, economic model synopses, prices/rebates, and evidence dossiers are published (with minimal justified redactions), with direct citizen oversight of meetings.

Real-world safety & effectiveness. Post-market outcomes and adverse events feed a public, de-identified audit log, with fixed-interval re-assessments and delisting for low net benefit.

Non-Pharmaceutical Modalities

Nutritional, herbal, and lifestyle interventions with strong evidence are eligible for coverage when proven safe and cost-effective, assessed on the same comparative framework as drugs.

Clinical Autonomy

The WAMS guides; it does not dictate. Clinicians retain off-schedule discretion with reason-giving and informed consent, subject to safety.

Conflict Firewalls

The independent Medicines Schedule Committee (MSC)advises the NWA; members have strict conflict-of-interest rules (no equity/paid roles with applicants), with all disclosures published.

5.6.2 Reforms

The reforms to the present system that are required to implement this new vision include introducing WellnessCare Item Numbers for preventive and integrative services; shifting GP funding toward outcomes-based payments (e.g., improved nutrient levels);covering essential tests (e.g., vitamin D, zinc, vitamin C, omega-3 index) and core supplements under WellnessCare; and creating a "WellnessCare Wellness Card" giving every citizen access to hub services.

5.7 Risk Management

Transformation of this scale carries risks. Anticipated challenges include:

1. Resistance from vested interests (pharmaceutical, processed food industries).
2. Political short-termism undermining long-term reforms.
3. Public skepticism fuelled by decades of failed promises.

These risks can be mitigated by the use of pilot hubs and early wins to build momentum; the anchoring of reforms in legislation and citizen oversight, and transparent communication through the NWA and community councils.

6. Safeguards & Ethics

Every great reform carries within it the seeds of unintended consequences. The introduction of artificial intelligence, blockchain auditing, and centralised wellness governance brings immense opportunities but also profound risks. Without clear ethical boundaries and enforceable safeguards, a system designed for wellness could be distorted into surveillance, coercion, or corporate exploitation.

Western Australia's real wellness and health care system must therefore be built not only on principles and architecture, but on a robust ethical framework. This framework ensures that citizens retain their medical freedom, that data remains private, that AI remains accountable and under human assessment and control, and that health care remains grounded in compassion and patient service rather than control.

6.1 Human-In-The-Loop

Every clinical decision, even when supported by technology, must involve human oversight.

1. AI recommendations must always be validated by a qualified practitioner, with the reasoning explained to the patient.
2. Individuals autonomously decide (in consultation with family as appropriate) whether to act on AI-powered advice. No life-or-death decisions may be automated. Emergency care must remain under full human judgment.

Such safeguards ensure that technology enhances care rather than replacing the human relationship and responsibility for wellness.

6.2 Informed Consent & the Right To Refuse

The covid crisis revealed how quickly informed consent can be undermined under "public health emergency" narratives. In the new wellness system, informed consent is non-negotiable.

Every intervention, whether a vitamin D supplement, an AI-recommended lifestyle protocol, a vaccine or a surgical procedure, requires voluntary, informed agreement

Citizens retain the right to refuse treatments without penalty, and .

AI and clinicians must communicate risks and benefits in terms citizens understand, free of jargon or coercion.

Western Australia's Constitutional Medical Freedom provisions make informed consent the default and bodily integrity non-derogable. Wellness policies must therefore:

1. Present clear alternatives, risks, and benefits;
2. Respect the right to decline without penalty to unrelated entitlements; and
3. Support and fund independent second opinions whenever a patient requests them.

Where an AI or bureaucratic decision affects access to care, individuals will have notice, reasons, and a right of review before the Human Rights Tribunal.

6.3 Data Sovereignty & Decentralisation

Our proposed new system features citizen-owned data, decentralised data storage using blockchain verification and with citizen oversight, and opt-in systems for sharing anonymised data to the health data commons.

By giving citizens control of their own data, the system aims to build trust and prevent the abuses that have plagued digital health projects worldwide.

6.4 Transparency & Auditability

The new system makes transparency a structural feature, not a political promise, embedding open AI algorithms (including for fraud detection) and publicly accessible dashboards containing documented spending, contracts and outcomes.

Transparency becomes both shield and sword, protecting citizens from abuse while actively deterring bad actors.

6.5 Guarding against Pharmaceutical & Corporate Capture

The greatest risk to building a successful real wellness system is organised action taken by the very industries it seeks to subjugate to the needs of citizens: pharmaceutical companies, ultra-processed food companies, and insurers.

Many direct citizen oversight mechanisms and protocols that disseminate power, such as peer-to-peer accreditation coordinated but not directed centrally, help to guard against capture. In addition, conflict-of interest declarations will be mandatory for all advisors, regulators, and researchers; cooling-off periods will be mandatory; and professionals exposing corruption in good faith will enjoy world-class legal whistleblower protections, with rewards for validated disclosures. The Western Australian Anti-Corruption Commission will have jurisdiction over health contracts and research grants.

6.6 Balancing Rights & Responsibilities

Wellness is is not only a state of being, but its pursuit is also a responsibility for pro-social community members. A real wellness system properly designed will encourage active participation by citizens. Public health campaigning will emphasise the benefits of a healthy body and community, encouraging citizens to visit their local Wellness Hub to take advantage of state-sponsored regular wellness check-ups, without scaring them into over-focusing on health to the detriment of achieving their broader life goals. Citizens are also a foundational component of wellness delivery and quality assurance, not only through their roles with the NWA but also via local community service roles in support of elderly, disabled and socioeconomically disadvantaged community members.

6.7 Cultural & Indigenous Respect

The new nation will honour Indigenous wisdom and cultural diversity where appropriate and promoting of citizens' health. For example:

Indigenous Integration. Holistic concepts of health, including traditional Indigenous perspectives, will be incorporated into Wellness Hub protocols and guidance.

Cultural Adaptation. Wellness coaching will be tailored to local settings, including into multiple languages and cultural contexts as needed.

Respect for Autonomy. No cultural group will be forced into a wellness model or intervention of any sort that contradicts its traditions.

6.9 The Moral Foundation

Ultimately, the ethical foundation of this new system is not technological but moral. It rests on the beliefs that:

Health is the natural state of humanity, not a commodity.

Citizens are free, not subjects.

Medicine is a calling, not an industry.

Transparency is the default, not the exception.

Wellness is both an individual and collective good.

7. Why Western Australia?

Every transformation needs a birthplace. The wellness revolution could begin in many nations, but Western Australia is uniquely positioned to pioneer it. Its size, history, geography, and culture provide the ideal conditions for developing a real wellness and health care system—one that is comprehensive, scalable, and credible to the world.

7.1 A Manageable yet Meaningful Population

Western Australia's population of nearly 3 million is large enough to test reforms at scale, but small enough to implement them swiftly. Countries with populations in the hundreds of millions face enormous inertia; pilot programs often struggle to scale nationally. By contrast, WA can trial innovations in a few regions, refine them, and then roll them out nationwide within a few short years, not decades.

This "Goldilocks scale" makes Western Australia the perfect laboratory: neither too small to matter, nor too large to move. Success here will resonate globally, offering a proven model that others can adopt.

7.2 WellnessCare as a Foundation

Unlike many nations, Western Australia comes from a long history of universal health under Australia's Medicare. While Medicare has its flaws—incentivising volume over prevention, and offering limited support for integrative services—it provides Western Australia with a universal framework upon which to build a new system.

WellnessCare ensures that every Western Australian citizen continues to have access to care. Western Australia will extend the framework of WellnessCare by embedding prevention, integrative medicine, and nutrition into a revamped system rather than creating one from scratch.

This is a crucial advantage. Countries such as the United States, with fragmented private insurance systems, face almost insurmountable barriers to reform. Western Australia, by contrast, can transform Medicare into WellnessCare—a wellness-first system with fewer structural obstacles.

7.3 A Legacy of Integrative Innovation

Australia has a strong, if under-recognised, history of integrative medical innovation. The Australasian College of Nutritional and Environmental Medicine (ACNEM), founded in 1982, fought against the powerful entrenched opposition from medical colleges, bureaucracies, government and pharmaceutical interests. Despite these obstacles, ACNEM pioneered education in nutrition, nutritional and environmental medicine, and integrative therapies for doctors and health professionals.

This legacy demonstrates both the capacity and the courage to innovate. Australian practitioners have shown that integrative approaches can be very effective, evidence-based, and safe, even when orthodoxy resists. Building on this foundation, the real wellness system of an independent Western Australia can elevate these once-marginalised insights into the mainstream, nationwide.

7.4 Cultural Diversity as Strength

WA is one of the most multicultural societies in the world. Nearly one in three Western Australians was born overseas, and more than 240 languages are spoken across the nation. Indigenous Western Australians add one of the world's oldest continuous cultural perspectives, with profound wisdom about land, community, and holistic health.

This diversity is not a challenge but a strength. It allows Western Australia to test wellness models across multiple cultural contexts: from Indigenous bush medicine to Mediterranean diets, from Asian herbal traditions to Western nutritional science.

If a wellness-first model can work in Western Australia's diverse society, it can work almost anywhere. This makes WA an ideal proving ground for a system aspiring to global export.

7.5 Geography & Environment

Western Australia's geography provides further advantages. Its vast distances and dispersed population have already pushed the health system to experiment with tele-health, remote medicine, and innovative service delivery. These lessons can be applied to digitally-supported wellness hubs health coaching.

At the same time, Western Australia faces pressing environmental health challenges: water scarcity, bushfires and pollution. Addressing these within a wellness framework ensures the system is resilient not only to disease but to environmental shocks. In this way, WA can model how wellness and sustainability intersect.

7.6 Economic &Geopolitical Independence

Western Australia's new economic and geopolitical independence further strengthens its position. While global institutions such as the WHO have drifted toward pharmaceutical dependence, Western Australia's new sovereignty enables it to chart an alternative course. It will not be bound by the same entanglements as Australia and many some European nations or the same corporate dominance as the United States.

Moreover, Western Australia has a history of exporting systems and standards—from environmental policies to education models—that other nations adopt. A real wellness and health care system would not only improve domestic health but holds the possibility of becoming one of Western Australia's most valuable exports: a model of health governance, AI-driven wellness, and integrative wellness and medicine.

7.7 Public Appetite for Change

Western Australian society is ready. Public trust in traditional institutions has eroded, particularly following the covid response, where coercion, censorship, and pharmaceutical dominance undermined confidence. Citizens are looking for alternatives that are ethical, transparent, and genuinely oriented towards their individual wellbeing.

Surveys consistently show that Western Australians want more choice in health care, with strong demand for integrative and preventive services. Nearly two-thirds of Australians already use complementary medicine in some form. By embedding these services within a national framework, Western Australia can meet a demand that is already surging.

7.8 Western Australia as Global Leader

Western Australia's health reforms could have global implications. By piloting and perfecting a real wellness and health care system, WA can show the world that prevention-first models reduce disease burden and costs; pilot pro-human uses of AI and blockchain in creating wellness; and become a world leader in integrative medicine training.

Just as Finland became a global model for education reform, Western Australia can become the global model for Wellness reform.

7.9 Summary

Western Australia is uniquely positioned to design and lead a real wellness and health care system because it combines:

1. A manageable population size with universal WellnessCare coverage.
2. A legacy of integrative innovation through the Australasian Council for Nutritional and Environmental Medicine and other pioneers.
3. Geographic challenges that foster digital and preventive innovation.
4. Economic independence and public appetite for change.

No other nation brings this precise combination of conditions. Western Australia has the opportunity to become not just a participant in global health but its pioneer and architect –the birthplace of a wellness revolution that the world urgently needs.

8. The Outcome: A New Era in Global Health

By shifting from a model of illness management to one of health creation, WA can demonstrate that societies need not be trapped in the endless spiral of chronic disease, spiraling costs, and declining trust. The outcomes span three domains: economic, social, and global.

8.1 Economic Benefits

Chronic disease consumes more than 80% of health budgets in developed nations, yet most of it is preventable. By addressing root causes—diet, micronutrient deficiencies, sleep, stress, toxins, inactivity—the system cuts costs before they escalate.

Reduced Health Expenditure

Diabetes. Reversal programs save thousands per patient annually compared to lifelong metformin and insulin therapy.

Cardiovascular Disease. Nutrition-first interventions reduce admissions for heart attacks and strokes, which are among the most expensive hospital events.

Cancer. Integrative oncology reduces symptom burden and hospital stays, saving millions in palliative care costs.

Productivity Gains

A healthier workforce means fewer sick days, longer careers, and reduced disability claims.

Cognitive health benefits from nutrition and lifestyle interventions enhance educational and workplace outcomes. Studies suggest that every $1 spent on prevention yields $5–$10 in long-term savings. If even 20% of hospital admissions in Western Australia were prevented, billions could be redirected toward other worthy goals.

In short, wellness is not just good for people—it is good for the economy.

8.2 Social Benefits

The benefits of wellness cannot be measured only in dollars. The deeper transformation is social: the way people live, relate, and flourish. Transparency, citizen oversight, and informed consent rebuild trust in institutions. Citizens need no longer feel like subjects of pharmaceutical empires but become participants in a shared health commons. Wellness hubs can serve not only as clinics but as community anchors. They may host workshops, connect generations, and provide resilience during crises. In this way, health care strengthens the social fabric rather than fraying it. Children grow up learning nutrition, sleep, and stress management as life skills. Adults feel confident interpreting their own biomarker data and making informed choices. Health becomes a matter of agency, not dependency. Culturally adapted AI health coaches and Indigenous integration ensure that no community is left behind. Access to prevention is universal, not dependent on income or geography.

Perhaps the most profound benefit is dignity. Patients are no longer reduced to “cases” or “conditions.” They are treated as whole persons—with body, mind, and spirit acknowledged and supported.

8.3 Global Benefits

The Real Wellness and Health Care System is not merely a national project. It is a blueprint for humanity.

8.4 The Risks of Inaction

If Western Australia does not seize this opportunity, the risks are clear. Chronic disease will continue to rise, consuming an ever-larger share of budgets. Hospitals will buckle under demand. Pharmaceutical dependence will deepen. Public trust will erode further, opening the door to populist backlash and social fragmentation.

8.5 A Call to Action

Designing and implementing a real wellness and health care system is ambitious but achievable. It does not require tearing down everything that exists; rather, it requires reorienting resources, incentives, and governance toward wellness.

The roadmap is clear:

Establish the National Wellness Authority.

Pilot and expand Community Wellness Hubs.

Embed AI and blockchain tools as appropriate.

Reform medical education.

If successful, Western Australia can begin the journey to establishing a World Wellness Council to replace the WHO.

What if we built a system not for illness, but for wellness?

A real wellness and health care system, designed in Western Australia, has the power to change not only a nation but the world. It promises economic sustainability, social renewal, and global leadership. It restores dignity, trust, and sovereignty to citizens. It offers a path out of crisis and into resilience.

Glossary Of Terms

Term	Definition
AI	Artificial Intelligence, a core technology for simulation, clinical support, and patient engagement in the wellness system.
AI Health Coach	Personalised AI-driven conversational agent providing ongoing wellness guidance.
AI-assisted oversight	Artificial intelligence tools for real-time anomaly detection in governance.
AI triage systems	Algorithms directing patients to appropriate care levels.
ANAO	Australian National Audit Office, involved in compliance and risk-based health auditing.
Australasian College of Nutritional and Environmental Medicine (ACNEM)	Organisation pioneering Nutritional, Environmental and Integrative Medicine approaches.
Comparative-effectiveness review	Process for assessing medicine superiority over standard care.
Covid pandemic	Global health crisis highlighting systemic weaknesses.
Covid Truth Commission	Inquiry into medical, regulatory, and pharmaceutical failures during the pandemic.
Crisis-driven	Health systems reactive to emergencies rather than proactive in prevention.
Cultural adaptation	Tailoring AI to languages and traditions.
Data sovereignty	Individual control over personal health data.
Decentralised technologies	Distributed systems like blockchain for data privacy and control.
Drug Supply Chain Security Act (DSCSA)	U.S. law for pharmaceutical tracking.

Term	Definition
Environmental medicine	Field focusing on environmental determinants of disease; addresses toxins and ecological factors in health.
Evidence synthesis	AI compilation of research findings.
Explainable outputs	AI results with clear, understandable reasoning.
HbA1c	Glycated haemoglobin test measuring average blood glucose for diabetes management.
Health Determinants Budget (HDB)	Ring-fenced funds for social factors like nutrition access.
Hospital-based	A care approach emphasising treatment in hospitals for acute or late-stage illnesses.
Human-in-the-loop	Requiring human review of AI outputs.
Hyperbaric Oxygen Therapy (HBOT)	Oxygen therapy under increased pressure for tissue repair and healing.
Informed consent	Voluntary agreement to medical interventions after full disclosure of risks, benefits, and alternatives.
Integrative Hospitals	Reimagined facilities combining acute and integrative care.
Integrative medicine	Blending conventional, nutritional, and complementary approaches.
Integrative Oncology Units	Hospital units for combined cancer treatments including natural therapies.
Integrative doctors	Practitioners combining conventional and complementary medicine.
Integrative oncology	Combined conventional and natural cancer treatments.
Intravenous vitamin C (HDIVC)	High Dose Intravenous Vitamin C for redox (reduction-oxidation) support and adjunct therapy.
Item numbers	Billing codes for covered interventions.
KSI blockchain	Keyless Signature Infrastructure for tamper-proof records.
Magnesium	Essential mineral for stress reduction, sleep, and cardiovascular health.
Micronutrient monitoring	Testing levels of vitamins and minerals like vitamin D and zinc.
Mistletoe extract	Herbal therapy used in integrative oncology.
Model cards	Documentation detailing AI model training, biases, and performance.
National Health Data Commons	Open repository of anonymised health research.
Naturopaths	Holistic providers using natural therapies.
NHS	UK's National Health Service, a model for counter-fraud and AI strategies.
Nutritional and environmental medicine	Approaches addressing diet and environmental root causes.
Nutritional psychiatry	Diet-based mental health interventions.
Nutritionists	Experts in dietary interventions.
OECD	Organisation for Economic Co-operation and Development, provider of AI governance guidance.
Omega-3 index	Blood test measuring omega-3 fatty acid levels for heart, brain and immune health.
Open source	Freely available and modifiable software or knowledge resources.

Term	Definition
Outcomes-based payments	Funding tied to health improvements, not volume.
Patient-relevant outcomes	Measurable benefits directly impacting quality of life.
Pharmaceutical-centreed	Describes a health model focused primarily on drug-based treatments rather than prevention.
Predictive analytics	AI forecasting population health risks.
Privacy impact assessments	Evaluations of data risks in AI systems.
Public dashboards	Real-time displays of health metrics.
Real Wellness and Health Care System	The proposed preventive, integrative model for Western Australia.
Rehabilitation	Recovery programs incorporating lifestyle changes.
Risk communication	Skills in conveying health risks and benefits clearly.
SECOP II	Colombia's e-procurement system for transparency.
Smart contracts	Blockchain-based automated agreements.
Sortition	Random selection for oversight roles to ensure impartiality.
Subsidiarity principle	Local adaptation of national standards.
Targeted nutraceuticals	Supplements designed for specific health needs.
Wellness Hubs	Local centres for preventive and integrative care (also "Community Wellness Hubs").
Wellness Physicians	Dual-trained doctors in conventional and integrative care.
WellnessCare	Western Australia's universal public health system, reimagined for prevention.
WellnessCare Wellness Card	Access tool for preventive services.
WHO	World Health Organization, critiqued for pharmaceutical-centric approaches.
World Wellness Council	Proposed global alternative to WHO for integrative health leadership.
Vitamin D	Essential nutrient for immune resilience and bone health.

Sources

Unless otherwise stated, online materials were viewed on 27 January 2026.

Prevention ROI

1. World Health Organization, *Saving Lives, Spending Less: The Case for Investing in Noncommunicable Diseases* (2021) <https://www.who.int/publications/i/item/9789240041059>.
2. Masters, R, Anwar, E, Collins, B, Cookson, R and Capewell, S, 'Return on Investment of Public Health Interventions: A Systematic Review' (2017) <https://pubmed.ncbi.nlm.nih.gov/28356325/>.
3. Turner, H C, Hori, Y, Revill, P, Rattanavipapong, W, Arai, K, Nonvignon, J, Jit, M and Teerawattananon, Y, 'Analyses of the Return on Investment of Public Health Interventions: A Scoping Review and Recommendations for Future Studies' (2023) <https://pmc.ncbi.nlm.nih.gov/articles/PMC10471881/>.

4. NIHR Evidence, 'Public Health Interventions May Offer Society a Return on Investment of £14 for Each £1 Spent' (2017) <https://evidence.nihr.ac.uk/alert/public-health-interventions-may-offer-society-a-return-on-investment-of-14-for-each-1-spent/>.

ACNEM

5. Australasian College of Nutritional and Environmental Medicine (ACNEM), *About ACNEM* (2024) <https://www.acnem.org/about/our-story/>. Annotation: confirms founding in 1982 by medical practitioners focused on nutritional and environmental medicine.

Prevalence of complementary/integrative medicine use (Australia)

6. Xue, C C, Zhang, A L, Lin, V, Da Costa, C and Story, D F, 'Complementary and Alternative Medicine Use in Australia: A National Population-Based Survey' (2007) <https://pubmed.ncbi.nlm.nih.gov/17718647/>.
7. Harnett, J E, McIntyre, E, Adams, J, Addison, T, Bannerman, H, Egelton, L, Ma, J, Zabakly, L and Steel, A, 'Prevalence and Characteristics of Australians' Complementary Medicine Product Use, and Concurrent Use with Prescription and Over-the-Counter Medications: A Cross-Sectional Study' (2023) <https://www.mdpi.com/2072-6643/15/2/327>.
8. Harnett, J E, McIntyre, E, Steel, A, Foley, H, Sibbritt, D, Wardle, J and Adams, J, 'Use of Complementary Medicine Products: A Nationally Representative Cross-Sectional Survey of 2019 Australian Adults' (2019) <https://bmjopen.bmj.com/content/9/7/e024198>.

WA Demand for Integrative Services

9. Sustainable Health Review, *Final Report* (WA, 2019) <https://ww2.health.wa.gov.au/~/media/Files/Corporate/general-documents/Sustainable-Health-Review/Final-report/sustainable-health-review-final-report.pdf>. Annotation: system reform directions including prevention and person-centred models.

Blockchain & Transparency

10. e-Estonia, 'e-Health Records' <https://e-estonia.com/solutions/e-health-2/e-health-records/>.
11. e-Estonia, 'e-Health Authority Partners with Guardtime to Accelerate Transparency for Patients' (2016) <https://e-estonia.com/ehealth-authority-partners-with-guardtime-to-accelerate-transparency-and-auditability-in-health-care/>.
12. e-Estonia, *KSI® Blockchain in Estonia: Frequently Asked Questions* (2024) <https://e-estonia.com/wp-content/uploads/faq_ksi_blockchain.pdf>.
13. U.S. Food & Drug Administration, 'Drug Supply Chain Security Act (DSCSA)—Pilot Project Program' <https://www.fda.gov/drugs/drug-supply-chain-security-act-dscsa/dscsa-pilot-project-program>.
14. U.S. Food & Drug Administration, 'Drug Supply Chain Security Act (DSCSA) Pilot Project Program' (2023) <https://www.fda.gov/media/168307/download>.
15. IBM, KPMG, Merck and Walmart, *DSCSA Blockchain Interoperability Pilot: Final Report. U.S. FDA DSCSA Pilot Program* (2021) <https://www.fda.gov/media/147174/download>.
16. MediLedger Project, '2019 DSCSA Pilot Project: An Interoperable Blockchain Solution to the Track-and-Trace Requirement—Project Results and Final Report' (2024) <https://www.fda.gov/media/168283/download>.
17. World Bank, 'Open Contracting Reforms in Colombia: Case Study' in *Enhancing Government Effectiveness and Transparency: The Fight Against Corruption* (World Bank, 2021) 84 <https://documents1.worldbank.org/curated/en/235541600116631094/pdf/Enhancing-Government-Effectiveness-and-Transparency-The-Fight-Against-Corruption.pdf>.
18. Open Contracting Partnership, 'Impact: Colombia' <https://www.open-contracting.org/impact-stories/impact-colombia/>.

AI, Accountability & Program Integrity

19. NHS Employers & NHS Counter Fraud Authority, *NHS Counter Fraud Strategy to Implementing and Using AI* (2024) <https://www.nhsemployers.org/system/files/2024-08/20240723%20NHS%20counter%20fraud%20strategy%20to%20implementing%20and%20using%20AI%20%282%29.pdf>.

20. U.S. Government Accountability Office, 'Medicare and Medicaid: Additional Actions Could Help Strengthen Program Integrity' (2024) <https://www.gao.gov/products/gao-24-107487>.
21. Centers for Medicare & Medicaid Services, 'Fiscal Year 2024 Improper Payments—Fact Sheet' (2024) <https://www.cms.gov/newsroom/fact-sheets/fiscal-year-2024-improper-payments-fact-sheet>.
22. Australian National Audit Office, *Managing Health Provider Compliance* (2021) <https://www.anao.gov.au/work/performance-audit/managing-health-provider-compliance>.
23. Organisation for Economic Co-operation and Development, *G7 Toolkit for Using Artificial Intelligence in the Public Sector* (2024) <https://www.oecd.org/en/publications/g7-toolkit-for-artificial-intelligence-in-the-public-sector_421c1244-en.html>.

WHO Model List of Essential Medicines

24. World Health Organization, *WHO Model List of Essential Medicines, 21st List* (2019) <https://www.who.int/publications/i/item/WHOMVPEMPIAU2019.06>.

Health Insurance Fraud & Machine Learning

25. Hamid, Z, Khalique, F, Mahmood, S, Daud, A, Bukhari, A and Alshemaimri, B, 'Healthcare Insurance Fraud Detection Using Data Mining' (2024) <https://bmcmedinformdecismak.biomedcentral.com/articles/10.1186/s12911-024-02512-4>.
26. Aoufi, S, Sun, Y, Elazab, A and Wang, S, 'Explainable Unsupervised Anomaly Detection for Healthcare Insurance Data' (2024) <https://bmcmedinformdecismak.biomedcentral.com/articles/10.1186/s12911-024-02823-6>.

Global Health Spending & Chronic Disease Burden

27. World Health Organization, *Global Spending on Health: Weathering the Storm* (2020) <https://www.who.int/publications/i/item/9789240017788>.
28. Centers for Disease Control and Prevention, 'Fast Facts: Health and Economic Costs of Chronic Conditions' (2025) <https://www.cdc.gov/chronic-disease/data-research/facts-stats/index.html>.
29. Organisation for Economic Co-operation and Development (OECD), *Health at a Glance 2023: OECD Indicators* (2023) <https://www.oecd.org/en/publications/2023/11/health-at-a-glance-2023_e04f8239.html>. Annotation: notes preventive care spending averages 2-5% in OECD countries, including Australia.

Chronic Disease Prevalence in Australia

30. Australian Institute of Health and Welfare, 'Chronic Conditions' (2024) <https://www.aihw.gov.au/reports/australias-health/chronic-conditions>.

Global Mortality Statistics

31. World Health Organization, 'Cardiovascular Diseases (CVDs)' (2025) <https://www.who.int/news-room/fact-sheets/detail/cardiovascular-diseases-%28cvds%29>.
32. World Health Organization, 'Cancer' (2025) <https://www.who.int/news-room/fact-sheets/detail/cancer>.

Linguistic Diversity in Western Australia

33. Office of Multicultural Interests, *WA's Linguistic Diversity Census 2021* (2021) <https://www.omi.wa.gov.au/docs/librariesprovider2/2021-census/was-linguistic-diversity708970098a51485ea4fb0e120029c649.pdf>.
34. Australian Bureau of Statistics, 'Snapshot of Western Australia, 2021' (2022) <https://www.abs.gov.au/articles/snapshot-wa-2021>. Annotation: reports 32.2% born overseas in 2021, consistent with "nearly one in three".
35. Australian Bureau of Statistics, 'Census of Population and Housing: Cultural Diversity—Western Australia' (2022) <https://www.abs.gov.au/statistics/people/people-and-communities/cultural-diversity-census/latest-release>. Annotation: reports proportion born overseas.

Exporting Systems & Standards

36. World Bank, *State and Trends of Carbon Pricing 2019* (2019) <https://openknowledge.worldbank.org/handle/10986/31755>. Annotation: notes Australia's carbon pricing mechanisms influencing global environmental standards.

37. Chapman, B, 'Income Contingent Loans for Higher Education: International Reforms' in Eric Hanushek and Finis Welch (eds), *Handbook of the Economics of Education* (Vol 2, 2006) <https://brucejchapman.com/wp-content/uploads/2018/12/Ch-25-ICL-for-HE-International-Reforms.pdf>.
38. Sahlberg, P, *Finnish Lessons: What Can the World Learn from Educational Change in Finland?* (Teachers College Press, 2011) <https://www.pedocs.de/volltexte/2015/11098/pdf/CEPSJ_2011_3_Franko_Rezension_Sahlberg_Finnish_lessons_what_can.pdf>.

Eroded Trust In Government

39. Australian Election Study (ANU), 'Australian Election Study 2022: Trust in Government and Institutions' (2022) <https://australianelectionstudy.org/>. Annotation: data and trends.
40. Australian Government Department of the Prime Minister and Cabinet, *COVID-19 Response Inquiry Summary Report: Lessons for the Next Crisis* (2024) <https://www.pmc.gov.au/resources/covid-19-response-inquiry-summary-report-lessons-next-crisis>. Annotation: documents erosion of public trust in institutions due to inconsistencies in covid responses.

Diabetes Reversal Programs

41. Diabetes Prevention Program Research Group, 'The 10-Year Cost-Effectiveness of Lifestyle Intervention or Metformin for Diabetes Prevention: An Intent-to-Treat Analysis of the DPP/DPPOS' (2012) 35(4) *Diabetes Care* 723 <https://pubmed.ncbi.nlm.nih.gov/22442395/>. Annotation: shows lifestyle reversal programs save ~$1,700-2,500 per patient annually vs. metformin/insulin.
42. Lean, M E J et al, 'Primary Care-Led Weight Management for Remission of Type 2 Diabetes (DiRECT): An Open-Label, Cluster-Randomised Trial' (2018) 391(10120) *The Lancet* 541 <https://www.thelancet.com/journals/lancet/article/PIIS0140-6736(17)33102-1/fulltext>.
43. Xin, Y et al, 'Economic Evaluation of the DiRECT/Counterweight-Plus Intervention for Remission of Type 2 Diabetes in Primary Care' (2020) *Diabetic Medicine* <https://onlinelibrary.wiley.com/doi/10.1111/dme.14208>.

Cardiovascular Disease Prevention

44. Estruch, R et al, 'Primary Prevention of Cardiovascular Disease with a Mediterranean Diet Supplemented with Extra-Virgin Olive Oil or Nuts' (2018) 378(25) *New England Journal of Medicine* e34 <https://www.nejm.org/doi/full/10.1056/NEJMoa1800389>. Annotation: PREDIMED trial shows nutrition interventions reduce cardiovascular events by 30%, lowering hospital admissions; notes high costs of such events.
45. Estruch, R et al, 'Primary Prevention of Cardiovascular Disease with a Mediterranean Diet (PREDIMED)' (2013) 368 *New England Journal of Medicine* 1279 <https://www.nejm.org/doi/full/10.1056/NEJMoa1200303>.
46. Australian Institute of Health and Welfare, 'Cardiovascular Disease: Cost and Impact' (2024) <https://www.aihw.gov.au/reports/heart-stroke-vascular-diseases/cardiovascular-disease>.
47. Stroke Foundation, *The Economic Impact of Stroke in Australia* (Report, 2024) <https://strokefoundation.org.au/>.

Integrative Oncology

48. Kligler, B et al, 'Cost Savings in Inpatient Oncology through an Integrative Medicine Approach' (2011) 17(12) *American Journal of Managed Care* 779 <https://pubmed.ncbi.nlm.nih.gov/22216749/>.

WA's New Education System

Introduction

Here we set the constitutional anchor. This chapter proceeds directly from the constitution's Title 16: Human Law & Medical Freedom in Chapter 15, where Article 4—Social Guarantees—commits the new nation to provide free public education, alongside other social guarantees.

Article 4—Social Guarantees

"The Western Australian Government guarantees free public education . "

Article 4 is not a ceiling but a floor. It directs government to deliver education to every child, and it empowers a broad, innovation-friendly remit to build a world-leading system: locally led institutions, clear community standards, transparent public reporting, and statewide checks on fundamentals, with the State funding the mission while communities steward quality.

What follows is a practical blueprint for that system. Stewardship sits with the Ministry of Education and Civic Integrity, pursuing core goals: to raise well-rounded young citizens with a strong sense of civic duty, and to prioritise literacy, numeracy, civics, ethics, health and practical skills. Community mechanisms—including crowd-sourced quality verification and community-set standards—give parents and citizens a direct role in assuring outcomes for Western Australia's young.

The core goals of the new Western Australian education system are as follows:

Support children and young adults' development into well-rounded individuals with a strong sense of civic duty, high self-esteem, and orientation towards promoting their own wellbeing and that of their community.

Reinforce the nationhood paradigm and responsibility of every citizen to contribute to their community and to provide a check on the power of those in authority who serve the population (including via mandatory civil service).

Provide fundamental education in:

Literacy.

Numeracy.

Civics. Including the motivation for setting up new Western Australia as it is, the mechanisms of governance and citizen oversight, and the basic foundations upon which the West has been built.

Ethics. Including the basic tenets of Christianity, the traditional source of ethical guidance for the West.

Practical skills. Including the basics of:

- Human health, exercise and nutrition
- Human physiology and self-care
- Chemistry
- Communication and relationship skills
- Self-reflective and self-management skills, and
- Tactile and mechanical skills.

Nurture the curiosity of the human spirit and catalyse the innovation it can create by supporting pro-social research by diverse teams that approach their subjects using different lenses, guided only by peer-enforced principles of ethical research.

Support continuous learning within communities by knowledge dissemination programs (such as lecture series, seminars, skills-building workshops and other events) convened at the local level, in community-stewarded venues (e.g., community halls, community gardens, public parks, and beaches).

The basic structure of the Western Australian education system is sketched below, organised by citizen age. Common elements across age groups include:

- Crowd-sourced quality verification of care and education providers, modelled on what is presently used to elicit consumer ratings for hotels and restaurants (to be organised by the Ministry using bespoke, developed technology).
- A high degree of local control by the leadership of institutions of learning over resource expenditure, to cater to their different strengths, foci and approaches to supporting learning.
- Minimal use of screens for content delivery, homework, or other non-administrative purpose (with exceptions for technology-focused high schools).
- Community-set standards and community and market-led enforcement of those standards, coupled with state funding and periodic state-wide testing of fundamental skills.
- The recognition that children are best served when their family is strong and secure, and supported in a strong community.

Integration of community activities, including community-led standard-setting, inspections and audits that are the charge of the community education civic referred to herein, into the broader Western Australian model of allocating one day per week for all citizens to contribute toward the life and enrichment of their communities, and requiring a significant civil service contribution from every citizen. The community education civic body shall be composed of a rotating group of 12-15 citizens who have opted to fulfill their civil service via serving on this body, with term lengths of no more than one year and no repeat terms possible.

Conception to 2: Pregnancy Care, and Family Care or Family Daycare

Babies and young infants develop best when they are cared for in a secure, loving, stimulating home or home-like environment. Every family is expected to make its own choice, based on its own local situation, about whether to care for its youngest members at home or in another home-like environment (whether paid or unpaid).

Partial supply-side government subsidies will be offered to family daycare providers, expected to consist mainly of mothers or grandmothers operating out of their own homes, who agree to adhere to their local community education civic body's one-page guidelines surrounding family daycare.

The default for such guidelines, which each community is invited to customise, is as follows:

- The family daycare provider agrees not to take into her care any child younger than 6 weeks of age.
- The family daycare provider is trained in the administration of first aid to infants and toddlers (via the Western Australian health system), in developmentally appropriate

interaction with young children, and in the preparation of nutritious foods for infants and toddlers.

- The family daycare provider agrees to have in her sole care no more than one child under 6 months of age and no more than one additional child between the ages of 6 months and two years, at any one time. She agrees to care for a maximum of four children under school age, and a maximum of six children in total, at any one time.
- The family daycare provider agrees to have her care site inspected unannounced no more than six times per year by nominated members of the community education civic body and/or state, at the community's absolute discretion.
- The family daycare provider participates in a crowd-sourced quality verification system, whereby all parents who visit her location or hire her services must provide brief, anonymous feedback about the quality of care provided, which in turn is made public via a website for other parents to be informed of the community daycare options around them.
- Government supply-side subsidies will cover the full cost of at least three days of full-time family day care for any child, regardless of economic circumstances.

Some overlap between the health system and the education system occurs between the moment a prospective mother announces her pregnancy and the first six months of a child's life, when a series of state-sponsored home visits to the pregnant/new mother and newborn by community health and education providers will include training and support in self-care during pregnancy, breastfeeding and other healthcare, interacting in developmentally appropriate ways with the new baby, caring for the parents, the parental partnership, and other family members, and preparing to support the baby's future developmental stages. The potential roles of grandparents and other extended family and community members in the care of the new baby now and into the future will also be discussed at these visits.

A special note is in order about women who fall pregnant in difficult circumstances. Western Australia affirms the necessity of placing moral decisions in such cases, which are often complicated, into the hands of informed local actors, including but not limited to the pregnant woman herself within whose body the new life is developing. Western Australia also affirms the sanctity of life and of maintaining a set of support structures for pregnant women such that pregnancy terminations, while safe and legal, are extremely rare and happen only in the first trimester or to save the life of the mother. In pursuit of that goal, all women who announce their pregnancy will be entitled to an array of state-sponsored services, including healthcare for mother and child, counselling and information services, adoption and shared-care referrals (with specific options for adoption and shared-care arrangements coordinated locally by the community education civic body), time-limited relocation services, and time-limited financial support in case of demonstrated need. Pregnant women will be honoured and supported unconditionally and compassionately, regardless of their circumstances.

2-4: Pre-School

In addition to family daycare, another paid option that families may consider for the care of their slightly older pre-school children is a formal pre-school. This option should be seriously considered for gifted or developmentally advanced children from 2 years of age, and for older children (i.e., 3-4 years of age).

Partial supply-side government subsidies will be provided to public or private pre-schools that enroll between 6 and 32 children at all times and whose leadership agrees to adhere to their local community education civic body's one-page guidelines surrounding pre-schools.

The default for such guidelines, which each community is invited to customise, is as follows:

- The pre-school may enroll children from the age of 2 years until the day before a child's first day of primary school.
- All staff directly interacting with children are trained in the administration of first aid to infants and toddlers (via the Western Australian health system) and in developmentally appropriate interaction with young children. All staff involved in preparing and serving food are trained in the preparation of nutritious foods for infants and toddlers.
- Pre-school leadership agrees to maintain a coal-face-staff: child ratio of 1:8 or greater at all times (note: administrative or support staff who are not working directly with children do not count towards satisfying this ratio).
- Pre-school leadership agrees to have the pre-school inspected unannounced no more than six times per year by nominated members of the community education civic body and/or state, at the community's absolute discretion.
- Pre-school leadership agrees to participate in a crowd-sourced quality verification system, whereby all parents who visit the pre-school or use its services must provide brief, anonymous feedback about the quality of the experience for children provided there, which in turn is made public via a publicly run website for other parents to review.
- Government supply-side subsidies will cover the full cost of at least three days of full-time pre-school for any child, regardless of a family's economic circumstances.

It is at the pre-school level that different philosophies about how best to help children develop start to become meaningful in the design and implementation of activities. Citizens may propose leading the establishment of pre-schools that implement their preferred philosophies, and on approval from the community education civic body, the proposed leaders will be awarded three months' worth of government supply-side subsidies to demonstrate that their philosophy is sufficiently appealing that the pre-school attains a viable size. After the three-month trial period, if six or more children are enrolled (to be verified by the community education civic body), the pre-school will enter the regular community-oversight system described above; if fewer than six children are enrolled, the proposed leaders of the pre-school will be ineligible for government subsidies for two years, whereupon they may re-apply for approval from the community for another three-month trial period.

5-12: Primary School

The over-arching goals of primary education are to embed fundamental numeracy, literacy, and practical skills into children; to begin to make them aware of the broader society and their present and potential places in it; and to teach them how to comport themselves and how to treat others in loving and productive ways.

Primary schooling will be provided by a mix of public and private providers, with both options available to all families via the distribution of educational vouchers that can be redeemed, supply permitting, at any private school that receives public subsidies. It is the choice of the leadership of each private school whether to accept vouchers and public subsidies (the latter equal to a fraction (.5?) of the per-pupil operational costs paid to public schools), or whether to decline both. Private schools that accept vouchers must not charge additional fees to students who attend via the voucher system, must enroll no fewer than 20% of their student body via vouchers (with an initial grace period of one year to establish viability), and must accept any voucher student who applies while capacity for voucher students is still available (i.e., until the 20% threshold is reached). Apart from these stipulations, private schools may charge whatever fees they like, and may be established or closed by citizens according to their preferred educational philosophies and market signals. However, to be eligible for public subsidies, private schools must not only fill at least 20% of their student body with voucher students, but also must participate in state-wide testing, public reporting of test results, community-infused governance (with a body modelled on the current "P&C Committee" being mandatory) and a crowd-sourced quality verification system similar to that described for daycare and pre-schools (including at the teacher level, with community evaluations of teachers feeding into promotion decisions)—all of which all public schools will also participate in as conditions of operation.

State-wide testing will focus on basic literacy and numeracy, using four of the five NAPLAN test types as the initial template (spelling will not be included), in years 3, 5, and 7. Results reporting will initially follow the present Australia-wide mySchool website reporting structure. Except for schools in exceptional and explicitly documented circumstances, such as those established to serve entirely learning-disadvantaged student bodies, any publicly funded school that does not test more than 97% of its enrolled students in any given year (whether due to withholding, exemption, or absence) will automatically by audited by the community education civic body and, at the auditors' absolute discretion, a referral will be made to the Ministry for possible cessation of public funding.

Local leadership of both public and private primary schools will have wide latitude to run school operations and design and implement curricula according to their principles and experience, while omitting from classrooms and leaving to families and communities the responsibility of providing religious, ideological, and spiritual education and guidance. At the primary level, school leadership is encouraged to provide both in-class and community-linked extension and support for gifted and learning-disabled students, respectively, rather than separate ability-streamed classes within the school, with an example of an opt-in state-sponsored extension program provided below. Regardless of their particular focus or philosophy, all publicly funded primary schools are expected to offer, at a minimum, physical education (including at least one full year of swimming lessons for each student), community outreach, and aesthetic programming (visual and performing arts) to all students in addition to academic programming. Template page-limited curricula for different subjects will be provided by the Ministry, but it is not compulsory for any primary school, principal, or teacher to follow these curricula. Teachers of different subjects will be supported by the state to share their lesson plans and interactive activities with other teachers on peer-to-peer online resource-sharing platforms administered by the Ministry, with awards provided (and given significant weight in promotion decisions) for the development and sharing of excellent teaching materials.

To support future Western Australian leaders, publicly funded schools may choose to participate in a state-sponsored Primary Extension and Challenge (PEAC) enrichment program for students with high intellectual potential modelled on and run as per the PEAC program in place in WA during the 1990s. The program will be organised and managed by schools within a district in concert with the community education civic body. PEAC testing will occur for all students during grade 3, with a maximum of 5% of students from each school accepted into the program. The program consists of extension opportunities in different subjects provided each term from grades 4 to 6. Transportation will be provided to bus students to and from PEAC classes.

Year 7 students in all publicly funded primary schools are expected to prepare for the transition to high school and for increasing civic responsibility by mentoring younger students and taking on other leadership roles and responsibilities, performing basic assistance of teaching staff, contributing toward the organisation of events, representing the student body in school governance, and serving as the first port of call for mediation and arbitration in case of non-violent or minimally violent conflict between students.

13-17: High School

High school is the level of schooling at which students begin to substantially diverge from one another in terms of interests and aptitudes, as they prepare to fill different paid and unpaid roles in adulthood. Accordingly, high schools are expected to provide a range of elective subjects, and to catalyse work experience opportunities, extension opportunities, and support programs such that every student can develop his or her potential to the fullest extent. High school is a place for young people to build their psychological wellbeing and to discover themselves, including what they are interested in and good at, and how best they can contribute to their community.

The basic setup of high schooling will be as for primary schooling:

> Public and private providers, with minimum-fraction voucher-student requirements for private schools to receive public subsidies, and all other requirements as stated for primary schools except that following a minimum set of state-level curricula in core subjects (English, mathematics, civics, and ethics) will be mandatory for the receipt of government funding. State-wide testing will occur in years 9 and 11, with the year 11 test being optional and focused on a range of practical skills, based on which students may be offered places in TAFE or other non-university tertiary education institutions.

18-22: Tertiary education

Western Australia's system of tertiary education will be made up of (1) TAFE and other skills-focused, degree-granting tertiary education institutions (the default destination for students who wish to continue their education beyond high school), and (2) universities (for a small fraction of high school graduates, e.g., 10%, who have demonstrated outstanding academic potential).

Admission to TAFE and other non-university institutions of higher learning will proceed on the basis of the Year 11 optional state-wide testing mentioned above, plus entrance exams (practical or written) of the tertiary institution's choosing. Admission to university undergraduate programs will proceed on the basis of review by a rotating panel of academic staff of the high school academic and extracurricular records, personal statements, and letters of reference of high school graduates from within Western Australia or Australia (minimum 90% of enrolment) or similar materials from overseas applicants (maximum 10% of enrolment), the latter of whom must also, to be eligible for admission, score sufficiently well on a written and oral test of English-language skills taken in a Western Australian-supervised location. Universities may charge whatever fees they like to overseas students, but to be eligible for public funding of domestic student places, universities must run all undergraduate classes on campus and in person, and must make all student records available for public scrutiny in anonymized form.

TAFE and other non-university tertiary providers may offer training and certificates in the following types of areas (this is an illustrative rather than an exhaustive list):

- Agriculture
- Bricklaying
- Electrical
- Forestry
- Glazier and glassblowing skills
- Gas fitting and turning
- Leatherworking
- Mechanics and machine operation
- Metalworking
- Plumbing and sanitation
- Textiles
- Woodworking

Existing WA universities will either remain universities (if their research is both sufficiently voluminous and sufficiently pro-social in nature, and they have sufficiently populous post-graduate programs and research facilities) or will be converted into, and/or spin off separately, skills-focused tertiary providers delivering degree-granting programs in one or more of the following types of areas (this is an illustrative rather than an exhaustive list):

- Accounting

- Applied chemistry and materials science
- Architecture
- Aviation
- Business administration
- Computer science
- Construction
- Creative writing
- Dance
- Ecology and environmental science
- Education
- Hospitality and event management
- Hydrology
- Community nursing
- Information management and digital technology
- Legal studies
- Marine science
- Midwifery
- Military officer studies
- Music (composition and/or performance)
- Nutrition
- Physiology and exercise science
- Public administration
- Solar technology
- Theatre studies
- Visual art

Universities will shrink in number and size, and will increase their focus on providing research and training in core academic disciplines, including the following (this is an illustrative rather than an exhaustive list):

- Anthropology
- Archeology
- Biology
- Chemistry
- Economics
- Engineering
- History (including art history)
- Western literature
- Non-Western literature
- Law

- Linguistics
- Mathematics
- Medicine
- Philosophy
- Physics
- Political science
- Psychology
- Sociology

Government research funding will be provided to universities in tranches of six-year-long support for research groups within universities that propose and defend, on pro-social grounds, a particular approach to their discipline (a particular school of thought). At least two divergent schools of thought will be funded in each discipline, within or across universities, at any time; if only one application or one school of thought in a given discipline is deemed worthy of funding at any given time, no applications will be funded in that discipline until a second viable application in a divergent school of thought is found. Funding levels will be determined based on projected personnel, equipment, and research-training costs. Applications for funding will not exceed five pages, must nominate at least three academics to form the core group, and will be accepted on a rolling basis from academics in all disciplines. Funding recipients must write a report of not more than ten pages at the close of each year of funding, demonstrating the achievements of the research group. Research groups will be audited by the community education civic body both randomly and based on the contents of these reports, with members of groups that fail the audit referred to the Ministry and possibly stripped of funding and of the opportunity to apply for research funding for the ensuring three years. The sole administrative requirements of research funding receipt are to submit these yearly reports and to adhere to the Western Australian statement on the ethical conduct of research, which will be verified via peer-to-peer auditing of research practices.

Community Education Programming

In addition to the formal structures above designed to support developing young people, Western Australia recognises community education as a valuable source of lifelong personal and social development. To that end, the state will fund knowledge dissemination programs such as lecture series by touring tertiary educators, artists, authors, and others, seminars or skills-building workshops by skilled community members, community dance, music, theatre and visual art classes, and other events convened at the local level by the community education civic body, in community-stewarded venues (e.g., community halls, libraries, community gardens, public parks, and beaches). Each community that has no modern, air-conditioned community hall will be provided a subsidy to build or renovate such a hall (payable on the completion of renovations or construction).

Civil Service

All Western Australian citizens have the responsibility to contribute to the health and development of their community through their own personal efforts. These efforts can take many forms, from bearing and/or raising natural or adopted children or grandchildren, to taking care of elderly family or community members, to volunteering at local philanthropic, religious, or service organisations (e.g., the local fire service). In addition to these ongoing contributions, every Western Australian citizen is expected to devote a minimum of six months of his or her life to the community in his or her choice of an array of ways. At least three months of this service must be completed before the age of 30, and all forms of service will be remunerated at reasonable rates. An initial list of options is provided below.

- Service on community civic bodies (such as the community education civic body described herein) —terms of not less than six months and not more than 1 year.
- Service in a citizen media organisation—terms of not less than three months and not more than 1 year.
- Service on a citizen jury to appoint the head or deputy head of a Ministry—term of three months.
- Service in the armed forces—terms of not less than six months.
- Service on criminal jury rolls—terms of not less than 1 year.

Enabling Legislation

Recall, Article 4 is not a ceiling but a floor. It both guarantees free public education and empowers Parliament to legislate ambitiously to realise a world-leading system that is locally led, transparent, community-stewarded, and accountable for fundamentals. A new Western Australia Education Act should be enacted to give effect to that constitutional mandate. The following is a legislative blueprint:

EDUCATION ACT—SCHEMATIC OUTLINE

Part I—Objects & Principles

State the core goals. raise well-rounded young citizens with civic duty and high self-esteem; prioritise literacy, numeracy, civics, ethics, health and practical skills; nurture curiosity and pro-social innovation.

Operationalise the constitutional guarantee of free public education, combining community stewardship with state checks on fundamentals.

Part II—Institutions & Governance

Establish the Ministry of Education and Civic Integrity as system steward.

Constitute a Community Education Civic Body in each district (rotating 12–15 citizens; one-year, non-renewable terms) to set local standards, conduct inspections/audits, and participate in appointments and reviews of school leadership.

Part III—Quality Assurance & Transparency

Mandate crowd-sourced quality verification for providers (including teacher-level feedback where appropriate), published on a public website.

Require periodic state-wide testing of fundamentals with public reporting; trigger audit if <97% of enrolled students sit tests (with narrow, documented exceptions).

Tie state funding to compliance with standards, transparency and community-governance conditions.

Part IV—Early Childhood (Conception–2; 2–4)

Enable supply-side subsidies for family day-care and pre-schools that meet one-page community guidelines (first-aid training; nutrition training; staff:child ratio ≥1:8; up to six unannounced inspections per year; participation in public ratings).

Fund at least three days per week of full-time family day-care or pre-school for any child, regardless of income.

Provide trial support for diverse pre-school philosophies, with three-month viability tests overseen locally.

Part V—Primary Education (5–12)

Guarantee parental choice via vouchers redeemable at eligible private schools; require participating private schools to:

(a) enrol ≥20% voucher students;
(b) charge no top-ups to voucher students; and
(c) comply with testing, public reporting, community governance and crowd-verification.

Preserve wide local autonomy over operations and curricula; offer optional, page-limited state templates and peer-to-peer resource-sharing with recognition and promotion weight for excellent materials.

Require minimum offerings: physical education (including a full year of swimming), community outreach, and aesthetic programmes.

Authorise a district-run Primary Extension and Challenge (PEAC) programme for high-potential students (test in Year 3; up to 5% intake; term-based extensions with transport provided).

Part VI—Secondary & Tertiary Pathways

Align secondary schooling with the primary model of choice and accountability; embed core academic requirements and clear progression pathways into TAFE/skills-focused institutions and universities.

Fund university research through multi-year support for divergent schools of thought, audited by the community civic body and governed by a Western Australian ethical research statement.

Part VII—Community Education & Civil Service

Finance continuous community learning: local lecture series, seminars, skills workshops and arts programmes in community-stewarded venues, with capital support where halls are lacking.

Integrate education civics into the national civil-service duty (e.g., service on community bodies, citizen media, juries, armed forces), remunerated at reasonable rates.

Part VIII—Funding & Procurement

Tie funding to compliance with transparency, testing and community-governance conditions; publish machine-readable, school-level dashboards.

Part IX—Enforcement, Review & Regulations

Provide inspection, remedial direction, funding suspension and referral powers.

Require a five-year statutory review with public consultation.

Authorise regulations to update standards, instruments and administrative arrangements.

Rollout

The new nation's education system must be crafted from the existing system, which features amongst other things a significantly more prominent role for the central government, a differently balanced and subsidised tertiary sector, and less emphasis on community-based quality assurance and educational programming.

The rollout of the new model for education will proceed in three phases:

Phase 1 (0–3 years)

Establish the Ministry of Education and Civic Integrity and all community-level education and childcare-related civic bodies, write and disseminate to schools all new national education guidelines, significantly deregulate childcare, design and implement support programs for pregnancy; design and pilot crowdsourced quality assurance of childcare and schools and all national quality dashboards, evaluate existing universities, grandfather out old research grants, plan new "schools of thought"-based funding system for pro-social research plus how to transition each university's disciplines; take a census of existing community spaces and work with selected communities to plan construction of new community spaces; form all education-related civic bodies; selected communities design and pilot an initial suite of community education programs and enrichment activities for school students.

Phase 2 (3–7 years)

Further rollout of crowdsourced quality assurance system and dissemination of successful community education and school enrichment programs; transition all disciplines within universities to TAFE, skills-focused tertiary institutions, and/or downsized universities, initiating peer review of research quality to replace centralised research quality assurance; implement new university research funding plan; embed full community review of all local schools and childcare facilities; resurrect PEAC-style extension programs and implement additional work experience and enrichment programs locally for public school students, with assistance from education-focused civic bodies; complete construction of all new community spaces; extend citizen oversight of education to the periodic review of national education guidelines.

Phase 3 (7–15 years)

Further reduce the role of the Ministry and enhance the role of communities in directing educational choices, retaining for the Ministry by Year 15 only the role of custodian of national education guidelines, administrator of all education and childcare-related public dashboards, and administrator of block education grants and pro-social research grants to public educational establishments.

Final Thoughts

Western Australia can do more than restore free public education; we can restore confidence in what education is for. The present system has not adequately prepared Western Australia's youth for the twenty-first century. This blueprint offers a practical path to fix what is broken: the State funds the mission; communities steward quality; and every child is seen, challenged, and supported to become a capable citizen. With Article 4 as our constitutional floor and a clear legislative scaffold, Western Australia can build a schooling culture that prizes literacy and numeracy, civic and ethical understanding, health and practical competence, and the curiosity that fuels innovation—with parents and citizens directly shaping standards and outcomes. Communities lead; the next generation thrives.

WA's New Anti-Corruption Framework

Executive Summary

As a nascent nation, Western Australia will commit to eradicating corruption to safeguard its legitimacy, foster public trust, and ensure economic prosperity for all citizens. Drawing on the exemplary models of Hong Kong's Independent Commission Against Corruption (ICAC, established 1974) and Singapore's Corrupt Practices Investigation Bureau (CPIB, established 1952), Western Australia will establish the Western Australian Anti-Corruption Commission (WAACC) as a singular, independent authority to enforce a unified legal framework across public and private sectors. This framework will be anchored by the Western Australian Anti-Corruption Commission Act 2029 (WAACCA), which will criminalise bribery, illicit enrichment, and related offenses with severe penalties, including reverse-burden-of-proof provisions for unexplained wealth. Constitutionally mandated cutting-edge blockchain technology will create tamper-proof records of government actions, ensuring transparency, while artificial intelligence (AI) will provide 24/7 monitoring for fraud detection and continuous system improvements. A Communications Transparency System (CTS) will offer citizens near-real-time access to official correspondence, reinforcing accountability. A robust whistleblower protection regime, citizen-driven judicial oversight, and a lifelong civic education program will embed integrity into Western Australia's cultural fabric. Implementation, commencing in late 2029, will deliver a governance model where corruption is both illegal and nearly impossible to conceal, positioning Western Australia as a global exemplar of transparent and accountable governance.

Foundational Principles

Corruption undermines the social trust, economic prosperity, and moral authority of any nation. Western Australia's founding charter will confront this existential threat by adopting a "one society, one set of rules" principle, ensuring that no individual or entity—whether public official, corporate executive, or private citizen—is exempt from scrutiny. Inspired by Singapore (Transparency International Corruption Perceptions Index score 84) and Hong Kong (CPI score 75), which transformed high-graft societies into global integrity leaders through consistent enforcement and cultural reinforcement, Western Australia's framework will integrate rigorous enforcement, systemic prevention, and comprehensive public education. The WAACC, modeled on Hong Kong's ICAC holistic strategy of enforcement, prevention, and education, and Singapore's CPIB relentless independence, will operate outside civil service hierarchies, reporting directly to the public, Citizen Oversight Committee (COC) and President to ensure impartiality. The World Bank and OECD emphasize that transparency and citizen engagement are critical to making corruption difficult to hide, a principle Western Australia will embed through public access to government records and participatory oversight mechanisms, including the COC. By combining legal rigor, technological innovation, and civic participation, Western Australia will forge a governance model where integrity is not merely an aspiration but a lived reality, ensuring that every citizen's share in the nation's wealth is protected for future generations.

Building on these principles, Western Australia will prioritise transparency and citizen participation as core design elements, drawing from World Bank and OECD guidelines to ensure public access to records and participatory oversight. Advanced technologies like tamper-evident ledgers and AI will enhance detection while upholding due process, aligning with United Nations Office on Drugs and Crime (UNODC) standards to create a system where corruption is nearly impossible to conceal.

Institutional Framework

Western Australian Anti-Corruption Commission (WAACC)

The WAACC will be the cornerstone of Western Australia's anti-corruption regime, established as a single, independent agency with authority to prevent, investigate, and refer cases for prosecution across public and private sectors affecting the public interest, as mandated under Constitutional Title 18: Anti-Corruption Framework (see Chapter 15: A New Nation's Constitution). Its design reflects the strengths of Hong Kong's ICAC and Singapore's CPIB, which operate outside bureaucratic influence to ensure impartiality. Key features include:

> ***Full Independence.*** Commissioners are appointed by the President from a COC-nominated shortlist, protected by security of tenure and strict conflict-of-interest rules. A guaranteed budget from the Western Australian Reserve Authority (WARA) ensures operational autonomy, with monthly public reports.

Mandate. Empowered to obtain information, examine accounts, search/seize under warrant, freeze assets, conduct covert operations, and cooperate internationally. It includes unexplained-wealth orders and civil recovery on a balance of probabilities.

Sanctions. Powers for disgorgement, fines (including turnover-linked penalties), treble damages, debarment from public office/contracts, imprisonment, professional notifications, and extraterritorial reach.

Judicial Accountability Integration. Judicial integrity is overseen by the COC's Judicial Appointments & Integrity Subpanel; alleged criminality is referred to the WAACC/WAACCP (Western Australian Anti-Corruption Commission Prosecutor) for investigation and (where sanctioned) prosecution.

The WAACC's "no one is above the law" mandate will ensure swift enforcement, even for high-ranking officials and corporates. For citizens, this means a trusted institution pursuing justice without favour; for scholars, it offers a model of centralised, independent governance, supported by global precedents like Rwanda's Ombudsman.

Citizen Oversight Committee

A 29–30 member Citizen Oversight Committee (COC), elected non-partisan from electoral districts in alternating cohorts to ensure geographic separation and impartiality, will monitor political finance, governance, and integrity, as established under Constitutional Title 18: Anti-Corruption Framework. Members serve four-year terms (max two), must be at least 40 years of age with professional qualifications, and have no political party registration or government contracts. The COC is independent, with immunities for good-faith acts and a PRA-guaranteed budget.

The COC has jurisdiction to oversee political finance, procurement, and transparency obligations; issue compliance notices, penalties, and corrective orders, with referrals to WAACC/WAACCP for suspected illegality

For citizens, the COC ensures voices hold leaders accountable.

COC Emergency Powers Oversight

The COC's Emergency Powers Review Subpanel operationalises Constitutional Article 7 of Title 16: Human Law & Medical Freedom, providing citizen-led oversight of emergency declarations that restrict freedoms (e.g., lockdowns, rights suspensions). As detailed in Chapter 9, A New Fourth Branch: Human Law & Medical Freedom, the Subpanel reviews measures for necessity and proportionality, with authority to uphold, modify, suspend, or revoke them. Comprising qualified COC members, it ensures emergencies serve the public interest without abuse. All reviews and decisions are published on the public blockchain, reinforcing transparency and aligning with Western Australia's commitment to protecting liberties even in crises.

Legal Framework

Constitutional Foundation

Title 18 constitutionally establishes the WAACC, the WAACCP, and the Citizen Oversight Committee (COC) as an integrity triad, hard-wiring independence (appointments, tenure, conflicts, and protected funding), enforceable transparency obligations, and citizen-led oversight with judicial review on questions of law. The Constitution sets the minimum powers and safeguards and requires enabling legislation to specify offences, investigatory tools, confiscation mechanisms, and procedural protections—implemented through the WAACCA specimen provisions that follow.

Western Australian Anti-Corruption Commission Act 2029 (WAACCA): Specimen Legislation

The WAACCA will be the keystone statute, streamlining Hong Kong's Prevention of Bribery Ordinance and Singapore's Prevention of Corruption Act into a unified law covering public and private sectors. It will operationalise Western Australia's "high-risk, zero-reward" approach, integrating severe criminal offenses, civil recovery tools, and whistleblower protections to deter and punish corruption effectively. The following is specimen legislation demonstrating the scope and depth possible under Title 18 of the new Constitution.

PART I—PRELIMINARY

Short Title & Commencement. This Act may be cited as the Western Australian Anti-Corruption Commission Act 2029 and will come into force on the day fixed by proclamation.

Objects. (a) Safeguard the integrity of public and private dealings affecting the public interest; (b) deter, detect, and punish corruption by individuals and entities; (c) provide civil recovery tools where criminal proof is unavailable, ensuring no safe harbor for illicit gains.

Definitions. Defines "gratification" (any benefit, monetary or non-monetary), "public official" (elected or appointed officials, including contractors), "unexplained wealth" (assets disproportionate to lawful income), "associate" (family or business affiliates), and "adequate procedures" (corporate compliance measures), aligning with Hong Kong and Singapore standards.

PART II—CORE OFFENCES

Bribery (active and passive). Any person who corruptly solicits, receives, agrees to receive, offers, promises, or gives gratification—directly or through an intermediary—to influence the performance of a public or corporate function commits an offence. Penalty: up to 10 years imprisonment and/or up to $WAT 2,000,000 fine.

Trading in Influence. Using real or ostensible influence over a decision-maker for a benefit, such as securing contracts or favours. Penalty: Up to 7 years imprisonment and/or up to $WAT 1,000,000 fine.

Abuse of Functions. Misusing a public position for private gain, including favouritism or negligence. Penalty: Up to 15 years imprisonment and/or $WAT 2,000,000 fine.

Embezzlement. Misappropriating public property or funds. Penalty: Up to 12 years imprisonment and/or up to $WAT 2,000,000 + triple value compensation to the state.

Illicit Enrichment. Possession of assets disproportionate to lawful income creates a rebuttable presumption of corruption, shifting the burden to the accused to prove legitimacy, as in Hong Kong's model. Penalty: Up to 10 years imprisonment and/or full forfeiture.

Corporate Failure to Prevent Bribery. Strict liability for organisations failing to prevent bribery by associates, modelled on the UK Bribery Act s.7. Penalty: Up to $WAT 20,000,000 or 10% of global turnover, whichever is higher.

Obstruction & Retaliation. Hindering investigations, destroying evidence, or retaliating against whistleblowers. Penalty: Up to 20 years imprisonment and/or up to $WAT 5,000,000 fine.

Note: Courts may impose both fines and imprisonment; bribe values will be forfeited; repeat offenders face sentence enhancement of one-third.

PART III—INVESTIGATION & ENFORCEMENT

WAACC Powers. Designates WAACC, in coordination with the WAACCP, as the lead agency with authority to arrest without warrant where reasonable suspicion of commission of Part II Core Offence, search premises, freeze assets, examine bank and cryptocurrency accounts, and require document production, ensuring rapid response to corruption allegations.

Special Warrants & Covert Tools. Permits surveillance, undercover operations, and data analytics; blockchain audit logs will be admissible as prima facie evidence of data integrity, facilitating prosecution.

Extraterritorial Reach. Offences by Western Australians abroad or affecting public interest will be triable locally, preventing evasion through foreign transactions, as per UNODC conventions.

Deferred Prosecution & Leniency. Allows penalty discounts for corporate self-reporting, full restitution, and compliance overhaul, encouraging proactive reform, as seen in Singapore's model.

PART IV—CIVIL RECOVERY & UNEXPLAINED-WEALTH ORDERS

Unexplained-Wealth Order (UWO). On reasonable suspicion, WAACC may order a person or related entity to explain asset origins, and make determinations using a balance of probabilities standard, as in Hong Kong's approach.

Civil Forfeiture. Assets unexplained by a UWO will be forfeited to the Consolidated Fund without requiring a criminal conviction, ensuring swift recovery of illicit gains.

Asset Freezing & Management. Interim 180-day freezes, extendable; WAACC may appoint receivers to preserve asset value during investigations.

Forfeiture Appeals. Limited to questions of law; the appellant bears the burden to prove assets were lawfully obtained.

PART V—PROTECTION & INCENTIVES

Whistleblower Immunity & Rewards. Adopts the whistleblower framework (see below), with corruption-specific bounties of 10–20% of recovered funds, capped by regulation, paid within 60 days of judgment.

Witness Protection. Courts may order voice/image alteration, relocation, or identity change for witnesses, ensuring safety.

PART VI—SANCTIONS & COLLATERAL CONSEQUENCES

Mandatory Disgorgement & Treble Damages. WAACC must order repayment of benefits or thrice their value, whichever is greater, maximising deterrence.

Lifetime Debarment. Convicted offenders (individuals or entities) will be barred from public office, government contracts, and regulated licenses for up to 15 years to life, depending on offense severity.

Professional Disqualification. Mandatory notice to professional bodies (e.g., bar, accounting) for potential striking-off, ensuring career consequences.

Publication of Convictions. Judgments and recovery statistics will be hashed on the public blockchain within 24 hours.

Deterrence Features. Reverse burdens for gratuities and illicit enrichment ensure no safe harbor; dual criminal-civil recovery claws back assets; severe corporate liability compels robust compliance; blockchain publication makes corruption visibly futile; and treble damages and lifetime bans strip profit and prestige, creating a "high-risk, zero-reward" calculus.

PART VII—COMPLIANCE & DEFENSES

Adequate Procedures Defence. Corporates may avoid liability by proving risk-based controls, including blockchain-logged payments and AI-vetted vendor due diligence, as per UK Bribery Act standards.

Facilitation Payments. Abolished, eliminating loopholes for small bribes.

Legal Privilege. Preserved but cannot shield ongoing crimes or fraud.

This comprehensive statute integrates with supporting laws, providing a clear, enforceable framework that citizens can rely on, and scholars can analyse, drawing on precedents from Singapore, Hong Kong, and the UK.

Technological Enablers

Blockchain-Enabled Transparency

Western Australia will pioneer blockchain technology to create a tamper-proof governance system, as mandated by Title 18: Anti-Corruption Framework's requirement for real-time, tamper-evident ledgers like MonetaNet. Drawing on pilots in Colombia (e.g., blockchain-based public procurement), India (e.g., land registry and financial pilots), and Estonia, this system ensures transparency and verifiability:

> ***Public Ledger.*** All government actions—budgets, contracts, licenses, grants, and case records—are recorded on a permissioned blockchain (e.g., Hyperledger Fabric or Estonia's KSI model), operated by a neutral state IT authority under COC oversight. Citizens access a user-friendly web portal with data visualisation tools and APIs, enabling real-time auditing of transactions, such as contract awards or budget allocations. Smart contracts automate bid execution and payments, preventing tampering.
>
> ***Public Registers.*** Land titles, mining licenses, and beneficial ownership registries are blockchain-based, reducing manipulation risks, as seen in Sweden and Georgia. Citizens can trace ownership chains via public dashboards, deterring hidden assets.
>
> ***Case Records.*** WAACC investigations are hashed on-chain, ensuring evidence integrity and visibility. Public dashboards, inspired by Singapore's reporting, display case statuses, conviction rates, and recovered assets, reinforcing credibility.
>
> ***Open-Source Architecture.*** Open-source platforms (e.g., Hyperledger) allow independent audits, with critical hashes written to a public chain, creating a "single view of truth," as recommended by the World Economic Forum.

AI-Assisted Oversight

AI serves as an impartial, 24/7 guardian of Western Australia's governance. It monitors government business, detects fraud, and drives improvements, addressing skepticism through transparency and ethical safeguards:

> ***Passive Audits.*** AI reviews investigative reports, prosecutions, and contracts in real time, ensuring compliance with WAACCA clauses and flagging inconsistencies (e.g., statutory errors). For example, AI verifies WAACC case files for legal adherence, delivering feedback instantly, per U.S. NIST AI principles.

Anomaly Detection. Machine-learning algorithms scan blockchain feeds, financial transactions, and communications for red flags (e.g., bid-rigging, asset spikes), as seen in OECD procurement studies. Alerts trigger human review by the COC's Technology Subpanel, catching schemes early.

System Improvements. AI analyses case outcomes and performance to recommend enhancements, feeding insights into WAACC/WAACCP training. By 2030, generative AI will improve pattern recognition across diverse data, per OECD projections.

Transparency and Ethics. The COC's Technology, Data and AI Audit Subpanel oversees system integrity, publishing "Model Cards" detailing AI purposes and metrics. All AI actions are blockchain-logged, with human review required for alerts, ensuring no unchecked bias, per Deloitte's guidelines.

Public Trust. Education campaigns explain AI's supportive role, with third-party audits published on the blockchain. Dashboards show AI's impact (e.g., fraud cases flagged), building confidence.

Communications Transparency System (CTS)

The CTS, tied to Constitutional Title 19: Freedom of Disclosure Framework, ensures near real-time monitoring of official actions, building on U.S. "Capstone" archiving and Sweden's public access principles:

Default Openness. Official emails, memos, and approved-platform communications are published on the blockchain, redacted for privacy/security, via a public portal with search and API functionality. Citizens can query, e.g., "Project X emails," to monitor compliance, as advocated by the Sunlight Foundation.

Audit Trail. Blockchain timestamps prevent tampering, logging document existence, sender, and timing. Redacted logs note activity, ensuring transparency, as in Estonia's e-government systems.

Security Limits. Sensitive communications (e.g., defence, judicial) are embargoed per Title 19: Freedom of Disclosure Framework, Article 2, but AI-logged internally, with metadata published. Content releases post-embargo.

Infrastructure. A central server encrypts emails, with keys controlled by a judicially independent office. AI scans for anomalies (e.g., "side deal" keywords), feeding alerts to WAACC, logged on the blockchain.

Citizen Engagement. Civic tech groups develop tools to scan CTS data, enabling collaborative oversight, e.g., NGO bots flagging irregular contracts.

Together, the ledger, AI monitoring, and publication-by-default communications create an auditable integrity stack: they increase the probability of detection, reduce opportunities for concealment, and preserve due process by keeping final decisions with accountable officials and courts.

Civic Engagement & Integrity Promotion

Whistleblower Protection & Bounty Framework

Western Australia's whistleblower regime, overseen by the COC's Whistleblower Protection Sub-panel, encourages citizens to expose wrongdoing without fear, aligning with Article 3's right to report and protections. Drawing on OECD, South Korea's ACRC, and U.S. False Claims Act models, it offers robust protections and incentives:

> ***Scope.*** Covers public officials, contractors, and private actors in public business (e.g., procurement), per Article 3. Good-faith reports of corruption, fraud, or public harm are protected, ensuring early detection, as in the EU Whistleblower Directive.
>
> ***Confidentiality.*** Reports can be anonymous or via legal proxy, with government-funded legal support. Identities are confidential, with breaches incurring up to 5 years imprisonment or $WAT 500,000 fines, mirroring South Korea's Anti-Corruption and Civil Rights Commission.
>
> ***Anti-Retaliation.*** Retaliation (e.g., dismissal, harassment) is void, with victims entitled to reinstatement, back pay, and damages. Retaliators face fines up to $WAT 500K or 5 years imprisonment, per Article 3's severe penalties.
>
> ***Immunity.*** Good-faith reporters face no liability for disclosures, even if incorrect, provided no independent wrongdoing occurred, per EU standards (Directive (EU) 2019/1937).
>
> ***Safeguards.*** False reports forfeit protections and incur fines (e.g., $WAT 50,000), but honest mistakes are protected, per EU guidelines.
>
> ***Technology.*** Reports are blockchain-logged for auditability, per Title 18: Anti-Corruption Framework, Article 4. AI triages submissions, detecting keywords (e.g., "bribery"), with progress tracked via anonymised case numbers.

This regime ensures safe reporting with rewards, offering a world-leading model for experts, aligned with global practices.

Integrity Education & Corporate Engagement

Integrating anti-corruption themes into primary and secondary curricula is appropriate, teaching honesty, transparency, and civic duty through stories, debates, and practical exercises to foster ethical citizens.

The government should engage corporations, especially foreign ones, to adopt voluntary Model Anti-Corruption Charters, promoting compliance with WAACCA standards like zero-tolerance policies and blockchain logging, without mandates.

Implementation Strategy

Western Australia's anti-corruption framework will roll out in phases from late 2029, balancing immediate action with long-term innovation, as mandated by Title 18: Anti-Corruption Framework, Article 5:

> ***2029–2030.*** Establish WAACC and WAACCP, enact WAACCA and supporting laws (e.g., Digital Transparency Act), launch pilot blockchain procurement projects, deploy early AI tools (e.g., anomaly detection), and expand open-government initiatives (e.g., budgets, agendas). Officials begin asset declarations, with campaigns introducing transparency tools. COC oversees implementation via its subpanels.
>
> ***2032+.*** Transition to advanced AI analytics (e.g., generative AI) and full CTS deployment, leveraging Hyperledger Fabric and open-source tools (e.g., TensorFlow). Nationwide body cams, CCTV, and ISO 27001-compliant cloud infrastructure roll out for police/customs, integrated with AI/blockchain for oversight.
>
> ***Governance & Evaluation.*** Independent review boards, including foreign experts, conduct annual audits, measuring corruption indicators (e.g., Transparency International rankings). COC's Technology Subpanel reports systemic issues to WAACC/WAACCP, with data-sharing protocols feeding AI/blockchain systems. Privacy safeguards (e.g., encryption, judicial oversight) protect data while ensuring auditability, per Article 4. By 2035, Western Australia aims to rank among the least corrupt nations, with public trust reflected in rising corruption perception indices, as seen in Singapore and Hong Kong.

Expected Outcomes

Western Australia's Anti-Corruption Framework will:

> ***Deter Corruption.*** Severe penalties, reverse-burden laws, and blockchain transparency, as mandated by Title 18: Anti-Corruption Framework, make graft high-risk and low-reward, mirroring Singapore's near-zero corruption rates.
>
> ***Build Trust.*** WAACC/WAACCP enforcement, COC oversight, and public dashboards foster confidence, as seen in Hong Kong's ICAC-driven trust gains.
>
> ***Embed Integrity.*** Education and corporate charters normalise ethical conduct, creating a cultural shift, as in Rwanda's Integrity Clubs.

Set a Global Standard. The fusion of WAACC, WAACCP, COC, and technology positions Western Australia as a model for transparent governance, inviting global study.

Conclusion

Western Australia's anti-corruption framework will be a covenant of integrity, uniting robust institutions, enforceable laws, advanced technology, and universal civic participation in a shared vision for a just nation. The WAACC, WAACCA, blockchain, AI, and CTS will ensure that corruption is both visible and futile, deterring wrongdoing before it erodes trust.

By embedding integrity in every classroom, workplace, and corporate charter, Western Australia will empower every citizen to protect the wealth of the nation. As a chapter in the nation's political manifesto, this framework signals Western Australia's resolve to begin its journey as a shining new light—a nation whose prosperity springs from probity, whose global stature rests on moral authority, and whose citizens can trust in a future secured by impeccable governance.

Sources

Unless otherwise stated, online materials were viewed on 6 February 2026.

1. Independent Commission Against Corruption (Hong Kong), *Homepage* (n.d.) <https://www.icac.org.hk/en/>.
2. Corrupt Practices Investigation Bureau (Singapore), *Homepage* (n.d.) <https://www.cpib.gov.sg/>.
3. Transparency International, *Corruption Perceptions Index 2024* (n.d.) <https://www.transparency.org/en/cpi/2024>.
4. World Bank, *Global Program on Anticorruption for Development* (n.d.) <https://www.worldbank.org/en/programs/anticorruption-for-development>.
5. Organisation for Economic Co-operation and Development (OECD), *Anti-Corruption and Integrity* (n.d.) <https://www.oecd.org/en/topics/policy-issues/anti-corruption-and-integrity.html>.
6. United Nations Office on Drugs and Crime (UNODC), *Corruption and Economic Crime Branch* (n.d.) <https://www.unodc.org/unodc/en/corruption/index.html>.
7. Open Government Partnership, *Homepage* (n.d.) <https://www.opengovpartnership.org/>.
8. Office of the Ombudsman (Rwanda), *Homepage* (n.d.) <https://www.ombudsman.gov.rw/>.
9. *Bribery Act 2010* (UK) <https://www.legislation.gov.uk/ukpga/2010/23/contents>.
10. *Directive (EU) 2019/1937 on the Protection of Persons Who Report Breaches of Union Law (Whistleblower Directive)* (European Union) <https://eur-lex.europa.eu/eli/dir/2019/1937/oj>.
11. Anti-Corruption & Civil Rights Commission (South Korea), *Homepage* (n.d.) <https://www.acrc.go.kr/en>.
12. Department of Justice (United States), *The False Claims Act* (n.d.) <https://www.justice.gov/civil/false-claims-act>.
13. e-Estonia, *KSI Blockchain Model* (n.d.) <https://e-estonia.com/solutions/cyber-security/ksi-blockchain/>.
14. 'Blockchain-Based Land Titling Project in the Republic of Georgia' (MIT Press Article) <https://direct.mit.edu/itgg/article-pdf/12/3-4/72/705280/inov_a_00276.pdf>.
15. Hyperledger, *Hyperledger Fabric* (n.d.) <https://hyperledger-fabric.readthedocs.io/>.
16. World Economic Forum, *The Digital Commons: How to Harness Blockchain for Better Governance* (2025) <https://www.weforum.org/stories/2025/02/digital-commons-blockchain-governance/>.

17. National Institute of Standards and Technology (United States), *Trustworthy and Responsible AI* (n.d.) <https://www.nist.gov/trustworthy-and-responsible-ai>.
18. Deloitte, *ISO 42001 Standard for AI Governance and Risk Management* (n.d.) <https://www.deloitte.com/us/en/services/consulting/articles/iso-42001-standard-ai-governance-risk-management.html>.
19. Sunlight Foundation, *Homepage* (n.d.) <https://sunlightfoundation.com/>.
20. World Economic Forum, 'Exploring Blockchain Technology for Government Transparency: Blockchain-Based Public Procurement System' (2020) <https://www.weforum.org/reports/exploring-blockchain-technology-for-government-transparency-blockchain-based-public-procurement-to-reduce-corruption>. Annotation: Colombia procurement focus.
21. Government of India, 'National Blockchain Framework' (2025) Press Information Bureau <https://www.pib.gov.in/PressReleasePage.aspx?PRID=2182023>. Annotation: covers RBI pilots and land registry in states like Andhra Pradesh/Telangana.
22. National Archives and Records Administration (NARA), 'White Paper on The Capstone Approach and Capstone GRS' (2015) <https://www.archives.gov/files/records-mgmt/email-management/final-capstone-white-paper.pdf>.
23. Government of Sweden, 'Public Access to Information and Secrecy—The Legislation in Brief' (2009) <https://www.government.se/contentassets/2ca7601373824c8395fc1f38516e6e03/public-access-to-information-and-secrecy.pdf>.
24. Organisation for Economic Co-operation and Development (OECD), 'Exploring Possible AI Trajectories Through 2030' (2024) <https://www.oecd.org/en/publications/exploring-possible-ai-trajectories-through-2030_cb41117a-en.html>. Annotation: covers generative AI as a general-purpose technology with projections for pattern recognition and system improvements.
25. Gong (et al), 'Unpacking Public Perceptions of Effectiveness in Anti-Corruption Agencies: The Case of Hong Kong' (2022) *Public Integrity* <https://www.tandfonline.com/doi/full/10.1080/10999922.2022.2068902>. Annotation: discusses ICAC's campaigns to restore trust, with surveys showing 95-99% support.
26. World Bank, 'Rwanda's Anti-Corruption Experience: Actions, Accomplishments, and Lessons' (2018) <https://openknowledge.worldbank.org/server/api/core/bitstreams/3b31c79a-0636-5536-805e-7ff7e27d5d96/content>. Annotation: mentions Ombudsman organising anti-corruption clubs in schools.

NEW WA'S FREEDOM OF DISCLOSURE FRAMEWORK

The Global FOI Illusion

Around the world, Freedom of Information (FOI) laws were introduced with the promise of empowering citizens, ensuring accountability, and checking government overreach. Yet decades later, many of these systems are broken. Citizens face excessive delays, arbitrary refusals, overbroad redactions, and bureaucratic stonewalling. In the United States, more than 267,000 FOIA requests remain backlogged, with some responses delayed by years. Australia spends over $86 million annually on FOI administration, yet only 21% of requests are granted in full. In Canada, average wait times exceed 90 days, well beyond statutory limits, while watchdogs warn the system is "broken." In the UK, journalists face politically-vetted FOI denials, and civil society describes a "secret war on transparency." Even in countries like New Zealand, cultural resistance and friction among agencies over time and cost undermine statutory ideals.

The result is the inversion of democracy: those elected to serve, instead shield themselves from those who elected them. Information that rightly belongs to the public is withheld by those paid by the public to govern. Western Australia categorically rejects this inversion. Government in Western Australia shall be transparent by constitutional design and operational default.

Foundational Principle: The People own the Information

Government information is not the possession of public servants but the property of the people. This principle has deep legal and philosophical roots.

Thomas Jefferson stated:

> *"When a man assumes a public trust, he should consider himself as public property."*

The UN Office on Drugs and Crime (UNODC) emphasises that access to public information is a key tool for citizen participation and accountability, treating it as an essential public asset under the United Nations Convention Against Corruption.

The OECD and UN UDHR Article 19 confirm the right to information is a fundamental right, not a privilege.

Leading nations enshrine this:

Sweden (Freedom of the Press Act, Ch. 2, Art. 1):

> *"Everyone shall be entitled to have free access to official documents, in order to encourage the free exchange of opinion, the availability of comprehensive information and freedom of artistic creation."*

Finland (Constitution, Sec. 12):

> *"Documents and recordings in the possession of the authorities are public, unless their publication has for compelling reasons been specifically restricted by an Act. Everyone has the right of access to public documents and recordings."*

New Western Australia follows suit but surpasses these models through digital and institutional innovation.

Citizen Benefits & Everyday Impact

For Western Australians weary of opaque government processes, Western Australia's framework will deliver tangible, life-changing benefits. Imagine a parent in a mining town querying "Show me the latest environmental impact report for the local processing site"—and receiving it instantly via voice command on their phone, complete with AI-summarised highlights. No forms, no waits, no fees. This empowers families to hold officials accountable, ensuring resource revenues benefit communities, not hidden deals. Businesses can verify tender fairness in real-time, fostering competition and economic growth without corruption's shadow. Retirees might check "How is my pension fund invested?" to confirm ethical use of royalties. By 2029+, this system—built on blockchain's unalterable records and AI's intuitive interfaces—eliminates the frustration of traditional FOI, where Australians waited months for partial answers. It deters misconduct: officials know every email is public, reducing graft risks as seen in Nordic models. For secession, this means a government that works for you, transparently—boosting trust, investment, and prosperity. Experts note such systems could elevate Western Australia to top Transparency International rankings within years, as proactive disclosure correlates with lower corruption perceptions.

Metric	Denmark	Finland	New Zealand	Norway	Sweden	WA (Proposed)
Avg. Response Time	7-10 days	14-30 days	20 days	1-5 days	Prompt (days)	24 hours max
Full Grant Rate	90%	85%	75%	>80%	90%	99% (proactive default)
Tech Integration	Digital portals	Suomi.fi portal	Govt.nz open data	Altinn.no real-time	Opengov.se	Blockchain/AI voice portals
Request as Exception**	Partial	Partial	No	Partial	Yes	Yes, with COC review

**Request as Exception: This metric shows whether governments treat formal information requests as rare occurrences ('exceptions') because most data is already shared publicly without needing to ask. 'Yes' means proactive sharing is the norm, reducing the need for requests; 'Partial' or 'No' means citizens often must file requests, leading to delays and bureaucracy.

Legal Framework

Constitutional Provision

Western Australia's Constitution (Chapter 15: A New Nation's Constitution) establishes a groundbreaking right to public information, declaring that all citizens are the legal and moral owners of government-held data: Title 19: Freedom of Disclosure Framework. This means information is held in trust for the people and must be proactively shared by default, with access being timely, free, and in user-friendly formats. Public authorities are required to create and preserve detailed records of all official actions and communications, extending these duties to contractors handling public functions or funds.

To protect this right, the Constitution allows only narrow, time-limited restrictions—such as for national security, active investigations, or personal privacy—ensuring they are the least intrusive possible and justified publicly. Proactive publication is mandated for key areas like contracts, budgets, policies, and health standards, so citizens rarely need to request information.

Oversight is entrusted to the Citizen Oversight Committee (COC), which can issue disclosure orders and penalties, with appeals to the Human Rights Tribunal (HRT) or courts for fairness. Sanctions for destroying or concealing records are severe, including disqualification from office, to deter abuse.

These provisions empower and require Parliament to enact enabling legislation that operationalises the mandates, such as creating infrastructure for automated disclosure. The Western Australia Freedom of Disclosure Act 2029 (WAFDA) serves as specimen legislation, naturally flowing from these constitutional powers and directives to build a transparent system integrated with anti-corruption tools like blockchain and AI.

Western Australia Freedom of Disclosure Act 2029 (WAFDA)

Legislative Preview: Essential Specimen Sections

The WAFDA reorients the information paradigm. Information is to be proactively published; requests are the exception. Deriving from Article 9's implementation duty, it establishes timelines and mechanisms, with the Open Records Authority as the core operator of the Public Records Network per Article 7.

PART I—PRELIMINARY

High-level. Defines key terms like "public information" mirroring Article 1, "official communication" as in Article 2, and "embargo" per Article 4. Objects emphasise proactive disclosure to fulfill constitutional ownership principles, accessible to all readers as "ensuring every Western Australian can see how their government works daily."

Short Title & Commencement. This Act may be cited as the Western Australia Freedom of Disclosure Act 2029 and commences within 12 months of constitutional force, aligning with Article 9.

Objects. To guarantee immediate and proactive public access to all government communications, records, and decisions, operationalising the people's ownership.

PART II—PROACTIVE PUBLICATION & DUTIES

Strict alignment with Article 5. Mandates publication registers for contracts, tenders, budgets, etc. High-level description: Agencies must upload records to the Public Records Network within 24 hours, with AI assisting machine-readable formats for easy citizen access.

Proactive Publication Registers. All public authorities shall maintain and publish registers as prescribed in Article 5, including real-time dashboards for grants and performance data.

Duty to Preserve Records. Public officials must capture all communications per Article 2; willful destruction incurs penalties up to 10 years imprisonment, as in Article 8.

PART III—ACCESS & REQUESTS

Thematic. Requests as exceptions, with 24-hour responses. Understood to mean: "If something isn't already public, ask once—and get it fast."

Right of Access. Any person may access public information free of charge; requests must be fulfilled within 24 hours unless embargoed under Article 4.

Exemptions and Embargoes. Restrictions limited exactly to Article 4 categories, with automatic expiry and partial disclosure where possible.

PART IV—INSTITUTIONAL FRAMEWORK & OVERSIGHT

Merges WAFDA into Open Records Authority per Article 7; COC handles reviews as in Article 6, integrating anti-corruption referrals to WAACC.

Open Records Authority. Establishes an independent authority to operate the Public Records Network, with guaranteed funding and standards for verifiability and APIs.

COC Transparency Panel. Empowered to issue orders and penalties per Article 6; referrals to WAACC for criminal spoliation.

PART V—ENFORCEMENT & SANCTIONS

High-level. Fines up to WAT$100,000 for delays; disqualification for serious breaches, aligning with Article 8.

Appeals and Emergency Measures. As per Article 6, with HRT review for rights issues.

PART VI—MISCELLANEOUS

Implementation timelines and reviews every 5 years, entrenching via supermajorities per Article 9.

Technological Infrastructure

Blockchain Ledger. All government communications are automatically recorded on a permissioned, auditable blockchain.

AI Search and Redaction. Citizens can query the database using natural language (e.g., "Show me the last mining contract signed"). AI assists by redacting private data and flagging anomalies for review.

User Interface. Information is accessed via a publicly maintained portal and mobile application, ensuring real-time, equitable access.

Challenges & Safeguards

While transformative, Western Australia's system anticipates challenges like privacy risks and misuse. Security threats are mitigated by permissioned blockchain with quantum-resistant encryption, and regular third-party audits. Privacy balances openness: AI auto-redacts personal data under strict rules, with COC vetoing over-redactions. Misuse triggers penalties under WAFDA, with AI monitoring abusive queries. National security exemptions are time-bound and COC-reviewed, preventing abuse. These safeguards ensure robustness, drawing from Estonia's e-gov lessons where similar tech has significantly reduced security risks and built trust. For citizens, this means safe, user-friendly access; for experts, a resilient model advancing Right to Information (RTI) evolution.

Cultural Transformation & Civic Education

The WAFDA is supported by a national Civic Transparency Curriculum. All school students and the general public will have a working understanding of:

Their right to information.

How to access and interpret government records.

How to participate in oversight via the COC or audits.

These initiatives, though not mandated, are essential recommendations to embed disclosure awareness, ensuring citizens fully exercise their constitutional ownership.

Implementation & Evaluation

Rollout begins late 2029: Phase 1 launches blockchain logging and basic portals, with Open Records Authority training agencies. Phase 2 (2030) integrates AI voice interfaces and COC operations.

Conclusion

New Western Australia's Freedom of Disclosure Framework breaks with the global pattern of opacity cloaked in the rhetoric of FOI. It guarantees what others only promise. Citizens will no longer request information—they will possess it.

Sources

Unless otherwise stated, online materials were viewed on 29 January 2026.

"It deters misconduct: officials know every email is public, reducing graft risks as seen in Nordic models."

1. *Freedom of the Press Act* (Sweden) <https://www.riksdagen.se/globalassets/05.-sa-fungerar-riksdagen/demokrati/the-freedom-of-the-press-act-2023-eng.pdf>
2. *Constitution of Finland* (Finland) <https://www.finlex.fi/en/legislation/translations/1999/eng/731>
3. *Access to Public Administration Files Act 1987* (Denmark) <https://danishbusinessauthority.dk/sites/default/files/2023-10/The-danish-Access-Public-Administration-Files-Act-1987_U.pdf>
4. Meijer, 'Understanding the Complex Dynamics of Transparency' (2013) *Public Administration Review* <https://onlinelibrary.wiley.com/doi/abs/10.1111/puar.12032>
5. Bajpai et al, *Enhancing Government Effectiveness and Transparency: The Fight Against Corruption* (World Bank, 2020) <https://www.worldbank.org/en/topic/governance/publication/enhancing-government-effectiveness-and-transparency-the-fight-against-corruption>
6. The Northern Voices, 'Nordic Countries (and Estonia) Lead the World in Clean Governance (2025 Rankings)' <https://www.thenorthernvoices.com/post/nordic-countries-and-estonia-lead-the-world-in-clean-governance-2025-rankings> Annotation: Describes how Nordic transparency traditions, including open public records, close avenues for corruption by making wrongdoing hard to hide.
7. Policy Options, 'Trust and transparency: is Sweden still a model?' <https://policyoptions.irpp.org/2025/02/sweden-trust-transparency> Annotation: Links Nordic public transparency to reduced corruption perceptions, with officials accountable via open records.

FOI USA

8. CREW (USA), 'The FOIA is Broken, but is it Beyond Repair?' <https://www.citizensforethics.org/reports-investigations/crew-investigations/the-foia-is-broken-but-is-it-beyond-repair/>
9. U.S. Department of Justice Office of Information Policy, 'Summary of Fiscal 2024 Annual FOIA Reports' <https://www.justice.gov/oip/media/1398111/dl?inline=> Annotation: Confirms a government-wide backlog of 267,056 requests at the end of FY 2024, with processing delays often extending into years due to increased demand.
10. Brechner Center for Freedom of Information, 'FOIA Requests, Denials, Backlogs, Delays, Costs Surge in FY 2024' <https://brechner.org/2025/04/30/foia-requests-denials-surge-fy-2024/> Annotation: Notes a 33% increase in backlogs to 267,056, with average response times rising and some delays spanning years.

FOI UK

11. Rob Evans, 'UK Government "Waging Secret War Against Transparency"' (2021) *The Guardian* <https://www.theguardian.com/politics/2021/oct/25/uk-government-waging-secret-war-against-transparency>
12. David Pegg, 'UK's FOI Laws are Being Undermined, Warn Journalists' (2022) *The Guardian* <https://www.theguardian.com/politics/2022/apr/07/uk-foi-transparency-laws-are-being-undermined-warn-journalists>

FOI Australia

13. Australian Senate, *The Operation of Commonwealth Freedom of Information (FOI) Laws* (2023) <https://www.aph.gov.au/Parliamentary_Business/Committees/Senate/Legal_and_Constitutional_Affairs/CommonwealthFOI2023/Report>
14. Rushton and Black, 'Information is a National Resource: Crikey's Submission to the FOI Senate Inquiry' (2023) *Crikey* <https://www.crikey.com.au/2023/05/29/freedom-of-information-crikey-senate-inquiry-submission/>
15. Anton Nilsson, '"Australia is an Outlier": Sluggish FOI System Sets Secrecy as the Default' (2023) *Crikey* <https://www.crikey.com.au/2023/05/29/redacted-series-freedom-of-information-australia-outlier/>

16. Christopher Knaus, 'Former Information Commissioner Claims in Senate Inquiry He Was "Manhandled" and "Gaslighted" by Leadership' (2023) *The Guardian* <https://www.theguardian.com/australia-news/2023/aug/29/leo-hardiman-foi-freedom-of-information-backlog-senate-inquiry>
17. The Australia Institute, *The Price of Freedom* (Report) <https://australiainstitute.org.au/report/the-price-of-freedom> Annotation: Reports that the FOI system cost $86 million in 2023–24, with only 21% of requests granted in full (down from 81% in 2006–07).
18. IDM Magazine, 'FOI System Costs Soar $A61 Million' <https://idm.net.au/article/0015391-foi-system-costs-soar-a61-million> Annotation: Confirms annual costs around $86 million, with low grant rates contributing to inefficiencies.

FOI Canada

19. The Globe and Mail, 'Opposition MPs United in Call for Overhaul of Access to Information System' (2023) <https://www.theglobeandmail.com/canada/article-parliament-mps-access-to-information/>; 'Canada's Access-to-Information Law Has Entered a Painful Midlife Crisis' (2023) <https://www.theglobeandmail.com/opinion/article-canadas-access-to-information-law-has-entered-a-painful-midlife-crisis/>; 'Federal Review of Access to Information Law "Doesn't Have Credibility," Expert Says' (2025) <https://www.theglobeandmail.com/canada/article-federal-review-access-to-information-law-lacks-credibility-expert-says/>
20. Yves Faguy, 'Canada's Broken Access to Information System' (2023) *National Magazine* <https://nationalmagazine.ca/en-ca/articles/law/rule-of-law/2023/access-to-information-delays-are-eroding-our-trust-in-democracy>
21. Office of the Information Commissioner of Canada, *Access at Issue: The Unsustainable Status Quo* <https://www.oic-ci.gc.ca/en/resources/reports-publications/access-issue-unsustainable-status-quo> Annotation: Notes average response times of 90 days for key agencies like IRCC, exceeding the 30-day statutory limit, with backlogs contributing to a "broken" system.

FOI New Zealand

22. Peter Boshier (Chief Ombudsman of New Zealand), 'Outgoing Chief Ombudsman Releases "Reflections" Report on Official Information Act' (2025) <https://www.ombudsman.parliament.nz/news/outgoing-chief-ombudsman-releases-reflections-report-official-information-act>
23. Wikipedia, 'Official Information Act 1982' <https://en.wikipedia.org/wiki/Official_Information_Act_1982> Annotation: Notes constant friction between requesters and state agencies over time and cost, leading to reluctant disclosure and undermining the Act's ideals.

Blockchain & AI

24. World Economic Forum, *Exploring Blockchain Technology for Government Transparency: Blockchain-Based Public Procurement to Reduce Corruption* (Insight Report, June 2020) <https://www3.weforum.org/docs/WEF_Blockchain_Government_Transparency_Report.pdf>
25. OECD, *Governing with Artificial Intelligence: The State of Play and Way Forward in Core Government Functions* (September 2025) <https://www.oecd.org/en/publications/2025/06/governing-with-artificial-intelligence_398fa287.html>

Thomas Jefferson

26. Oxford Reference, 'Thomas Jefferson 1743–1826 American Democratic Republican Statesman, 3rd President 1801–9' <https://www.oxfordreference.com/display/10.1093/acref/9780191843730.001.0001/q-oro-ed5-00005878>

FOI United Nations

27. UN Office on Drugs and Crime, 'Access to Information: A Condition for Citizen Participation' <https://www.unodc.org/e4j/en/anti-corruption/module-10/key-issues/access-to-information_-a-condition-for-citizen-participation.html> Annotation: UNODC's resources emphasise that public information and records are essential public assets for accountability, aligning with the United Nations

Convention Against Corruption (UNCAC), which UNODC administers and promotes as treating information access as a tool for public ownership over governance.

28. United Nations, *Universal Declaration of Human Rights* art 19 <https://www.un.org/en/about-us/universal-declaration-of-human-rights> Annotation: 'Everyone has the right to freedom of opinion and expression; this right includes freedom to hold opinions without interference and to seek, receive and impart information and ideas through any media and regardless of frontiers.'

FOI OECD

29. OECD, *Institutions Guaranteeing Access to Information: OECD and MENA Region* (2019) <https://www.oecd.org/content/dam/oecd/en/publications/reports/2019/10/institutions-guaranteeing-access-to-information_b3c047a4/e6d58b52-en.pdf> Annotation: "The right to access information is an essential element of open government, and should be considered in the framework of ongoing public governance reforms and a transparent and participatory government."
30. OECD, *Seizing the Productive Potential of Digital Change in Estonia* <https://www.oecd.org/content/dam/oecd/en/publications/reports/2020/12/seizing-the-productive-potential-of-digital-change-in-estonia_63752f80/999c7d5a-en.pdf> Annotation: Praises Estonia's e-government for enhancing security and trust, reducing risks through systems like X-Road.

Transparency International Rankings

31. OECD, *Recommendation on Open Government* <https://www.oecd.org/content/dam/oecd/en/about/programmes/grc/grc-see/integrity/Policy-Briefing-Note-on-Open-Government.pdf>
32. Transparency International, *Corruption Perceptions Index* (2024) <https://www.transparency.org/en/cpi/2024> Annotation: Top performers like Nordic countries attribute lower corruption perceptions to disclosure practices.

Further Reading

33. Seth F Kreimer, 'The Freedom of Information Act and the Ecology of Transparency' (2008) *Penn Journal of Constitutional Law* <https://scholarship.law.upenn.edu/jcl/vol10/iss5/2/>
34. Pozen et al, *Troubling Transparency: The History and Future of Freedom of Information* (Columbia University Press, 2018) <https://scholarship.law.columbia.edu/books/8/>

WA's Political Lobbying & Donations Reform

Introduction

Western Australia's bid for sovereign nationhood rests on an ironclad pledge to exemplary governance, where transparency reigns supreme and corruption finds no foothold. This chapter unveils a new framework for political lobbying and campaign finance, meticulously crafted to fortify democracy against covert manipulations. By adopting and amplifying rigorous standards from exemplars like Canada and Ireland—including exclusive citizen donations, stringent caps, and comprehensive registries—Western Australia pioneers advancements such as instantaneous disclosure systems, AI-enhanced monitoring, and robust citizen-led oversight. Grounded in the new Constitution's Title 20: Political Lobbying and Donations, this blueprint not only bolsters the Anti-Corruption Framework but elevates Western Australia to the forefront of global integrity, affirming that true power derives from public trust, not purchased allegiance.

Learning from Global Best Practices

Post-secession WA's system adopts and exceeds the most rigorous international regulations. Key inspirations are summarized below.

Comparison Table: Western Australia vs. Global Models

Feature	Western Australia (Proposed)	Canada 2025	Ireland 2025
Donation Sources	Citizens/residents only; no entities.	Citizens/residents only; no corporations/unions/foreigners.	Citizens/residents; corporate limited to €200 unless registered; foreign/anonymous banned above €100.
Annual Caps	WAT $1,000 per recipient.	CAD $1,750 annually per donor to each party (aggregate across party and related entities).	€1,000 per candidate; €2,500 per party.
Cooling-Off**	5 years for officials.	5 years under Lobbying Act for designated public office holders.	1 year for designated public officials, requiring consent for certain lobbying activities.
Disclosure	Real-time Register.	Monthly for lobbying communications; annual/periodic for donations.	Returns within 21 days post-period (typically every 4 months).
Sanctions	Up to 5 years prison; fines up to WAT $1,000,000; election void.	Fines up to CAD $5,000 and/or 6 months' imprisonment for minor offenses; higher fines (up to CAD $200,000) and imprisonment up to 2 years for serious violations.	Fines up to €25,000 and/or up to 2 years' imprisonment (on indictment); disqualification for up to 2 years possible.

****What is a "Cooling-Off" Period?***

- It's a required wait time after leaving public office to stop ex-officials from lobbying on their old work.
- This prevents the "revolving door" where insiders use knowledge for private gain, harming trust.
- In WA's system (Title 20, Article 6), it lasts at least 5 years from the last day in office.
- Covers Ministers, department heads, regulators, chiefs of staff, and other key roles.
- During this time, no paid lobbying on former portfolios or using non-public information.

- The Citizen Oversight Committee (COC) can allow exceptions if truly for public good, with rules to avoid conflicts.

Western Australia's model aligns with Organisation for Economic Co-operations and Development (OECD) recommendations for transparency in lobbying (OECD/LEGAL/0379), which advocate for public registers and conflict-of-interest safeguards, while exceeding them through real-time AI analytics. Similarly, it embodies the United Nations Convention Against Corruption (UNCAC) Article 7.3's call for enhanced political party funding transparency, with severe sanctions to deter corruption.

Constitutional Provisions

Western Australia's new Constitution enshrines a robust framework for political lobbying and donations under Title 20: Political Lobbying and Donations, (Chapter 15: A New Nation's Constitution), designed to uphold the integrity of public office and prevent undue influence.

At its core, Article 1 mandates that public officials exercise power solely for the public good, rejecting any form of private gain—a principle that sets a high bar for ethical governance and inspires confidence in democratic processes. Complementing this, Article 2 guarantees citizens' right to transparency, requiring a Public Transparency Register for all donations and lobbying activities, accessible to all with minimal exceptions. Oversight is vested in the Citizen Oversight Committee (COC) and the Open Records Authority, as outlined in Article 3, ensuring independent monitoring without creating new commissions.

Building on these foundations, the Constitution restricts donations to natural persons who are citizens or permanent residents, imposing caps and banning foreign, corporate, or anonymous sources to level the playing field (Article 5). Lobbying is tightly regulated through Article 6, which mandates registration, a code of conduct, and a five-year cooling-off period for former officials to close the "revolving door." Real-time disclosure of all interactions is required under Article 7, integrating with the broader Freedom of Disclosure Framework to foster accountability.

Anti-circumvention measures in Article 8 prohibit indirect influence through intermediaries, while extending rules to third-party campaigners. Sanctions under Article 9 are severe, including fines, possible imprisonment, and disqualification from office, with the power to void elections tainted by violations. This comprehensive approach not only protects democracy but also positions Western Australia as a model of principled governance, where influence is earned through ideas, not wealth.

These constitutional articles establish binding mandates and direct the new WA Congress to implement these protections effectively and transparently.

Strict campaign finance rules ensure elections reflect broad citizen support, not elite interests. Caps, funding source bans, and blockchain disclosure prevent dominance by wealth, with robust COC and WAACC enforcement.

These reforms position Western Australia as a beacon of democratic purity, blending legal rigor, technology, and citizen empowerment. In a world plagued by corruption, Western Australia's system—

exceeding global benchmarks—affirms a commitment to governance for the people, strengthening our case for sovereignty and international recognition.

Sources

Unless otherwise stated, online materials were viewed on 29 January 2026.

Canada

1. Elections Canada, *Limits on Contributions—2025* (Web page, 2025) <https://www.elections.ca/content.aspx?section=pol&dir=lim&document=lim2025&lang=e>. Annotation: outlines federal contribution limits at CAD 1,750 annually for citizens/residents only; prohibits corporate, union, and foreign donations
2. *Canada Elections Act* (SC 2000, c 9) <https://laws-lois.justice.gc.ca/eng/acts/e-2.01/>. Annotation: Section 363 (prohibits corporate, union, and foreign donations; restricts contributions to citizens/permanent residents)
3. Office of the Commissioner of Lobbying of Canada, *Interpretation Bulletin—Significant Part of Duties: Registration Threshold for Organizations and Corporations—July 2025* (Web page, 2025) <https://lobbycanada.gc.ca/en/rules/the-lobbying-act/advice-and-interpretation-lobbying-act/significant-part-of-duties-registration-threshold-for-organizations-and-corporations/>. Annotation: lowers the threshold from 32 hours per month to 8 hours in a rolling 4-week period, effective January 19, 2026; details implications for in-house lobbyists
4. *Lobbying Act* (Canada) <https://lobbycanada.gc.ca/en/rules/the-lobbying-act/>. Annotation: details the five-year post-employment ban and lobbyist registration requirements

Ireland

5. Standards in Public Office Commission (Ireland), *2024 General Election Guidelines for Candidates and Political Parties* (Web page, 2024) <https://www.sipo.ie/en/collection/30d00-2024-general-election-guidelines/>. Annotation: covers donation caps, corporate donor rules, foreign/anonymous bans; applicable in 2025
6. Standards in Public Office Commission (Ireland), *Guidelines for Political Parties—Steps to be Taken Concerning Donations and Prohibited Donations* (Web page, 2023) <https://assets.sipo.ie/media/283819/11286dbb-e208-4fd8-abd4-ef00c0b15127.pdf>. Annotation: confirmed no 2025 changes; outlines €1,000 candidate/€2,500 party caps, corporate registration, and foreign bans
7. *Regulation of Lobbying Act 2015* (Ireland) <https://www.irishstatutebook.ie/eli/2015/act/5/enacted/en/html>. Annotation: establishes mandatory lobbyist register, disclosure rules, and enforcement; enhanced with 2024 administrative sanctions
8. Standards in Public Office Commission (Ireland), *Annual Report 2024 under Regulation of Lobbying Act* (Report, 2024) <https://www.lobbying.ie/>. Annotation: published June 2025; details compliance, returns within 21 days post-period, and penalties up to €25,000

OECD

9. OECD, *Recommendation of the Council on Transparency and Integrity in Lobbying and Influence* (OECD/LEGAL/0379, revised May 2024) <https://legalinstruments.oecd.org/en/instruments/OECD-LEGAL-0379>. Annotation: recommends disclosure of lobbying activities, foreign influence safeguards, and public registers
10. OECD, *Public Integrity Indicators: Regulatory Framework for Transparency in Lobbying, Conflict-of-Interest, and Political Finance* (Web page) <https://oecd-public-integrity-indicators.org/indicators/1000097/subindicators/1000402>. Annotation: framework for assessing transparency; aligns with chapter's emphasis on real-time registers

United Nations

11. United Nations, *Convention Against Corruption* (full text) <https://www.unodc.org/documents/brussels/UN_Convention_Against_Corruption.pdf>. Annotation: Article 7.3 emphasises measures to enhance transparency in political party funding
12. Transparency International, *UNCAC CoSP10—Enhance Transparency of Political Finance* (Web page, December 2023) <https://www.transparency.org/en/press/uncac-cosp10-enhance-transparency-of-political-finance>. Annotation: calls for global standards on donation disclosure and preventing undue influence under Article 7.3.

A New Nation's Constitution

Opening Reflections

As Western Australia emerges from the shadows of federation, this Constitution crystallises the aspirations articulated throughout our inquiry—from the historical grievances over union in 1901 and the unheeded 1933 referendum's call for independence, to the economic blueprint for fiscal autonomy in Chapter 4. Here, we reclaim powers once surrendered to the Commonwealth, empowering a sovereign governance model that serves the People first. At its core stands a unicameral Congress, led by an elected President and supported by nominated Secretaries of state across eleven founding departments, from Treasury managing prudent budgets to Resources and Energy stewarding our mineral wealth. This streamlined structure, departing from bicameral traditions like Australia's Senate, integrates executive efficiency with devolved authority to local councils under subsidiarity principles outlined in Chapter 5, ensuring decisions remain close to those affected and countering centralisation's perils.

Parallel to this, revolutionary independent oversight bodies—embodying the manifesto's anti-corruption covenants in Chapters 12-14 and the fourth branch for human law (no longer human rights, but *laws*) in Chapter 9—provide citizen-led checks, correcting governmental stray before it entrenches. These mechanisms, unique in their proactive remedies, safeguard the supreme rights of man drawn from UDHR and ICCPR (Annexure D), including medical freedom and non-derogable protections against torture or arbitrary detention. Together, this framework resumes responsibilities borne adeptly pre-secession, forging a nation where Congress directs resources toward global prosperity while prioritising domestic needs.

Central to this endurance are constitutional mandates for unbridled self-sufficiency, transforming Western Australia's inherent abundances—iron ore exports exceeding $143 billion annually, agricultural outputs feeding nations with 40% of Australia's grain—into pillars of stability (Chapter 7). Domestic energy expansion from petroleum and solar secures independence, while broadened water capture, irrigation, and farming sustains exports and local resilience. An FX-backed currency (Chapters 6) diminishes past fiscal volatilities, writing away federal burdens like GST inequities that returned only 70 cents per dollar, ensuring present excesses do not indebt future generations. These opportunities, long denied under federalism's Loan Council constraints and redistribution skews, now find eloquent exposition in constitutional articles that solidify the labours of prior chapters into enduring law.

We invite all with a stake in Western Australia's future to undertake their civic duty: read these articles which articulate the Social Contract between Citizens and their chosen servants. Affirm your acceptance, seek clarifications, or propose refinements through ongoing discussions—this manuscript's very purpose—to secure prosperity not just for ourselves, but for our children and theirs.

The Constitution of Western Australia

Preamble

In solemn remembrance of Western Australia's secession referendum of 1933, and mindful of the long decades within the Commonwealth of Australia that have shaped and tested us, we, the People of Western Australia—heirs to the ancient lands and coasts of the west—now unite to found a sovereign and self-determined Nation. We honour the First Peoples—the Noongar, Yamatji, and custodians whose care for Country spans millennia across red deserts, rugged ranges, and turquoise seaways—acknowledging their enduring connection as a cornerstone of our shared life. Learning from our history's aspirations and trials, we choose a future written by our own hand.

With the spirit of the outback rider galloping free across wide brown lands, through droughts and flooding rains, we affirm the liberty of every individual, the equal dignity of all, and justice under the rule of law. Like eucalypts blooming in autumn's glow, we commit to representative self-government, honest stewardship of public power, and institutions that serve the People—city and bush, coast and inland—united in mateship and a fair go for all. As trustees of this land's beauty and bounty, we pledge to conserve its riches for generations yet to come.

Open to the world yet rooted in our iron-rich soil, we declare our peaceful intent: to live in cooperation with all nations, to carry our share of global responsibility, and to foster prosperity and human dignity. With courage and hope, we hereby adopt and enact this Constitution as the supreme law of Western Australia, securing freedom, justice, and unity for the present age and posterity.

Founding Principles of Western Australia

In solemn affirmation of our Western heritage, forged in the Enlightenment's light and proven to uplift humanity through centuries of progress, we, the People of Western Australia, establish these Founding Principles to guide the interpretation and application of this Constitution. Rooted in individual freedoms—of thought, speech, inquiry, movement, religion, and the press—we champion a society of private property, market vitality, and families thriving in vibrant local communities that nurture social bonds, healthcare, education, and economic resilience, countering the pull of centralised power.

We embrace the virtues of separation of powers to avert tyranny; diversity of mind and experience to foster strength; grace in accepting human frailty, freeing the spirit from unproductive burdens;

universality in ethics, science, art, and literature that transcends time and uplifts all; and personal expression to ignite innovation and growth. Observing history's lessons, we hold these truths self-evident: power corrupts, demanding vigilant decentralisation and citizen oversight; wealth concentrates naturally under capitalism, requiring balanced mechanisms that reward endeavour without stifling liberty; human creativity drives prosperity, warranting space for exploration amid seeming inefficiency; and decisions distant from consequences breed peril, thus favouring subsidiarity and local councils as the default.

All Western Australians stand equal under law, endowed from birth with inalienable rights to life and core freedoms, expanding in adulthood to civic duties like voting and stewardship of our shared legacy. Our unique human rights regime, with enforceable remedies and a fourth branch for integrity, ensures dignity trumps overreach. As trustees of iron-veined earth and turquoise shores, we pledge honest governance, medical freedom, and anti-corruption covenants, harmonising with our Preamble's call to liberty, mateship, and global peace.

These principles bind leaders, jurists, and citizens alike, securing Western Australia's enduring sovereignty for posterity.

Commencement Day means the day this Constitution enters into force: **1 January 2030**

Title 1: Congress

Article 1—Unicameral Congress

Legislative authority is vested in a single-chamber Congress of Western Australia comprising fifty-nine (59) members, with one member elected from each of the electoral districts. Congress shall represent the people of Western Australia and is the sole national legislative body.

Article 2—Enumerated Powers of Congress

Congress may make laws only in the areas expressly enumerated in Annexure A. All national legislation must only be founded on an enumerated power. Congress has no authority beyond these heads of power, except that it may legislate strictly necessary measures to meet a formally declared national emergency, subject to oversight by the Citizens Oversight Committee (COC). Congress shall not enact any law permitting the digital or other surveillance of citizens except where a court has authorised such surveillance for a limited and defined national security or criminal law investigation.

Article 3—Subsidiarity & Lean Governance

In exercising its powers, Congress shall adhere to the principles of lean government and subsidiarity. National laws and programs must be limited to what is necessary for the peace, order, and good government of Western Australia, and matters that can be effectively handled by Local Councils or by the private sector should there remain as a priority. Congress shall not legislate in a manner that usurps Local Council or private sector responsibilities unless such legislation is essential. All powers and freedoms not expressly granted to the Western Australian Government remain with Local Councils or the People of Western Australia by default, and any ambiguity shall be resolved in favour of individual liberty and local autonomy.

Title 2: Legislative Process

Article 1—Public Exposure & Deliberation of Bills

Every Bill must be published as an exposure draft for public comment at least thirty days before a first reading, to allow transparency and citizen input. All Bills shall undergo at least two separate readings in Congress, with a minimum period of fourteen days between the first and final readings. A shorter exposure or expedited passage is permitted only for narrowly defined Urgent Bills addressing emergencies or essential budgetary matters. Urgent Bills require a special majority vote of four-fifths of the total membership of Congress to be enacted. All Congressional deliberations on Bills shall be open to the public.

Article 2—Independent Review & Certifications

No Bill may be passed into law without undergoing independent scrutiny for its financial, human rights, and integrity impacts. A fiscal analysis of each Bill's costs and revenues shall be prepared by the Western Australian Reserve Authority (WARA) and provided to Congress before a final vote. An integrity assessment shall be prepared by the Western Australian Anti-Corruption Commission (WAACC) and provided to Congress before a final vote. A statement of compatibility with Human Rights shall be prepared by the Human Rights Tribunal (HRT) and provided to Congress before a final vote. Every Bill concerning public procurement, government contracts, political finance, or other matters of public trust, require an Integrity Certificate prepared by the Citizens Oversight Committee provided to Congress before a final vote. These expert reviews and certificates are to inform lawmakers and the public, and their absence or negative findings pause the legislative process until addressed.

Article 3—Special Majority Legislation Categories

Certain categories of legislation shall require more than a simple majority of Congress of no less than four-fifths of the total membership of Congress to be enacted, recognising their fundamental importance. In particular, any Bill that (a) changes national electoral laws, (b) grants or governs emergency powers, (c) regulates political donations, campaign finance or the functioning of political parties, (d) establishes or amends the core powers or independence of key integrity institutions including the Anti-Corruption Commission (WAACC), the Human Rights Tribunal, or the Citizen Oversight Committee, or (e) alters the framework of the WARA or the Sovereign Wealth Fund. Laws in respect of (d) and (e) also require a referendum approval and must achieve a "double majority"—a majority of the national popular vote and a majority of voters in a majority of the electoral districts must vote in favour.

Article 4—Presidential Assent & Veto Override

A Bill passed by Congress shall become law only after receiving the President's assent. The President may refuse assent and return it to Congress with written reasons. Congress may override a regular presidential veto by re-passing the Bill with the support of at least three-quarters of all its members in a vote taken no sooner than fourteen days after the Bill's return. However, if the President's veto message certifies that the Bill unnecessarily expands government functions, bureaucracy or spending contrary to the Constitution's lean governance principles, then the veto can be overridden only by a higher consensus, namely, at least four-fifths of all members of Congress, and only if the Citizens Oversight Committee formally concurs that overriding the veto is in the national interest.

Article 5—Citizen Referendum Safeguard

If, within sixty (60) days of a law's commencement, a petition is lodged with Congress bearing verified signatures of at least ten percent (10%) of enrolled electors nationwide, including signatures from electors in at least one-half of all non-metropolitan electoral districts, with not less than five percent (5%) of enrolled electors signing in each counted district, the operation of that law is suspended upon the certification that these thresholds are met. A prompt referendum shall then be held, offering all citizens a *yes/no* vote on whether the law should take effect. The law will only commence if a majority of voters in a majority of electoral districts in the referendum approve it; otherwise, it is repealed by the popular vote. This citizen "circuit-breaker" mechanism shall not apply to annual appropriations or budget supply laws essential to the continuity of government services.

Title 3: Office Of The President

Article 1—Head of State & Executive Power

The executive power of Western Australia is vested in the President, who shall serve as both Head of State and Head of Government. The President's powers and responsibilities are enumerated in Annexure B to this Constitution. All executive actions of the Western Australian Government are taken in the name of the President, who shall ensure that the Constitution and laws are faithfully observed.

Article 2—Duty of Lean Governance & Qualified Veto

The President has a fundamental duty to ensure lean and efficient government. He or she shall scrutinise all legislation and withhold assent from any Bill that, in the President's considered judgment, unnecessarily expands government functions, increases public bureaucracy, or encroaches on areas where the private sector or local communities can perform effectively. This "lean governance veto" is an exercise of the President's constitutional responsibility to prevent unnecessary government expansion and protect the subsidiarity principle. If the President vetoes a Bill on these grounds, the veto message shall explicitly state that the Bill violates the efficiency or subsidiarity mandates or involves unnecessary expansion under this Constitution. Such a vetoed Bill shall not become law unless the override conditions in Title 2 Article 4 are met. In carrying out this duty, the President shall act as a steward of the public trust to keep the central government focused, affordable, and limited to its necessary roles. In all events the President must assent or veto a Bill within 30 days of being presented.

Article 3—Oversight of Executive Administration

The President shall supervise and direct the operations of the national executive government and its departments to ensure faithful execution of the laws. The President appoints and may require reports from the Secretaries of each executive department, and shall hold them accountable for performance, legality, and alignment with national policy. It is the responsibility of the President to co-ordinate the work of all executive agencies, to eliminate waste and duplication, and to ensure that government services are delivered effectively. The President may, in accordance with this Constitution and law, issue directives or executive orders to the departments to carry out policies consistent with Acts of Congress. All executive authorities and their personnel answer to the President's leadership. Regular oversight mechanisms including reports to Congress, appearances by Secretaries before Congressional committees, and cooperation with the Citizens Oversight Committee and Western Australian Anti-Corruption Commission and Human Rights Tribunal, shall be respected and facilitated by the President to maintain accountability in governance.

Article 4—Vice President

1. **Election and Term.** Each candidate for President shall, before close of nominations, designate a Vice President. If elected, the Vice President holds office with the President for the same four-year term. The Vice President may not sit in Congress but may be invited to address Congress.
2. **Eligibility.** The Vice President must meet the same eligibility requirements as the President under Title 5, Article 1(1).
3. **Functions and Duties.** The powers and authority of the Vice President shall be those powers and authority of the President delegated to the Vice President by the President. In all other respects, it shall be the duty of the Vice President to assist, aid, support, and facilitate the President in the discharge of his or her duties and the performance of his or her office, including but not limited to advising on matters of executive authority, foreign affairs, defence, and national

policy; representing the President in ceremonial or diplomatic capacities; and undertaking specific assignments related to the oversight of executive departments or emergency preparedness.

4. **Succession to Presidency.** If the office of the President becomes vacant due to removal, death, or resignation, the Vice President shall immediately become President for the remainder of the term and shall take the Oath of Office without delay. The new President shall then nominate a new Vice President in accordance with the vacancy provisions of this Article.
5. **Filling Vacancies.** If the office of Vice President becomes vacant due to succession, removal, death, or resignation, the President shall nominate a successor who meets the eligibility requirements under this Article. The nominee shall take office upon confirmation by a majority vote of all Members of Congress, following any required hearings or integrity checks as provided by law. If Congress is not in session, the President may make a recess appointment, which shall expire at the end of the next session unless confirmed.
6. **Temporary Assumption of Presidential Powers—Voluntary Transfer.** The President may, at any time, transmit to Congress a written declaration of inability to discharge the powers and duties of the office. Upon receipt of such declaration by Congress, the Vice President shall immediately assume the powers and duties of the office as Acting President. The President may resume the powers and duties by transmitting to Congress a written declaration of recovery. Upon receipt of such declaration, the President shall immediately resume the powers and duties, unless contested under the involuntary provisions of this Article.
7. **Temporary Assumption of Presidential Powers—Involuntary Declaration.** The Vice President, together with a majority of the Secretaries heading the principal departments, may transmit to Congress a written declaration that the President is unable to discharge the powers and duties of the office. Upon receipt of such declaration by Congress, the Vice President shall immediately assume the powers and duties of the office as Acting President. Congress shall convene within forty-eight hours if not already in session to consider the matter.
8. **Resolution of Disputes.** If the President transmits to Congress a written declaration contesting an involuntary declaration of inability, the Vice President shall continue to discharge the powers and duties as Acting President. Congress shall, within twenty-one days of receiving the President's contesting declaration, decide the issue by vote. If Congress determines by a two-thirds vote of all Members that the President is unable to discharge the powers and duties, the Vice President shall continue as Acting President. If Congress fails to sustain the declaration by such vote or fails to vote within the twenty-one-day period, the President shall immediately resume the powers and duties of the office.

Title 4: Appointment and Oversight of Secretaries

Article 1—Selection & Confirmation of Secretaries

The President shall nominate a Secretary to lead each principal executive department of the Nation. Secretaries shall be chosen on the basis of their department-centric expertise, merit, and integrity, and must be citizens eligible to hold high public office. To ensure separation of powers, no sitting member of Congress may serve as a Secretary. Each nominated Secretary must be confirmed by Congress before assuming office. Confirmation shall require an affirmative vote by a majority of the Congress, after the nominee has been subject to any required Congressional hearings or integrity checks. Congress shall establish a fair and prompt confirmation process, including public hearings before the relevant departmental oversight committee, to assess the nominee's qualifications and any potential conflicts of interest. Once confirmed and sworn in by the President, a Secretary begins the duties of that office for the term of the President.

Article 2—Accountability & Oversight of Secretaries

Secretaries are accountable to both the President and Congress for the performance of their departments. Each Secretary is responsible for administering their department's portfolio in accordance with the Constitution and laws, and for advancing the policies set by the President within their domain. Secretaries must regularly report to Congress on their department's activities, budget expenditures, and outcomes. Congress shall establish standing departmental oversight committees empowered to summon Secretaries for testimony, require the production of documents, and evaluate departmental performance and compliance with law. Secretaries have a duty of candour and transparency when dealing with oversight bodies and must disclose any significant issues, failures, or irregularities in their departments. If a Secretary willfully misleads Congress, fails to comply with the law, or is grossly ineffective or corrupt in office, he or she may be subjected to investigation by the appropriate oversight bodies including the WAACC for corruption matters, and to removal mechanisms as provided in Article 3 of this Title or by general law.

Article 3—Tenure & Removal of Secretaries

Secretaries serve at the pleasure of the President. The President may dismiss any Secretary at any time, for any reason or no stated reason, as an exercise of executive prerogative to ensure the effective functioning of the administration. The President shall promptly notify Congress of the removal of a Secretary and the reasons for that decision, unless national security concerns justify limited disclosure. In addition to Presidential removal, Congress retains the power to hold Secretaries accountable for misconduct: a Secretary may be removed through impeachment proceedings or disciplined or other mechanisms provided by law if he or she commits a serious violation of the law or abuse of public trust. Impeachment of a Secretary shall require substantial evidence of serious wrongdoing and a vote of no less than four-fifths of the total membership of Congress. The removal or resignation of a Secretary shall not absolve that person from legal liability for any unlawful acts committed in office.

Article 4—Founding Departments

The principal executive departments of Western Australia at the commencement of this Constitution shall be the eleven (11) Founding Departments listed in Annexure C. Each Founding Department is headed by a Secretary and covers a broad functional area of national administration. The number of core departments shall not exceed eleven (11) without explicit authorisation as described in Article 5. The President may by executive order rename, consolidate or internally reorganise these departments for operational efficiency, provided that such changes do not create new principal departments beyond the authorised number or fundamentally alter the scope of powers as set by law. All such changes must be reported to Congress and remain subject to Congressional approval and legislation.

Article 5—Creating or Altering Executive Departments

Any proposal to establish an additional principal department shall require an extraordinary level of approval. No new executive department may be created unless the proposal is passed by at least four-fifths of the total membership of Congress and is thereafter approved by the People of Western Australia in a referendum. The referendum approving a new department must achieve a "double majority"—that is, a majority of the national popular vote and a majority of voters in a majority of the electoral districts must vote in favour.

Title 5: Elections & Candidacy Requirements

Article 1—President: Eligibility & Ballot Access

1. The President must be a natural-born citizen of Western Australia, not hold dual citizenship at nomination or while in office, be at least 35 years of age, and have at least 15 years lawful residence in Western Australia.
2. Ballot access requires a petition to the Independent Electoral Commission with 20,000 verified signatures of enrolled electors nationwide, including signatures from electors in at least one-half of all non-metropolitan electoral districts, with not less than five percent (5%) of enrolled electors signing in each counted district, as classified by the Commission at the last general election.
3. No nomination may require endorsement by an incumbent, a political party, or any officeholder.
4. A person may only be elected to serve as President for no more than two terms. Each term shall be for four years.

Article 2—Congress: Eligibility & Ballot Access

1. A member of Congress must be a citizen of Western Australia, not hold dual citizenship at nomination or while in office, be at least 35 years of age, and have at least 15 years lawful residence in Western Australia.

2. A candidate for a district seat must be an enrolled elector of that district and have been in residence and domiciled in the district at least 5 years.
3. Ballot access for a district seat requires 100 verified nominators who are enrolled electors of that district and a $WAT 2,000 deposit, refundable upon receiving more than 10% of the formal votes cast in that district.
4. No nomination may require endorsement by an incumbent, a political party, or any officeholder.
5. A person may only be elected to serve in Congress for no more than two terms. Each term shall be for four years.

Article 3—Further Exclusions & Rulemaking

1. Congress may by law prescribe objective and reasonable grounds of ineligibility or exclusion, consistent with best international standards and practice, on recommendation of the COC and with COC approval.
2. Any such law must be necessary to protect electoral integrity and proportionate and must provide for prompt review by an independent tribunal or court.

Article 4—Congress Voting System

1. Members of Congress are elected in single-member districts (59).
2. **Ballot.** Voters may mark 1, 2, 3, ... for as many or as few candidates as they choose; a ballot showing a single "1" is valid.
3. **Counting (Instant Runoff Voting).** If no candidate has more than 50% of continuing ballots, the lowest-polling candidate is excluded and each affected ballot is transferred at full value to the highest next available preference. The process repeats until a candidate attains a majority of continuing ballots.
4. **Exhausted ballots.** A ballot with no further available preference at any stage is exhausted and is not counted in later rounds.
5. **Administration.** An Independent Electoral Commission shall prescribe ballot form, scrutiny, recounts, tie-breaking, and publication of results consistent with this Article.
6. **Declaration.** The elected ticket is declared Congressman/Congresswoman-elect and assumes office as provided by law, upon taking their Oath of Office.

Article 5—Presidential Election Voting System

1. **Ballot and ticket.** The President and Vice President are elected on a single national ballot as a paired ticket (per Title 3, Art 4(1)). Voters may mark 1, 2, 3, ... for as many or as few tickets as they choose; a ballot showing a single "1" is valid.
2. **Counting (Instant Runoff Voting).** If no ticket has more than 50% of continuing ballots, the lowest-polling ticket is excluded and each affected ballot is transferred at full value to the highest next available preference. Repeat until a ticket attains a majority of continuing ballots nationwide.

3. **Exhausted ballots.** A ballot with no further available preference at any stage is exhausted and is not counted in later rounds.
4. **Tie-break.** If the final round is tied: (a) the ticket with the higher total of first-preference votes is elected; if still tied, (b) the ticket with the greater number of district first-preference pluralities is elected; failing that, (c) the Independent Electoral Commission shall determine the result by lot.
5. **Administration.** An Independent Electoral Commission shall prescribe ballot form, scrutiny, recounts, and publication of results consistent with this Article.
6. **Declaration.** The elected ticket is declared President-elect and Vice-President-elect and assumes office as provided by law, upon taking their respective Oath of Office.

Title 6: International Obligations and Treaties

Article 1—Limits of Treaty Power

The making of treaties or international agreements by Western Australia's government shall not be used to expand the legislative powers of Congress beyond the bounds set by this Constitution. No treaty, convention, or other international instrument can confer upon Congress any new law-making authority that it does not otherwise have under Annexure A or other provisions of this Constitution. In domestic law, treaties shall have effect only through legislation duly enacted by Congress under an enumerated power. Any law made to fulfil an international obligation must still fall within Congress's constitutional powers and is subject to all constitutional limits. If a treaty provision touches on matters outside Congress's jurisdiction, it shall not be given legal effect unless and until this Constitution is amended to allow it. In sum, while Western Australia may responsibly engage with the international community and honour its commitments, such commitments cannot be used to override or circumvent the constitutional distribution of powers or protections of citizens.

Article 2—Sovereignty in International Organisation Membership

Western Australia's participation in international or supranational organisations is to be approached with caution and with due regard to national sovereignty and the will of the People. The government may join or remain a member of only those international organisations that are consistent with Western Australia's constitutional principles and enumerated powers, and that do not infringe upon the nation's sovereign right to self-government. Any proposal for Western Australia to join a new international organisation or alliance which entails significant obligations or commitments beyond routine cooperation shall require the approval of Congress by law and must be submitted to the People for approval in a referendum. Membership in an organisation that would impose binding rules or policies on Western Australia in areas beyond the national powers enumerated in this Constitution shall have no effect unless the People have expressly agreed to such terms. This means, for example, that joining any political or economic union that could make laws for Western Australia, or any defence alliance that could obligate Western Australia to act, must be endorsed by a referendum achieving a "double majority"—that is, a majority of the national popular vote and a majority of voters in a majority of the electoral districts must vote in favour. All international engagements must be transparent, and treaties or membership agreements shall be tabled in Congress for scrutiny. In every case, the primacy of the Western Australian Constitution and the direct consent of its People remain paramount when engaging internationally.

Title 7: Digital Identity and Civil Registry

Article 1—Prohibition of National Digital Identity

Congress shall not establish or impose any universal national digital identity system or biometric identification registry of the population. Any attempt to create a nationwide system that electronically tracks or verifies individuals across all aspects of life is prohibited. This does not prevent the use of voluntary identity documents for specific purposes.

Article 2—Permissible Civil Register and Sectoral IDs

The government may maintain a basic civil registry for limited civic purposes, and it may provide or recognise sector-specific identification mechanisms, with appropriate safeguards, to ensure effective governance, provided the information collected is limited to what is necessary and is protected by strong privacy laws. Government departments and authorised bodies may also issue sectoral identification documents or numbers strictly for their respective services, but each of these identifiers must be confined to its specific context and not serve as a de facto national ID. Sectoral IDs shall not be unified into a single tracking system, nor shall data from different sectoral IDs be combined to profile individuals without their consent and due process.

Title 8: Lean Governance

Article 1—Mandatory Sunset Clauses

All Acts of Congress must include, without exception, a sunset provision that the Act will automatically expire and cease to have effect after five years of operation unless renewed by Congress. An independent review shall be conducted before the renewal of any sunsetting Act by the Citizens Oversight Committee to assess whether the law remains necessary, efficient, and effective in serving the public interest. That review's findings must be presented to Congress and made public. If the COC determines a sunsetting Act to no longer be necessary or efficient or effective, Congress is expected to let the Act expire or amend the Act to make it necessary, efficient, and effective in serving the public interest. All standing programs established by law are also subject to performance evaluation: all major continuing programs must define clear Key Performance Indicators or metrics of success within the Acts establishing them prior to assent by the President, and if a program subsequently fails to meet its objectives over two successive review cycles, its funding and authority shall be immediately suspended pending a specific Congressional vote to repeal the enabling Act or reform the enabling Act providing for the standing program.

Article 2—Necessity & Efficiency Statements

Every Bill introduced in Congress must be accompanied by a Statement of Necessity and Efficiency prepared by its proposers. This statement must plainly explain why the proposed government action or intervention is essential and cannot be achieved adequately by existing means or by the private sector or Local Councils. It shall include a "Market Alternatives Assessment," describing any non-governmental solutions to the issue and why they are insufficient or less suitable than the proposed government action. The statement must also detail the expected outcomes of the Bill, how it will solve the identified problem, and why these outcomes cannot be accomplished without enacting new law. Congress shall develop with the Citizen Oversight Committee, and revise annually, standard guidelines for these statements to ensure they are concise, factual, and focused on the core question of "Why must the government do this?". By constitutional design, no expansion of government activity shall occur without this question being asked and answered.

Article 3—Efficiency Commissions

At the inception of every Presidential term, a comprehensive Government Efficiency Commission shall be convened composed of non-partisan private sector experts appointed by the President, to review the structure and performance of each executive department and major statutory program. The Commission's mandate is to identify functions, services, and contracts that could be eliminated, streamlined, or transferred to the private sector or local councils for better outcomes. The Commission will produce a public report with recommendations. The President and Congress are required to formally consider these recommendations: within a set time after the report, the President shall respond with an action plan, and Congress shall hold hearings and, where appropriate, enact reforms.

Article 4—Private Sector Preference

In furtherance of minimal government and encouragement of enterprise, there is a constitutional presumption that if a service or function can be effectively performed by the private sector or civil society, it should not be undertaken by the Western Australian Government.

Article 5—No Unfunded Mandates

The Western Australian Government shall not impose new obligations, duties, or responsibilities on Local Councils or other public bodies without providing the resources necessary to fulfill those obligations.

Title 9: Referendums

Article 1—Referendum Mechanism

Congress shall establish and maintain a national referendum system to enable the People's direct exercise of sovereignty on constitutional amendments or other questions requiring a public vote. This system must be secure, timely, and cost-effective. The total cost per voter of conducting a referendum, including associated government information campaigns in respect of each referendum, must be kept low to not burden the public finances. As a benchmark, total direct and indirect cost should not exceed five Western Australian Talents (~$WAT 5) per eligible voter per annum.

Title 10: Universal Royalty Rate and Taxation

[Chapters 3&4]

Article 1—Enumerated & Limited National Taxing Power

1. The Western Australian Government may levy taxes only as expressly authorised by this Article. All other forms of taxation are prohibited.
2. For the avoidance of doubt, no law may impose a tax on personal income, wages, salaries, dividends, interest, capital gains, or corporate profits. Any such law is void.
3. **Unified Property Rates System (UPRS).** Property rates on land shall be levied and collected nationally under a uniform, unimproved-land-value base.
   (a) A Local Services Share of UPRS receipts shall be credited directly to Local Councils under a law establishing objective, transparent funding formulas, with at least annual publication and audit.
   (b) No Council may levy a general property rate in addition to the UPRS. A Council may impose special rates or charges for a specified local work, service, or facility within its district, where (i) the charge is proportionate to special benefit, and (ii) ratepayers affected approve by the threshold prescribed by law.
   (c) The National Valuer determines valuations for UPRS purposes under uniform rules; appeals lie to the courts as provided by law.
   (d) For the avoidance of doubt, Local Councils are statutory authorities of national law with

devolved service functions; their financing is primarily through the Local Services Share and such grants as Congress provides.

Article 2—Zero-Income-Tax Guarantee

Western Australia is a zero-income-tax nation. Neither the People nor businesses shall be taxed on income or profits.

Article 3—URR Fiscal Primacy & WARA Collection

1. The Universal Royalty Rate (URR) is the primary revenue instrument of the Nation and shall be collected and verified in real time by the Western Australian Reserve Authority (WARA), credited to the Consolidated Fund.
2. URR receipts are applied first to fund essential national services and constitutional functions. Analyses underpinning the fiscal design inform but do not bind the constitutional rule.
3. Explanatory Note. For fiscal-feasibility modelling, a base Universal Royalty Rate of twenty per cent (20%) applied to an indicative resource-sales envelope yields ~A$48 B in annual receipts (2026). This Constitution establishes URR fiscal primacy but does not entrench a numerical rate; the 20% figure is a modelling assumption to guide policy, subject to future calibration by law consistent with this Title's transitional architecture (Articles 4–5).

Article 4—Transitional, Broad-Based, Non-Regressive Tax Bases

1. Where URR receipts are temporarily insufficient to fund the Essential Budget, Congress may, by a Special Majority Act, enact only:
   (a) a general consumption tax (e.g., GST);
   (b) the UPRS described in Article 1(3), including the Local Services Share to Councils;
   (c) selective excises on luxury or harmful goods and services.
2. Any instrument under subclause (a) or (c) above must include regressivity safeguards (exemptions/rebates for basic food, essential medicines, primary residences up to a protected threshold, and low-income households).
3. Rates, bases, exemptions, rebates, valuation rules and the Local Services Share formula must be stated in a Special Majority Act and may not be expanded by delegated legislation.

Article 5—Transitional Taxes & Surplus Allocation

1. Net-URR Coverage Ratio (NUCR) is defined as: URR receipts over the prior 12 completed quarters ÷ Essential Budget over the same period.
2. Transitional taxes under Article 4 shall be maintained as the basic tax structure to ensure ongoing fiscal stability and funding requirements, including the guaranteed Local Services Share to Local Councils under the Unified Property Rates System (UPRS).

3. Where the WARA certifies that the NUCR has exceeded 1.0 over a sustained period prescribed by law, indicating surplus URR receipts exceeding Essential Budget requirements, such surpluses shall be allocated first to the Sovereign Wealth Fund (SWF) under Title 12, as certified by the WARA.

Article 6—WARA Remittance Hierarchy & Sovereign Wealth Fund Priority

1. Until all Article 4 taxes are fully abolished under Article 5, no WARA surplus may be transferred to the Sovereign Wealth Fund (SWF) except to the minimum stabilisation tranche provided by Title 12: The Currency of Western Australia.
2. Once Article 4 taxes are fully abolished, enduring WARA surpluses are remitted to the SWF in accordance with Title 12 and invested for inter-generational equity and macro-stabilisation.
3. This Article prevails over any inconsistent law or fiscal directive.

Article 7—Rate Caps, Uniformity & Non-Duplication

1. Taxes under Article 4 must be uniform across Western Australia unless the Special Majority Act provides an objective equalisation mechanism.
2. Double charging is prohibited: no public authority may impose a second general property rate on the UPRS base. Special local rates/charges permitted by Article 1(3)(b) are not a duplication.
3. Congress shall not hypothecate debt service as a ground to re-impose any tax on income or profits.

Article 8—Transparency, Real-Time Verification & Audit

1. The WARA shall publish real-time URR and tax dashboards (MonetaNet) and monthly ledgers of Article 4 receipts, exemptions, and rebates, machine-readable and freely accessible.
2. Annual independent audit is mandatory; the Western Australian Anti-Corruption Commission (WAACC) has full investigatory access to systems and flows.
3. Any citizen or legal person has standing to seek judicial review of compliance with Articles 3–7.

Article 9—COC-Centred Emergency Revenue Clause

1. In a declared national emergency under the COC, Congress may, by a two-thirds vote of the total membership, temporarily suspend the phase-down schedule in Article 5 or apply a surcharge to an Article 4 instrument.
2. Any such measure:
   (a) must be narrowly tailored and may not tax income or profits;
   (b) expires automatically after 180 days, renewable once for a further 180 days by a two-thirds vote;
   (c) is subject to immediate Human Rights Tribunal (HRT) and judicial review.
3. Upon expiry, Article 5 resumes its automatic operation.

Article 10—Tax Innovation Lock & Referendum for New Bases

No new category of national tax beyond those enumerated in Articles 3–4 may be enacted except by:
(a) a four-fifths vote of Congress and concurrence of the COC; and
(b) approval at a national referendum by an affirmative vote of four-fifths of electors.

Article 11—Definitions

1. Essential Budget means the annually appropriated outlays for constitutionally required national functions, as certified by the Auditor-General under law.
2. Transitional tax means a tax authorised solely by Article 4.
3. URR means the constitutionally prescribed royalty charge levied on the value of resource production as provided by law, collected by the WARA with real-time verification.
4. MonetaNet means the national public ledger and disclosure platform operated or commissioned by the WARA.
5. Special Majority Act means an Act:
   (a) passed by at least two-thirds of the total membership of Congress (vacant seats counted against the tally);
   (b) assented to in the ordinary manner; and
   (c) not amendable by delegated legislation.
   An Act that states on its face that it is a Special Majority Act and records the final vote satisfies paragraph (a).
6. Unified Property Rates System (UPRS): the nationally administered property-rates regime on unimproved land value with uniform valuation rules, national collection, and crediting of the Local Services Share to Councils.
7. Local Services Share: the hypothecated portion of UPRS receipts distributed to Local Councils according to formulae set by law and published annually.
8. Local Council: a local government body constituted by national law, with powers and functions as devolved by Congress.
9. Special rates or charges: a levy by a Council to fund a defined local work, service, or facility that confers a special benefit within the district, subject to approval thresholds set by law.

Article 12—Entrenchment & Judicial Enforcement

1. Articles 1–11 are entrenched. Any inconsistent law or executive instrument is ultra vires and of no effect.
2. Amendments to Articles 1–11 require the process in Article 10(1).
3. Courts shall give these provisions a purposive interpretation favouring: (a) zero income taxation; (b) URR fiscal primacy; (c) non-regressive, temporary taxation only where strictly necessary; and (d) automatic phase-out toward a tax-free citizenry.

Title 11: Local Councils

[Chapter 5]

Article 1—Continuity of Local Government Law

1. The Local Government Act 1995 (as it stood immediately before Commencement Day) continues as the law of Western Australia, subject to the Constitution and to amendment or repeal by Congress in conformity with the Constitution.
2. All Local Councils, districts, by-laws, officers, assets, liabilities, proceedings, delegations, rates and elections continue unaffected.
3. Congress shall revise the Local Government Act within a reasonable period to align it with this Constitution while preserving institutional continuity.

Article 2—Constitutional Status & Purpose of Local Councils

1. Local Councils are bodies politic established by law for the self-government of communities within defined districts.
2. Their purposes are to: (a) deliver local public services including education and health services; (b) plan and manage local infrastructure and amenity; (c) promote community wellbeing, safety and environmental stewardship; (d) administer local regulation; and (e) represent community interests to the Western Australian Government and other bodies.
3. Within their constitutional functions, Councils enjoy institutional autonomy and are accountable to their electors and the law.

Article 3—Principle of Subsidiarity & Devolution

1. Public functions shall be allocated to the lowest competent level of government, closest to the people, unless demonstrably requiring national scale, externality management, or uniformity.
2. Devolution is the default: where a function can be effectively delivered by a Council under national minimum standards, it shall be devolved.

Article 4—Devolution Mandate & Schedule

1. Congress shall enact a Devolution Act that establishes a standing Functional Allocation Framework and a Devolution Schedule specifying phased transfer of functions from national (formerly State government, pre-independence) ministries and agencies to Councils.
2. The responsible Secretary must table the Initial Devolution Schedule within 180 days of Commencement Day, with phases and dates certain. Any function classified "local in character" in the Framework is deemed devolved on its scheduled date unless Congress disallows by a two-thirds majority with published reasons.
3. A Council demonstrating readiness may petition for early assumption of a scheduled function; approval is by the Secretary responsible, with reasons published.

4. The Devolution Schedule must eliminate administrative duplication and reduce national-level personnel commensurate with the transfer.

Article 5—Minimum National Standards; Methods Left Local

1. Congress shall set outcome-based minimum standards for devolved services (including accreditation, safety, quality, access and timeliness) and establish an independent Standards and Audit Office to monitor compliance through digital reporting.
2. Councils choose methods and delivery models to meet those outcomes. Congress shall not prescribe operating methods except where necessary for safety or interoperability.

Article 6—Funding, Rates & Collection (Anti-Duplication)

1. Councils may impose special rates or charges for specified local works/services and service charges within their districts, subject to law, and consistent with Title 10.
2. To eliminate duplication and lower cost, Congress may provide for centralised collection of council rates and land-based charges by the WARA as agent for Councils. Amounts collected shall be credited in full, at least daily, to each Council's ring-fenced account; any service fee must be cost-based and transparent.
3. No double-charging: where a national land-based tax or charge is imposed on the same base, law must provide automatic credits, offsets or revenue-sharing so that (a) households and businesses are not charged twice on the same base, and (b) Councils are not financially disadvantaged.
4. Funds standing to the credit of a Council are ring-fenced and shall not be appropriated for national purposes save by a law of general application that ensures the Council is no worse off under a published formula.

Article 7—Grants, Equalisation & Fair Access

1. Congress shall maintain a transparent, formula-driven Local Services Grant system to ensure capacity to meet minimum standards in all districts, with weightings for population, remoteness, disadvantage and infrastructure backlog.
2. Grants are unconditional as to method but conditional as to outcomes and reporting.
3. Any structuring intended to evade grant conditions or obscure end-use is unlawful.

Article 8—Budget Autonomy; Prohibition on Parallel Administrations

1. Councils set their budgets, rates, plans and implementation strategies, subject to minimum standards and audit.
2. On and from each Devolution Schedule date, any parallel national administrative unit for that function shall be wound down within a reasonable period and its employees, assets and contracts re-allocated under Article 10.

Article 9—Digital Interoperability & Open Data

1. The Western Australian Government shall provide and maintain a shared digital backbone for payments, permits and records to which all Councils shall connect; standards shall be open and machine-readable, and privacy protected by law.
2. Council budgets, contracts and performance data for devolved functions shall be published to the national FOI portal in near real time to enable public scrutiny and oversight.

Article 10—Transitional Employment & Assets

1. Employees substantially engaged in devolved functions shall be offered transfer to Councils on terms and conditions no less favourable, with portable entitlements. Where roles are redundant, fair severance shall be provided by law.
2. Assets, liabilities, records and contracts necessary for devolved functions vest in Councils by operation of this Constitution or by Allocation Order under the Devolution Act.

Article 11—Emergency Assistance & Temporary Re-Assumption

1. In a declared emergency under the Citizens Oversight Committee, the Western Australian Government may temporarily assume direct control of specified devolved functions for the minimum period necessary, not exceeding 90 days without Congressional renewal; actions must be proportionate and are subject to post-event audit and judicial review.
2. On cessation, control, assets and unspent funds revert to Councils, with full reconciliation.

Article 12—Periodic Review & Entrenchment

1. The Functional Allocation Framework shall be reviewed at least every five years by a congressional committee with citizen representation; recommendations shall be tabled and responded to within 60 days.
2. The principles of subsidiarity, anti-duplication, ring-fencing of Council funds and formula-based equalisation are entrenched; a law substantially derogating from them has no effect unless enacted by the extraordinary majorities prescribed for constitutional amendments.

Article 13—Purpose & Scope of Congressional Oversight

1. Each Member of Congress holds a narrow fiscal guardianship over local councils within their electorate to uphold legality, prevent material waste or fraud, and ensure compliance with conditions attached to national grants. Where a local council overlaps electoral districts, the electoral district containing most of the land area of the council shall be responsible for fiscal guardianship.
2. Oversight is not execution: Members of Congress must not award contracts, direct council staff, or substitute policy preferences for those of elected councils. Intervention is exceptional and proportionate.

Article 14—Grounds & Emergency Freeze

1. A Congress person may object to a council budget, by-law, procurement, or disbursement only on recorded evidence of: (a) illegality/ultra vires; (b) material misstatement or omission at or above statutory thresholds; (c) fiscal risk likely to cause structural deficit beyond a set ratio; (d) breach or evasion of grant ring-fencing; (e) corruption or maladministration.
2. A Congress person may issue a 7-day Emergency Spending Freeze (ESF) where irreversible loss or illegality is imminent, subject to Local Governance Review Tribunal (LGRT) review confirming, amending, or nullifying the ESF.

Article 15—Procedure & Transparency

1. A Congress person must issue a Reasoned Objection Notice within statutory time limits, stating grounds, evidence, and remedy sought after issuing an ESF.
2. All objections, evidence, LGRT outcomes, and freeze orders must be published within 48 hours on the FOI portal, with only strictly necessary redactions provided by law.

Article 16—Local Governance Review Tribunal

1. **Establishment & Status.** A Local Governance Review Tribunal (LGRT) is established as an independent tribunal of the Western Australian Government, exercising judicial powers of review within its statutory remit. The LGRT's secretariat forms part of the administration of the Western Australian courts, as prescribed by law, without prejudice to the LGRT's decisional independence.
2. **Jurisdiction.** The LGRT has original jurisdiction to determine objections and referrals under Articles 14–15 and related laws, including orders to prohibit, modify, surcharge, or claw back unlawful or wasteful council expenditures or decisions; to confirm, vary or set aside Emergency Spending Freezes; and to make ancillary or consequential directions.
3. **Composition & Appointment.** The LGRT shall consist of a Chair and not fewer than four (4) Members, appointed by the President on a shortlist nominated by the Citizens Oversight Committee (COC) and vetted for integrity and conflicts in accordance with law. Members must be acknowledged experts in Local Council administration or allied fields (local government law, public finance, procurement, audit, infrastructure delivery). Terms are staggered and fixed for a period of four years; a maximum of three terms only can be served by a Chair or Member; remuneration and conditions shall not be reduced during tenure.
4. **Independence & Removal.** Members act impartially and shall not be directed by any person or authority. Removal is only for proved misbehaviour, gross incompetence, or permanent incapacity, on address to Congress following an open hearing, or by order of a superior court on application as prescribed by law.
5. **Procedure & Timelines.** Proceedings are fast-tracked, with time-limits for filing, evidence exchange, hearing, and decision fixed by law. The LGRT may receive evidence on affidavit, hold

remote hearings, and adopt inquisitorial case-management where appropriate, consistent with natural justice.

6. **Powers.** The LGRT may issue interim and final orders, require production of information, summon witnesses, compel attendance and testimony under oath, and award costs on a principled basis. Orders are binding on all persons and authorities, including Congress persons and Councils, and take effect on publication unless stayed by the LGRT for stated reasons.
7. **Funding.** The LGRT shall have a guaranteed, non-lapsing appropriation charged on the Consolidated Fund, sufficient for effective discharge of its functions; administrative support is provided through the court administration, with a separately identified budget line.
8. **Publication & Transparency.** Decisions with reasons must be published promptly, with necessary and narrow redactions for privacy or legitimate confidentiality.
9. **Review.** Appeals lie on questions of law to the Constitutional Court within a short, fixed period, consistent with Article 17. No appeal or review operates as a stay unless ordered by the LGRT or the appellate court.

Article 17—Citizen Triggers, Appeals, and Metrics

1. Citizen petitions to the LGRT are available at low thresholds set by law.
2. Appeals lie on questions of law to the Constitutional Court within a short, fixed period.
3. The FOI Commissioner maintains a public dashboard; the Auditor-General reports annual metrics to Congress.

Article 18—Definitions

For the purposes of this Title:

Council or Local Council means a local government constituted under the Local Government Act 1995 as continued by this Constitution.

Devolution Act means a law enacted under Article 4 establishing the Functional Allocation Framework and Devolution Schedule.

Functional Allocation Framework means the criteria and methodology for allocating public functions between the Western Australian Government (WAG) and Councils.

Devolution Schedule means the phased timetable or instrument transferring specified functions to Councils.

Standards and Audit Office means the independent body established by law to monitor compliance with outcome-based minimum standards for devolved services.

Ring-fenced means legally segregated funds held for a Council that are not available for national appropriation except as expressly permitted by a law of general application that ensures the Council is no worse off under a published formula.

Western Australian Reserve Authority (WARA) means the independent authority established by this Constitution to receive and verify URR and perform functions assigned by law.

COC means the Citizens Oversight Committee established by this Constitution.

FOI portal means the national public-access platform for proactive disclosure and records publication as provided by law.

Title 12: The Currency of Western Australia

[Chapter 6]

Article 1—Currency & Legal Tender

The official currency of Western Australia is the Western Australian Talent (WAT). The sole issuer of the WAT shall be the Western Australian Reserve Authority (WARA), an independent authority established under this Constitution. The WAT shall be the sole legal tender for all debts, public and private, within Western Australia, subject to the transitional provisions in Article 15.

Article 2—Rule-Bound Issuance

The WAT shall initially operate under a currency board model with 100% coverage of the monetary base by eligible foreign exchange reserves. All currency in circulation must be fully backed by verified eligible FX reserves. The money supply may expand or contract only against net inflows of eligible FX reserves according to non-discretionary rules prescribed by law, anchored in reserve coverage and public-interest stability objectives. This prohibits unbacked issuance or deficit monetisation.

Article 3—Western Australian Reserve Authority

1. **Establishment & Independence.** The Western Australian Reserve Authority (WARA) is established as an independent monetary authority to issue the WAT solely against inflows of eligible FX reserves (AUD, USD, RMB, JPY or other determined currencies) in a currency board style, maintaining 100% coverage of the monetary base initially. Decisions shall be non-partisan, transparent, and auditable as prescribed by law. The WARA's functions under this Title shall be exercised consistently with its duties under Title 10: Universal Royalty Rate and Taxation.
2. **Governance.** The WARA shall be governed by a board of seven members nominated by the Citizens Oversight Committee (COC) and confirmed by Congress. At least three members shall possess expertise in monetary policy, and two in financial technology, to ensure competent oversight of issuance, reserves, and MonetaNet. Terms shall be staggered, with initial appointments of three, five, and seven years, thereafter seven years, to promote continuity. Removal of board members requires demonstrated cause, such as misconduct or incompetence, proven by a

four-fifths vote of Congress upon COC recommendation, safeguarding independence from political interference.

Article 4—Budget Financing from URR

1. **Cap on Year-on-Year Growth.** Total releases by the WARA to finance the Western Australian Government's annual appropriations must not exceed one hundred and five percent (105%) of the amount released in the immediately preceding financial year.
2. **WARA Gatekeeping Within the Cap.** The WARA must refuse any submission that would breach clause 1 above. Further, even where a proposed budget is within that cap, the WARA has absolute discretion—subject only to clause 3 below—to disallow, in whole or in part, any requested increase over the prior year; a partial disallowance reduces the authorised ceiling accordingly, and disallowed items have no effect until resubmitted and accepted.
3. **Override in Extraordinary Circumstances.** Congress may authorise a temporary exceedance of the cap, or require the WARA to accept specified increases, for a defined and exceptional purpose (including disaster recovery, defence exigency, or a one-off national priority) by a four-fifths majority of all Members, subject to concurrence by a reasoned resolution of the WARA Board confirming consistency with monetary stability and reserve integrity; the Citizens Oversight Committee shall review the justification and sunset provisions and publish its opinion. Any override lapses at year-end. For this Title, "WARA Board" means the governing body of the WARA constituted by law.
4. **SWF Integrity First.** Even where clause 3 applies, measures shall favour preservation of the Sovereign Wealth Fund's capital and long-term returns over expedience; draws, where permitted by law, shall preferentially use earnings rather than principal.
5. **Reasons and Publication.** The WARA shall publish reasons for any disallowance or concurrence, including quantitative assessment of compliance with the cap and effects on reserves.

Article 5—Consolidated URR Account & Priority of Releases

1. **Consolidated URR Account.** The WARA shall maintain a Consolidated URR Account into which all URR receipts (converted to eligible FX) are credited. Funds are held on trust for the People of Western Australia and released only as authorised by this Constitution and law. URR receipts in major currencies contribute to eligible FX reserve inflows supporting WAT issuance; physical in-kind deliveries are not eligible reserves.
2. **Priority of Use.** URR receipts shall be applied in the following order: (a) costs of administering this Title as prescribed by law; (b) due servicing of any bonds or instruments lawfully secured against URR streams consistent with Article 11; (c) releases to the Consolidated Fund for appropriations within the annual cap in Article 4; (d) transfer of all residual to the Sovereign Wealth Fund (SWF) as prescribed by law.
3. **Periodicity and Transparency.** Releases shall occur at intervals prescribed by law (ordinarily monthly), and a real-time public dashboard of receipts and releases shall be maintained, subject only to narrow lawful redactions for commercial or security sensitivities.

Article 6—Enforcement, Offences & Remedies

1. **Anti-Subversion.** No organ or official may, directly or indirectly, circumvent Articles 3–5; any device or arrangement having that purpose or effect is void.
2. **Justiciability.** Without limiting Article 9, a person with sufficient interest may seek declaratory and injunctive relief to enforce Articles 3–5; courts shall give such proceedings priority.
3. **Offences.** Knowingly authorising, directing, or executing releases or measures in breach of Article 4 is an offence defined by law, in addition to any civil or criminal liability.

Article 7—Prohibition on Monetary Financing

1. **No Direct or Indirect Financing.** The WARA shall not directly or indirectly finance government expenditure except as permitted by this Title; no law or executive order may compel it to do so.
2. Prohibited Practices. Without limiting clause 1, the WARA is prohibited from providing overdrafts, advances, guarantees, or primary-market purchases of government securities, save only as expressly authorised under Articles 12-14 for a defined, time-limited purpose and subject to Congressional control.
3. **Releases Only via Article 4.** Budget financing shall occur only by releases in accordance with Article 4.

Article 8—Accountability, Transparency & Audit

1. **Reporting.** The WARA must report at least quarterly on currency in circulation, reserve status and composition, issuance rule compliance, and URR receipts and releases; quarterly statements shall be published in detailed form and in summary.
2. **Independent Audit.** The WARA's financial statements, reserve holdings (including custody confirmations), and the integrity of the verification systems in Article 3 shall be independently audited as prescribed by law.
3. **Congressional and Civic Scrutiny.** Reports and audit opinions shall be tabled in Congress for committee scrutiny and made public. The Citizens Oversight Committee may issue opinions and recommendations on transparency and compliance.
4. **Real-Time Transparency.** The WARA shall maintain and expand the public dashboard mandated by Article 5(3), releases under Article 4, and reserve metrics, incorporating a national blockchain ledger for real-time auditing, subject only to narrow lawful redactions for commercial or security sensitivities.

Article 9—Entrenchment & Judicial Enforcement

1. **Entrenchment.** Articles 3–9 are entrenched; any inconsistent law, instrument, or executive action is ultra vires and void.
2. **Justiciability and Remedies.** In addition to Article 6, courts may grant declaratory and injunctive relief to enforce Articles 3–9; proceedings shall be given priority.

3. **Amendments.** Amendments to Articles 3–9 require the extraordinary majorities and procedures prescribed by this Constitution, consistent with the entrenchment provisions in Title 10: Universal Royalty Rate and Taxation, Article 12.

Article 10—Sovereign Wealth Fund

1. A Sovereign Wealth Fund is hereby established as a permanent, ring-fenced public trust to convert non-renewable and strategic revenues into enduring public wealth.
2. **Sources.** The WARA shall by law dedicate defined shares of resource royalties, concession fees, privatisation proceeds, fiscal surpluses and other prescribed windfalls to the SWF.
3. **Objects.** The SWF shall (a) preserve intergenerational equity; (b) stabilise public finances against commodity and business-cycle volatility; and (c) support counter-cyclical fiscal policy within the limits of the debt and fiscal rules of this Constitution.
4. **Governance.** The SWF shall be managed by an independent Board appointed on a Citizen Oversight Committee-nominated shortlist, with staggered terms, strict conflict-of-interest rules, and fiduciary duties to the People of Western Australia; appointments and removals shall be by law with cause only.
5. **Integrity & Custody.** Assets shall be held in segregated accounts; borrowing against the Fund, pledging it as collateral, or using it for off-budget spending is prohibited.
6. **Withdrawals.** Annual draws, if any, shall occur only under a formula prescribed by law that (a) protects the real value of the Fund and (b) respects the fiscal responsibility rules of this Constitution; extraordinary draws require a two-thirds vote of Congress upon a public report by the Fiscal Council first approved by a two-thirds vote of a specially convened fiscal experts panel of the Citizens Oversight Committee.
7. **Transparency.** Quarterly performance reports and audited annual statements shall be published; all holdings, benchmark policies and costs shall be disclosed subject only to narrowly tailored market-sensitivity delays set by law.
8. **SWF Integrity First.** Even where clause 3 applies, measures shall favour preservation of the Sovereign Wealth Fund (SWF).
9. The WARA shall establish and manage the SWF as a perpetual fund for intergenerational equity and economic stabilisation. Surplus URR receipts exceeding Essential Budget requirements, as certified by the WARA, shall be transferred to the SWF for investment in accordance with prudent, diversified strategies prescribed by law.
10. Congress shall enact laws providing for the allocation of SWF investment returns, prioritising reinvestment to ensure the SWF's growth and sustainability. Where investment returns exceed thresholds determined by law consistent with the preservation of the real value and long-term sustainability of the Fund, Congress must provide for the distribution of excess profits as a citizen dividend, conditional on demonstrated community contributions including, without limitation, civic service, volunteering, or other forms of societal participation, as defined by law.

Article 11—Fiscal Responsibility & Public Debt

1. **Golden Rule.** Structural operating budgets shall be balanced; borrowing is permitted only for net public investment (including national Defence procurement) and emergencies defined by law.
2. **Debt Brake.** Congress shall enact a statutory debt rule that caps general-government net debt within objective thresholds relative to GDP and to average own-source revenue; any proposal to exceed the cap must be approval at a national referendum by an affirmative vote of four-fifths of electors following a Citizens Oversight Committee impact statement.
3. **Medium-Term Framework.** Congress shall publish a rolling multi-year fiscal strategy with expenditure ceilings, investment envelopes, and contingency buffers consistent with the debt rule.
4. **Fiscal Council.** An independent Fiscal Council shall be established by law to (a) assess macro-fiscal forecasts; (b) certify compliance with rules; (c) cost major proposals; and (d) report publicly. Members are appointed via a Citizen Oversight Committee-nominated shortlist with security of tenure.
5. **Transparency & Correction.** Budgets, quarterly updates and outcomes shall be published with reconciliations to rule compliance. Any breach triggers a mandatory correction plan and reporting to Congress.

Article 12—Emergency Currency Powers: Declaration & Trigger

1. **Trigger.** Congress may by law authorise a time-limited declaration of a Monetary Emergency where a severe external or internal shock threatens the peg basket or payment system.
2. **Scope.** A declaration shall specify the threat and include guidance measures for the WARA. A declaration shall not exceed 30 days. A declaration may be renewed by Congress.
3. **Publication.** All measures undertaken by Congress and the WARA pursuant to a declaration shall be published immediately. The Citizens Oversight Committee shall be notified without delay of all measures prior to execution. Measures not communicated to the COC prior to execution will be subject to review as actions constituting serious criminal or civil offenses.

Article 13—Emergency Currency Powers: Temporary Measures

1. **Temporary Exchange Measures.** During a declared Monetary Emergency, the WARA may adopt proportionate, least-restrictive measures prescribed by law, including temporary wideners to the peg band, targeted capital-flow tools, liquidity support against high-quality collateral, and settlement-system safeguards.
2. **Safeguards.** Measures must (a) preserve property and contract rights to the maximum extent; (b) avoid discrimination; (c) be technically justified with written reasons; and (d) be reversible to the maximum extent possible. In all events the wealth and resources, including financial resources, of the People of Western Australia held and managed in trust by the WARA, SWF, and Congress shall not be exploited, extended, or used to save, secure, or rescue private sector commercial or financial mismanagement that was avoidable with reasonable foresight.

Article 14—Emergency Currency Powers: Oversight, Review & Sunset

1. **Continuous Review.** The WARA shall report daily to Congress and the Citizens Oversight Committee on conditions, measures taken, and an exit plan back to the constitutional peg regime.
2. **Sunset & Audit.** All emergency measures lapse upon expiry of a Monetary Emergency declaration unless renewed by Congress; a post-event independent audit shall be published within 90 days, with any rights impacts reviewed by the Human Rights Tribunal.

Article 15—Peg Basket & Price Stability

1. **Peg Mandate.** The WARA shall maintain a transparent rules-based initial peg to a trade-weighted basket of foreign currencies (e.g., RMB 50%, AUD 40%, USD 10% or calibrated to major trade partners) to anchor the Western Australian currency, with approximate 1:1 parity to the AUD at launch. Peg weights and review cycles shall be prescribed by law and published.
2. **Price Stability Objective.** The primary objective of monetary policy is price stability consistent with long-run purchasing-power integrity; secondary objectives, where compatible, are financial stability and employment.
3. **Rule Transparency.** The WARA shall publish the operating rule, intervention thresholds, and minutes with reasoned decisions; deviations from the rule require contemporaneous reasons and a dated re-entry path.
4. **Western Australian Price Index.** Congress shall by law establish the Western Australian Price Index (WAPI) as the official price-monitoring index maintained by the WARA. The WARA shall publish its methodology, inputs and quarterly values with at least 60 days' notice for any methodological change and conduct a formal review no less frequently than every year. The Index serves transparency and rule-trigger purposes and does not authorise monetary financing or deviation from the 100% FX reserve rule.
5. **Transition to WAT.** The transition from the Australian Dollar shall include an initial FX-reserve-backed peg, a dual legal tender period of 6–12 months, conversion of bank accounts and contracts at the prevailing market rate on the fixed end date, local licensing of Australian banks with a grace period, and shift of public-sector payroll and transactions to WAT as soon as practicable.

Article 16—AI Monetary Oversight

1. **Establishment.** Congress shall by law establish an AI-assisted oversight system (MonetaNet) within the WARA to monitor reserve holdings, FX inflows, WAT issuance, and macro-financial risks impacting the peg and payments system. MonetaNet leverages blockchain for an immutable ledger recording all FX reserve deposits, WAT issuances, and related transactions in real time. Integrated AI analyses data streams for anomalies (e.g., unusual issuance or reserve discrepancies), triggering alerts to WARA officials, the COC and the WAACC. Public dashboards provide real-time aggregated reserve metrics, coverage ratios, and compliance reporting.

2. **Human-in-Command.** MonetaNet shall provide alerts and recommendations; it shall not make binding decisions. Any critical alert classification and action remain the responsibility of named WARA officials.
3. **Integrity & Safety.** Law shall mandate secure development and operation standards, including model registers, audit logs, change-control, adversarial testing, red-team exercises, and strict access controls; tampering, data poisoning, or disabling lawful alerts shall be serious criminal offences.
4. **Transparency & Review.** Model cards, impact assessments, and annual effectiveness reviews shall be published with necessary redactions. The Citizens Oversight Committee shall provide for periodic independent evaluation and sunset review.

Article 17– Transition to Floating Exchange Rate Regime

1. **Objective.** The WAT shall initially operate under a currency board with a pegged exchange rate to provide stability and build public trust during the nation's early years. The long-term objective is a transition to a floating exchange rate regime, enabling full monetary sovereignty and flexible responses to domestic economic conditions, once minimum metrics for institutional and economic readiness are met. This pathway shall be pursued cautiously to avoid risks associated with underdeveloped markets or external shocks.
2. **Minimum Metrics for Transition.** Congress may legislate a transition from the pegged regime only upon WARA certification, endorsed by the Citizens Oversight Committee (COC), that the following metrics have been sustained for at least three consecutive years:
   a) Inflation rate below 3% annually, measured by the Western Australian Price Index (WAPI), demonstrating effective price stability;
   b) Foreign exchange reserves covering at least six months of imports, ensuring resilience against external shocks;
   c) Fiscal deficit not exceeding 2% of GDP, with public debt below 40% of GDP, reflecting disciplined budgeting;
   d) Banking system capital adequacy ratio above 12%, with non-performing loans below 5%, indicating a robust and liquid financial sector;
   e) Demonstrated market depth, including average daily FX turnover exceeding 5% of GDP and diversified investor participation, to support independent rate determination without excessive volatility.
3. **Process and Safeguards.** The WARA shall annually review and publish progress toward these metrics. Any transition legislation requires a special majority of four-fifths of Congress and referendum approval by (a) a majority of the national popular vote and (b) a majority of electoral districts. During transition, the WARA may implement gradual measures, such as widening peg bands, subject to real-time MonetaNet monitoring. If metrics deteriorate post-transition, the WARA shall reinstate pegged elements temporarily to protect stability.

Title 13: Banking

[Chapter 6]

Article 1—Legislative Competence over Banking

Congress may make laws with respect to banking and financial services within Western Australia.

Article 2—Institutions & Allocation

1. A Western Australian Monetary Supervisor (WAMS) shall be established by law as the national banking regulator. The WAMS exercises licensing, supervisory, investigatory, and resolution powers provided by law, and coordinates with the Western Australian Reserve Authority (WARA) on matters affecting monetary stability and the payments system, consistent with Title 12.
2. National Bank. Congress shall by law establish, maintain, and regulate a national bank to be known as the Bank of Western Australia (BWA), wholly owned by the Western Australian Government. The BWA shall be constitutionally limited to providing simple, low-fee checking and savings accounts, simple mortgages for owner-occupiers, and simple small-business loans, as prescribed by law. The law may provide for the acquisition and operation by the BWA of banking branches and infrastructure located in Western Australia, as prescribed by law.

Article 3—Reserves, Lending Requirements & Segregation Rule

1. **Tiered Reserve Requirements.** Deposit-taking institutions must maintain liquid reserve holdings in Western Australian Talent (WAT) or other WARA-approved reserve assets against deposits and other short-term liabilities at ratios prescribed by law, calibrated to preserve the integrity of the WAT's reserve-backed issuance under Title 12.
2. Lending Priorities. The law must provide that lending to owner-occupiers (including first-home buyers) and to small businesses (including micro-finance) attracts the lowest reserve requirements (e.g., around 5%), and that lending to overseas clients, property investors, and large businesses attracts materially higher reserve requirements (e.g., around 20% or higher).
3. **Hard-Currency Safeguard.** During the period in which the WAT operates under an FX-reserve-backed peg, the law must provide that any credit created for low-priority borrowers is tethered fully to verified eligible foreign exchange reserves.
4. **Operational Segregation.** Transaction-banking functions must be operationally segregated from lending and investment activities as prescribed by law. To the extent lending is funded from deposits, the law must ensure that withdrawable-on-demand deposits are not used to fund long-term lending except within the reserve, liquidity, and stability safeguards established under this Article and Title 12.

5. **Prudential Controls.** Deposit-taking institutions must maintain capital ratios prescribed by law, having regard to the objective of materially higher resilience than legacy fractional-reserve regimes (e.g., equity-to-assets around 20%).

Article 4—Credit Creation & Denomination

1. **Disciplined Credit Expansion.** Money creation via bank lending may occur only within the reserve, liquidity, capital, and lending-priority requirements established under Article 3 and law, and in a manner that does not undermine the WAT's FX-reserve-backed issuance under Title 12.
2. **Denomination.** All retail deposits and loans to residents must be denominated in WAT. Foreign-currency loans to residents are unlawful.
3. **Minimum Downpayment.** The law must provide that the downpayment on all mortgages and business loans (excluding micro-finance) is not less than fifteen per cent (15%).
4. **Penalties.** A law shall provide civil and criminal penalties, including licence revocation, for contraventions. This Article operates subject to Title 12.

Article 5—Licensing & Foreign Banks

1. No person may carry on banking in Western Australia without a banking licence issued in accordance with Article 2 and law.
2. **Foreign banks.** A foreign bank wishing to operate in Western Australia must incorporate a Western Australian subsidiary, hold local capital and reserves as prescribed, maintain books and data locally, and comply with the reserve, denomination, and lending requirements of this Title.
3. **Transition and Conversion.** The law must require banks operating physically in Western Australia after secession, including Australian banks and other foreign banks, to transition Australian Dollar holdings and inflows to WAT over the dual-legal-tender transition period in Title 12 (ordinarily 6–12 months), and to redenominate local assets and liabilities to WAT on terms that protect depositors and preserve financial stability.
4. **Audit and Enforcement.** The law must provide for annual audits of licensed institutions, and for proportionate enforcement including licence revocation for non-compliance. In cases of persistent or wilful non-compliance threatening monetary stability, the law may provide for compulsory acquisition as prescribed by law.

Article 6—Payments & Settlement

Congress may designate payment, clearing and settlement systems as systemically important and provide for finality of settlement, interoperability, fair access, and operational resilience. The WAMS may issue binding standards accordingly.

Article 7—Reporting & Transparency

Licensed institutions shall comply with uniform reporting and disclosure standards set by law. The WAMS and WARA shall publish periodic summaries and audit results, including machine-readable disclosures via MonetaNet, with lawful and narrowly tailored confidentiality exceptions.

Article 8—Enforcement & Resolution

1. The WAMS may issue directions, require remedial plans, impose administrative penalties, appoint a statutory manager or receiver, transfer assets and liabilities, and revoke licenses, in accordance with law.
2. An emergency measure restricting depositor access, including any temporary suspension or withdrawal limit, may be taken only pursuant to a proclamation of the Citizen Oversight Committee. The WAMS shall bring the submission to the COC for consideration; the Western Australian Reserve Authority may join as co-applicant.
3. Standing before the COC on such a submission is confined to the WAMS and the WARA. No Secretary, political officeholder, or political staff member may appear.
4. The COC may issue a proclamation only where satisfied on the material before it that there exists a serious and imminent risk to the integrity of the payments system or to depositor funds. A proclamation shall state its scope and duration, which shall not exceed fourteen (14) days; renewal requires a fresh submission meeting the same threshold.
5. Decisions to issue, refuse, renew, or revoke a proclamation under this Article are not reviewable by any court. Measures taken under a proclamation remain subject to the jurisdiction of the Human Rights Tribunal, whose relief shall not invalidate the proclamation.
6. The COC shall cause a record of its decision and reasons to be kept. A detailed decision shall be published as soon as reasonably practicable, with lawful redactions for financial stability, national security, and confidentiality.

Article 9—Definitions

For this Title:

Bank of Western Australia (BWA) means the national bank established by law under Article 2;

Bank or deposit-taking institution means a person authorised by law to accept deposits or funds repayable on demand;

Demand deposit means a deposit payable on demand or on short notice without material loss;

Term deposit means a deposit with a fixed term not withdrawable on demand;

Foreign bank means a body corporate incorporated outside Western Australia;

WAMS means the Western Australian Monetary Supervisor established by law.

Title 14: Eight Pillars of Self-Sufficiency

[Chapter 7]

Article 1—National Self-Sufficiency

Self-sufficiency is a foundational expression of sovereignty. Western Australia must develop and maintain independent capabilities in critical sectors necessary for security, resilience, and long-term prosperity.

Article 2—Domains and Duties

1. Congress shall take legislative, fiscal, scientific, and technological measures to progressively expand sovereign capacity in:
    (a) Mining and resource exploration;
    (b) Defence manufacturing;
    (c) Energy;
    (d) Food and agriculture;
    (e) Healthcare;
    (f) Transport and infrastructure;
    (g) High-tech innovation with export capacity; and
    (h) Strategic reserves.
2. Detailed quarterly update reporting to the People is required.

Article 3—Permanent Sovereignty over Natural Resources

The Western Australian Government exercises permanent sovereignty over natural resources, administering them exclusively in the interests of the Western Australian people and converting resource wealth into domestic capability.

Title 15: Defence & War Force

[Chapter 8]

Article 1—Purpose & Character

The Western Australia Defence Force (WADF) defends the sovereignty, territorial integrity, constitutional order, and vital interests of Western Australia, and shall act consistently with international law.

Article 2—Civilian Primacy

The President is Commander-in-Chief. A Secretary accountable to the President and Congress exercises day-to-day control.

Article 3—Transparency

Defence appropriations and procurement are tabled and audited, with classification only where strictly necessary; an independent Defence Audit Board reports quarterly to Congress.

Article 4—Remote-Warfare & Technological Sovereignty

Western Australia prioritises unmanned and autonomous systems with meaningful human control; core components are domestically designed and produced wherever feasible.

Article 5—Domestic Deployment

During domestic deployments, service members remain subject to this Constitution and civilian courts, save as provided for military discipline by law.

Article 6—Rights and Duties of Personnel

WADF members enjoy Constitutional rights subject only to strictly necessary limits for discipline and security; no special courts outside lawfully constituted military courts subject to civilian court appellate review.

Article 7—Defence Industrial Base

Western Australia shall foster a resilient domestic defence industrial base; Congress shall enact a Defence Industrial Act to promote R&D, protect sensitive IP, and reduce foreign dependency.

Article 8—Anti-Corruption Safeguards

Defence spending is subject to the Constitution's anti-corruption framework, including public ledgers and WAACC jurisdiction.

Article 9—Armed Engagements Abroad

Overseas hostilities require four-fifths Congressional approval, with limited 48-hour urgent action for armed attack and mandatory four-fifths Congressional approval within that time; deployments beyond 90 days require four-fifths Congressional approval for renewal.

Title 16: Human Law & Medical Freedom

[Chapter 9]

Article 1—Human Law as Supreme Law

1. Fundamental human rights listed in Annexure D to this Constitution are recognised as Human Law in Western Australia with the highest legal authority binding all persons and organs of state.
2. All branches and citizens must respect and uphold these laws; Congress shall provide civil and criminal remedies against violations. Official position is no defence.
3. Standing extends to all persons under Western Australia's jurisdiction.

Article 2—Non-Derogation & Emergencies

1. Non-derogable rights include life; freedom from torture or cruel, inhuman or degrading treatment; freedom from slavery or servitude; no retrospective punishment; recognition as a person before the law; freedom of thought and conscience and speech; freedom to work; freedom of movement; bodily integrity and informed consent; freedom from arbitrary detention and the right to habeas corpus; and the right of the People to acquire, keep and bear small arms, including pistols, rifles, and semi-automatic firearms, is guaranteed. Any purported derogation of these rights is void.
2. Other rights may be temporarily limited only by clear law and only to the extent strictly required, subject to prompt COC oversight. The COC may reverse any law or measures temporarily limiting one or more rights. A reversal order or decree by the COC of any law or measures temporarily limiting one or more rights, shall be reviewable by the HRT only, upon application by the Attorney-General only.

Article 3—Interpretation

Courts and the Human Rights Tribunal may consider international law as persuasive, giving priority to Western Australia's democratic values; directive principles under Annexure D guide but are not justiciable.

Article 4—Social Guarantees

1. The Western Australian Government guarantees free public education and free public healthcare; paid maternity and paternity leave; and a maximum four-day ordinary workweek fixed by statute for employment other than the remote rotational operations contemplated in sub-article (2).
2. Remote rotational operations (FIFO/DIDO). The four-day ordinary workweek guarantee in clause 1 does not apply to specified remote resource operations requiring rotational rosters

(including FIFO and DIDO), as prescribed by law for geographically remote resource extraction and related operations. Rosters and shift patterns for such operations are governed by enterprise agreements and may provide for extended consecutive workdays and weeks.

Article 5—Human Rights Tribunal

1. **Establishment & Status.** There is established a Human Rights Tribunal as a superior court of record constituted under this Constitution with exclusive original and appellate jurisdiction over matters of Human Law as defined in Article 1 and Annexure D. The HRT is independent and not subject to the direction or control of the Executive or of any person or authority, save as provided by this Constitution.
2. **Jurisdiction: Civil and Criminal.** (a) Civil. The HRT has jurisdiction to hear and determine civil complaints alleging violations or threatened violations of Human Law and to provide effective remedies. (b) Criminal. The HRT has jurisdiction to try offences created by or under law constituting egregious breaches of Human Law (including, as prescribed by law, torture; enforced disappearance; cruel, inhuman or degrading treatment; excessive use of force; slavery or servitude; arbitrary detention; false arrest; wrongful arrest; false imprisonment; wrongful imprisonment; persecution; and other grave deprivations of non-derogable rights under Article 2).
3. **Powers & Remedies.** The HRT may grant declarations, injunctions (including interim relief), orders for release, restitution, compensation, and exemplary damages; set aside, vary, or suspend any act or decision inconsistent with this Constitution; invalidate a law to the extent of inconsistency; impose criminal penalties for offences within its jurisdiction; and punish for contempt. All organs of state must assist and comply with its lawful orders.
4. **Citizen Governance & Juries.** (a) Appointments are subject to citizen governance in accordance with clause 5; (b) In criminal proceedings above thresholds fixed by law, trial shall be by jury, with eligibility, summons, and protections prescribed by law; (c) The HRT may convene Citizen Panels on Human Rights, drawn by lot and trained under statute, to assist in systemic inquiries and to make non-binding recommendations published with reasons.
5. **Composition, Appointment, Tenure & Removal.** (a) Composition. The HRT consists of a President and other Judges as prescribed by law; it may sit in Divisions (Trial, Appeals, Inquiries) constituted by Rules of Court. (b) Appointment. Judges are appointed by the HRT President from a shortlist publicly nominated by the Citizens Oversight Committee (COC) following open, merit-based selection.

   (c) Tenure. Judges hold office for a fixed renewable term prescribed by law, not less than five nor more than nine years, with security of remuneration; renewal requires re-vetting by the COC against published criteria. (d) Removal. A Judge may be removed only for proved misbehaviour or incapacity, upon a two-thirds vote of Congress following an open hearing, on a motion supported by a COC report. Interim suspension may be ordered by the HRT Appeals Division on COC application. (e) Disqualifications and conflicts are prescribed by law and enforced by the HRT and the COC; undisclosed conflicts void affected decisions unless the Appeals Division determines otherwise in the public interest.

6. **Institutional Independence & Funding.** (a) The HRT shall control its own listing, registries, security, and administration, and shall make Rules of Court consistent with this Constitution and law. (b) Appropriation. The Western Australian Reserve Authority shall provide to the HRT a guaranteed, non-lapsing annual appropriation charged on the Consolidated Fund, not less than a statutory floor or formula, and disbursed in equal monthly instalments free from Executive discretion. Multi-year commitments for essential operations shall not be reduced mid-term except by a four-fifths vote of Congress on public reasons certified by the Citizen Oversight Committee. (c) Salaries, pensions, and conditions of Judges and key officers shall not be reduced to their disadvantage during term.
7. **Procedure, Access & Celerity.** (a) Proceedings are public save for narrowly tailored orders necessary to protect life, safety, or fair-trial rights. (b) Standing is broad: any person within Western Australia's jurisdiction or acting on behalf of a person unable to act, may bring a matter; representative and class actions are permitted. (c) The HRT may act on its own motion (suo motu) to inquire into systemic or urgent threats to Human Law, including by appointing independent counsel and experts. (d) Causes raising substantial rights questions in ordinary courts shall be promptly stated for authoritative determination by the HRT (reference procedure prescribed by law). (e) Time limits and summary procedures shall ensure expeditious relief; unreasonable administrative or judicial delay itself constitutes a remediable breach.
8. **Finality & Review.** (a) Decisions of a Trial Division are appealable to an internal Appeals Division for error of law, jurisdictional error, or manifest miscarriage of justice. (b) No court other than the Constitutional Court may review or set aside a judgment, order, or process of the HRT; the Constitutional Court has jurisdiction only on a question of constitutional law certified by the HRT Appeals Division. (c) Interim relief ordered by the HRT remains in force pending appeal unless varied by the Appeals Division.
9. **Duty to Defer & Refer; Supremacy in Human Law Matters.** (a) Where a human-rights question within Article 1 arises elsewhere, judicial and administrative authorities must defer to or promptly refer the question to the HRT as prescribed by law. (b) Failure by an official to refer in good faith constitutes a breach of constitutional duty and, where willful and substantial, a serious offence prescribed and punishable by law.
10. **Human Rights Prosecutions & Investigations.** (a) An independent Director of Human Rights Prosecutions (DHRP) is established by law, appointed from a COC-nominated shortlist with security of tenure, to prosecute offences in the HRT; the DHRP may appoint a team of Human Rights Prosecutors, according to law; prosecutorial discretion must be exercised in accordance with published guidelines. (b) The HRT may issue commissions and compel production of documents and testimony, consistent with fair-trial rights, and may refer evidence of corruption or other offences outside its jurisdiction to competent authorities. Upon application by the DHRP, the HRT may issue search or arrest warrants, to be executed by authorised court officers.
11. **Co-operation & Comity.** The HRT may request the assistance of other courts and agencies; its orders are registrable and enforceable in ordinary courts. Where the HRT finds a statute incompatible with Human Law, it shall declare the incompatibility and transmit reasons to Congress; Congress shall consider appropriate amendment or repeal without delay.

12. **Enabling Act & Transition.** Congress shall enact a Human Rights Tribunal Act consistent with this Article to prescribe offences against Human Law, procedures (including juries, references, and suo motu inquiries), the constitution of Divisions, Citizen Panels, the office of the Director of Human Rights Prosecutions, and ancillary matters.

Article 6—Plea Practice in Serious Human Law Offences

No plea bargain or charge reduction is permitted in prosecutions for serious Human Law offences; a timely, pre-listing guilty plea may yield a limited sentencing discount set by law.

Article 7—Oversight of Extraordinary Emergency Powers

1. **Immediate Notification.** Any declaration of a state of emergency and all rights-restricting measures shall be notified to, and published for, the Citizens Oversight Committee at once; secret directives and declarations are void.
2. **COC Review Power.** The COC may review, amend, suspend, or nullify any emergency measure that is not strictly necessary, proportionate, and time-limited; its determinations take immediate effect, subject to judicial review by the HRT Appeals Division on questions of law.
3. **Non-Derogable Rights & Sunset.** Measures may not infringe non-derogable rights; every declaration shall include a fixed sunset not exceeding 30 days unless renewed by law and further Citizens Oversight Committee approval.
4. **Post-Emergency Accountability.** After any emergency, a public report shall be issued; the COC may refer abuses to the Human Rights Tribunal or prosecutorial authorities.

Article 8—Sanctity of the Doctor–Patient Relationship

1. **Informed Consent.** Every person has the right to bodily autonomy and to free and informed consent; emergency exceptions shall be narrowly defined by law and guided solely by an individual patient's best interests.
2. **Clinical Independence & Confidentiality.** Practitioners owe independent clinical judgment free from undue interference; doctor–patient communications are confidential save for narrowly tailored, lawful court orders concerning serious crime.
3. **Freedom of Medical Expression.** No law, directive, or action shall abridge good-faith professional discourse or the communication of information necessary for informed consent.
4. **Medical Exemptions.** Licensed medical practitioners may issue bona fide exemptions where interventions are contraindicated or deemed by a medical practitioner to be unduly risky; neither the State nor employers may retaliate against practitioners or patients for exercising rights under this clause.
5. **Anti-Coercion & Remedies.** No person shall be coerced into treatment against informed refusal; Congress shall legislate civil and, for willful egregious breaches, criminal remedies; affected persons may seek relief before the Human Rights Tribunal.

Title 17: A Wellness-First Nation

[Chapter 10]

Article 1—National Wellness Authority

1. **Status & Mandate.** There shall be an independent National Wellness Authority (NWA) invested with paramount authority for standards, professional accreditation, safety, and transparent public reporting across the Wellness System. A National Wellness Authority Act shall be created pursuant to this Tile and Title 16.
2. **Independence & Funding.** The NWA shall be insulated from Congressional direction in its assurance functions and receive multi-year appropriations not reducible below a formula-based floor except by a two-thirds vote of Congress.
3. **Appointments & Removal.** A National Wellness Commissioner (NWC) shall be appointed by the President from a COC-nominated shortlist; removal only for proved misbehaviour or incapacity after an open hearing before Congress.
4. **Accountability & Review.** The NWA shall publish quarterly reports and is subject to judicial review for legal error; where constitutional rights are engaged, parties may seek remedies in the Human Rights Tribunal.

Article 2—Medicines & Therapeutics: Western Australia Medicines Schedule (WAMS)

1. **Establishment.** The WAMS is established and maintained by the NWA; the Western Australian Essential Medicines List (WAEML) shall form the guaranteed coverage floor.
2. **Decision-Making.** An independent Medicines Schedule Committee advises the NWA; law shall provide transparent criteria, disclosure of reasons, public participation procedures, and strict conflict-of-interest rules governed and applied by the COC with power to disqualify committee members, reviewable on points of law by the Human Rights Tribunal.
3. **Evidence & Review.** Listings beyond the WAEML require superiority on patient-relevant outcomes, with real-world evidence considered; decisions are reviewable on points of law and, where rights are engaged, by the Human Rights Tribunal.
4. **Clinical Discretion.** The NWA shall guide but will not dictate clinical care; lawful clinical discretion remains, subject to proportionate audit.
5. Implementation Duty. Government must fund and operationalise WAMS listings in conformity with NWA standards and integrity rules.

Article 3—Independent Pharmacovigilance Safety Monitoring Board

1. **Establishment & Status.** A Pharmacovigilance Safety Monitoring Board (PSMB) is hereby established as a standing sub-committee of the Citizen Oversight Committee, institutionally and operationally independent of the NWA and of any national regulator or department.

2. **Appointments & Qualifications.** The COC shall appoint not fewer than five (5) suitably qualified members for fixed, staggered terms prescribed by law. Appointees must possess demonstrated expertise in clinical trials, pharmacology, toxicology, epidemiology, biostatistics, or related disciplines, meet strict conflict-of-interest standards, and owe a primary duty to public safety. Members may be terminated by the COC for any perceived or actual conflict of interest.
3. **Mandate.** The PSMB shall (a) conduct continuous, proactive pharmacovigilance over all drugs, therapeutics, and substances distributed in Western Australia; (b) design, operate, and maintain a pharmacovigilance safety system that is institutionally, technically, and procedurally independent of any NWA system; (c) act on its own motion or upon referral to guard against regulatory capture or undue influence by manufacturers, distributors, or related interests; and (d) protect the health and wellbeing of the Western Australian People by detecting, assessing, and responding to safety signals, including where a product is subsequently found to be unsafe.
4. **Access to Information.** The PSMB and its delegate experts shall have prompt and unrestricted access to all data it deems relevant to safety assessment, including raw datasets, adverse-event reports, risk-management plans, manufacturing and quality records, and confidential commercial information, subject to lawful protections for personal privacy.
5. **Compulsion.** The PSMB may compel timely production of information and cooperation from any public authority or company or private person involved in manufacture, importation, distribution, supply, marketing, or monitoring.
6. **Protective Actions.** Where, in the PSMB's judgement, risks outweigh benefits, it may, by written determination, suspend, restrict, cancel, or revoke any approval or authorisation for manufacture, import, distribution, supply, advertising, or use, and may impose conditions, warnings, and labelling changes. Interim measures may be issued immediately where necessary to prevent harm.
7. **Effect & Binding Nature.** PSMB determinations take immediate effect and are binding on all persons and authorities, including the NWA. Any review provided by law shall not operate as a stay unless the PSMB consents.
8. **Transparency.** The PSMB shall publish timely statements of reasons and de-identified supporting analyses, to the extent consistent with privacy and legitimate commercial confidentiality.
9. **Resourcing & Immunity.** The PSMB shall control its budget and secretariat under the COC, and members acting in good faith shall have the immunities necessary for the independent discharge of their functions.

Title 18: Anti-Corruption Framework

[Chapter 12]

Article 1—Western Australian Anti-Corruption Commission

1. **Establishment.** An independent Western Australian Anti-Corruption Commission (WAACC) is established with authority over prevention, investigation, and prosecution referrals for corruption in public and private sectors affecting the public interest.
2. **Western Australian Anti-Corruption Prosecutor.** A Western Australian Anti-Corruption Prosecutor (WAACP) is established as an independent public office to conduct anti-corruption investigations and prosecutions under this Title and law. The WAACP acts in the public interest.
3. The WAACC President appoints the WAACP from a COC-nominated shortlist, on merit and integrity, for a fixed, non-renewable term prescribed by law; removal is only for proved misbehaviour, gross incompetence, or permanent incapacity by a process set by law.
4. The WAACP may open or continue an investigation when sanctioned by at least two (2) WAACC Commissioners by formal minute or instrument recorded (with necessary, lawful redactions) on the public ledger. Nothing prevents the WAACC from conducting preliminary inquiries to decide whether to sanction a WAACP investigation.
5. In sanctioned matters, the WAACP may investigate, compel information, seek warrants from the WAACC, charge, and prosecute offences created by or under the Western Australian Anti-Corruption Commission Act and cognate statutes, and pursue civil recovery where provided by law. Prosecutorial discretion must accord with published guidelines.
6. The WAACP may appoint Deputy Prosecutors and authorised officers, subject to COC vetting and clearance for integrity and conflicts under procedures set by law.
7. All government officers and agencies must afford the WAACP prompt assistance in sanctioned investigations, including access to records, systems, and premises (all under warrant), and technical support, subject to lawful privileges adjudicated by the WAACC.
8. The conduct and administration of the WAACP's office is subject to unrestricted oversight by the COC, including audits of timeliness, integrity safeguards, conflicts management, and publication obligations, without prejudice to the WAACP's decisional independence in individual cases.
9. The WAACP shall publish quarterly statistics and annual reports (with necessary, lawful redactions) to the tamper-evident public ledger.
10. **Powers.** Law shall confer the WAACC with investigatory powers to obtain information, examine financial accounts, search and seize under warrant, freeze and manage assets, conduct covert operations, and cooperate internationally.
11. **Unexplained Wealth & Civil Recovery.** Congress shall authorise Unexplained-Wealth Orders and civil forfeiture on a balance of probabilities, with appeals limited to points of law.
12. **Sanctions & Consequences.** Law shall provide the WAACC powers for mandatory disgorgement; fines (including turnover-linked corporate penalties and 'failure-to-prevent' offences); up to treble damages; long-term debarment from public office and contracts; civil recovery and unexplained-wealth orders with a rebuttable burden for illicit enrichment; imprisonment for

minor and serious offences; professional notification following conviction; publication to the public ledger; deferred-prosecution/leniency for full cooperation; and extraterritorial reach with mutual legal assistance.

13. **Governance.** Commissioners are appointed by the President from a COC-nominated shortlist with security of tenure and strict conflict-of-interest rules; the WAACC reports publicly at least quarterly, otherwise in real-time.
14. The Western Australian Reserve Authority shall solely and reasonably determine and provide the WAACC with a guaranteed, non-lapsing annual appropriation charged on the Consolidated Fund, not being less than a floor prescribed by WARA rules.

Article 2—Citizen Oversight Committee

1. **Establishment and Nature.**
    - (a) There shall be established an independent constitutional body to be known as the Citizens Oversight Committee (COC). The COC is a body corporate with perpetual succession and a common seal, capable of acquiring, holding and disposing of property, and of suing and being sued in its corporate name. In performing its functions, the COC shall act impartially, without fear or favour, and in accordance with this Constitution and the law. Furthermore:
    - (b) Subpanels composed of appropriately qualified COC Members shall be formed, tasked with carrying out constitutional and, where relevant, statutory duties allocated to the COC.
    - (c) The COC may constitute standing and ad-hoc Subpanels to discharge its functions within defined subject remits. A Subpanel is an organ of the COC; acts taken within a Subpanel's delegated remit are acts of the COC.
    - (d) A Subpanel comprises five to nine COC Members appointed by resolution of the COC having regard to Members' expertise and the avoidance of conflicts of interest. The COC may appoint non-voting expert advisers of recognised standing to assist a Subpanel.
    - (e) The COC may delegate to a Subpanel the power to conduct inquiries, issue notices, make determinations and orders, and refer matters to competent authorities within the COC's remit. The COC may, by majority of all Members, call-in any live matter from a Subpanel for plenary determination.
    - (f) Subpanels must apply the due-process rules of Article 2(6). Quorum is a majority of appointed Subpanel Members; decisions are by majority of Members present and voting.
    - (g) The following Subpanels are established:
        - i. Emergency Powers Review Subpanel.
        - ii. Political Finance, Lobbying and Gifts Subpanel.
        - iii. Procurement and Public-Interest Contracts Subpanel.
        - iv. Transparency and Records Subpanel.
        - v. Appointments and Integrity Vetting Subpanel.
        - vi. Pharmacovigilance Safety Monitoring Board.
        - vii. Whistleblower Protection and Anti-Retaliation Subpanel.

viii. Technology, Data and AI Audit.
ix. Judicial Appointments and Integrity Subpanel.

(h) Subpanels must refer suspected illegal conduct (civil or criminal) to the WAACC; nothing in this Article limits the WAACC's independent powers of investigation and prosecution.

(i) Members appointed to a Subpanel must disclose relevant interests and refrain from participation where a conflict exists. The COC must maintain and publish rules on conflicts, recusals, and expert selection applicable to all Subpanels.

(j) Each Subpanel must report its activities, decisions and statistics to the COC and publish them on the public tamper-evident ledger with necessary, lawful redactions.

2. **Composition and Election.**

(a) The COC shall comprise one Member elected from each electoral district allocated to the current cohort under subclause B. At any time, the number of sitting Members shall be thirty in one cycle and twenty-nine in the next, alternating.

(b) Cohort design and objective geographic separation.
At the commencement of this Constitution, the Electoral Commission shall assign the fifty-nine electoral districts to two cohorts—Cohort A (thirty districts) and Cohort B (twenty-nine districts)—so as to maximise geographic separation between districts eligible in the same election cycle. For this purpose, the Commission shall prefer an assignment that, so far as practicable, places neighbouring districts in different cohorts and shall publish the assignment and a short statement of reasons. COC elections shall be conducted every four (4) years, alternating between Cohort A and Cohort B; at each such election only the cohort assigned for that cycle is elected. Upon the swearing-in of the newly elected cohort, the prior cohort demits office. No overlap between cohorts shall occur.

3. **Redistribution and continuity.**
Upon any redistribution, creation, abolition or renaming of districts, the Electoral Commission shall, by notice in the Gazette, re-apply subclause (B) to produce a revised assignment that maintains, so far as practicable, the alternation and near-equal size of the cohorts and the objective of geographic separation; no re-assignment shall shorten a sitting Member's term.

4. COC elections shall be conducted on non-partisan ballots. No party label or endorsement shall appear on the ballot paper.

5. A candidate for election to the COC:

(a) must be at least forty (40) years of age at the time of nomination; and

(b) must have attained at least a bachelor's degree (or equivalent qualifications) and/or not less than fifteen (15) years of professional experience meeting criteria prescribed by law; and

(c) is prohibited from being a registered member of any Western Australian national political party; and

(d) must meet integrity, residency and disclosure requirements prescribed by law.

6. A person is disqualified from nomination or service if the person:

(a) is a sitting Member of Congress, Minister, judicial officer, WAACC officer, member of the defence forces or police, or holds any office of profit under the State; or
(b) holds a beneficial interest in a contract with the State, save as a member of a class and as permitted by law.

7. Each elected Member shall, before assuming office, take and subscribe an oath or affirmation of impartiality and faithful performance as prescribed by law.
8. **Tenure and Vacancies.**
   (a) The term of office of a COC Member is four (4) years and a Member may serve no more than two (2) terms, whether consecutive or otherwise.
   (b) Staggering shall be achieved by the cohort system in clause 2; there shall be no drawing of lots.
   (c) The office of a Member becomes vacant upon expiry of term, death, resignation, disqualification, or removal as provided by this Article.
   (d) A vacancy shall be filled by special election in the affected district within ninety (90) days, or as otherwise provided by law. A Member elected at a special election serves for the remainder of the term attached to that district's cohort, and the cohort cycle is not thereby altered.
9. **Independence, Privileges and Removal.**
   (a) The COC and its Members are independent and shall not, in the exercise of their functions, be subject to the direction or control of any person or authority, save as provided by this Constitution.
   (b) A Member may be removed from office only for proven misconduct, gross incompetence, corruption, or permanent incapacity:
      i. Upon a finding by a superior court constituted for that purpose on application by the COC by a two-thirds vote of its other Members or by the Western Australian Anti-Corruption Commission (WAACC); or
      ii. By a recall election in the Member's district conducted in the manner and on the threshold prescribed by law.
   (c) A Member and officer of the COC shall have such immunities as are reasonably required for acts done in good faith in the performance of official functions.
10. **Secretariat and Funding.**
   (a) The COC shall appoint a Secretary-General as chief executive and may appoint such staff and engage such professional and technical assistance as are necessary for the proper discharge of its functions.
   (b) The Western Australian Reserve Authority shall solely and reasonably determine and provide the COC with a guaranteed, non-lapsing annual appropriation charged on the Consolidated Fund, not being less than a floor prescribed by WARA rules.
   (c) Remuneration and conditions of service of Members and staff shall be fixed by law.
11. **Jurisdiction and Core Powers.**
   The COC shall have jurisdiction and powers, exercisable on its own motion or on complaint, to:
   (a) Emergency Powers Oversight: exercise the authority provided by Title 16: Human Law & Medical Freedom, Article 7.

(b) Political Finance, Lobbying and Gifts: oversee compliance with constitutional and statutory rules on political donations, election spending, lobbying, gifts and conflicts of interest; issue compliance notices and administrative penalties as provided by law, and refer suspected serious breaches to the WAACP.
(c) Procurement and Public Interest Contracts: review and audit procurement and public-interest contracts; where a serious, prima facie breach is indicated, issue a Corrective Action Notice and, if necessary, a provisional suspension not exceeding 30 days; if unresolved, refer to the WAACC/WAACP for set-aside, debarment, or other remedies.
(d) Transparency and Records: monitor compliance with open-government obligations including the Communications Transparency System (CTS) and public-records laws; order disclosure, correction or publication of records, subject to lawful limitations for security and privacy.
(e) Ethical Standards and Vetting: promulgate codes of conduct for public officials consistent with this Constitution; issue advisory opinions; vet senior appointments for integrity and conflicts as assigned by law and provide candidate short-lists where required.
(f) Whistleblowing and Retaliation: supervise protected-disclosure systems; order protective and restorative measures.
(g) Judicial Integrity Interface: The COC monitors compliance by judicial officers with disclosure, gifts, and integrity obligations. Where a complaint discloses reasonable grounds of corruption or serious misconduct by a judicial officer, the COC shall promptly refer the matter to the WAACC or the WAACP for investigation and, where appropriate, prosecution.
(h) Investigatory Tools: The COC can compel the production of documents and data, including encrypted and digital records; compel testimony under oath; administer oaths; enter premises under warrant issued by a competent court or the WAACC, executed by authorised officers.
(i) Referrals: The COC must refer evidence of suspected serious misconduct (civil or criminal) to the WAACP/WAACC or courts; nothing in this Article limits the WAACC's independent powers of investigation and prosecution.
(j) Technology and Audit: access and audit State blockchain ledgers, CTS archives and AI audit trails for the purposes of oversight; require agencies to maintain technical standards prescribed by or under law.

12. **Procedure and Decisions.**
(a) The COC shall adopt its own rules of procedure consistent with due process, including provisions for notice, hearing, reasons and publication.
(b) A quorum is a majority of all Members, and, unless otherwise provided by law, decisions are taken by a majority of Members present and voting; orders imposing disqualification, debarment, or suspending a public contract shall require not less than three-fifths of all Members.
(c) An order of the COC imposing an oversight remedy takes effect on publication and is binding, subject to judicial review on questions of law and to HRT review where rights are implicated.

13. **Accountability and Reporting.**

   (a) The COC shall publish on a public, tamper-evident ledger its quarterly reports, decisions and statistics, with necessary redactions strictly limited by law.

   (b) The COC shall lay its annual report before Congress and appear when requested before the appropriate committee to answer questions on administration, without prejudice to the confidentiality of investigations.

14. **Incompatibilities and Cooling-Off.**

During service and for three (3) years thereafter, a Member shall not:

   (a) Hold or seek elected political office; or

   (b) Accept employment or remuneration from any entity over which the COC has imposed sanctions within the preceding three (3) years, save with leave of the COC granted on stated reasons.

15. Members shall file annual asset and interest disclosures in a manner prescribed by law.

16. **Transitional.**

   (a) The first elections to the COC shall be conducted within one hundred and eighty (180) days of the commencement of this Constitution for Cohort A (as assigned under clause 2.

   (b) The second elections shall be conducted four (4) years after the first for Cohort B, and thereafter elections shall continue every four (4) years alternating between the cohorts.

   (c) Upon the election and swearing-in of Members from the first cohort, the COC is constituted and may exercise all its functions.

   (d) Until the first cohort assumes office, Congress must provide by law for an interim panel to exercise urgent oversight powers under Title 16: Human Law & Medical Freedom, Article 7. Upon constitution of the COC, all interim acts shall be subject to review by the COC.

Article 3—Right to Report & Protections for Whistleblowers

1. **Right to Report.** Every person has the right to report corruption or serious wrongdoing affecting the public interest, with confidentiality and immunity in good faith. Congress shall by law provide rewards for good-faith disclosures that materially prevent serious wrongdoing, recover public assets, or secure convictions for public-interest offences.
2. **Anti-Retaliation.** Retaliation against Whistleblowers unlawful; Congress shall create severe civil and criminal penalties for unlawful retaliation, including imprisonment for up to 25 years.

Article 4—Integrity Technology & Transparency Infrastructure

1. **Mandate.** Congress shall establish and maintain a national integrity technology stack comprising a tamper-evident public ledger, a communications-transparency system, and AI-assisted oversight and audit tools to serve this Title's objectives and to operationalise Title 19: Freedom of Disclosure Framework. An independent statutory authority, Western Australia Disclosure Authority (WADA), shall be created and staffed by legal, civic, and technical experts responsible for

system architecture, public interface integrity, and ensuring all government communications are properly recorded and published.

2. **Technology-neutrality.** The system is technology-neutral and may incorporate successor or complementary technologies that meet or exceed requirements for verifiability, auditability, interoperability, security, and privacy.
3. **Application and access.** The WAACC, WAACP, COC and all public authorities and contractors performing public functions shall connect to and use the system as prescribed by law. The COC is entitled to real-time, read-only access to logs, models, and audit trails necessary to discharge its mandate.
4. **Publication and safeguards.** Records prescribed by law shall be published in near real-time with only narrow, lawful redactions; design and operation must protect whistleblower confidentiality, lawful privilege, and personal privacy.
5. **Standards and audit.** Open standards, model registers, security controls, and periodic independent audits shall be prescribed by law. Tampering, evasion, data-poisoning, or disabling lawful logging or alerts is an offence.

Article 5—Implementation Duty and Timelines

1. Congress shall enact a:
   (a) Western Australian Anti-Corruption Commission Act to effectively operationalise the WAACC; and
   (b) Citizens Oversight Committee Act to effectively operationalise the COC.
2. **Timelines.** The statutes in clause (1) shall be introduced within six months of this Constitution coming into force and fully commenced within twelve months.
3. **Entrenchment.** Amendments that seek to dilute the independence or core powers of the WAACC or COC require a four-fifths vote of Congress confirmed by a national referendum and majority vote after presenting proposed amendments to the People of Western Australia.

Title 19: Freedom of Disclosure Framework

[Chapter 13]

Article 1—Right to Public Information

1. All citizens of Western Australia are the legal and moral owners of all information created and held by their government. Every person has the right to timely access to public information. Public information is held in trust for the People and shall be proactively published by default.
2. This right is individually and collectively justiciable and may be limited only by narrowly tailored restrictions in Article 4 and by time-limited emergency postponements declared under Article 6.

3. Access shall be free of charge save for reasonable reproduction costs prescribed by law, and shall be provided in accessible, machine-readable formats.

Article 2—Duty to Create & Preserve Records

1. Public authorities and officeholders have a positive duty to create, capture, and preserve contemporaneous records of all official actions and communications.
2. "Official communication" includes, without limitation, emails, messages, audio, video, drafts, instructions, decisions, disclosures, and communications including those made on third-party or ephemeral platforms when used for public business.
3. Congress shall prescribe minimum retention periods not less than ten (10) years for ordinary records and longer for archival classes, and shall criminalise willful destruction, concealment, or alteration of public records.

Article 3—Application to Contractors & Delegates

1. Any person or entity performing a public function, receiving public funds above thresholds prescribed by law, or holding public information on behalf of the State, is bound by this Title as if a public authority.
2. Contracts for public services shall include disclosure covenants and audit rights to ensure compliance with this Title.

Article 4—Narrow Restrictions & Embargoes

1. Restrictions on access must satisfy all of the following:
   (a) lawful and necessary to prevent a specific, foreseeable, and substantial harm;
   (b) the least-restrictive means, with partial disclosure where practicable; and
   (c) justified in writing with reasons published.

2. Subject to (1), Congress may prescribe time-limited embargoes for:
   (a) national security and defence capabilities—maximum five (5) years from origin;
   (b) intelligence operations—maximum five (5) years from origin;
   (c) active criminal investigations—for the duration of proceedings;
   (d) fiscal, monetary or currency deliberations prior to public announcement, with a post-announcement tail not exceeding ninety (90) days;
   (e) law-enforcement methods whose disclosure would substantially prejudice their effectiveness—maximum five (5) years;
   (f) legally protected personal data—permanently restricted except to the data subject;
   (g) legitimately confidential supplier trade secrets during live procurements—embargo ends at award save for narrowly-defined secrets, with all contracts, pricing, and performance data disclosed.
3. Embargoes expire automatically and affected records are published without further order.

Article 5—Proactive Publication

1. Congress shall mandate publication registers covering, at minimum: contracts and variations; tenders and evaluation reports; safety and environmental reports; standards; medicines, therapeutics, and health standards; national statistics; budget and spend; policies and drafts; meeting calendars and minutes; lobbying contacts; grants; datasets; and performance dashboards.
2. No person shall be required to make a request for material encompassed by publication registers once operational.

Article 6—Oversight, Appeals & Emergency Postponements

1. The Citizens Oversight Committee (COC) shall maintain a standing Transparency & Records Panel with powers to:
   (a) issue binding disclosure orders;
   (b) require retroactive and category-wide proactive publication;
   (c) impose administrative penalties prescribed by law; and
   (d) refer suspected criminal offences to the Western Australian Anti-Corruption Commission (WAACC).
2. **Appeals:**
   (a) rights-implicating matters may be brought before the Human Rights Tribunal (HRT);
   (b) questions of law may be reviewed by the WAACC, HRT, or courts;
   (c) COC findings of primary fact are final absent manifest error.
3. **Emergency postponements.** The COC may, by public proclamation stating reasons, postpone specific disclosures for up to thirty (30) days where immediate publication would cause the substantial harms. Renewals require fresh reasons, and all postponements are subject to prompt HRT review upon application.

Article 7—Open Records Infrastructure

1. Congress shall establish an independent Open Records Authority to operate a secure, auditable, technology-neutral Public Records Network that automates capture, integrity, and publication of public records, with an appropriations floor guaranteeing operational independence overseen and administered by the WARA.
2. Technical standards shall favour verifiability, audit trails, open formats, and public APIs; the choice of technologies is not to be entrenched in this Constitution, and shall be subject to COC oversight, recommendations, reports, and approval.

Article 8—Spoliation & Sanctions

1. Willful destruction, concealment, unauthorised alteration, or unlawful delay of public records is a serious offence. Conviction carries disqualification from public office for a period prescribed by law and other penalties including imprisonment and significant fines.

2. Good-faith whistleblowing about spoliation or unlawful secrecy is protected by this Constitution and statute.

Article 9—Implementation & Entrenchment

1. Implementing legislation shall be introduced within six (6) months of Commencement Day and fully operational within twelve (12) months.
2. Any amendment that narrows access rights, expands exemptions, introduces fees beyond reasonable reproduction costs, or weakens COC/WAACC/HRT oversight or jurisdiction requires a four-fifths vote of Congress and approval by a majority of voters at a referendum.

Title 20: Political Lobbying & Donations

[Chapter 14]

Article 1—Integrity of Public Office

No holder of public office may seek or permit undue private gain or influence. The public interest is paramount.

Article 2—Right to Transparency in Politics

Citizens have an inalienable right to information on political finance and lobbying. A Public Transparency Register shall record donations and lobbying interactions for free public inspection, with only narrow, lawful national-security exceptions.

Article 3—Oversight

1. The Citizens Oversight Committee (COC) monitors compliance with political-finance and lobbying laws.
2. The Open Records Authority operates the Political Finance & Lobbying Registers within the national integrity technology stack under Title 19.

Article 4—Entrenchment & Supremacy

1. After a referendum passed by a majority of Western Australian citizens, Congress shall enact legislation meeting or exceeding international best-practice standards for monitoring political finance and lobbying, including laws creating serious criminal offenses and severe civil consequences for persons and organisations found in breach of political finance and lobbying laws and rules; amendments require a three-quarters vote of Congress confirmed by a majority national referendum vote.

2. Timelines. The laws and rules in clause 1 shall be introduced within six months of this Constitution coming into force and fully commence within twelve months.

Article 5—Donations: Sources & Caps

1. Only natural persons who are citizens or permanent residents may donate; no entity may donate.
2. Prohibited sources. Donations by foreign principals, corporations, unions, trusts, foundations, or anonymous sources are prohibited; Congress shall criminalise the making, soliciting, concealing, or receiving of such donations.
3. Caps and aggregation. Congress shall set annual per-recipient caps and aggregation rules for monetary and in-kind contributions, applicable to parties, candidates, and third-party campaigners.
4. Public portal. All donations must be processed through an official public portal recording donor identity, amount, date, and recipient for real-time public inspection, subject only to narrow, lawful redactions.

Article 6—Lobbying Integrity & Cooling-Off

1. Lobbying is registrable and subject to a statutory code of conduct, including disclosure of interests and bans on gifts and inducements.
2. Both the lobbyist and the public official must report lobbying contacts for inclusion in the Public Transparency Register.
3. A cooling-off period of not less than five (5) years, commencing on the person's last day in public office or employment, applies to lobbying activities.
4. Who is covered. At a minimum this applies to Ministers, Cabinet Secretaries, heads and deputy heads of departments, regulators and statutory authorities (including state-owned enterprises with licensing, contracting or enforcement powers), chiefs of staff and senior executives at prescribed bands, and any additional designated public officials prescribed by law.
5. Scope of restriction. During the cooling-off period a covered person must not, for remuneration or on behalf of another, engage in lobbying activities directed to Western Australian public authorities on matters within their former portfolio, regulatory remit, or official responsibilities, or on matters where they had access to relevant non-public information.
6. Public-interest waiver. The Citizens Oversight Committee (COC) may grant a limited, reasoned waiver where demonstrably in the public interest, subject to published conditions and a conflict-management plan.
7. Declarations and register. Covered persons must file an exit declaration and periodic post-separation declarations for the cooling-off period; these are published on the Public Transparency Register.

Article 7—Real-Time Disclosure

Donations and lobbying contacts must be recorded and published promptly on the Public Transparency Register in machine-readable form; these registers form part of the proactive publication regime under the Freedom of Disclosure Framework, including the "lobbying contacts" publication register.

Article 8—Anti-Circumvention and Third-Party Campaigners

No person may do indirectly, through intermediaries or affiliated entities, what this Title forbids directly. Congress shall regulate and require disclosure by third-party campaigners and in-kind contributors to prevent evasion of caps, bans, or disclosure duties.

Article 9—Sanctions & Disqualification

1. Congress shall provide serious criminal and civil penalties, confiscation of unlawful funds, and disqualification from public office for proven serious contraventions of this Title or laws made under it.
2. The WAACC may void or set aside an election or appointment procured by serious unlawful influence, per standards prescribed by law.

Annexure A: Enumerated Powers of Congress

1. Congress may make laws for the peace, order, and good government of Western Australia only with respect to the matters enumerated below, with each subject to the subsidiarity principle and other limitations in this Constitution. Each head of power listed includes laws incidental to that subject. Any matter not listed here is outside the legislative authority of Congress and remains for Local Councils or the People or the private sector.
   i. Trade and commerce with other countries: Regulation of international trade and commercial activities, including exports, imports, tariffs, and trade agreements.

ii. Bounties on the production or export of goods or services: Authorisation of incentives, subsidies, or reward schemes to encourage the production or export of specified goods or services.

iii. Postal, telegraphic, telephonic, and other like services: Establishment, operation, and regulation of postal services; telecommunications systems including space and satellite; broadcasting services; and analogous communication networks for connecting Western Australia domestically or internationally.

iv. Defence of the nation: Raising, organising, and maintaining Western Australia's armed forces; protecting national security; regulating military installations and training; Defence procurement and military justice systems; and measures for civil defence and emergency preparedness in the face of external threats. This power excludes legislating compulsory military service or Defence training.

v. Lighthouses, lightships, beacons, and buoys: Management and funding of maritime navigation aids and coastal safety installations to ensure safe passage of ships.

vi. Astronomical and meteorological observations: Establishment of national services for weather forecasting, climate monitoring, and astronomical observation. This includes maintaining meteorological stations, satellites, and research facilities, and disseminating weather warnings for aviation, shipping, agriculture, industry, and disaster readiness.

vii. Quarantine: Protection of public health, agriculture, and livestock through biosecurity measures.

viii. Fisheries in waters beyond territorial limits: Regulation and conservation of fishing and marine resources in the Exclusive Economic Zone (EEZ) and on the high seas as permitted by international law. This includes licensing of Western Australian fishing vessels, quotas and methods for sustainable fishing, and cooperation in regional fisheries management. Fishing rights and aquaculture within territorial waters may be managed by local authorities unless impacting national or international obligations.

ix. Census and statistics: The taking of periodic national censuses of population, and the collection, analysis, and publication of statistical data on matters of national importance.

x. Insurance: Regulation of insurance and reinsurance businesses, including prudential standards for insurers, consumer protection in insurance contracts, and oversight of insurance products.

xi. Weights and measures: Establishment, inspecting and certifying of uniform standards of weights and measures for use across Western Australia.

xii. Bills of exchange and promissory notes: Laws governing negotiable instruments such as bills of exchange, cheques, and promissory notes, including electronic equivalents.

xiii. Bankruptcy and insolvency: Legislation on insolvency for individuals and companies, including processes for bankruptcy, liquidation, restructuring, and the distribution of insolvent estates to creditors.

xiv. Copyrights, patents of inventions and designs, and trademarks: Registration systems and protection of intellectual property (IP) rights on a national basis, while aligning with international IP treaties.

xv. Naturalisation and aliens: Laws concerning how non-citizens (aliens) may enter and reside in Western Australia and how they may become citizens.

xvi. Foreign corporations and financial corporations: Laws, rules, and regulation of corporations formed outside Western Australia that operate within Western Australia, as well as domestic trading or financial corporations. Congress can set rules for corporate governance, securities and stock exchanges, foreign investment, mergers and acquisitions, and ensure that companies operate fairly and transparently.

xvii. Marriage: The creation of a uniform law of marriage for Western Australia. This covers who can marry, the formalities of marriage, and recognition of marriages.

xviii. Divorce and matrimonial causes; parental rights and responsibilities: Laws regarding the dissolution of marriage and related family law matters.

xix. Pensions and social welfare benefits: The provision of income support and social services on a national basis. This may cover invalidity pensions, old-age pensions, unemployment benefits, disability services, maternity and parental leave payments, widows' pensions, child endowments or family allowances, public health insurance or benefits (pharmaceutical, dental, medical, hospital benefits), and support for students or other vulnerable groups.

xx. Immigration and emigration: Control over the entry of persons into Western Australia, and the departure of persons from Western Australia.

xxi. The influx of criminals: Measures to refuse or expel persons with serious criminal backgrounds from entering or remaining in Western Australia.

xxii. External affairs: Management of Western Australia's external relations and obligations. This broad power includes making and implementing treaties with other nations or joining international organisations, subject to the limitations of Title 6.

xxiii. Acquisition of property on just terms: Whenever the Western Australian Government exercises a power that involves compulsorily acquiring property (whether land, goods, or intangible property) from an individual or entity, it must do so on just terms.

xxiv. Justice and courts: Congress shall create a unified court system comprising the Western Australian Constitutional Court, the Supreme Court of Western Australia, and Local Courts, for criminal justice and civil dispute resolution, and shall define crimes and penalties, and establish a national law enforcement body and correctional institutions.

xxv. Education and training: To give effect to Title 16 by setting national minimum standards, funding frameworks for free public education, accreditation and qualification frameworks, transparency and public reporting, and state-wide testing of fundamentals; delivery remains devolved to local institutions and community providers, subject to subsidiarity.

xxvi. Health and public welfare: to give effect to the guarantee of free public healthcare, (including basic dental care limited to emergency relief of pain or acute infection when strictly necessary), by setting national minimum standards and funding frameworks, accreditation and safety rules, the medicines schedule and essential medicines list, and independent pharmacovigilance, with transparent public reporting; delivery remains devolved under subsidiarity and all measures are subject to Title 16: Human Law & Medical Freedom.

xxvii. Environment and conservation: Protection of the environment and conservation of natural resources and the effective and efficient exploitation of natural resources, at a national and intergenerational level.

xxviii. Transport and infrastructure: Development and regulation of national transport and other major infrastructure systems, including highways, main roads, inter-city railways, airports and civil aviation, seaports and shipping, and any infrastructure of national significance. It also covers standards for vehicle safety, traffic rules on national highways, and coordination of infrastructure that spans multiple local council jurisdictions.

xxix. Matters incidental to the execution of any enumerated power: Congress can legislate on matters that are not themselves listed above only if they are a necessary incident of implementing the powers listed above. Any incidental law must be a reasonable means to give effect to a primary enumerated power.

xxx. Impeachment and removal of senior national officers: Congress may impeach the President, Vice-President, and senior civil officers for Treason, Bribery, or other serious Crimes and Misdemeanours. Impeachment is initiated by an Act of Impeachment passed by at least four-fifths of all Members. Upon passage, three senior members of the WAACC shall promptly publish an Opinion on the Evidence and Merits of the allegations particularised in the Act. After considering that Opinion and hearing the person(s) named for Impeachment—who must be afforded up to five days to present evidence and submissions before Congress—Congress may, by four-fifths of all Members, resolve to submit the impeachment to a national referendum. The referendum succeeds only if approved by (a) a majority of the national popular vote and (b) a majority of electoral districts; upon approval, the officer is removed forthwith. Removal is without prejudice to any criminal or civil liability. Laws may provide for procedure and incidental matters.

2. The listing of a power here does not obligate Congress to legislate on it; indeed, under the subsidiarity principle, Congress should leave many of these matters to local or private action unless uniform national legislation is truly necessary. However, if needed for the nation, Congress can act in these domains, and these alone.

Annexure B: Powers & Duties of the President

1. The President of Western Australia is endowed with the following powers and responsibilities:
   i. Executive Authority: The President holds the supreme executive power of the Nation. He or she is responsible for ensuring the Constitution and all laws enacted by Congress are faithfully executed, and for providing leadership and direction to the executive branch of government. This includes issuing necessary directives to departments, managing national administration, and taking care government operations are conducted effectively.
   ii. Head of State Functions: The President serves as the Head of State, representing Western Australia both at home and abroad. In this capacity, the President performs ceremonial duties, such as opening sessions of Congress, receiving the credentials of foreign ambassadors, and officiating at important state occasions. The President embodies the unity and continuity of the Western Australia.
   iii. Commander-in-Chief: The President is the Commander-in-Chief of the Western Australia Defence Forces. The President has supreme command over the nation's military forces and any reserve or militia forces lawfully established. This power includes the authority to direct military operations, oversee defence policy, and ensure the security of the nation. The President may deploy the armed forces for the Defence of Western Australia or in support of civil authorities during emergencies, subject to any requirements of law. The President commissions all officers of the armed forces and can appoint or remove top military commanders.
   iv. Granting of Pardons and Reprieves: The President may grant pardons, reprieves, commutations, and amnesties to persons convicted of offences under national law. This clemency power allows the President to show mercy or correct injustices by forgiving a crime, postponing a punishment, reducing a penalty, or offering a group pardon. This power cannot be used in cases of Congressional impeachment and must be exercised transparently, reasonably, and be accompanied with written reasons for its exercise. Any pardon, reprieve, commutation, or amnesty granted must be reported to Congress.
   v. Treaty-Making Power: The President has the authority to negotiate and sign treaties, conventions, and other international agreements with foreign states or international organisations. However, any such instrument or agreement does not take effect internally without the requisite approval of Congress or, where relevant, approval by the People via referendum.
   vi. Appointment of Officials: The President appoints, either directly or by delegation, the principal officers of the Western Australian Government. This includes nominating Secretaries of Departments (subject to Congressional confirmation as per Title 4), ambassadors and high commissioners to other countries, judges of the Constitutional Court and Supreme Court and any national courts (with the advice of Congress), and other key senior public officials as specified by the Constitution or statutes (such as the Auditor-General, heads of independent commissions, etc.). The President can also make interim appointments if Congress is not in session (acting appointments), which expire unless later confirmed. In making appointments, the President should strive for individuals of integrity, competence, and reflect Western Australia's diversity.

vii. Removal of Officials: The President has the authority to remove or dismiss executive officials he or she has appointed, particularly Secretaries and ambassadors, when the President loses confidence in them or for misconduct, except where the law provides a specific tenure or removal process for independent officers. Judges may only be removed by the process described in Title 18.

viii. Legislative Participation and Veto: Although the President is not a member of the legislature, he or she plays a crucial role in the legislative process. The President may recommend legislation or policy measures to Congress. All Bills passed by Congress must be presented to the President for assent. The President can approve the Bill by signing it into law or refuse assent (veto the Bill) and return it with reasons. The President's veto can be overridden by Congress only under the conditions specified in Title 2. If the President neither signs nor vetoes a Bill within the constitutionally prescribed period of 30 days after presentation, it may become law without the President's signature, unless Congress is not in session. The President also has the power to withhold assent specifically to fulfil the duty of lean governance (see Title 3).

ix. Informing and Convening Congress: The President shall have the right and duty to address Congress and to provide information on the state of the nation. At least once a year, the President shall deliver an address to Congress reporting on the condition of the nation, outlining the executive's achievements, challenges, and legislative agenda. The President may also send written messages to Congress on specific issues. Furthermore, the President can convene Congress on extraordinary occasions. If Congress is in recess or has adjourned sine die and an urgent matter arises, the President can call it back into session.

x. Receiving Ambassadors and Foreign Dignitaries: The President has the exclusive (delegable) authority to receive foreign diplomats, ambassadors, and high commissioners. By accrediting foreign ambassadors, the President formally recognises foreign governments on behalf of Western Australia. The President also may enter into executive agreements or understandings with foreign leaders, consistent with Western Australia's laws and treaties. All official communications with foreign states are conducted through the President or the President's delegates in the Foreign Affairs department.

xi. Commissioning Officers: The President commissions all officers of Western Australia, both civil and military. This means that judges, military officers, and other specified senior officeholders receive their formal appointment from the President's hand. The commissioning power signifies the start of authority in office. The President's signature on a commission or instrument of appointment is the legal act that vests the office in the appointee.

xii. Foreign Affairs and Policy Leadership: As the country's chief diplomat and head of government, the President directs Western Australia's foreign policy. This includes recognition of foreign governments, directing ambassadors and consular officials, protecting Western Australian citizens abroad, and shaping responses to international developments. The President may impose or lift diplomatic sanctions, propose international initiatives, and generally act as the primary voice of Western Australia in international affairs.

xiii. Emergency Powers: In times of grave national crisis—such as war, natural disaster, or a severe internal emergency—the President may take urgent executive actions to safeguard the nation, even if not explicitly authorised by prior statute or the Constitution. These actions can include issuing executive orders, mobilising resources, and directing departments to extraordinary tasks. However, the President's emergency powers are not unchecked: any such measures must be necessary and proportionate to the crisis and are temporary. They are subject to review or disallowance by the Citizens Oversight Committee (COC) under the emergency oversight clauses, and to judicial review to prevent abuse. The President must inform Congress as soon as possible of any significant emergency actions taken and seek retroactive approval or enabling legislation for continuance of those measures beyond a brief initial period. Ultimately, the President is expected to lead the nation through crises with decisiveness but also with respect for democratic institutions—emergency authority cannot be used to undermine the Constitution or suspend fundamental rights except to the extent strictly required and for as short a duration as possible, while being subject to COC oversight, and final accountability to citizens.

xiv. Chief Public Communicator: Although not a formal power, it is understood that the President, by virtue of the office, has the responsibility to communicate truthfully and transparently with the People of Western Australia. This includes providing reassurance in crises, explaining policies, and maintaining public morale. The President should periodically hold press briefings or public forums and ensure the People are informed about significant governmental actions and national issues.

Annexure C: Founding Departments of the Executive

1. Upon the commencement of this Constitution, Western Australia's national executive shall be organised into the following eleven principal Departments, each led by a Secretary or Commissioner. These Founding Departments are structured to cover all essential functions of the Western Australian Government in a lean and efficient manner. Each Department's general domain is described.

   i. Treasury; Secretary of the Treasury: Sets fiscal strategy; prepares the Essential Budget and appropriations; manages public accounts and expenditure control; oversees taxation to the extent permitted by this Constitution; steers financial-sector regulation and economic reporting.

ii. Resources and Energy; Secretary of Resources and Energy: Resource policy and stewardship of minerals and petroleum; licensing, tenure and compliance; national energy policy, security, markets and infrastructure; coordination with Local Councils under subsidiarity.

iii. Foreign Affairs; Foreign Secretary: Conducts diplomacy and foreign policy under the President; represents Western Australia; manages embassies and consulates; protects citizens abroad; negotiates treaties and agreements; leads engagement with international organisations; oversees state-to-state aid, sanctions and export-control policy; public international law and protocol.

iv. Department of Justice; Attorney-General: Chief law officer; national legal policy; advice to the President and departments; legislative drafting and scrutiny; administration of policing, prosecutions and corrections as provided by law; extradition and mutual legal assistance; access-to-justice programs.

v. National Wellness Authority; National Wellness Commissioner: National health and social policy; funding frameworks for free public healthcare (WellnessCare); commissioning and coordination of services; hospital and primary-care support; aged care, disability and family services; public-health preparedness; transparency and outcomes reporting, delivered with Local Councils under subsidiarity.

vi. Education; Secretary of Education: National education policy; minimum standards and curriculum frameworks; accreditation and qualifications (school, vocational, tertiary); funding frameworks for free public education; national assessments and transparent outcomes reporting; teacher quality and training pathways.

vii. Transport and Infrastructure; Secretary of Transport and Infrastructure: National transport and infrastructure policy; planning, funding and delivery of major roads, rail, ports and aviation, and other nationally significant assets; network standards, safety and resilience; project appraisal, procurement and transparency; implemented with Local Councils under subsidiarity. Co-responsible with Interior and Regional Development for implementing Title 14: Eight Pillars of Self-Sufficiency—Transport leads corridor integration and national networks; Interior leads regional prioritisation and local delivery interfaces. Works in structured coordination with Labour and Commerce (workforce/industry capability), Environment and Conservation (approvals and safeguards), and Defence (dual-use, security and continuity)

viii. Environment and Conservation; Secretary of Environment and Conservation: National environmental policy and law; biodiversity and heritage protection; national parks and reserves; pollution control and standards; water and air quality; environmental impact assessment (EIA) and conditions; delivered with Local Councils under subsidiarity.

ix. Labour and Commerce; Secretary of Labour and Commerce: Workforce policy; employment and workplace standards; industrial relations and dispute resolution; skills, apprenticeships and industry capability; competition and consumer policy; business regulation simplification; SME growth, investment and innovation; domestic trade facilitation and market access.

x. Defence and Emergency Services; Secretary of Defence and Emergency Services: Defence policy; raise, equip and sustain the Armed Forces; readiness, operations and procurement; national security and critical-infrastructure protection (including cyber) as provided by law; civil defence and national resilience; whole-of-nation emergency management—planning, coordination and surge support for preparedness, response and recovery when events exceed Local Council capacity.

xi. Interior and Regional Development; Secretary of the Interior and Regional Development: National policy for regional development and cohesion; Local Council liaison; place-based programs, grants and capacity-building; land use coordination and community partnerships to support balanced growth, delivered under subsidiarity. Co-responsible with Transport and Infrastructure for implementing Title 14: Eight Pillars of Self-Sufficiency—Interior leads regional prioritisation, local delivery interfaces and place-based investment; Transport leads corridor integration and national networks. Works in structured coordination with Labour and Commerce (workforce/industry capability), Environment and Conservation (approvals and safeguards), and Defence (dual-use, security and continuity)

Annexure D: Human Law & Medical Freedom

This schedule provides a cross-reference between Western Australia's codified Human Law rights and the articles of the Universal Declaration of Human Rights (UDHR) and the International Covenants (ICCPR) for civil-political rights, ICESCR for economic-social rights from which they are drawn. It serves as the schedule in the Constitution that formally lists the rights and anchors them in international human rights instruments.

Part 1: Enforceable Fundamental Rights Known as Western Australian Human Law—Derived From UDHR/ICCPR:

1. Dignity, Equality, Non-Discrimination: UDHR Articles 1–2; ICCPR 2(1), 26.

2. Right to Life, Liberty & Security of Person: UDHR Article 3; ICCPR 6(1) (right to life), 9(1) (liberty/security).
3. Freedom from Torture and Cruel Treatment: UDHR Article 5; ICCPR 7 (plus ICCPR 10(1) on humane treatment of detainees; includes ban on non-consensual experimentation).
4. Freedom from Slavery and Servitude: UDHR Article 4; ICCPR 8(1)–(2).
5. Recognition as Person before the Law: UDHR Article 6; ICCPR 16.
6. Equal Protection of Law & Effective Remedy: UDHR Articles 7 and 8; ICCPR 2(3) (effective remedy obligation), 26 (equality before law).
7. Freedom from Arbitrary Arrest/Detention; Habeas Corpus: UDHR Article 9; ICCPR 9(1)–(4) (security of person, no arbitrary detention, right to habeas corpus), and ICCPR 10(1) (dignity of detainees).
8. Right to Fair Trial and Due Process: UDHR Articles 10–11 (fair hearing, presumption of innocence, no ex post facto laws); ICCPR 14 (detailed fair trial rights) and 15 (no retroactive criminal law).
9. Right to Privacy (family, home, correspondence, honour): UDHR Article 12; ICCPR 17.
10. Freedom of Movement (residence, travel, return): UDHR Article 13; ICCPR 12 (liberty of movement, right to enter one's country).
11. Right to Nationality (and not be arbitrarily deprived of it): UDHR Article 15; ICCPR 24(3) (child's right to nationality).
12. Right to Marry and Found a Family (with spousal equality): UDHR Article 16; ICCPR 23 (rights of family and spouses).
13. Right to Own Property (individual and collective): UDHR Article 17; UDHR 27(2) (protection of authors' moral and material interests). (Note: Property rights per se are not in ICCPR; Western Australia includes intellectual property here as per UDHR 27(2)).
14. Freedom of Thought, Conscience, and Religion: UDHR Article 18; ICCPR 18 (includes freedom to change religion/belief and manifest it).
15. Freedom of Opinion and Expression: UDHR Article 19; ICCPR 19 (freedom to seek, receive, impart information and ideas). (ICCPR Article 20's requirement to prohibit incitement of violence/hatred is addressed under Western Australia's free expression limits consistent with that article.)
16. Freedom of Peaceful Assembly: UDHR Article 20(1); ICCPR 21.
17. Freedom of Association (including forming/joining trade unions): UDHR Article 20(1); ICCPR 22; (ICESCR 8 also covers trade unions; Western Australia protects core of union rights via ICCPR and treats strike rights as statutory).
18. Right to Participate in Government (Democracy Rights): UDHR Article 21; ICCPR 25 (right to vote, be elected, access public service).
19. No Imprisonment for Debt: (Implicit in UDHR 9 and 11; explicit in ICCPR 11 which states no one shall be jailed merely for inability to fulfill a contract.)—Western Australia upholds ICCPR 11.
20. Humane Treatment of Detained Persons: ICCPR 10(1) (also UDHR's spirit of dignity).
21. Rights of Minorities: ICCPR 27 (ensuring ethnic, religious, linguistic minorities can enjoy their culture, religion, language). (UDHR 2's anti-discrimination clause also broadly covers this.)

22. Non-Derogable Core Rights (during Emergencies): As per ICCPR 4(2): right to life (ICCPR 6), freedom from torture or cruel inhuman treatment (ICCPR 7), freedom from slavery (ICCPR 8(1),(2)), no retroactive criminal laws (ICCPR 15), recognition before law (ICCPR 16), freedom of thought, conscience, religion (ICCPR 18). Western Australia adds freedom from non-consensual medical experimentation (implied in ICCPR 7) as part of these core rights and generally treats the above rights as absolute.

Part 2: Directive Principles: Socio-Economic & Cultural: Drawn from UDHR/ICESCR—Not Enforceable:

1. Right to Social Security: UDHR Article 22; ICESCR Article 9. (Western Australia: guiding principle for basic social support.)
2. Right to Work & Favourable Conditions: UDHR Article 23(1)–(4); ICESCR Articles 6, 7, 8. (Western Australia: some aspects binding via civil rights—e.g. no forced labour, union freedom—others (safe conditions, fair wages, strike) as directives.)
3. Right to Rest and Leisure: UDHR Article 24; ICESCR Article 7(d).
4. Right to an Adequate Standard of Living: UDHR Article 25(1) (incl. food, clothing, housing, medical care); ICESCR Article 11 (and freedom from hunger in Article 11(2)). (Western Australia: directive to progressively improve living conditions.)
5. Right to Health: UDHR Article 25(1) ("health and well-being"); ICESCR Article 12. (Western Australia: directive—pursue healthcare access, but via mixed system and with emphasis on medical freedom.)
6. Protection of Family, Mothers, Children: UDHR Article 25(2); ICESCR Article 10(1)–(3). (Western Australia: binding ban on child exploitation; directive support for parental leave, family welfare.)
7. Right to Education: UDHR Article 26; ICESCR Articles 13 & 14. (Western Australia: directive—free compulsory primary education; goal of accessible secondary/higher education; free tertiary for citizens as policy.)
8. Right to Participate in Cultural Life & Benefit from Science: UDHR Article 27(1); ICESCR Article 15(1)(a) and (b). (Western Australia: directive—promote and not impede cultural and scientific activities.)
9. Protection of Intellectual Property (Authors' Rights): UDHR Article 27(2); ICESCR Article 15(1)(c). (Western Australia: implemented as binding under property rights above.)
10. Right to Asylum: UDHR Article 14(1). (Western Australia: acknowledges principle—commit to humane asylum process, not a guarantee of entry.)
11. Right to a Social and International Order for Realising Rights: UDHR Article 28. (Western Australia: guiding principle—committed to international cooperation and building domestic order that supports all rights.)
12. Duties to Community & Limitations Clause: UDHR Article 29(1)–(2). (Western Australia: reflected in constitutional interpretation—individuals have duties to respect others' rights; any rights limits must be by law, for legitimate purpose, necessary and proportionate.)
13. Prohibition on Destruction of Rights: UDHR Article 30. (Western Australia: incorporated as interpretive principle—rights cannot be used to extinguish rights.)

Note: Rights marked as enforceable under Title 16 are binding Human Law. Where a right appears in both enforceable and directive contexts (e.g. property or intellectual property rights), the enforceable version takes precedence and governs legal interpretation.

An Invitation To The People Of Western Australia

In concluding this manifesto, we extend a humble invitation to all who have journeyed through these pages: reflect upon the ideas presented, share your thoughts, and engage in the vital discussions that will shape Western Australia's path. Your voices, as stewards of this new nation, are essential to refining and realising the vision of sovereignty, integrity, and shared abundance for generations to come.

www.ingramcontent.com/pod-product-compliance
Lightning Source LLC
LaVergne TN
LVHW071412210926
848486LV00004B/255